A Volunteer in the Regulars

A
VOLUNTEER
in the
REGULARS

The Civil War Journal and
Memoir of Gilbert Thompson,
US Engineer Battalion

EDITED BY MARK A. SMITH

Voices of the Civil War   Michael P. Gray, SERIES EDITOR

Knoxville / The University of Tennessee Press

Unless otherwise noted, all photographs and all sketches are from the Gilbert Thompson Journal, Manuscript Division, Library of Congress, Washington, DC. The sketches were executed by Thompson himself except where noted.

 The Voices of the Civil War series makes available a variety of primary source materials that illuminate issues on the battlefield, the home front, and the western front, as well as other aspects of this historic era. The series contextualizes the personal accounts within the framework of the latest scholarship and expands established knowledge by offering new perspectives, new materials, and new voices.

Library of Congress Cataloging-in-Publication Data

Names: Thompson, Gilbert, 1839–1909. | Smith, Mark A., 1972–editor.
Title: A volunteer in the regulars : the Civil War journal and memoir of
 Gilbert Thompson, US Engineer Battalion / Mark A. Smith.
Description: First edition. | Knoxville : The University of Tennessee
 Press, 2020. | Series: Voices of the civil war | Includes bibliographical
 references and index. | Summary: "At the outbreak of the war, Gilbert
 Thompson joined the regular army and was assigned to the engineer
 battalion. He began writing a journal of his service. After the war,
 Thompson took his three wartime journals and interleaved them into
 a single volume, adding some of his postwar reflections along the way.
 Thus, the text he left to posterity is both journal and memoir, and he
 maintains a clear delineation between these two perspectives throughout.
 Thompson was also an accomplished artist and topographer, and his
 sketches from the field add a unique visual narrative to this book. His
 service, including activity at Chancellorsville, Gettysburg, the
 Wilderness, and Petersburg, extended well into 1864"— Provided by
 publisher.
Identifiers: LCCN 2020015404 (print) | LCCN 2020015405 (ebook) | ISBN
 9781621905592 (hardcover) | ISBN 9781621905608 (pdf)
Subjects: LCSH: Thompson, Gilbert, 1839–1909—Diaries. | United States.
 Army of the Potomac. Engineer Battalion. | United States—History—Civil
 War, 1861–1865—Engineering and construction. |
 Soldiers—Massachusetts—Diaries. | Military
 engineers—Massachusetts—Diaries. | United States.
 Army—Officers—Diaries. | United States—History—Civil War,
 1861–1865—Personal narratives. | Massachusetts—History—Civil War,
 1861–1865—Personal narratives.
Classification: LCC E492.7 .T475 2020 (print) | LCC E492.7 (ebook) | DDC
 973.7/444092 [B]—dc23
LC record available at https://lccn.loc.gov/2020015404
LC ebook record available at https://lccn.loc.gov/2020015405

Contents

Illustrations

MAPS

Editor's Introduction

This volume contains Gilbert Thompson's record of his experiences in the American Civil War. He served a three-year enlistment with the Union army, rising to the rank of corporal before the expiration of his service in late November 1864. Born in South Mendon (later Blackstone), Massachusetts, on March 21, 1839, he was the only child of William Venner Thompson and William's second wife, Harriet Gilbert Thompson.[1] William was a bootmaker by trade who apparently abandoned his family about 1849, settling into a new life with Catharine Welch, née Mann, with whom he seems to have lived as a common law spouse in Blackstone. Gilbert appears to have been estranged from his father after this point, remaining instead very close to his mother, as his wartime journals attest.[2]

The same year that his father started a new life, Thompson and his mother relocated to the Hopedale community. Established by Adin Ballou and his followers in 1842 within the town limits of Milford, Massachusetts, Hopedale was one of many experimental or utopian communities founded in the first half of the nineteenth century. Its founders sought to establish a peaceful and godly mill town based on what Ballou called Practical Christianity. To achieve their goals, Ballou and his followers adopted a collective oversight of property through a joint stock organization that owned and managed community assets but in which members invested by buying shares. Since shareholders earned profits relative to the number of shares they owned, they were incentivized to work hard, but the cooperative control of property insured that the work of all members was applied as best benefitted the community as a whole. Hopedale's members sought first and foremost to improve themselves morally and religiously and to promote the education necessary to produce upright citizens who shared their values. These objectives had clear connections to antebellum reform movements, and while the reform impulse at Hopedale ran the gamut from vegetarianism to refraining from shaving, the community was particularly committed to abolition, non-resistance, and complete abstinence from alcoholic beverages. All of these aspects of Hopedale influenced Thompson to some degree or another, even though by the outbreak of the Civil War, the community had been hijacked by two textile manufacturers, who slowly turned it into little more than a company town.[3]

Thompson wrote little about temperance, though he generally set himself apart from those episodes he described that involved strong drink. He admitted consuming only for what he described as health reasons, an exception in line with the tenets of Hopedale's Practical Christianity.[4] He had even less to say about women's rights, which was another popular reform in antebellum Hopedale. Nevertheless, when he wrote of the bloomers that were popular with some early women's rights advocates, he did so without rancor or judgment, perhaps because of his earlier exposure to this style of dress, which had been popular with some of Hopedale's women.[5]

The community's acceptance of abolition may have had a larger impact on Thompson. Ballou's Practical Christianity incorporated a commitment to equality that engaged Hopedale with both women's rights and abolition, experiences that made Thompson exceptional among white northern men of his era. Every August, Hopedale held annual abolition meetings that brought to the community white speakers such as William Lloyd Garrison and Wendell Phillips and black abolitionists (and formerly enslaved people) like Frederick Douglass, Henry "Box" Brown, Sojourner Truth, and William and Ellen Craft. While there were only two African American residents of Hopedale, these regular abolition meetings and the relatively common community practice of harboring fugitive slaves likely gave Thompson more progressive ideas about race than most of his contemporaries. This is not to say that he was free of all racial prejudice. He never employed the n-word, already by the mid-nineteenth century the most virulent slur against African Americans, but he did occasionally use other racially fraught terms, such as "darky." He also displayed some prejudice in his negative assessment of black teamsters when compared to whites, but at the same time he recognized that the alleged failings he identified in these particular African Americans might have been a result of their life experiences under slavery rather than any particular racial inheritance. Moreover, he appears to have been committed to the end of the South's peculiar institution from a very early period, remarking with pride in February 1862 that "we were all John Brown men."[6]

Of course, there were limits to the influence that specific community values had on Thompson. After all, Hopedale's Practical Christians were non-resisters who rejected all forms of violence in general and resolved to maintain that principle during the Civil War. Thompson, on the other hand, enlisted in the army, like several young men from the community.[7]

Hopedale's education system, though, was more influential in shaping the young man's character. Adin Ballou believed everyone capable of achieving goodness with the proper instruction, so education was always a focus. In 1848 the community set up a board to oversee its schools, and the new organization put the educational institutions under the founder's daughter, Abigail Sayles Ballou (later Abigail Sayles Ballou Heywood). "Miss Abbie," as all the students called her, was only nineteen, but she had just graduated from Massachusetts's normal school and was by all accounts a brilliant teacher. Her small district school was supplemented in 1854 by a coeducational boarding and day school for children of all races. First established by Morgan Bloom and his wife, this new institution became the Hopedale Home School in 1856, when William and Abbie Ballou Heywood bought it and took over its management. Under the Heywoods, the school offered a broad college-preparatory curriculum that sought to encourage self-reliance, independence, and cultural appreciation. These institutions provided Gilbert Thompson with his early education, and in terms of cultural awareness they seem to have succeeded, helping him to become an extremely well-read young man by the time he enlisted in late 1861. His journal is littered with literary and artistic references, and his wartime reading list was impressive. Though he did not always have perfect recall of previously read materials, he clearly remembered enough to approximate appropriate passages, and in the lulls between campaigning, he even made his own attempts at original poetical, musical, and theatrical compositions. To top it all off, he bought a cello over the winter of 1863–1864 and carried it with him for the rest of his active service. By all accounts, Thompson was an extraordinarily well-rounded individual.[8]

As a young man in Hopedale, Thompson also cultivated two particular skills that influenced his later life. Shortly after his arrival, when he was just ten years old, his appreciation for the written word and a desire to become an editor led him into a four-year apprenticeship as a printer with the *Practical Christian*, the community's biweekly newspaper. Following his apprenticeship, Thompson continued in the printer's trade, working in that capacity for Michael Blunt.[9] At the same time, he also learned to draw at the Hopedale Home School, and he employed this skill throughout the record of his wartime experiences, producing both formal drawings (some in ink) and dozens of informal sketches that litter the margins of his journals.[10]

Thompson's artistic training, however, gives the lie to his later claim of having entered a new profession purely by chance. During the postwar years, he supported himself as a topographer and geographer for the federal government, a position he acquired based on his wartime activities. When asked how he came to that occupation, however, Thompson liked to tell a tale of his Civil War enlistment. According to him, when he signed up, he gave his profession as a printer but was misunderstood and assigned to the topographical engineers because the recruiting officer had heard "painter." When the alleged error was discovered, according to Thompson, he was hastily taught the basics of surveying and topographical drawing rather than be reassigned.[11] Instead, Thompson already possessed some artistic skill, and as is clear from his wartime journal, he enlisted specifically in the topographical engineers.

Regardless of how he joined the service, Thompson kept a wartime record of his experiences in three journals that are preserved in the Library of Congress and that have been digitized and made available online.[12] This record stands apart from other Civil War diaries and journals in several ways. In addition to producing a written record, Thompson used his talents as an artist to provide a plethora of sketches that illustrate the daily lives of Union soldiers. Moreover, this visual record is supplemented with photographs that Thompson collected both during and after the war. All the sketches used to illustrate this volume have been drawn from the journal, and with just a few clearly marked exceptions, all the photographs are those that Thompson selected.

In addition to the remarkable visual record, Thompson's reminiscences combine elements of a wartime record and a postwar memoir into a single document. Beginning about fifteen years after the war and continuing for approximately a decade thereafter, Thompson returned to his journals, supplemented them with postwar recollections, and corrected both place and personal names where lack of information during the conflict had introduced errors. It was, presumably, during this period when he also inserted photographs of men with or under whom he had served, of places he visited, and of roles his unit fulfilled during the war. The only real gap in the record is left by Thompson's wartime correspondence. He did not preserve the letters he received on campaign, and his correspondents apparently did not save the letters he sent them. The only exceptions were his wartime journals, which he sent home to his mother as he filled each individual volume. Sometime after the war, Thompson interleaved those three journals into a single bound volume to which he subsequently added his postwar thoughts on some issues. Most of this commentary seems to have been added after 1879, the year he dated his postwar introduction and noted that he had combined his journals so he could incorporate illustrations and notes. These additions appear to have been intended entirely for himself, as he gave no indication that he was preparing the work for publication, a supposition supported by his arrangement of materials. While Thompson tried to place his recollections close to the wartime entries to which they corresponded, the alignment was not always precise, leaving his record confusing and disjointed. This has been remedied by a judicious rearrangement of materials and a clear differentiation of all postwar additions so that they are immediately distinguishable from Thompson's wartime journals.

A clear delineation of Thompson's wartime and postwar writings is required because of his tendency to offer postwar assessments of wartime events. Most of his later additions merely incorporated additional anecdotes he had neglected to record during the conflict, but in several cases he adopted a more reflective tone. The quality of these latter postwar ruminations is decidedly mixed, with some astute analysis, some useful thoughts on leading figures and events of the war, some misplaced exculpatory remarks, and some inflation of the importance of his unit and its parent organization. All of it, however, has been included because it presents a unique view of how one veteran considered his service long after its conclusion and because Thompson's postwar thinking may prove enlightening about the ways former Union soldiers remembered their service.

Another feature that sets this collection apart from other soldiers' accounts derives from the nature of Thompson's service. Unlike most young men in the Union forces, he did *not* join one of the numerous volunteer units that provided the vast majority of northern manpower. Instead, Thompson enlisted in the United States Army and ended up in the newly established US Engineer Battalion. From 1831 to 1863, engineering duties in the American military were divided between two separate departments. The Corps of Engineers was responsible primarily for the design and construction of both permanent and field fortifications, the conduct of sieges, and the construction and repair of roadways and bridges, while the Corps of Topographical Engineers oversaw the production of maps and the collection of topographical information. Until 1846, however, both organizations consisted entirely of officers.[13]

From 1846 to 1861, the only body of engineer troops in the army was a single hundred-man company known variously as the engineer company, the company of sappers and miners, the company of sappers, miners, and pontoneers, or, officially, Company A, Corps of Engineers. Congress had authorized this unit just after its declaration of war against Mexico. Once it was recruited and trained, the company joined Winfield Scott's army for his campaign against Mexico City, where it provided valuable engineering expertise and fought in nearly every engagement of the campaign from Veracruz to the Mexican capital.[14]

When the Civil War began, most of the engineer company was at its regular peacetime post at the United States Military Academy, except for a small detachment serving on the Pacific Coast. The company, however, was quickly drawn into the crisis of secession winter. On January 18, 1861, Brigadier General John E. Wool ordered it to Washington, where its men camped on the National Mall and helped secure public property in the city. In early March, amid rumors of assassination plots against president-elect Abraham Lincoln, Major General Winfield Scott ordered the engineer troops to serve in the force escorting Lincoln and the outgoing president, James Buchanan, to and from Lincoln's inauguration. As a result, the company of sappers and miners was the only regular army unit in Lincoln's escort, though they were assisted by the Washington Volunteers and shadowed by other regular units moving along parallel streets as the presidential party traveled from Willard's Hotel to the Capitol building and back.[15]

A few weeks after the inauguration, Company A was ordered to Fort Pickens as part of the reinforcement of that lightly held and beleaguered work that guarded the entrance to Pensacola harbor from its position on Santa Rosa Island. The engineers first traveled from Washington to New York, where they joined the force bound for Fort Pickens under Major Harvey Brown. On April 7, the steamer *Atlantic* departed for Pensacola with Brown, the engineer company, Company C of the 2nd Artillery, and Companies C and E of the 3rd Infantry. Arriving at the fort in the early morning hours of April 17, Brown added his force to Lieutenant Adam Slemmer's Company G of the 1st Artillery, which was in Pensacola when the secession crisis began; about thirty seamen from the Pensacola Navy Yard, which had recently been surrendered to Confederate forces; and Captain Israel Vogdes's Company A of the 1st Artillery, which had earlier been sent to reinforce the fort. While Major Brown was in overall command, for the next five months the engineer soldiers directed the work of strengthening Pickens's defenses. They tore down all wooden structures to prevent them from catching fire during a bombardment, built bomb-proof shelters and traverses to protect the men and limit the damage inflicted by any single breach, and worked to place the fort's heavy guns so that an effective defense could be mounted. And they did all of this work under siege conditions and on tight rations, circumstances that took their toll. When the engineer company departed in mid-September, its men were not in the best of health, and two of them did not return at all, having found their final resting place beneath Fort Pickens's glacis.[16]

After spending a few weeks at West Point following their departure from the Florida fort, the sappers and miners were back in Washington on the last day of October. There they were joined by the detachment that had been on the Pacific, and all of the company's men were put to work overseeing the construction of Washington's extensive Civil War defenses.[17]

Despite its early contributions, this single engineer company was insufficient for the Union's needs in the Civil War. This is unsurprising since its small size had not even been adequate for the Mexican-American War or the peacetime demands of the 1850s. As a consequence, in August 1861 Congress authorized an expansion of engineer soldiers. The legislature enlarged the one company to 150 men and authorized three new 150-man companies, expanding the Corps of Engineers' total enlisted complement to 600 men in four companies. Together these four companies eventually constituted the US Engineer Battalion. Even this enlarged number of engineer troops, however, was grossly insufficient for the demands of the

Civil War, as is made plain by the fact that the battalion served only one of the many Union armies. Its entire wartime service was with the Army of the Potomac, and its size was insufficient for even that single army. About half a dozen volunteer engineer regiments were raised to close this gap, and two of them, the 15th and 50th New York Volunteer Engineers, formed the Army of the Potomac's Engineer Brigade, occasionally joined by the US Engineer Battalion.[18]

The four companies of the Engineer Battalion, however, were not the only regular engineer troops authorized by Congress at the start of the war. Three days after increasing the enlisted component of the Corps of Engineers, Congress also authorized a 150-man company of topographical engineers. Recruiting for this unit began in Boston on November 8, but the company was never organized and the dozen or so men recruited for it, including Gilbert Thompson, were transferred to Company B of the Engineer Battalion when they arrived in Washington in January 1862.[19]

At that early stage of the war, only the original Company A and the new Companies B and C of the battalion had been recruited, and all three were well below their authorized strength of 150 men each. By July 1862, after the Peninsula campaign and the Seven Days' Battles, the three companies had slightly less than 300 men. Their situation was not improved that month when the heretofore unrecruited Company D was created by the expedient of transferring men into it from the first three companies (one of the men transferred from Company B was Thompson, the only man to join Company D who had originally enlisted in the topogs). The battalion remained severely understrength until October when the War Department authorized regular army units to recruit up to their authorized complements by enlisting men from the volunteer regiments. At that point, the Engineer Battalion was quickly fleshed out to nearly its full strength.[20]

Even before it was fully recruited, the battalion provided critical support for the Union military effort. In conjunction with the volunteer engineer regiments, it performed the types of duties in the spring and early summer of 1862 that it would fulfill throughout the war. Its men built bridges, both floating and fixed. They made swampy, muddy, or marshy roads passable for all arms of the service. They built all manner of military constructions for sieges and defense. They surveyed for and produced much-needed maps, and they supported reconnaissances by their officers.

And on a few occasions, they laid down their tools and took up their rifle muskets to stand as infantry.

In addition to performing such valuable military service, the wide variety of duties undertaken early in the war by the men of the Engineer Battalion, by their officers in the Corps of Engineers, and by the topographical officers all highlighted the unnecessary division of military engineering within the US Army between construction-related services and mapping. This situation, along with the need for a wartime expansion in the number of engineer officers and a desire to provide them sufficient rank to undertake their duties, led Congress to abolish the Corps of Topographical Engineers in March 1863 and fold its officers into the Corps of Engineers, bringing all elements of military engineering into a single, enlarged organizational framework.[21]

As a result of the nature of his service with the Union's military engineers, Thompson's recollections provide a view of life in the regular army during the war, even though he considered himself and most of his colleagues to be "volunteers in the regular army."[22] These recollections also provide a view from the ranks of a highly specialized unit, offering an occasional glimpse at the role of field engineering in the American Civil War. Admittedly, Thompson did not consistently detail the varied activities of military engineers in the Civil War, but he did offer a few scattered insights, like his accounts of bridging operations at Harpers Ferry and along the Chickahominy in 1862, his frequent references to time spent on the topographical surveys required for Union mapmaking, and perhaps most significantly, his frequent if abbreviated references to the supervisory role played by engineer soldiers in the construction of the Federal lines around Petersburg. In this latter area, Thompson notes that the sappers of the battalion directed the fatigue parties from the line that built the Union siege works in the summer of 1864. Still, these comments are only isolated gems in an account that provides a much broader window into regular army life on campaign.

Perhaps the most valuable of Thompson's contributions were his repeated discussions of certain home-like aspects of soldier life between major military operations that might be called "soldier domesticity." Much of what he recounts in this area will be familiar, like march life, reading and music to pass the time, and discussions of the value of correspondence from home. Some of his descriptions, though, add nuance to the current understanding of camp life, such as his many treatments of the variety of semi-permanent shelters the men constructed or, especially, his repeated discussions of the system of bunkmates, or "bunkys" as Thompson often called them, and its importance to him and others.

Gilbert Thompson's wartime musings and postwar recollections, then, have much to offer any student of the American Civil War. They are presented here in the belief that they will resonate with students of this particular conflict and, perhaps, of the human condition in general.

—⊱•⊰—

In pursuit of the twin goals of presenting Thompson's recollections to a wide audience while also rendering them useful to future scholars, I have adopted several editorial processes in the preparation of this volume. Punctuation has been modernized where it was possible to do so without altering Thompson's voice. Likewise, his misspellings of place and personal names have been corrected, as has his occasionally erratic capitalization. Where Thompson employed unique or often inconsistent abbreviations, they have been spelled out wherever their meaning can be determined. Abbreviations that have fallen out of favor since the mid-nineteenth century have been adjusted for clarity. In particular, his usage of "12 a.m." or "12 m." has been altered to "12 noon" and "12 p.m." has been converted to "12 midnight" to avoid confusion. Where entire words have been added to clarify Thompson's meaning, they are enclosed in brackets. In a few instances, the interleaving of his wartime journals into a new volume has obscured a line of text entirely; these omissions are noted in editorial brackets.

The headings of Thompson's journal entries have all been standardized in format. The location and a state abbreviation have been placed on a single line; the date, day, and, if provided, the time of day have been set on the line immediately below the location of the entry. Thompson's musings then begin on the next line after the date. If, however, he left an element out in his journals, it has been omitted here, except for the year, which has always been supplied.

As Thompson was most intent on recording his thoughts and activities and less concerned with organizing his writing in his wartime journals, he often shifted topic multiple times within a single long paragraph. Where there are natural topical breaks within them, these long paragraphs have been broken up to maintain flow and signal topic changes to the reader.

Where Thompson employed underlining for emphasis, all of it, whether single, double, or (occasionally) triple, has been rendered as single underlining, except where an entire phrase is underlined singly but one word or phrase has been double (or triple) underscored for additional emphasis. In these latter cases, the words with extra emphasis have been both underlined and italicized to preserve Thompson's intent. Likewise, the varied symbols that Thompson used to indicate where he inserted material after his initial draft have all been replaced, either by including short additions in parentheses within the main text or by using an asterisk as a standard insertion symbol to indicate where he added longer remarks. Where Thompson made two longer addenda to a single paragraph, the second one is marked by a double asterisk. The text of these larger insertions marked by one or two asterisks has been added below the relevant entry or paragraph. Where Thompson provided supplemental information in brackets, these have been converted to parentheses to avoid confusing them with editorial additions.

The memoir recollections that Thompson added after the war have been identified by the indentation of their left margin and the placement of a unique typographical symbol at their start, though in a few instances where he inserted just a word or two, those have been added in parentheses and italics. Where two separate postwar musings have been placed in sequence between Thompson's wartime entries, the different postwar writings are separated by a blank line. All of this has been done to make his postwar writings clearly identifiable from his wartime musings. Postwar insertions have been identified with the same distinctive text, though they have been marked with an asterisk and located below the relevant paragraph or entry just like Thompson's wartime additions.

The illustrations in the volume are nearly all those selected or produced by Thompson. All the sketches are his except where noted. Those sketches not drawn by Thompson were collected by him from his fellows in the Engineer Battalion both during and after the war; the artist, when not Thompson, has been identified. Nearly every photograph in the volume was chosen by Thompson as well, and the majority of them have been reproduced from the photos within his journal, unless a better quality copy of the exact same photograph could be obtained elsewhere; where replaced from another source, the photo credits identify the new source. There are only a handful of illustrations that Thompson did not select, and their captions clearly identify them as the choice of the editor and provide a rationale for their inclusion.

Where all of the editorial changes and alterations described above have been incorporated into Thompson's writing, they have, for the most part, been done silently. To maintain the voice and intent of Gilbert Thompson, however, his consistent, intentional, and emphatic misspellings have been allowed to stand without the addition of "[sic]." Moreover, some military engineering terms, like pontoon and abatis, had multiple accepted spellings in the nineteenth century, and Thompson was inconsistent in their usage. Those words have been left as Thompson spelled them.

In addition to all of the editorial changes described above, when Thompson mentioned an individual, battle, or campaign only briefly, the editor has supplied any necessary context in an endnote annotation.

—✠•✠—

No work of this nature is the product of a single individual. Throughout this project, I have incurred numerous debts, and I would be remiss if I did not at least attempt to acknowledge them. My former department chair at Fort Valley State University, Fred R. van Hartesveldt, consistently supported all of my scholarly endeavors until his retirement from the institution in the summer of 2014, and even after that he continued to serve as a sounding board for the earliest stages of this particular project. His friendship has been equally important, and occasional dinners with him and his wife Mary Ann have provided a much-needed respite from many ongoing projects. Michelle Krowl, the Civil War and Reconstruction Specialist at the Library of Congress's Manuscript Division, expedited the digitization of Gilbert Thompson's journal when I expressed interest in obtaining scans of the collection, and she subsequently provided continuing support and assistance in response to my many queries. Her willingness to help and her attention to detail saved me considerable trouble and expense. In addition, several people provided invaluable assistance in deciphering particularly difficult words and identifying obscure terms. Both Laura Botts and Kathryn Wright from the Archives and Digital Initiatives of Mercer University Library helped decode some of the least legible handwriting. Molly Kernan, Mercer's Catalog and Government Information Librarian as well as the best of friends, used her extensive knowledge of music to identify some key words and clarify the meaning of some musical discussions and notations for a largely tone deaf historian. My mother-in-law, the Reverend Carol Rahn, ensured the accuracy of my biblical interpretations. Rick Herrera at the US Army Command and General Staff College, Randy Sparks at Tulane University, Karen Kehoe at St. Vincent College, and several other members of the Historians Facebook group also provided critical help elucidating abstruse abbreviations with only minimal context.

Scot K. Danforth at the University of Tennessee Press and Michael P. Gray at East Stroudsburg University, both of whom oversee the Voices of the Civil War series, offered continuing support and encouragement for this project, and the press's Jon Boggs patiently shepherded me through the publication process. John Logel of the Naval War College and Thomas F. Army Jr. of Quinebaug Valley Community College both read the entire manuscript and offered sage advice on every aspect of it. Without their guidance, it would be a much weaker work. Erin Kirk has my gratitude for the book's beautiful design, inside and out, and Tim Kissel's clean and precise maps are a welcome addition. Finally, my wife, Gretchen, has been a part of this project at every step, from its inception through the submission of the final page proofs. She has consistently encouraged me and provided invaluable assistance, reading multiple drafts and suggesting changes and improvements throughout. Without her this book would never have seen the light of day and, more importantly, my life would be considerably less rich.

Author's Introduction

✢— I have collected and had bound together here the three volumes of Journals kept by me from November 22, 1861, until November 22, 1864, during my service in the U.S. Engineer Battalion, which organization was with the Army of the Potomac throughout the war for the suppression of the Great Rebellion. The original has been interleaved for the purpose of the introduction of illustrations and notes. It is, with this and few exceptions, left as it was written.

I wonder now I wrote as much and as well, and am thankful I was so fortunate as to have the opportunity to do so.

In bringing them into this more permanent form, it was because, although containing very much that is poor and irrelevant, they were too valuable to be subject to division and loss, and maybe will reveal some things not to be found in more correctly and elegantly written narratives.[1]

Gilbert Thompson

Washington, D.C.
November 22, 1879.

Off to the Wars with Other Intelligent Men

November 1861–March 1862

The main portion of the company . . . remained at West Point until January 20, 1861, when it was ordered to Washington to guard the public buildings, stores, and arsenals during the excitement preceding the rebellion. It formed part of the escort of President Lincoln at his first inauguration.[1] *It remained at Washington till April 3, when it left at 6 a.m. for Fort Hamilton, N.Y., arriving at Fort Lafayette at 6 p.m. on the same day.*

On the afternoon of the 7th the company embarked on the steamer Atlantic, which sailed next morning under sealed orders. The Atlantic arrived at Santa Rosa Island, April 16. The company disembarked at 11 p.m., and reached Fort Pickens between 12 and 3 next morning.

While at Fort Pickens, the company was engaged in putting the works in a state of defense, building traverses, bomb proofs, and exterior batteries. It left Fort Pickens September 17, 1861, reaching West Point on the 30th, where it remained during the month of October and left on the 31st for Washington.

By Act of Congress of August 6, 1861, the U.S. Engineer troops were increased by the addition of three companies of 150 enlisted men each. One company of topographical engineers was allowed by the same act. This latter company was not organized till after the war and the men enlisted for it (only some half dozen) were sent to the engineer companies.[2]

Of the additional companies, one (Company C) was organized at Boston, and one (Company B) at Portland. These joined the old company (A), at Washington in the fall of 1861. The third additional company (Company D), was organized by transfer from Companies

*A, B and C, while the Army of the Potomac lay at Harrisons Landing
(July 4, 1862).*

*During the winter of 1861–62 the engineer troops were engaged in
the construction of works in the vicinity of Washington and in building a ponton bridge at Harpers Ferry.*

—LIEUT. TURTLE'S ESSAY[3]

November 21, 1861.

Thanksgiving Day. Well, my dear old journal, we must now bid Good
Bye to each other.

Too-morrow morning I am for Boston, thence to Fort Independence
as a soldier.[4] I was down yesterday and was examined. I am to go in the
Topographical Engineers (Company A).

TOPOGRAPHICAL ENGINEERS ! !

WANTED—150 Carpenters, Machinists, Bridge Builders, Riggers, and other
intelligent men, for the Company (A) of Sappers and Miners and Pontoniers,
attached to the U. S. Corps of Topographical Engineers. A proper proportion must be skillful mechanics, and all strong, able-bodied unmarried men,
at least 5 feet 3½ inches high, of good character, able to read and write, and
familiar with the four grand rules of arithmetic. Enlistment for three years;
pay from $13 to 34 per month, according to the rank attained in the com-
pany by merit; to which is added clothing, rations, medical attendance, and a
Bounty of One Hundred Dollars at the expiration of the term of enlistment.

As soon as the company is formed it will be assigned to active duty in the
field, will be commanded by officers of the Corps of Topographical Engineers, graduates of the West Point Military Academy, and when organized will
consist of 10 Sergeants at $34 per month, 10 Corporals at $20 per month,
64 Artificers at $17 per month, 64 Privates at $13 per month, 2 Musicians
(buglers), all to be enlisted as privates, and afterwards promoted according
to capacity, soldierly bearing and good conduct. From the most worthy of
the Sergeants selections will be made from time to time, as the wants of the
service require for promotion to the rank of commissioned officers of the
regular Army. Apply at No. 13 Franklin street, over the United States Quartermaster's office, between 9 a.m. and 5 p.m. daily.

Charles Turnbull,
1st Lieut. Topographical Engineers, Recruiting Officer.
—*Boston Journal,* November 8, 1861.

I have not time to tell how dear, a thousand times dearer everything seems to me when thus parting from them. I am going to do my duty, my man-life is begun.

I shall see two weddings to-night, Charlotte Percy,[5] Adaline Adams,[6] so-it-goes, joy, sorrow. Good Bye—Good Bye.

G. Thompson

November 22, 1861.

Off to the wars with other intelligent men. I have joined the Topo-graphical Engineers (Company A) sworn in today. A fine day in prospect; Hopedale never seemed so gay as last night.[7] Two weddings and light and mirth, music and song, the chorus to an old song came from one house (see last page). Though I am going away to encounter I know not what, yet I feel a buoyancy, an exulting spirit; whether I am possessed or not I am happy.

✠— Hopedale was a Community of Practical Christians organized by Rev. Adin Ballou in [1841]. One of its cardinal principles was Non-Resistance, and when the war broke out, there was a debate in the minds of some as to their course of conduct. Its roll of honor was, however, great if not greater than any village of its size. W. F. Draper became a Brevet Brigadier General of Volunteers.[8] George Gay died at Andersonville.[9] Warren Adams died of disease contracted in the service.[10] Eli Ball, killed in a charge of the 25th Massachusetts at Cold Harbor, 1864.[11] Arthur Johnson also.[12]

Johnson, a colored boy, killed in the charge on Fort Wagner, South Carolina.[13] Julius Laderer was on a Monitor.[14] Daniel Messenger was in the Cavalry.[15] Joseph Harlow, I think, and am sure his brother Henry, were out three months.[16]

November 25, 1861.

Blustering day. I am at Fort Independence, Boston Harbor. Only three of us. Shall *probably* be here all winter as the Company fills up slowly. It is rather loafy, hanging round. I am as happy here as at home. In the morning after *reveille*, which is "Get up Boys" from White instead of a grand flourish of trumpets,[17] we black our shoes, wash our faces &c., and then comes breakfast of bread & coffee, we have milk by buying it at the fort of the Ordnance Sergeant.[18] Drill from 10 to 11, Dinner at 12½ of Beef-steak or boiled clams, or anything one please to conjure up. Drill in the afternoon, which is new to me. I go left when I ought to go right, and change step a step too late, and so on. I am getting familiarized to its difficulties somewhat. Supper = coffee & bread. We are quartered in a building on the northwest of the fort, in an upper room, where we sleep. This was formerly an old paint shop but is comfortable thus far. A room below we use for a kitchen, which I police, that is, sweep out and clean. From our windows I can see the Blue Hills that I can see from my own hills, Boston with its conspicuous State House, and on the other side of the Fort, you can see as good sunrises as they get up anywhere. Company C, Engineer Corps occupy the fort, and when they move out we *may* move in.

➤— When we landed at the wharf in Boston, I remember a baggage man took our extra luggage off our hands to send to our various homes; he made no charge, and every box went to its destination.

November 27, 1861.

A splendid day, still as ever possible. I can not help thinking what the contrast would be between 1620 & now. Only forests and sounding waves with now & then a canoe timidly venturing out on the waters, while now the air rebounds with the noise and rush of trade, steamers cleave the water destined to ports near and distant. Two recruits came to-day. *Ames.*[19] *Slater.*[20] Had cabbage, pork, potatoes, clams, bread, red currant jelly, &c.

November 29, 1861. Friday, morning.

Two more recruits yesterday. Oh! It is most amusing to see the different manner in which each recruit accommodates himself to the circumstances around him. One complains of bunches and turnips in their mattresses, sleeps cold, and a student recruit talks of the intense cold when it is the warmest night we have had, and discourses of the blood stagnating in his head from being without a pillow, etc. I went up last night to the fort, to procure some milk, and had a chair offered me, and for a while it seemed the "calling in" at home. The Sergeant's (Parr) wife is a pleasant lady— that is, it seemed so. Company C, Engineers, are going away from the fort (Monday they say), and we shall have better quarters. Thus far, I like military life. Every one is obliged to be polite and do his share of the work. The recruits of yesterday are good singers and we had a grand *matinee* last

Fort Independence. Thompson's sketch of Fort Independence in Boston Harbor, where he first joined the Company of Topographical Engineers that was later absorbed into the Engineer Battalion.

evening. Slater fortunately bringing a *Columbian Glee Book*.[21] John Brown's song went with an unction.

December 1, 1861. Sunday.

I can't swear to December 1st, but I'll call it so. The bells are chiming in South Boston for meeting, let me see, ¼ of 10, the girls and boys of H.—— are just going to the S. School, there is a little buzz in the corners where misses are telling each other of ———. If I should be home, I would be by the furnace bidding Good morning to this one and that one, &c. I cannot appreciate the feelings of those who are posted or imprisoned in a garrison and hear their own village bells ringing; it must have a peculiarly mournful effect on their heart.

✦— The first time I ever saw Benjamin F. Butler[22] was on a tug boat going to Fort Warren.[23] One of the Sergeants, Leas, was also on board,[24] and there were several boxes of choice liquors for Messrs. Mason & Slidell at Fort Warren.[25] It seems the mate was in doubt whether they should be put off at Fort Independence or not. Leas solved it with a

"Of course . . . ," and in due time they were inside the quarters and a "Down with Jeff. Davis" drank every time.

At Christmas, Lieutenant Turnbull sent down turkeys, etc., for a sort of dining, and in many ways he made our barrack life pleasant for us, all of which should be noted and long remembered.[26]

Fort Independence, Boston Harbor.
December 29, 1861. Sunday.
   A tolerably fine day.
   Well old Journal I have the pleasure of writing in your folds again, and where do you think you are.[27] If I could really personify you, how your eyes would look round and wonder where you were, thinking how different the surroundings are from the little kitchen with the pleasant west window.
   On the opposite side of the table (*pine table*) from me is a pleasant-look-ing young man, a tailor by trade, putting a pocket into a great-coat, others are reading Dickens's *Dave Copperfield* in numbers, and if my chirography is this and that way,[28] it must be attributed to keeping time with the foot to a lively tune our drill-corporal is playing on the accordion accompanied by another with bones that a few days ago probably graced a soup dish. A couple of Maine boys are gazing into the bright coal fire, thinking perhaps of bright fires at home, while others are sitting in the bunks looking on at the various attractions of this room. Altogether, friend Journal, it is a queer scene for you, and did you ever think the *boy* who used to bend over the preceding pages, writing of this and of that, should ever write a page or two in a plain old room on Castle Island [on] the sunny side of Fort Independence, Boston Harbor? Eh!
   Soldier's life here at present, or rather what it was, is as easy as possi-ble. Our only duties are cooking, policing and three hours' drill a day. Sunday morning at 11 o'clock we have Inspection, and in the afternoon, at least today, instead of attending service in Hopedale Chapel, we stood three-quarters of an hour or so hearing the very agreable Articles of War.
   There are at present 13 of us, and we have (only) notice of leaving here soon, perhaps too-morrow, for West Point; what we are to do, we can only surmise but hope for the best, and [we] are determined to be cheerful under whatever circumstances may be granted to our term of enlistment.

I went home Christmas, and it was fortunate I did so, or I might not have succeeded in procuring a furlough so advantageously (at least). I enjoyed it, but I was glad to get back to the old fort after all. Every one seemed pleasant and even more polite and attentive than ever before. They are interested in my welfare, after all their opinions on such matters; and the leaders never defined their cordial good wishes, viz: that they wished me health, &c., but that they could not wish me success in war, &c. Ah! well! well![29]

I wish to write more, and more yet, thinking that perhaps *this is* the last opportunity for a long time I shall have to write in this old book, and it is my almost saddest parting giving you up for awhile. My Journal is a link that brings me pleasant reminiscences to home, its familiar covers bring home even here; I seem in the kitchen as before, and this room with the cheerful talking men seems like some creation of my imagination, as I sit at the table, scribbling along. But old Journal you must tell in your way and cheer up with funny recollection my mother's heart, and tell her that my mind, my soul, my thoughts are here, that through you I talk to her in spirit, though my physical body be far away from the hill environed vale. There are but comparatively few pages left in this book, but they are numerous enough to tell a tale of fortune or misfortune, of goodness or wickedness, and should I fall or die by disease I trust some friendly hand will write on the next page my epitaph, appropriate as a finis, but I hope to write a tale of adventure yet in these very coming pages, Good Bye, Good Bye.

West Point.
January 1, 1862. Wednesday.

New Year's! New Year's! Well! Well! Last New Year's I little thought of passing the next new year's day at West Point. But I *am* here, surely and square. Come from Fort Independence, Monday afternoon (December 30, 1861), 2 o'clock about, and arrived here about 6:30 (December 31, 1861).

At Fort Independence, when we had knapsacks all slung and ready to leave our familiar quarters, we stood in a circle round the table, and sang the "Topog. Chorus,"[30] (Hallelujah!) and at the "Hip! Hip! Hip! Hurrah!" we uncovered heads, and if we had not been soldiers, a tear or two possibly might have been seen, but our Topog. Day is over.*

*Transferred to Company B, Engineers, January 13, 1862.[31]

West Point is a beautiful and interesting place, even in winter. It surprised me from its large extent, as I presumed it did all of the boys, as we marched and marched from the ferry to our quarters last night, with our shoulders aching from the unaccustomed weight and position of the knapsack, but in a week tramping I would be as easy with it as a dress coat; but I am digressing. It strikes a person peculiarly, to hear the agreable sound of instrumental music, to [see] dwelling houses lit up with generous light, and see girls and boys amusing themselves as in any town; indeed walking along by the parade ground, you can hardly realize you are in one of the strong holds of America. Cadets come stepping along by twos, and it is strange to think that [P. G. T.] Beauregard, [Jefferson C.] Davis, and [George B.] McClellan have walked along these walks and acted as the same grey suited boys are. Too-morrow we commence our "facings,"[32] and I cannot tell or presume what will happen; Christmas I surely thought Spring would find us at [Fort] Independence, but a few days after, a day called New Year's, found me commencing a Journal in a commodious room at West Point.

While on the cars (H.R.R.),[33] I conversed with a gentleman who was acquainted with [Washington] Irving, and [who] kindly pointed out his "Sunnyside."[34] It is indeed a cosy, sunny place.

West Point.
January 2, 1862. Thursday.

Rather chilly. I have read a little in *David Copperfield*, drew a picture for a letter to mother, which I send to-day.[35] A recruit, ([Edwin A.] Kimball, Company C) plays the flute finely, and we set together on a locker, I turning over the leaves, while he executed this gem and that of music.

We have a character in "Jake" a Bowery boy (Company A, Engineers) who is about as broad as he is long, [36] and is paying *devoirs* to a little fat jug at all available times, a perfect counterpart to himself.[37] Yesterday was his birthday, which he celebrated by going down to Buttermilk village with two of our boys,[38] and coming back home elevated,[39] and chased one of them round from Dan to Besheba because they would not go back again, but he is not ugly though a little rough in his mirth, and kept us roaring nearly all night with his manoevres; he brought down the house by telling of chasing a pet dog of one of the sergeants who was in some scrape, and

Engineer Buildings at West Point. This sketch depicts the location where Thompson and the other new recruits first joined the Engineer Battalion.

Jacob D. "Jake" Geyser, Company A (later Company D).

his being "obliged to drop the two jugs," and on being questioned farther, said there was "two jugs besides himself." To-night he has got the same dog drunk with a bottle of brandy, and is just this moment coaxing Kimball to play a jig, for him to dance. He ends all his stories and awful statements with the neatest and complacent laugh you ever heard. When the boys sing, he comes in occasionally on the chorus, without regard to time, melody or tune. *Vive la Jake.*

West Point.
January 3, 1862. Friday.

Cool, with a sharp keen breeze. Military life here makes a man lazy—lazy, that's the word exactly, for only a few are here, and we are not subjected to real strict discipline. We have to be decent, of course, and have reveille, tattoo, and roll calls, three times a day;[40] drill, three hours a day.

Yesterday, I went into the Laboratory and was reminded of old times by the *chevaux de frise* chain, stretched across the Hudson (in the Revolution),[41] guns captured at Saratoga, Stony Point, Monterrey, Vera Cruz, &c.;[42] how strange a story they might tell of struggles fierce and desperate, and now they seem so dumb beneath our cold sky. This afternoon, Page and myself rambled up to the graveyard of the Cadets, and then went on some farther,[43] and I had a free light feeling for the moment; it made me think of old rambles. The scenery is wild and picturesque, you cannot complain of sameness here; Highlands, dells, brooks, and a smooth flowing river. I mean to spend an artistic holiday here yet. *Au Revoir.*

West Point.
January 4, 1862. Saturday.

Cool. Took a sketch to-day of the opposite shore, for Miss Albee.[44] This afternoon had a grand regular clearing up time, washing up the floor, and cleaning and blacking the stove. Had a pleasant chat and sing this evening. Last night after tattoo, we—Thayer, Fickett, Currier, and my humble self—had a "Circus," with tumbling and posturing extraordinary, and witnessed by a highly select audience in the bunks, or private boxes, as they were facetiously termed, and at some of the feats they would once and awhile start out into the arena and try their fortune at turning flip flaps.[45] A spectacle rarely seen of the audience emulating [illegible words in margin] performances.

West Point.

January 5, 1862. Sunday.

A fine nice day. Attended the Episcopal service in the Cadet's Chapel, a very neat and tasty building,* I do not think I could endure the service, beautiful as it may be, for more than a week. There are two windows converted into niches, with flags—English and Mexican—[and] cannons from Monterey and Stony Point inserted in the wall.[46] The Cadets have a very fine appearance, their clothes being a blue gray and with their white gloves and belts, chevrons and side arms, they look the very personification of neatness. Baked beans for dinner, a very pleasant reminiscence of home indeed.

* There is nothing more charming than the bugle-call for service from the heights of West Point on a clear, still Sunday morning.

In the afternoon I took a sketch, and went up with a party to old Fort Putnam, a work of the revolution.[47] The view from its ramparts is very extensive, embracing a bird's eye view of West Point and a good strip of the Hudson, with the Highlands high and rough before you and stretching away on the right, looking blue and enchanting in the purple distance; bringing to mind Irving's exquisite description of this river with the associations and Indian legends connected with its bank and clear flowing stream. The workmanship of Fort Putnam is rude but strong, and it seems yet even in its decay to be breathing forth from its very old rocks and ramparts the spirit of '76.

West Point.

January 6, 1862. Monday.

Snowing and blustering. It seems more like camp life here than at Fort Independence, and chiefly from one circumstance; after *reveille*, we go down to the brook near by, and wash up, although a little wintry it smacks so of the rustic and healthy age, I like it nevertheless. This building was built for the Company's 150 men (Engineer Company A), and is a fine structure, with a Library and kitchen and dining room, officer's rooms. At present there are only a few of the Company here, the remainder being on duty at various points, and I have been interested in personal accounts of the Company's operations at Fort Pickens. They had a hard time, working night and day, with poor food, and came home sick and worn out.[48]

West Point.

January 7, 1862. Tuesday.

A very fine day. Received a letter from mother, and there is nothing stirs the old heart—for we get a new heart when we enlist—like writing letters to and receiving letters from friends. Some recruits for Company B & C (Boston) came to-night from Portland. Progress quite well in drill, through some are bothered occasionally, and the one who makes the least mistake, is seldom spoken to when he does make a mistake.

West Point.

January 8, 1862. Wednesday.

Another fine day. In the morning the river was covered with dense fog, and when the Highlands were lit up by the morning's rosy beams just peering above the fog [it] was splendid! It is curious to see how we relate this anecdote to one and omit while talking to another, and show him some fine sentiment in poetry or prose instead. We have had a *very* grand time indeed, dancing, quarreling about flanking, jib dancing, schottische &c., and we are ending by a sergeant and corporal either half seas over or a very good imitation.[49]

West Point.

January 9, 1862. Thursday.

Another fine day, very. The day has gone in the usual manner, roll-call, eating, drill, roll-call, eating, drill, roll-call, eating, roll-call, and then sleeping. After the last eating time, about 5¼, Thayer and I started on a little walk, making an alignment for Cold Spring.[50] We spoke to the Sergeant (Anderson)* about going,[51] and he said he could not give us a pass to go, but if we did, he advised us to be "careful and not get in!" The Hudson is frozen over and sleighs have gone across these three days. The sly advice of the sergeant set us off. The ice is broken up in confusion, with now and then a dark streak [that] would startle us, and occasionally looked rather "nasty," but it [was] strong and tough, and we got over in fine shape. At Cold Spring we walked up a long street, and seeing a cross street, T. asked a little boy by a little oyster saloon "where that road led to?" "Up to Mr. James'[52] and Gen. Morris's,"[53] was the reply. Of course we went up the cross road, and soon were walking in poetic "Undercliff."[54] As we stood there, the moon seemed even brighter and the evening star looked with benign radiance over the crest of old "Cro's nest," and the merry mirth of children came out to us with strange sweetness from those rooms gleaming with light and warmth. T—— said "Who could not write poetry here?" I said "yes" for words are poor weak things under such circumstances, and we moved away. I wonder if the possessor of that fair retreat will ever dream of two soldiers with long thoughts, gazing on all around, with the rhythm of an old song ringing in their memory by his noble portico, one moonlight night in January?

We came back in safety, remembering the kind advice of the Sergeant, and Thayer is drying his wet feet by the fire, happy as a lark. The damp don't seem to strike to his heart after all, and I am here writing about it.

>+— * Anderson is a General Service Clerk in the War Department, and a month or two ago, I introduced myself to him, and showed him this record which amused him. I wanted to find out about the Mexican War, but he had no records. He told me Farr was dead,[55] [and] Ayres had gone to the dogs.[56] *April 11, 1880.*

Anderson was in Company A during the Mexican War.[57]

West Point.
January 10, 1862. Friday.
A warm, thawy day. I have written home, and my thoughts are turned out of Journalizing. Quite a number have gone to a dance on pass down to Buttermilk. Some of the men are talking about —— matters. Ah! there is many a bit of poetry and fine feeling uttered here that will be burnished up and laid away by kind angels for our redemption.

West Point.
January 11, 1862. Saturday.
Same kind of weather as yesterday. The boys came home from the dance in usual style, jolly as kings, one being in the guard-house; we did not sleep much after they came, and the sentinel chased the one who was put in the Guard-house, and his sword dragging along the floor and stairs sounding queer enough. Whiskey is the very devil himself in a camp or barracks. I have not drank yet nor mean to; and we regularly send a delegation to get drunk every night. We scrubbed up the quarters as usual and had a regular "washing time," and the air had an innate aroma like mother's washing day.

West Point.

January 12, 1862. Sunday.

A foggy day. Nothing occurred of any great account [in] the day. Had a Debate in the Evening, on Slavery question with all the paraphernalia of President, Sergeant at Arms, &c.

West Point.

January 13, 1862. Monday.

A fine day. Called on one [of] the Band, and passed a very pleasant evening, his wife singing some very nice songs while he accompanied with guitar. Drew a Bird's eye View of West Point from Fort Putnam, which pleases me very much. Received a letter from mother, which shows she is endeavoring to be resolute in her struggle to be happy during my absence. Had no drill this afternoon, so to allow the men to wash their clothes, &c., before going to Washington Wednesday or Thursday. I am ready to go. Good Bye.

West Point from Old Fort Putnam. This is likely the sketch that Thompson made on January 13, 1862.

West Point.

January 14, 1862. Tuesday.

Cold, but fine. Had an Inspection this afternoon, and are away too-mor-row. The boys are nearly all gone to Buttermilk, and will have a *good* time.

Washington.

January 18, 1862. Saturday.

Well you & I are in the Capitol of the United States, Mr. Journal. Wednesday morning found us started in a nasty slush for a tramp to Washington with some twenty or so others. A pleasant ride to New York passed off successfully, and New York is meaner than Boston. At 5 o'clock we took the boat for Amboy, a ride of some three hours time. On the trip, our sergeant got into a discussion with some volunteer officers on handling arms. They were awkward and obstinate, and to show them bayonet drill! he routed out Farr, an eight year soldier,[58] who has been drunk a week or two, as well; he came up to the scratch by a promise from the Sergeant not to report him for previous conduct. He went in good, though he could hardly stand, and in a grand thrust he put his bayonet with a grand rush right through a window!

We staid in Philadelphia two nights and a day, by the Sergeant losing his papers in New York, and if it had not been for the generous liberality of the people in their Union Volunteer Refreshment Saloons we should have come short. I had the pleasure of talking with Mrs. Mary Grover, who gave me an account of their humble beginning and their success.[59] God bless them!! We stopped at the depot, and slept on the floor, but had a good time of it. I visited Independence Hall, a place of great in-terest to Americans, and went through the Navy Yard. Philadelphia is a model city.

Friday night found us here, and I remember how I felt when I saw the fog in the distance lit up by the gas lights of Washington, having a decid-edly mean idea of Baltimore being dirty and *stinky*. As we came towards W.—— the face of things gradually assumed a military aspect, the road being guarded [at] every yard from Perrysville to Washington. I can not give a great description of our ride, as we are in new quarters, &c.

We are at last settled. We are transferred from Company A, Topographical Engineers, to Company B, Engineers. I am quite sell satisfied so far. More Anon.

Company B Engineer Soldiers. This 1862 photograph of a group of soldiers from
Company B of the Engineer Battalion must have been taken between January and
July of that year, when Thompson was a member of Company B. This photograph
is not contained in Thompson's wartime journal or memoir, but he is standing at
the upper right. Atkins Higgins is at center left, and the soldier at the very center
appears to be George L. Cobb. Courtesy of Office of History, Headquarters,
US Army Corps of Engineers.

Washington is at present nothing but mud, mud, and the fog has only lifted so that I could see the other bank of the Potomac.

Washington.
January 19, 1862. Sunday.

Fog and mud. Mud and fog, and then ditto. Wrote a long letter home, and that is about all. In spite of dismal fog I am in good spirits.

Washington.
January 20, 1862. Monday.

Foggy as usual. Received our arms to-day, bright and new, and will entail a great amount of cleaning on us. In the afternoon we commenced the manual of arms. I get along tolerably well in it.

There are many things that show up human nature in a rather disagreable manner, the world is the same go where you will, I suppose.

We are quartered in a little room, 14 x 10; seventeen of us. The wind comes up rather raw and chill through the floor, but last night I slept more comfortable. We have no mattresses but sleep on the floor; we expect some soon, and we will be all right.

Washington.
January 21, 1862. Tuesday.

Weather same as usual, with the variation of a few snow-flakes. Inhabitants of this section of country state this as being the usual winter; mud and fog, with a wind that chills to the bone. Oh! give me the northern winter, with its ice and snow, and jinglings, sleigh-bells, bright eyes, gay hearts.

Drilled as usual, and in the evening we made a circle and Currier favored us with a superb jig dance, and we sang "Auld Lang Syne" to "Annie Lisle."[60] After this sport we went over to our Lieutenant (Reese),[61] and heard a recitation on "Field Fortifications" and will probably study ourselves.[62]

I am writing this laying flat on the floor, by the light of the fire, taps having sounded sometime ago; and I can hear the heavy breathing and now and then a subdued whispering from the sleepers around me, as they lay packed like herrings on the floor near by. So Good Night, and would it could go in sweet accents to my mother. Good Night.

Washington.

January 22, 1862. Wednesday.

Weather, ditto; only with the exception of seeing the sun about three minutes. Drilled as usual. One of [the] Company C men died this morning of delirium tremens. He was an old soldier—Jim Latson—but drank and drank.[63] A soldier's funeral—private's—is rather business-like and heartless. One of our men, Miller, is sick with a cold, and I tuck and "cuddle" him nights.[64] I trust I shall as be as comfortably and kindly cared for when I am thus. Evenings we recite on Field Fortifications, so I am busy as can be.

Washington.

January 23, 1862. Thursday.

At sunset it appeared like a change of weather; the mud is drying up somewhat, so we had Dress Parade at night.[65] I get along quite well in drill, at least, so well, the squad I am in will be reported as competent for guard duty.[66]

Washington.

January 26, 1862. Sunday.

A rare fine day for a Washington winter, but *muddy*, most d——bly muddy. I procured a pass, and went round Washington a little. Washington is truly "a city of magnificent distances,"[67] and you can but notice the fact of its being far different from Yankee cities. Big black hogs are rooting along on Pennsylvania Avenue, an animal that would soon be in the pound at home, though he were but on a back road. Everything seems unfinished, as though a great plan was laid out and designed, but only a patch here and a patch there was finished up to the design; like a new built house with the clap boards and refuse lying round, before everything is cleaned up, terrace made and garden established.

The Smithsonian Institute grounds are very fine with trees from every portion of the Union, and it was pleasant to hear the familiar sound of the singing pine, and to breathe the odor of the fragrant cedar. There is a view near it which is the finest view I ever had the pleasure of viewing. It must be seen in the morning, so the building will be in shadow, and the Capitol appears to fine advantage, with its marble columns in the distance. I intend to sketch it. I have not time to write all about what I saw, but the Capitol and other public buildings and statues look as though they were put there and left to the care of themselves, and look dusty and forsaken. Military matters as usual; appears like a *forward movement*!

Washington.
January 27, 1862. Monday.
    Quite a fine day. Washington presents but few attractions for me at present. The water is flat and tasteless, warm in the bargain. It is unhealthy for us, the air is cold and damp, raw and chilling. Some of our company that were here last summer say in the day it would be seething hot and in the night it would be as cold as it is now in January. We have slept until lately on the floor, not a bit more comfortable than a kitchen familiar to me, but I felt better in the morning after sleeping on the floor, than after a night's sleep on a mattress. Tis strange how a man will accustom himself to such things.

Washington.
January 28, 1862. Tuesday.
    A decent day. All goes as usual. Got a letter from home and Sara ——.[68] Oh! tis not telling how happy a letter here makes a man. I told Ames to make up our bed that I might read, and by candle and firelight I devoured them. It makes a man, a man.

Washington.
January 29, 1862. Wednesday.
    Another decent day. Went in the evening to hear Dr. I. I. Hayes at the Smithsonian Institute on "Arctic Travel."[69] It was quite interesting, but his fame would rest more on deeds than lecturing. After the lecture, I shook hands with him, introducing myself viz, "Excuse me, but I like to shake hands with a brave man!" He took my hand cordially and said he "was shaking hands with a brave man," and "that these men with bright buttons were to be envied." He is a slight built man with a simple manner reminding me of Joshua Hutchinson,[70] and his face showed the exposure of storm & disease; his hand was small and delicate.
    I had the pleasure of talking with a clerk of the Treasury, and looked around to see if "Mrs. Lincoln was there," reminding me of many a village, with their little hall, and a citizen would point out to you Mrs. Brown or Mrs. So & So, wife of one of our leading men of the town. It seems so strange, and think of the *President's wife* pointed with about the manner.

Washington.

January 30, 1862. Thursday.

Everything about the same, only so stormy we did not drill, and I wrote a bit of poetry for George H. Young.[71]

Washington.

January 31, 1862. Friday.

One more month gone to pot.

February 1, 1862. Saturday.

Mud & snow. We are having a mimic Court tonight in regard to Page stealing a blanket. The witnesses' stories being perfectly amusing.

Washington.

February 2, 1862. Sunday.

A fine day, with the remarkable phenomena of ice, some ¼ inch thick. Wrote a letter to ———, and home. In the evening we had a grand jaw about the cooking, then White read a chapter out of the Bible and sang a few religious airs. I cut up a log into fire wood and piled it on to the fire, and it loomed up nobly, lighting up the room finely, and made everything look cheerful; but soon the conversation went on the same old way. The boys sang "From Greenland's icy mountains,"[72] and it made me think of old times, when the singing of that constituted the morning's devotion of my dear old mother, when I was a wee boy about her knee.

Washington.

February 3, 1862. Monday.

Snowing to-day. The most note worthy thing is four of our *particular* squad going on guard, so we are in for it now. I saw my "bunky" walking Post 2, looking savage as a meat-axe, at supper time.[73]

Washington.

February 6, 1862. Thursday.

Had some pleasant days, but to-day is dull again.

Received some letters from home, all in one, good, good. I could have one a day and not be tired of them. Mother is getting along nicely. We have been going through the Bayonet Drill a little, but will see more of it.

The besetting sin of a soldier in quarters is one I hardly thought of contending against, viz, Idleness. We have actually got Lazy, we growl at even a drill-call, complain at even five minutes' duty; this will wear off, by & by, I guess. The sight of those huge Pontoon Bridge boats over on the Parade Ground make my shoulders ache in sorrowful prospective.[74]

Higgins and I have copartively bought a spider, much to the envy of all around, and we talk grandiloquently about "*Our* Spider!"[75] I have a little bottle of Syrup, which puts a good edge to the bread, and once and awhile I purchase a quantity of milk (1 ct's worth, Marm) of an old lady who comes to *Our Pizarro*, mornings, sir! which makes real coffee out of our stuff, sir!

One of our men (Smith) was in the Crimea,[76] [and] another (Pendleton) in the English navy in the China war and also on the vessel which the Prince went to H'old H'ngland in from his visit to America.[77]

Washington.
February 7, 1862. Friday.

A pleasant day. We are all going through the Bayonet Drill, and it takes hold terrifically of a body's legs. We were vaccinated and are told to take care of ourselves and not get cold. I have had very good health so far, but I expect to have my turn, as well as the rest. A man gets along in fine health then all at once down he goes to the Hospital for his quantrum of "flax-seed," and growls round as good as the rest of them.

Washington.
February 9, 1862. Sunday.

Fine weather for now. The last twenty-four hours I have passed as a sentinel.[78] It is a queer feeling, when you are left *all alone* on your beat, with the precaution "to look out sharp for the Officer of the Day." We are *not* allowed to take off our side-arms and clothes, reminding you of that description of the old feudal knights in "The Lady of the Lake;"[79]

"——— drank the red wine through the helmet barr'd."

I received a letter from S. P. Lillie;[80] rather a strange place to read a ——— letter in, but it made all smile there. I tell you, light heart.

Harpers Ferry.
February 27, 1862. Thursday.

A brisk cool day. Well Mr. Journal a new, strange place I write and date at! I have not had a chance to write before since last date, so I will recapitulate, and tell how and why I am here and what we have done.[81]

Atkins Higgins,
Company B.

An Honorable Member
of the Culinary Dept.
This sketch from later
in his wartime journal
may have been the
"spider" that Thompson
and Atkins Higgins
purchased together in
February 1862.

Sunday, February 23, about Guard Mount, we had the order to pack up and be ready to go at 10 o'clock the next day. All immediately assumed a lively and busy appearance at our quarters. Carpenters were detailed to assort tools and construct boxes for transportation, we busied ourselves in arranging everything necessary for our trip, wherever it was to be, which occupied our thoughts with rumors and vain surmises; all seemed pleased and exhilarated with the prospect before them. The night was vexed with our preparations; tents were brought forth, camp stoves, kettles, every-thing. Fortunately I was not detailed and had a fine night's sleep.

In the morning (Monday, 24 February) at 9 o'clock, we fell in line with knapsacks &c., with forty rounds of cartridges. With a "Good Bye," or so, to our companions to be left behind to guard our quarters, we marched, or rather wallowed off up to the Baltimore & Ohio Railroad depot. In due time we found ourselves at the Relay House.[82] Here we stopped awhile. Now was the time of deciding where we were going with me. *If* we went to Baltimore I couldn't tell where, then; *if* we went towards Harpers Ferry, I could guess nearer. Presently the cars moved backward a little, and finally went into a deep, rough cut and were off somewhere towards "Secesh." The scenery on this road is rude and wildly picturesque, like the Berkshire mountains, only surpassing them. We rode nearly all night, sleeping in the cars at Sandy Hook. In the morning (Tuesday, February 25) we marched a little, and finally were pitching our tents on a level place near the destroyed bridge at *Harpers Ferry*. What we were to do? was the next question! There was no boat train came with us! no, nothing, only ourselves! But a rumor got round there was a boat train coming for us! About 2 o'clock at night we heard a whistle, then "Turn out B & C Company," from old Gerber,* our Sergeant Major.[83] We turned out and went to the cars, and there was a fearfully long train, packed with boats and material. We worked on this, lugging balk,[84] chess,[85] boats, &c., until morning, down to the river side. The "boatmen & sailors" turned in for a little rest before the rest of us, and when the sun was out, we turned in, and they turned out; we had some breakfast, and took a rest. When they had four boats out, we went to work, and kept on until night.[86] A good long time and stretch of it. When the bridge was nearly completed (3½ o'clock p.m., Wednesday, 26th February), I had the pleasure of seeing McClellan and General Banks with their staff pass over our structure.[87] When the bridge was completed, the troops composing Banks's Division commenced going over. The sight seen in that half hour I shall long remember. Standing on the opposite shore, you could see the bridge was covered with Infantry, and on the railroad round under the cliff, was troops, troops, marching, marching on to "Dixie." As they touched the sacred soil, their enthusiasm knows no bounds, the bands played, and the air was filled with shouting. But while looking at all this I turned with stranger, deeper feeling to a little Engine House, where John Brown held his own one day awhile ago, and I could not help thinking after all, we were all John Brown men.[88] "Glory, Hallelujah, &c."

At this moment, troops are going over, some Fire Zouaves just now, and they itched to get hold of two fire-engines that were laying by the road, [they] even begged permission.[89]

Camping is not such a bad thing. Ours are Sibley tents,[90] and excepting the want of room, I had rather sleep here than at our Washington quarters. Last night, I slept splendidly.

This is a most woe-begone, desolate, God-forsaken place I was ever in. Everything is burnt & desolate. Only seven families are living in the town.[91]

They say we are to build another bridge.[92] Troops crossing yet. I can give but a faint sketch of all we have seen and done, but we have put out the longest pontoon bridge ever put out I believe. More Anon.

To-night at 7 or so, I will write again. All of us have been busy during the day, one detail at this, another unloading cars of lumber, &c.; a little while ago, I was with a detail for pulling a hawser taut, which is stretched

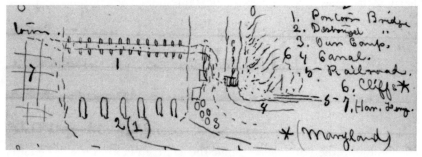

Pontoon Bridge at Harpers Ferry. Thompson's rough sketch of the bridge the battalion erected at Harpers Ferry in February 1862, showing its relation to the town. The number 2 marks the destroyed bridge and the parenthetical (1) refers to a marginal comment that "there are only five piers in the bridge," suggesting that Thompson drew one too many. Like many other sketches in Thompson's wartime journal, this one was included in or near the main text, as can be seen from the word "town" in the upper left corner.

across the river for the purpose of strengthening the bridge. It was the hardest work yet.

A company of Colonel Geary's Regiment captured a cannon and forty men (Secesh) who were preparing to shell us, but were fortunately prevented.[93] It is a wonder we were not troubled. We might have had a serious time of it. "How wondrous &c."

Looking from our tent door, or more properly slit, you can see far up the Maryland cliffs, a large white stone, with another laid across it, which has the appearance of a cross from the town. This has a peculiar significance to me, as it was put there by Cook, one of John Brown's men.[94] What it meant, who can tell; how many eyes have looked up and gazed with inward delight on that symbol, within that dark crevice, and hailed it, perhaps as a cross of fire to lead them from an Egypt of sin? There it stands, mute, but how impressive?

Soldiers are yet going over *our* bridge, Regiment after Regiment. It is some 825 feet in length, and floats in a current running at the rate of 10 miles an hour nearly. Harpers Ferry is lit up with light seeming like a thriving town to-night, contrasting strangely with "Put out your lights so as not to excite attention of the enemy," (the order we had the first night we came). Smoke was curling out of the chimneys this afternoon, suggesting household hearths, graced by homely friendship and cheer, but soldiers are round them!

I went up on to the hill by the town, and the sight from there is melancholy but impressive. All the splendid Government works are utterly ruined, ruined, the water-works being comparatively perfect, reminding me of a passage of eloquence, I think by Macaulay, referring to the fountains of some ancient city, surviving all the rack of ruin and time's decay.[95] More Anon.

✦— * Sergeant Gerber was a remarkable man in many respects. He was educated for a priest—was a bugler in the Mexican War—was detailed by General Scott to blow the "General's call" at the surrender of the city of Mexico[96]—he became Major J. C. Duane's *factotum* in executing his plans[97]—he drilled the volunteer engineers[98]—and kept up with the immense expansion of pontinering which was in an experimental stage in this country—he was a faithful intelligent assistant, as the first important bridge building at Harpers Ferry exemplified. He was

A Sketch View from Harpers Ferry. This sketch shows the pontoon bridge laid by the Engineer Battalion at Harpers Ferry in February 1862.

a man that any one would remember, and innumerable are the humourous stories related of him—he received a medal from Congress I think[99] (His medal shows him to [be] a G.A.R. comrade[100]). He fell sick at Alexandria, Virginia, in 1862 and never was in the field again on duty. He had a deep full voice, which could be heard in common conversation across a parade ground. He preferred to be the ranking non-commissioned officer of the U.S. army—than to receive a commission. His reading of the funeral service was most impressive. He died at Willets Point, New York. He kept a journal in a secret cypher—but left no key—it is at Willets Point, New York, I believe. He had a way of giving orders in a droll way.

Coolidge,[101] who was detailed, was at the burial of Latson;[102] He told me it was one of the most solemn scenes he ever witnessed. It was at a late hour in the night, and a dark, dismal rainy one at that. It was near some church, and when Sergeant Gerber read the Episcopal service for the dead, his remarkable deep and strong voice filled the whole space.

James C. Duane. Captain Duane commanded the Engineer Battalion from before Thompson joined the unit until August 1862.

Sergeant Frederick W. Gerber, Company A, US Engineer Battalion. Gerber enlisted in Company A in June 1846, just six weeks after its establishment, remaining with the company until after the Civil War. When he retired in 1871, he was awarded the Medal of Honor in recognition of his twenty-five years of service.

Harpers Ferry.

March 1, 1862.

Cool. My birth-month again. I would like to get hold of my old Journal, to see what I thought then.

Yesterday, we threw a Flying Bridge over the Shenandoah to pass troops.[103] It worked finely.

They (rebels) shelled a train car yesterday, near Berlin Heights, but did no harm. They were captured by Colonel Geary's command, and also some guns and forty men that were to pepper us, but were fortunately prevented, or it might have made trouble.[104] As it is, we have met with no accident, excepting two of our boys who tumbled into the [Chesapeake and Ohio] canal the night we moved the boats from the cars. It was a dangerous place anyway.

Thayer, Currier and myself went on a foraging scrape for wood. We took the liberty to go a good ways for wood! We went into five houses, and they were mean, miserable homes, indeed. The school-house was made of logs and a poor place it was for "ideas to shoot." You can judge of the character of a people by their school-houses. It is milder to-day.

Harpers Ferry.
March 2, 1862. Sunday.

Quite pleasant this morning, though cloudy. Our duties are not so tedious and hard as usual; but we are to do more yet.

I find nature has a language, a sort of spiritual language you might say, and it only requires acquaintance with her rocks and hills for a little while to have them talk to you. It is a regret with me that I cannot stop long enough to commune with these old cliffs, for I have caught their spirit here once and awhile in my haste and hurry for they have a solemn tale to tell to him who would hear. I am a child of nature. Rocks, hills, rivers, clouds, stars and the glorious sun improve with me on acquaintance. I can always find a new beauty every day. Oh! I long to talk with my old village hills again. To them I will hie for all the greetings of friends or relations; they are my friends, my kin.

Washington.
March 4, 1862. Tuesday.

Washington again. I am tired, so I won't write a lot now, but leave some room.

Monday night in a pelting rain storm, we struck tents and departed as suddenly as we came. We left a Corporal and two men to look after the bridge. At sunrise this morning we marched into our quarters, and have this day to recruit in, and scour and clean our guns which are terribly rusty.

Our comrades [who were] left here heard that we were cut to pieces and everything horrible and untrue.

The thing I notice particularly in this section of country, and I presume all Northerners do, is the difference in settlements and towns, and private residences. Instead of neat villages and cosy collections of houses, you [have] a large mansion with its plantation, and a collection of houses are like a dozen or so New England woodsheds and corn barns called together by the trump of some Belial;[105] miserable, nasty dens, all plainly telling there is no middle class full of energy and intelligence, but a high, haughty class and a low, degraded, spiritless set of poor whites and slaves. How different from the land of the North, the land of the free, the free!

Washington.
March 9, 1862. Sunday.
A spring-like day, balmy and genial like the days at home.

Since our Harpers Ferry raids, we have been working light and snug, loading boats on to wagons, and arranging all the this is and that is of a boat-train.[106] We shall soon be away again. Mrs. Rumor, who killed her husband by tattling, says we shall go to Budd's Ferry,[107] and moreover are going to build a bridge of a mile and a quarter in length! Whew, I don't believe it, and yet I can't say I don't.

Talking about some religious people I used this expression which I will note down, "They would steal the garb of an angel to hide their own sins."

Towards Fairfax Court House, Va.
March 11, 1862. Tuesday.
A splendid day. Another place, my friend. We received orders, and are about ten miles from Fairfax Court House. Marched with full rig, rather fatiguing, but stood it quite well.[108] A camp is a fine sight at night, & expect tattoo to sound, so I must cut short, More Anon.

Towards Fairfax Court House, Va.
March 12, 1862. Wednesday.
A very fine day indeed, far different from the old saw "if March comes in like a lion, &c." First, for facts and then for *fancy*. We started from Washington about 6½ *o'clock* Tuesday morning with knapsacks packed and usual ammunition, and by easy marching found ourselves about two miles distant from Fairfax Court House at 3½ o'clock p.m. We pitched our tents

and encamped for the night. This morning we struck tents and recommenced our march at 6 o'clock. When at Fairfax (*10 o'clock*) we encamped near a rebel epaulement, a poor piece of work at that.[109]

Now for description. The morning we started was fine as we could wish, mild and genial, and the songs of the Spring birds sounded sweetly to our hearts, Oh!

> Oh! cease your song, sweet birds
> Remind me not of other days
> In other vales your song I've heard,
> When other lips have spake your praise.
> Those other lips; rich, ruby lips and rare
> And she, Oh! she, who them possessed,
> Thy song, Spring birds, with hers could ne'er compare!
> Cease Spring birds, and let my morning rest!

We marched by short jaunts and with rests awhile. I got along finely and we could ask no better weather, warm but with a cool, fresh breeze blowing. The country is rough and hilly for about six miles from Long Bridge,[110] then the road is better and quite decent. When going over Long Bridge, I could not but help thinking of Winthrop, poor, good fellow.[111] The country is rather miserable, as far as houses go, and then think of "the rich and opulent citizens of Virginia, finding the tyranny of the North insupportable &c." They are mostly log, and the best are but poor, and all but two or three are gutted, windows gone and the very picture of desolation. The richness of the soil I cannot answer for, but the land is rolling and fine, with Northern energy, Virginia would be a splendid state.

When over Long Bridge I saw a lady standing on the banquette of a redoubt with a red hood on,[112] it started me, for my mother once wore such; it is the first time I have been reminded right at the heart of her. I am in good health, but a little footsore.

Again, at 7½ o'clock, I will write a little more, without regard to order and arrangement; this Journal will be a sort of grotto crusted with ideas, and in future time myself and others will amuse ourselves with this deformity or beauty.

The President (Lincoln) is here, and McClellan is farther on. Manassas is evacuated, and entirely deserted.[113] A man told me, who was there yesterday and 3 miles beyond. He represents everything in sad shape, even the dead unburied; one body half covered and the spade sticking in the ground beside the corpse. Where we are to go, I, of course, cannot tell. I have learned to pay no attention or fuss or worry about that point.

The Fairfax Court House itself is a time-worn, brick structure, and from its cupola, you have an extensive view. The chief interest is the portion of country being the scene of the revelries of Greenway Court, presided over by Lord Fairfax and graced by the presence of Geo. Washington,[114] and so pleasantly described by Washington Irving. My friend Kimball* says Washington has presided over the solemnities of the Court. At present instead of a splendid fox-hunt you can only see camps and camps. 200,000 men, I hear, probably over estimated, are congregated in this vicinity. "On to Richmond" will soon be the cry, if not now.

* Since honorably discharged by his application.[115]

We have been doing nothing of any account to-day, but looking at the scenes around us. There is such a day as this, a fascinating beauty in the movements and evolutions of war. The Cavalry drill interested me as much as anything, the Charge is magnificent, the blast of the bugle, the thunder of the rushing steed, the wild hurrah of the riders, the glitter of the flashing steel, the rush and roar excite the feelings of a beholder to the utmost extent.

➤— At about this time, we built some kind of rafts with the use of barges to land troops in shallow water, and we had it that we were [to] land troops to attack some fortifications on the lower Potomac. President Lincoln appeared very much interested in it, as he came down one day and looked at the arrangements. But nothing was ever done with them.[116]

Fairfax Court House, Va.
March 14, 1862. Friday.

A foggy morning and rather chilly. We changed our camp to about a half mile farther on, near McClellan's Head Quarters, who occupies a large building on our right.

We sleep well, though without a stove in the tent. With Hemlock and Cedar spray we "shingle" (in lumberman style) our tent floor of earth, and when finished it is as springy and easy as a Brussels carpet, and rivalling the Eastern censer in fragrant incense and aroma. I had a fine night's sleep, pleasant dreams, &c.

It is a striking sight at night from our quarters to see the flickering camp-fires of our troops,* behind trees and woods, near and distant, as far as eye can see.

* By "our troops" I mean *Federal Forces.*

Uncle Sam's Pontoon Shoes

The Peninsula Campaign, March–August 1862

From this time [early 1862] to the close of the war the engineer troops were on duty with the Army of the Potomac.

At the siege of Yorktown:

"The Battalion was engaged on the trenches and communications, from the beginning to the end of operations. It furnished superintending and instructing details for the entire parts of the line. The Battalion also assisted in making roads, and laid several bridges of pontons, three of the most important of which were composed of batteaux and crossed the north branch of Wormley Creek. The troops of the line at this early period of the war had received no practical instruction in making batteries and throwing up breastworks. The Battalion was drawn upon heavily in consequence, to furnish men, who always performed the duty of laying out the works, and imparting instruction to the troops of the line. Almost the entire line of trenches was in charge of Duane and his officers and men of the Battalion." From Letter of Bvt. Brig. Gen. C. B. Reece, Major, U.S. Corps of Engineers.

At Fair Oaks the Battalion was under arms during the entire night at New Bridge on the Chickahominy, awaiting orders to throw a bridge; and next morning was engaged in building one bridge and part of another, and in constructing roads leading to the same. During the construction of these bridges the rebel sharpshooters had possession of the opposite bank of the river.

A portion of the Battalion at the battle of Mechanicsville was ordered to New Bridge for the purpose of tearing up the bridge at that point as soon as the army had crossed. The Battalion was subsequently ordered to Gaines' Mills, where it threw up intrenchments on the right of Gaines' house. Portions of the Battalion were stationed at different bridges to destroy them as soon as the army should finish crossing. They were under arms all night, and destroyed the bridges just after daylight on June 28, the enemy appearing on the opposite bank before the work of demolition was fairly over.[1] *The roads to the rear were also put in proper condition for use, a portion of them being impassable, and to again render them impassable after the army had passed. At Malvern Hill, the Engineer Battalion was posted on the edge of a piece of woods to act as infantry. It received orders to slash this piece of timber in such a manner that by cutting a few trees the whole would fall. In this it was assisted by the 4th Maine Volunteers.*

—LIEUT. TURTLE'S ESSAY

✠— Throughout this book may be found notes of mine indicating criticism upon General McClellan. Among the soldiers, after his retirement there were sharp differences of opinion, so much so, at one camp we were ordered to stop the argument. There was a feeling, especially I think among some of the higher officers, that insisted on *posing* him as a martyr in some way of the administration, and that the war would never be brought to a successful issue except on "McClellan's plan"; but I believe as time goes by, and the war [is] more carefully studied, and especially without the attendant feeling of *impatience* so prevalent at that time, his campaigns will be found to be well conducted, and he fought Antietam, a decisive battle of the war, and the Wilderness campaign taught us that the "following up" was not so easy and trifling a performance with the Army of Northern Virginia, as our desires would prompt us, or the wishes of others so keen to point out.

I do not believe any successor of his had the *Entire* confidence and hearty aid of his officers as McClellan; with the soldiers it was also true, although they knew that it was their part to fight under anyone—John Pope or Pope John.

Gettysburg was the great decisive battle of the war, perhaps the only one, when we consider all the consequences that might have followed had [Robert E.] Lee been successful there, and the destroying of his army would not have made it much more so.

Therefore I feel that after all it will be found that McClellan fought successful campaigns, as the Peninsula, resolved itself into the extrication of that army, the Antietam [campaign], to foil Lee of his designs on northern territory, and both were successful. But I shall ever feel, that there were opportunities open to him that never again occurred to the Army of the Potomac, that had he possessed a quick *instinct* could have been improved upon, and at least would have created a great effect in the confidence of the troops, if of no durable effect; the war had to be fought out anyway, of course, but McClellan might have given us a "*crossing of the Delaware*" at Fair Oaks, and let Lee try to drive us from Malvern Hill, if he could try, and after he had given it up, then gone to Harrison's Landing as we pleased. The Army of the Potomac never could comprehend why it left the Malvern Hill battle-field or the position of Chancellorsville; it was a victorious army at the first and had not begun to fight at the second. General Washington was slow and conservative, but he could be audacious in the extreme when the occasion appeared.

And to close, I believe McClellan would have fought well to the very end, and we would not have had Fredericksburg or Chancellorsville, and he would have gained confidence in his powers as he learned what the Army of the Potomac could endure.

Washington, D.C.
March 15, 1862. Saturday.
At 7 o'clock to-night, it is raining like fun, "the Lord has lost the stopple," sure. Well, Mr. Journal you and I fly around like thistle-down, eh! Well, at 5 o'clock (March 14, Friday), we struck tents and walked the Bull Run ~~rout~~e step on to ~~Bailey's Cross Roads~~ Benson's Tavern, where we pitched tents for the night.[2] It was damp and foggy, with big drops at uncomfortably short intervals, but we had a good night's sleep after all, making our, at least mine, bed of a good sized board and some dry grass which I got by pulling it from underneath the uppermost grass; it is interesting to see how a soldier is put upon his own hook, it is No. 1, and yet with an eye to your "bunky's" welfare; I had to look out sharp for my board. We went right into the old building there, and almost finished the gutting of it. Reveille sounded at 4½ o'clock this morning and we struck tents and had breakfast and got away at 6 o'clock. We rushed through mud, rain and everything, one of our boys, an English chap, talked depreciatingly of the "'ills and 'allers." It is the hardest march we have had as yet, coming from

Fairfax here in about 5 hours, and we greeted our quarters with secret joy, for we did not talk much. Company B of course marched well.

We did not do anything this tramp, things turning out rather different from what was expected. The sudden and unexpected evacuation of Manassas has surprised all. Judging from the troops marching in that direction a movement of considerable character was expected, but Banks's coming down on one hand and this Advance on the other frightened them.[3] It is rumored the Rebels have retreated to Gordonsville and intend making a stand there,[4] and also to cut off Burnside, and the story to-night is that *he is cut up.*[5] Troops are coming rapidly from Fairfax Court House in this direction and to Alexandria, and we may move Monday, and a "roomy" just remarked that we were to go at eight too-morrow. One of our boys who was on guard at McClellan's Head Quarters says officers and all seemed in a quandary yesterday, and were running from here and there to get orders, but probably it was a new sight to him, and he probably exaggerated it. It seems so cheerful in our quarters to-night; I received a letter from mother. It did me [remainder of line illegible]

Washington, D.C.
March 16, 1862. Sunday.

Cloudy this forenoon. The old Commandment "Six days &c." is revered or rather parodized to-day and in fact there is no Sunday in the army, and it would read thus, "Six days shalt thou labor and on the seventh shalt thou labor like thunder." We are loading chess &c., tools, boats &c., on to steam-boats and tugs, preparing for some important move. Nothing but steamers are to be seen on the Potomac. Boston boats, North River boats, Philadelphia boats, with their familiar names, *Nelly Baker, Frances Skiddey* &c. I shall not spend time and occupy space in guessing where we are going, but probably down the river, somewhere.[6] Got a letter from mother.

Washington, D.C.
March 17, 1862. Monday.

Cool. Last part of yesterday afternoon I went with Sergeant Ayers on a trial trip at towing Ponton boats down to Alexandria and back.[7] They went well, and I had a good ride. The shores of the Potomac are anything but picturesque. I went on Guard, and it was a magnificent sight from No.

3 down the river, with the lights from the numerous steamers and craft. I saw the *Canonniers*, a Narragansett boat, and I saw the very places on her deck where I had chatted with a schoolmate and read newspapers, some—I can't think how many years ago down Narragansett bay.

To-day the packing of our tools and boats, &c. on the tugs &c., was completed, and we had an order to start, horses harnessed to our Company wagons, but after a while we unslung knapsacks and to-night I am sitting by our cheerful fire-place, scribbling this, pausing once and awhile to hear Slater, a veteran story-teller, hold forth, while Higgins is noting down notes beside me, and at the farther end of the table, a party of four are having a quiet game of "euchre."[8] How strange, perhaps in a few short days we may be exposed to every discomfort, while here we are as unconcerned, with no misgivings, no thought or care for what is to come, as we are here to-night. *Au Revoir.*

Washington, D.C.
March 22, 1862. Saturday.

Quite pleasant this morning. Yesterday was my birthday (twenty-third), which I celebrated by a sick time in the afternoon. I been having a cold, and it reached its culminating point and I had a sorry time of it. It is the first time I have been sick at all since I enlisted. There is nothing so grateful to a soldier, as the kind interest in your welfare by a comrade; home-folks can never appreciate or understand it. To-day I would like to be in a quiet, pleasant room with books to look at and a drawing or so to fuss over a little; and better still a cheerful, amiable ———— to talk with. I feel effeminate actually to-day in my tastes and disposition. I am improving finely and she's well as ever to-night.

Washington.
March 23, 1862. Monday.

Quite a decent day. I am feeling finely. I shall be glad when we are away, I am tired of hanging round here. Went to church yesterday forenoon. The choir sung "Hark ten thousand harps and voices, &c." It made me think of my choir days, but the old sweet familiar tenor and a pleasant alto I missed. I saw a fresh looking girl's face, and oh! my recreant heart will you never forget the one she resembled, say?

Frederick "Fritz" Vogel, Company C
(later Company D).

✠— Thursday, March 27, 3 a.m. Reveille. Went on board the steamer
Maryland, formerly a man of war sailing vessel, had a brig in tow.
Steamer *Herald* with two barges in tow. Companies A and B divided
among the two steamers.[9]

Friday, March 28. At 12 noon dropped anchor at Fort Monroe,
slept on board.

Saturday, March 29. . . . Disembarked and stacked arms. Our camp
is right alongside of Hampton Creek.

—Journal of Frederick Vogel[10]

Washington.
March 30, 1862. Sunday.

A dull, slashy mean day. Since last writing time considerable change has
taken place in our Battalion. Wednesday morning (March 26, 1862) they
went away on a couple of steamers with [a] boat train &c. strung along behind like the old Spanish Armada. Where they have gone I only guess, viz:,
Fortress Monroe. I was among the detail left behind to pack up and send
away our materials, which are being packed on board some canal boats by
ourselves and detail of Volunteer Engineers. We are having a good time of

it, especially in the eating line, we live high below stairs. I [have] been up the last two nights with White at the Hospital. I am excused from fatigue duty thereby, and I get along very well indeed. I think we shall change our Head Quarters to Fortress Monroe.

✠— With the Army of the Potomac were two Volunteer Regiments of Engineers, the 15th and 50th New York. They were a splendid collection of men, and did excellent service. In the beginning they were not as well posted in fortification as we, and were drilled by some of the Company A men in Washington, in Ponton drill; but they became as proficient in all branches as ourselves in time, and from their greater numbers they could detail men for [a] greater variety of work than our four companies, probably never exceeding 500 men at most. There was never any feeling between us more than a good natured rivalry, as between our own companies. We were volunteers in the regular army, as the re-enlistment list will abundantly prove; and nothing but a great national necessity brought us into the army, and when it no longer existed, we laid aside the blouse and went back to civil life as well as the Volunteers.[11]

Sunday, March 30. Rained hard all night and we were not called out until 11 a.m. unloading our trains and getting the pontoons on wagons.

—Journal of Frederick Vogel

Down to the Hospital. Washington, D.C.
March 30, 1862. Sunday, 10:30 p.m.
   Although I have made one entry to-day, I will write a little to-night. I am writing flat on my breast on the floor, the draft of air through the room rendering anything otherwise rather flickery with the candle. It is a rude looking night out, raining with rather a high wind, and clouds black as Erebus, with lightning the first of the evening and thunder. I saw an old soldier in here to-night by the name of Vickers. He [has] been in service some fifty years, thirty-five in the U.S. He was at Waterloo, and many of the 1812 engagements.[12]
   I have heard from the Engineers by the Captain who transported them to Fort Monroe. They are about five miles of the fort and were unloading the

train as fast as possible. There is an immense number of troops collected in the vicinity of that place, and *are moving on to Richmond.* We shall go by next Wednesday and will probably see some of the things of war. On! On!

Near Fortress Monroe.
April 4, 1862. Friday.

I must be brief. I am writing in a wagon body upside down on a canal boat, up by Hampton, Virginia. We started from Washington Wednesday about 3 o'clock. Corporal Thompson, Ames, [and] myself got left at Alexandria and rejoined our detachment here at Fort Monroe to-day.[13] Saw the famous *Monitor.* Hampton is a melancholy sight. We marched up a ways to rejoin the Battalion, found Boat-wagons but "nary" a Battalion, so we returned to the boat.

✠ Friday, April 4. Started at 12 towards Big Bethel. Got sick from drinking too much water and had to fall out, came up to camp quite late.

—Journal of Frederick Vogel

"Our House" at Hampton on a Canal Boat. Sketch depicting the canal boat accommodations described by Thompson in his April 4, 1862, entry.

Hampton, Va.
April 5, 1862. Saturday.

I can't tell what sort of weather. Weather is in the particular tense, transitive mode here. We are afflicted with sudden showers. To-night we had a beautiful sunset, and by twilight were easily discussing clams, &c., when there came a little flurry of wind which is bringing a thunder shower on the end of it as quick as possible. Peach trees are in blossom and the willows sprouting forth. Amid the melancholy waste of once beautiful Hampton, it is suggestive of a peculiar train of thought to see the trees budding forth the same, whatever ill betides their once possessor. Last night Ames and I were disturbed in our connubial felicity by a stream of water trickling down on our faces and clothes; we suddenly turned out like two snapping and snarling drowned out woodchucks and went round bare-headed and bare-footed "fixin'" the best we could and passed a very uncomfortable night, however to-day I have turned a wagon into a nice room with a table, sir! close and tight and this is written in it sir! too!

We are engaged in unloading one of our barges, which was obliged to be beached. Our Battalion went day before yesterday for Big Bethel at 3 o'clock, quite suddenly I should judge, as the boats are not all unpacked. Heavy firing was heard to-day in the direction of Yorktown, and it is not 4th of July firing, either. Alas!

⊱— Saturday, April 5. Started early. McClellan and staff passed us, the roads being blocked we marched until 2 a.m. of Sunday, April 6. Made me a bed of fence rails. Slept one hour when we started again, reached the large camp at noon. This camp is named McClellan and is the same field in which Cornwallis surrendered to Washington.[14]

—Journal of Frederick Vogel

Hampton, Va.
April 8, 1862. Tuesday.

Rainy. Last night we had to load a boat with tools, anchors, cordage, &c. It took us until 1 o'clock, and was a miserable job, rainy, muddy &c., etc. We were wet through but we were so fortunate as to have quarters on board the boat we loaded, and to-day are drying up and recruiting after our fatigue. It is the meanest job yet.

✟— Thursday, April 11. Went into the woods and made gabions.[15]

—Journal of Frederick Vogel

3½ miles of Yorktown, Va.
April 12, 1862. Saturday.

A splendid day, as was yesterday. Friday afternoon the 11th, 3½ o'clock we left the *Nastasket*, had a little lunch with the detachment at the Battalion's Head Quarters at Ship Point. It was pleasant to meet them, and one of them, although with poor variety of rations, slyly slipped a roasted sweet potatoe into my hand, it took hold of me. I felt weak and aily on starting; the water of Hampton gave me the diarrhea. I hardly thought I could get to our destination. The roads were positively awful. I went to my knees in mud. To-day I assisted in making gabions, and to-night feel much better. We can hear the peculiar ringing sound of Yorktown shells from here. We have a pleasant encampment, formerly a rebel one. The rebels' winter quarters are fine log huts, plastered with mud and comfortable. I could write a great deal more, but a sorry brief note *must* do. *More Anon.*

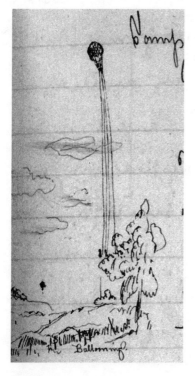

✟— Friday, April 12.[16] Prof. Lowe made a balloon ascension.[17] Marched off in a hurry and after a great deal of countermarching got on the right road and passed a little village of log huts formerly a rebel camp. About 2 miles beyond this we halted and pitched our tents on the banks of Black Creek.[18] We found here the remains of a former rebel camp, nice spring near camp. Immediately on our right is a strong rebel earthwork in very good order now held by one of our artillery Companies. [The] York River is right ahead about a mile, I can

Ballooning. Thompson's rough sketch of an observation balloon in use.

Virginia Outhouses. Thompson's sketch shows the location of the engineer camp near Wormley Creek in mid-April 1862, while its title also reflects Thompson's poor opinion of southern homes (see also his November 11, 1862, entry).

see the masts of three of our gunboats. The squad we left behind at Washington came in yesterday p.m. & such a handshaking!

—Journal of Frederick Vogel

Near Yorktown, Va.

April 16, 1862. Wednesday.

Fine weather, warm, *hot* days, very cool nights. I cannot write regularly, but with a scribble once and awhile and my letters home, I shall have an account of things after all. Since last date we have worked two nights, building bridges. We were obliged to keep quiet, as we were near the rebel lines. A number of bridges are being put across at that point, I should judge, so a rapid advance could be made when necessary.[19] A large train of Siege guns and heavy Artillery are near us. When the fire is opened on Yorktown, there will be a burning time of it.

Near Yorktown, Va.

April 20, 1862. Sunday.

Pouring down to-day. Just home from Cheeseman's Landing on duty. Went there Wednesday the 16th, weather was splendid till last night.

Cheeseman's Landing is as pleasant a place as I have seen in Virginia. Oysters in *abundance*. We were engaged in loading boats. Had a good time, got some letters too. This morning we came home in the rain, and the tent is quite agreable.

Near Yorktown, Va.
April 22, 1862. Tuesday.

A bright sunny day in prospect. We have had a spell of weather since last date. Sunday evening when I most desired a good "layout," I was put on guard at the bridges on Wormley's Creek.[20] Corporal Thompson was in charge of us. We went by road to our post, which we found after a great deal of inquiry &c.; when we got to the bridge the guard would not let us cross to our quarters [on] the other side (two of us were to be at one of the upper and two men at the lower). I was one to stop at the lower; we could not cross and the former guard went away and we made friends with the volunteer guard and their fire and sat there in the dark and mist and with strange feeling saw the fire gradually die out in our good quarters on the other side that we could not go to.* Bye and bye it began to rain and we passed a queer night of it. I managed to sleep a little towards morning, the tide came in extraordinary high and kept us moving our fire up and up. The two that went to upper bridge fared hardly as well as we. Corporal and the "bold, brave guard" slept in the centre of the bridge with their heads on the side-rail, right in the pitiless rain. In the morning we got a boat and went to the long looked at retreat. We fried some beef steak and with some chess built one additional L to our suburban residence. Here we passed a decent day, though we were wet and damp. Night came along in due time, but no relief, raining the while with all vengeance. We waited and waited, then finally made arrangements for another night on guard at the bridges. We drew lots for our 1st & 2d &c. Reliefs and then turned in to sleep. Just as I was nicely dozing in they came, wet and muddy, the new "Guard," we put on our "duds" and started for home at 9 at night. During the day we captured a *dug out*, and in it we were going by the creek home to our camp. It was dark and vast differences were in our minds in regard to the posé of the channel,[21] & the consequence was we went this side and that, got *stuck* and got off, then got to swearing a little, got challenged, got into strange inlets and coves, and even began to think we had got to Secessia, but when we had nearly given up, we came unexpectedly upon the point where we loaded our boats previous to taking up to where we built our bridges. After a great deal of mud tribulation we arrived at camp at 11 o'clock. I turned in the best I could and had a good sleep.

⊁— * While on this guard, I talked with some of the volunteers about the length of the war. One of them stated he expected "to be home by the 4th of July." I felt accordingly, that I was in for three years whether the war lasted that long or not; I considered they had the best of us.[22]

It was clear starlight when I turned in and this morning the sun has come with healing and balms in his rays for the wet soldiers. We could hear the shell burst in the rebel fortifications from our gun-boats, with a peculiar sound. Wormley's Creek is quite picturesque. I could sketch with profit there. Fine tall characteristic pines, bluffs and splendid woody backgrounds. Although I have been so exposed, I feel the best this morning since I left Washington.

It is amusing to see how politeness will wear off under misfortune. Last night when we were fussing along the extraordinary crooked creek, at first it was "Don't you think we had better go there," but the gravity of manner wore off, and came down the sharp bony ornery words, 'You d——n fool, why in hell don't you keep her off!" etc. &c.

Near Yorktown, Va.
April 23, 1862. Wednesday.

A fine day what little I have seen of it. Last night I lost my nice "lay out" again. About 6 o'clock, I found myself at Battery No. 3 and at dark commenced to work. The battery had to be rebuilt in the embrasures (6),[23] and the second tier of Gabions all had to come down. All we did was to set the Gabions and get the lines true &c., the Volunteers doing the shoveling. We were in close proximity to rebel batteries, and saw their camp fires flickering like any camp fire, and heard a roll of a drum. We had to work quietly, and when we got home when the east was gray with the morning and its reigning star shining brightly upon us, it seemed strange to speak freely above a whisper. I eat breakfast; washed up, went to sleep, and have just woke up about 3½ o'clock.

Before Yorktown.

April 28, 1862. Monday.

Fine to-day. It is delightful to see the genial sun after the long dismal N.E. storm we have had. Was out last night on the outworks, and ran a parallel.[24] Just about dusk we had three shells tossed at us, coming very near, the pieces coming over the redoubt like hail. A shell is a queer feeling tickler surely, it comes whipping like a fiend, when *whang* it bursts with a most heavy sound.

I saw E. M. Marshall[25] in the 40th N.Y. Mozart Regiment.[26] We had a pleasant chat, he being the first man I have seen since I enlisted that I was formerly acquainted with.

I think I could write a tolerable Article under the title of "A night in the Trenches."

Before Yorktown.

May 2, 1862. Friday.

Foggy this morning and quite warm. I am not on a detail this morning and I will catch at the chance. I have worked quite steady since last date; one day (yesterday) building a corduroy road, connecting two parallels.[27] It is something strange how human nature will accustom itself to any position. I cannot tell, but it may [be] ignorance, but a shell whizzing along and bursting fifty yards away scarcely occasions a turn of the head. Thus far none of our Battalion have been injured, though some narrow escapes have occurred.

Sweet May has come, how time flies. I wonder if any one plucks a flower and thinks of me.

Before Yorktown, Va.

May 4, 1862. Sunday.

A fine day with Yorktown evacuated![28] At 11 minutes of 7 o'clock this morning, our glorious old flag kissed the beams of the morning over the ramparts of Yorktown. Bands of music are airing themselves after a long interval [of] silence, smiles are seen where the muscles were set in firm, determined lines. I was curious to learn whether it has been a sudden or an evacuation of some length of time; but however it may be, this is the story the air is full of, "Yorktown has evacuated!" McClellan will doubtless receive his usual share of approbation and praise, but let statesmen criticise, editors disclaim and gloat over, let the sneering smile be passed along, the *mothers* of the North will send praise to God and invoke his blessing on our Commander; Oh! what heavy hearts will soon be made light. Troops are passing by, one singing "Glory Halle, hallelujah!" Oh! what changes in the camp in time of war. Stern, cold determination gives way to highest gayety and mirth. More by to-night. Good morn.

Before Yorktown, Va.
May 6, 1862. Tuesday.

A fine day in prospect. Yesterday was a miserable day, pouring rain all the time, and the sun comes with healing in its beams for the soldiers. We heard heavy firing in the direction of Williamsburg all day. I suppose our troops have overtaken them as they were retreating, as large bodies of Cavalry went away yesterday morning. A soldier who was near the action gave the account this morning, how correct I cannot tell but will enter it. "Our Cavalry overtook their main force, and by night had a severe battle, 180 Rebel prisoners."[29] I will not enter it after all. I'll wait and see. If we can keep them brimming along, and give them no time to intrench, we are well. They have fortified Yorktown with a year's labor, in a short four weeks we have rendered them untenable, without opening our batteries to any great extent, most of them unfinished.

Before Yorktown, Va.
May 7, 1862. Wednesday.

A glorious day. Last night about Tattoo we heard a great cheering above us, which came to us with considerable meaning and resulted in this news, how true I can't tell—

"*Magruder killed and his whole army captured!*"[30]

Oh! war has grown a pleasant thing to us since last Sunday; we have done but little fatigue and have cheered and heard news all the time. Our time is taken up mostly with cooking "little luxuries" for ourselves. "Our Spider" figures largely. Dandy funk, fritters, Johnny cakes, hasty pudding &c., is turned out in miraculous quantities just front of our tent; our appetites are like cormorants, one had a mess of fritters just after Tattoo! Everything is pleasant now. Sunshine, flapjacks and no work. Music regales our ears instead of the old lions whose roar is hushed and lieth quiet and still in No. 1 Battery.*

Yorktown Battery No. 4, Scene 1. Union Mortars in position near Yorktown, Battery No. 4. LC-DIG-cwpb-00135, Prints and Photographs Division, Library of Congress, Washington, DC.

Yorktown Battery No. 4, Scene 2. Another view of the mortars in Battery No. 4, near Yorktown. LC-DIG-ppmsca-08363, Prints and Photographs Division, Library of Congress, Washington, DC.

* The best shots made from No. 1 Battery, indeed *the best* of all the firing on our side, were by a man by the name of John Brown; that name seems to follow them like an avenging spirit! A strange coincidence truly.

Now the time of trial is passed, what have I to tell beside the meagre details along back. I could tell considerable, but I will tell a little disjointed at that. As some genuine wit said, "Spades were trumps" here, and surely they were, for our Engineers and picks &c. conquered Yorktown, as our batteries were not all completed and but little real firing was done, our formidable looking parallels appalled them and they recoiled from them. As a Mississippian rebel prisoner said, "The first day I came to Yorktown, you had no works, the next morning I woke up and looked out, and there was batteries all around us." He was not far out either, as our parallel seemed to grow in a night, as though some genie strewed seeds along and batteries, redoubts grew forth from the earth. Night work in the trenches is something I must write about elsewhere with more room and time, but it is a sight to be remembered, to see a thousand strung along like a train of busy ants in the night, shoveling away, with now and then a shell bursting near. It is strange feeling to have a piece of a shell come so near you, you can feel the wind, like feeling the wind from off the slowly moving wings of Death as he moves past you. The last night they held Yorktown (May 3, 1862, Saturday), I worked in Battery 14, on the right, on the river bank, and there was one gun from a shore battery that troubled us. The shells would come whizzing along, sometimes tipping the parapet[31] and ricochet into the field back. A man is placed in a safe and sightly position, who warns with "Down," "Over," and all goes on again like clockwork. Coming home from the batteries was the really most dangerous, as it brought us into one section where a large number of their shells burst. Just as we had got on to the bridge (Pontoon) from the Grist Mill, one burst just ahead of us over the water. I am tired. More Anon.

Beyond Williamsburg, Va.
May 10, 1862. Saturday.

More Anon, eh? A few minutes first. May 8th, Thursday. Left our camp at 2 o'clock, and encamped for the night between the two lines (Federal & Rebel) near the woods on a line with the two poplar trees designating the scene of Cornwallis' surrender. May 9th, struck tents and passed through Yorktown and by easy marches encamped about 8 miles of Williamsburg.

Yorktown Battery No. 1. This Union battery contained one 200-pound and five 100-pound Parrots and, according to Thompson, made some of the best shots of the brief siege there. LC-DIG-cwpbh-03379, Prints and Photographs Division, Library of Congress, Washington, DC.

May 10th, Struck tents 5½ a.m., reached Williamsburg at 10 o'clock a.m. At present, 3½ o'clock p.m., about 4 miles beyond Williamsburg, and will probably encamp.

Now for description. I must confess it was with queer feelings as I looked for the last time on a place grown quite interesting from associations, the heart will love where it goes; it bears transplanting. Our parallels indeed looked formidable as we passed them. I did not realize until we encamped the nearness of our works to theirs. It was spades and picks that took Yorktown. The Engineers have no chance for brilliancy of attack like Cavalry or Infantry, but our work though hidden is equally important.

We had many pleasant encampments, the 8th near some apples trees in a field of clover, literally "sleeping in clover." The field is celebrated as the scene of the surrender of Cornwallis, a small enclosure showing the place where Washington stood at the time. Of course there were all the camp rumors about encamping for a month &c., and they all were dissipated by the Order to "Strike tents" the next morning. Yorktown is a very strong position both by nature and artificial works, and our approach was splendid, all under the cover of a belt of woods with ravines that an immense number could be thrown forward on to the rebel works. The country from Yorktown to Williamsburg is the finest I have seen in Virginia. We had a good sleep, the 9th night. "March On &c.," at ½ past 6. Williamsburg has many pretensions to elegance and really looks the most interesting and attractive of any Virginia town (or city) I have yet seen. We had a tough hot march to-day, but a good wash in a splendid Spring and the breeze as it comes through the apple trees under which I am writing, has in a miraculous manner charmed my fatigue away. The scene of the battle of last Monday,[32] there was not much to remind you of it, only some scarred trees and some graves, "Sacred &c." Well I will stop.

Somewhere (Camp [at] Roper's Meeting House).
May 12, 1862. Monday.

A hot day yesterday, another in prospect. In consequence of our train (tool & luggage) (Company A left behind with the boat) having much difficulty getting through, (got in at 1 o'clock at night), we bivouacked for the night (May 10th) without tents. A shed near by shingled with corn stalks furnished us with a bed, and a large quantity of overcoats thrown away by the advance furnished us with bedding. I had a fine sleep, only too short. A battery was encamped near us, and in the morning (May 11th) I saw a negro take away a heaping ox load of coats, &c., the hot weather and fatiguing marches, occasions the throwing away of everything possible. A queer sort of top-dressing for a land surely.

The march yesterday was a very good one, of about 12 miles I should judge, and the road led through quite a fine tract of country, quite a number of fine plantations, with their stately mansions and the usual negro huts congregated around. Virginia roads are very fickle. We saw rebel Artillery caissons up to the hub in mud, which now is baked hard as brick around them, all this since last Tuesday. They are terribly dusty at present, and in a day's march we grow wonderfully venerably night, our beard, face, all, of a most exquisite gray. We had a good breeze yesterday. Quite a number of dead horses are along the road, left or shot by the rebels, which smell a *little* all ready. We left our airy residence of May 10th night, at 10 o'clock, encamped about 20 miles of ——— [at] 5 o'clock p.m., having marched between 11 & 12 miles. Had a good sleep, although it was very odd (comparatively). We cannot march *much* farther.

✄— At some camp, I think May 13th, as a test trial, we routed out, had roll-call, eat breakfast, struck tents—Sibleys—and were on the road in much less than an hour. It was very laborious; each Company had a wagon.

Between West Point, Va., & new Kent Court House (Cumberland Landing).
May 14, 1862. Wednesday.

That is, I think we are after quizzing the maps and judging from what I hear. We staid over a day at our encampment of May 11th night, and many of us improved the time in washing our clothes in a rather muddy brook, and a creamy whiteness was the nearest we could approach to a pearly lustre. By arranging some pines, we made quite an agreable place of a poor one. May 13th, Company B went in charge of the boat train, and with having our knapsacks carried on the teams and the good roads, conspired to make a pleasant jaunt of it for us. The country becomes finer as we go this way, more oak, chestnut, &c., than the inevitable pine, more pleasant residences. May 18th night we had a little sleep outdoors until ½ past 1 o'clock, when we started again in the dark and arrived here about 8 o'clock, and are enjoying a rest, how long may be shortly told. I cannot give even an outline, and from such a mass of stars crowding on me, I verily believe I succeed the pariel! We can hear steamboats or cars whistling which sounds awkward indeed.

White House Landing.
May 15, 1862. Thursday.

A rainy day. Last night we brought all our train, 70 wagons, through to here from White House Landing (*Cumberland,* familiarly among us).[33] It was a horrid job, coming about four miles. We are encamped in a large field near the river Pamunkey (or York),[34] steamers, gun boats thick as ever at Shipping Point. It is a striking sight here to-night, and in connection with the order to be in readiness to turn out in good fighting order on the first alarm reminds you of the night before Waterloo. Not that I think anything may happen, but I believe we have a warning from the rebels to leave the position in 24 hours.

Sketch of Company B Cook Tent, White House Landing, ca. May 1862.

White House Landing.
May 18, 1862. Sunday.

A fine sunshiny day. Since last date, we have been encamped in our present position. The White House which gives the name to this place is noted as the scene of Washington's Courtship. "The Lion in Love" loved here.[35]

Near Tunstall, Va.
May 20, 1862. Tuesday.

A fine day. Changed camp to this place (*Temple's Plantation*) this morning. Our present position is the most delightful we have been in. To the east we have a broad expansive landscape, and all the surrounding country is interesting; ravines, picturesque clumps of trees, fields of fresh springing grain, etc. I hope we can stay here some length of time. The country as well as the occasion grows more interesting as we near Richmond. Yesterday, early, the multitude commenced moving from White House, and by night nothing was left but a few Sutlers' tents and stragglers; the tented city had all disappeared.

Although there are many discomforts connected with active service, still there are many phases and incidents that smack of the poetical and romantic. I heard a bugler at the last camp near us, an old soldier from the English, who played "Put out Lights" (Taps) in a manner that I would not [have] believed possible, stirring strange and deep feelings in the heart of all. We often lingered outside the tent after Tattoo to hear him. Another little incident, on one of our marches, had a smack of poetry about it. We had been marching through a piece of wood, that on one side being burnt and thus rendering it close and very hot, and when we got out [of] the infernal place, we came to an open field, and just as we had got there, Oh! such a fresh, cool breeze, such as faint & weary men can appreciate, met us, and the boys immediately remarked "that seems like a New England (home) breeze," Oh! go where we will, we *will* think of our native hills and long for their cool and joyous breezes. Though we have met with no great hardships, yet there are times when we have thought of the cool, deep well by the apple trees, and the resting place by the door where we looked away on distant fields, wooded hills and flashing stream.

Last night I went to see the "White House;" it is a plain two story house, pleasantly situated on the banks of the river, surrounded by large trees, and the grounds indicate a *once* elegant and tasty management, seemingly done now more for reputation's sake than real genuine desire to render it what it might be. Where occurred one of the most pleasant incidents in Washington's life, it was with melancholy interest we looked on the old house and the avenue of trees, which like Napoleon's Old Guard "Die, but never surrender," beneath whose shade, perhaps, some words were spoken we would have given so much to hear, and then to speak not to gay ladies and gallant cavaliers, but only ask a few brief questions of a slowly pacing sentinel.

Heavy firing has just commenced towards Richmond, some skirmish.

Camp Cold Harbor.
May 24, 1862. Saturday.
Raining. May 22d [we] changed camp to this place, about twelve miles distant from Richmond. Quite a pleasant camping ground in a cornfield, but the corn will get sadly hoed in a queer way by Uncle Sam's pontoon shoes. We had a great march here, the first part being sweltering hot, and the last two-thirds the roads were transformed to complete Slough of Despond by a thundering shower. The sun rays have an unusual heat, it

fairly sears right into your flesh; the nights are quite even and agreable. It is comparatively quite cool to-day on account of the rain. The land is more elevated as we approach Richmond, and at our last camp I looked with satisfaction *back* on the Yorktown peninsula. Our Pontoon Train has been turned over to the 15th & 50th New York Volunteer Engineers, so we are rid of the boat job. Whiskey is dealt out twice a day, I think quinine is in it, as it is ordered by Government as a preventative of disease, chills & fevers &c. I take some occasionally. It is advisable to do so here, I think. We shall probably follow on the Advance with Head Quarters & the Reserve. I guess *our* fighting was all done at Yorktown. Beside Guard, Police and Garrison Police duty we do nothing but lay around and sleep, it is about *all* we can do on account of the heat. I have improved the cool of to-day in writing, &c. As far as news goes and the prospect ahead, the rebels are being broke up, both by the prestige of our arms and discontent among themselves. As far as Rumors and Camp Stories go we have plenty; a comical Sergeant of ours (Kendall[36]) keeps us posted on stunners of thema, last night he set the news-mongers going with the report that 10 Regiments of ours had been taken, together with Generals Casey,[37] Slocum,[38] &c., Whew!! I believe however we *drove* in the enemy some four miles by a *true account*.

Headquarters Gen'l. Porter, Camp Cold Harbor, Va. This sketch depicting the headquarters of Major General Fitz John Porter, commanding the Union V Corps, was at Camp Cold Harbor, where Thompson dated his May 24, 1862, journal entry.

Camp Cold Harbor, Va.

May 25, 1862. Monday.

A fine day. The order for to-day is, "Leave to-night with sixty rounds cartridges, three days' rations, leave knapsacks &c." More Anon.

Camp near Gaines's Mill (Near New Bridge).

May 29, 1862. Thursday.

Pleasant. May 25th, night, unloaded pontoon boats by the Chickahominy, worked all night, raining heavy all the time. One party being obliged to wade in the water to anchor them to bushes in the inlet where we launched them. Unknown to us a dead dragoon was near us, we thought it was a horse. Next day (May 26, 1862) at 3½ o'clock struck camp and came here; a good place.

Camp near New Bridge.

June 2, 1862. Monday, morning.

Going to be a searing hot day. June has come; how on eagle wings time flies. Two months gone since leaving Washington. Well may happiness, good fortune, peace, yet gild thy wings Oh! Time. Affairs are generally assuming a warlike aspect since the affair of Hanover Court House.[39] I went up to see the wounded of that battle, a fine mansion towards our front from us, with all its buildings being converted into a hospital. A pleasant path shaded with apple trees led us up to the house. On the small portico amputation was going on with appalling frequency. In the small barns were rebel and Federal wounded. The rebels, as would be supposed, were those who were so badly hurt as not to be able to get away, and were the worst of all. I will not attempt to describe the sickening sights seen there. Those who say "Storm! Storm!" would think different could they see them.

Our Battalion was out to work yesterday and the night before, building bridges. One of Company A on a reconnoitering party was shot in the breast, but we hope not mortally.[40] He is the first one injured at all so far. The stern reality of war is forcing itself on to us. A heavy skirmish* seemed to be going on our left; we could see the smoke of their pieces.

* The commencement of [the] Fair Oaks fight.[41]

✝— "June 1, 1862. 8:15 a.m. . . . . anxious to ascertain how practicable the route was, I directed Lieutenant Babcock[42] to proceed with a few of his sappers, as far as he safely could on the other side. He proceeded perhaps two hundred yards, when he was fired upon by sharpshooters ambuscaded in the vicinity, and one of his men shot through the lungs.[43] Supporting the wounded man himself, he withdrew, followed by repeated volleys. The intense anxiety I felt at this moment was partially relieved when I ascertained that it was not Lieutenant Babcock himself, as I supposed, who was shot."[44]

   J. G. Barnard and W. F. Barry,[45] *Report of the Engineer and Artillery Operations of the Army of the Potomac, From Its Organization to the Close of the Peninsular Campaign by Brig.-Gen. J. G. Barnard, Chief Engineer, and Brig.-Gen. W. F. Barry, Chief of Artillery* (New York: D. Van Nostrand, 1863), 24.

Front at Seven Pines. This photo shows Fort Richardson in the vicinity of Fair Oaks. LC-DIG-cwpb-00191, Prints and Photographs Division, Library of Congress, Washington, DC.

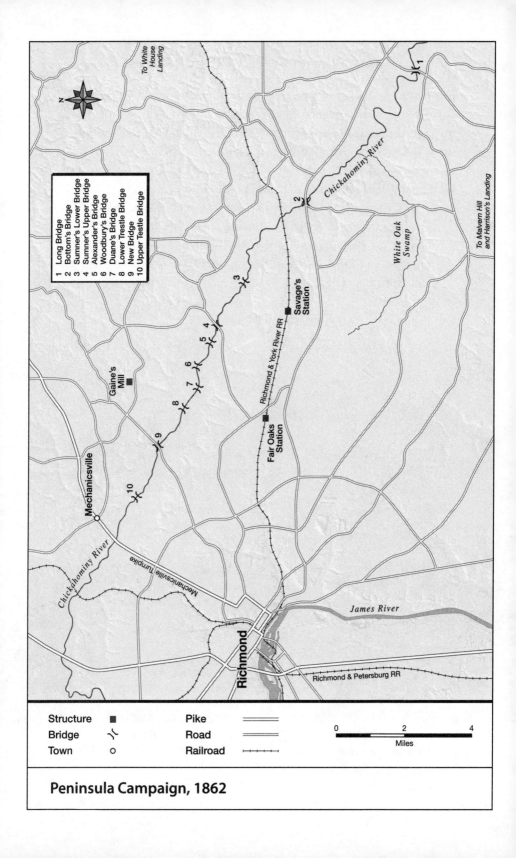

Peninsula Campaign, 1862

Legend:

1 Long Bridge
2 Bottom's Bridge
3 Sumner's Lower Bridge
4 Sumner's Upper Bridge
5 Alexander's Bridge
6 Woodbury's Bridge
7 Duane's Bridge
8 Lower Trestle Bridge
9 New Bridge
10 Upper Trestle Bridge

Structure	■	Pike	
Bridge	⅄	Road	
Town	○	Railroad	

0   2   4
Miles

Camp near New Bridge.
June 7, 1862. Saturday.

Since last date it has been rather more cool, on account of quite a storm. Fine to-day but a thunder shower has the floor now. We have been engaged mostly in building corduroy along the Chickahominy;[46] which is as dispisable a little river as I ever wish to meet with. After the dry spells before we came here, the correspondents were right no doubt in saying it was "insignificant;" but like all southern rivers it is subject to sudden over-flows. In a military point of view, it is a formidable obstacle to an invading force towards Richmond. It flows through a bottom land of perhaps a mile in width *here*, and its banks [are] fringed with close underbrush and heavy woods with occasional openings; on each side are high hills, so the rebels care not to cross it to reach us, and it will require considerable time and a great deal of labor to be crossable for us. Yesterday and day before we have been up to our arm-pits in its delectable waters. Yesterday we worked at the bridge below New Bridge;[47] we taking the lead, and by 5 o'clock or so had it so far advanced that the rebels could have a view of us and com-menced to fire at [us] with rifles. A dozen shots made us "skedaddle." One poor fellow was wounded within fifteen feet of me and died last night, I understand.[48] He was shot through the leg and hand. One bullet passed between two of us about four feet apart, and it gave me a queer sensation although it did not frighten me a bit. I had really rather be in a battle than work as we Engineers have to (as well as the details from the Infantry with us); we are targets for anything in the shape of a missile. It requires the highest kind of courage. I count myself lucky to be in my tent, and shall be happily disappointed if none of our party to-day are not injured. I shall be glad when the infernal river is past. One of Company A's men was wounded in the foot with a piece of shell at the bridge we were working at day before yesterday, nearly to our front.[49]

Camp near New Bridge.
June 15, 1862. Sunday.

Quite hot for the last few days. The 13th we broke camp and came to where we are at present which is south of Dr. Gaines's house, on an ele-vated field of wheat, which is the best encampment yet. We can look from the door of our tent on the famous Chickahominy with its bottom lands & hills. We have a splendid spring and a *big* brook to bathe in. We have been engaged in corduroying.

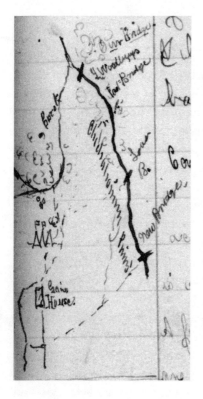

Wartime Sketch of the Chickahominy Bridges. This rough sketch from the margin of Thompson's June 15, 1862, journal entry shows several of the bridges over the Chickahominy River as Union forces prepared for operations outside of Richmond, but it is difficult to decode because north appears to be oriented toward the image's left. The bridge labeled "Our Bridge" by Thompson appears to be Duane's Bridge as identified on the map of the "Peninsula Campaign, 1862," while what Thompson labeled "Lower B." is the Lower Trestle Bridge. New Bridge is correctly identified.

Camp Lincoln.
June 19, 1862. Thursday.

Changed camp. Some two or three miles across the Chickahominy near McClellan's Head Quarters. Our bridge building is over I guess. What we are to do here I cannot guess, perhaps fortify a little. A forward movement will soon take place. Our bridge is a fine one.

There are a great many sick in the Battalion. Drum (of Company A) died at our camp.[50] There is something touching in those wayside graves to me, falling by the way, no one to remember them, soon forgotten by their comrades; but how many friends would fain wander in spirit to that lonely grave.

Camp Lincoln.
June 22, 1862. Sunday.

A fine hot day in prospect. Some details of ours have been out the last few days, having charge of works.[51] Things begin to look interesting, the two armies are so near together they can almost count noses. Skirmishes are occurring at intervals; last night I got up about twelve and there was a great popping and cheering ahead of us. I think a ground attack all at once will be the game, but there are other things to come about before that takes place. Burnside will have a hand in it. I saw him and General Prince at the other (New Bridge) camp.[52]

Camp Lincoln.
June 25, 1862. Wednesday.

A cool morning. Night before last worked on a battery (No. 3) by the river at the right of New Bridge. It was as bougerish a situation as I ever worked in. During the day it was shelled by three or four rebel batteries and why they did not in the night was strange. It was very dark with vivid flashes of lightning at intervals; at twelve we had a shower, the heaviest one yet. I cuddled down by a piece of Artillery and covered myself with my overcoat cape which shed the rain like a poncho. It was a strange sight when it lightened to see the men in all the cautious positions of a person walking in the dark. It would make a fine steel engraving, it was like some ghostly Pandemonium suddenly revealed to you.

I believe I have not made mention of one very interesting phase of camp life, viz: singing at night. It is very natural that men while sitting around the camp-fire to think of home, and to sing the songs of home. To appreciate the sound of music at night welling forth from the darkness and distance, it must be heard. I have heard old songs that reminded me of old times and pleasant hours, and of some who I may never see again. I notice with pleasure that the character of the songs are of an elevated character, "Home Again," "Do they miss me at Home," and patriotic airs in abundance. Sacred airs are great favorites with the soldiers; I do not remember of having ever heard anything so sweet and heart-touching as some airs sung by Germans of an Artillery Company, at the Camp near New Bridge. It carried me back to my choir days, and the neat quiet church where I used to sing. "Our days are as the grass," &c.[53]

Camp Lincoln.
June 26, 1862. Thursday.

Quite a pleasant day. Made Gabions in forenoon; quite good material for them is here. This afternoon very heavy firing commenced on our right which still continues. It is at Mechanicsville I understand, and it may lead to Richmond or [the] James river.[54] Ambulances are going rapidly to the rear, so as to give room for the freshly wounded, &c. We are in a state of suspense as to the result; men gather involuntarily together and talk in impressed tones, and every rumor is eagerly snatched at; I will not note them, for it would be useless. It is 8:30 and it hammers away as heavy as war.

✠— The night before we left Camp Lincoln, the Head Quarters Band played with great effect the air "On to the field of Glory." We thought we were for Richmond sure!

[During the night of June 27th, 1862, Fitz John] Porter crossed the Chickahominy at Sumner's Upper Bridge this being the one the detachment I was with was detailed to destroy.[55] Sometime before daylight [on June 28] Porter came along with a small rear guard and gave orders to "destroy the bridge when this brigade has crossed." His voice had a great deal of pathos in it, as it seemed to me; I was the one left awake and routed up the officer in charge to receive the order. We left the bridge open for the wounded long after daylight. During the night, I half carried one of about my own age across the bridge, and I still recall his look of gratitude; at daylight I found him dead. Our own pickets finally drew back from the head of the bridge, and the detachment sent to relieve us were obliged to put out some of their own number as skirmishers; two of the enemy's cavalry came down to reconnoitre and one was killed. When we left for camp, there were at least twenty pieces of artillery commanding the crossing.

As we went to the bridge by Trent's House,[56] we met the artillery coming in; they were quiet and looked as though they had had a rough fight. Some wounded officer, held in his saddle by a man with him, took us for reinforcements and said "God bless you my boys."

All was quiet and in good order, and I did not hear one word of complaint. June 27th evening. We came back to Savage Station; and after our incessant work, we did growl at digging a sink,[57] and only consoled ourselves that there must be some hidden stragetical meaning in it, that by some active and keen scented spy would be conveyed to General Lee.

We came from Savage Station and bivouacked at White Oak Swamp crossing; the next day we kept it in constant order, and I have no doubt we had as many men used up by that terrible swamp heat as if we had been in a line of battle. I corduroyed (!) a piece two rods long with blanks and overcoats, mixed with earth and brush; the wagons went over it as though it was india rubber and as tough. This same day at Retreat I went on guard, we camping a few miles beyond.

This crossing was the critical point of the whole movement, and the point of honor to keep it open. I do not think a single wagon was delayed a moment, but it was terrible, inexorable work to accomplish it. The rebels confidently believed the Army could never cross it, and on no other ground can be explained their neglect to hold it; I remember being anxious at the time about a road coming into the crossing from the direction of Richmond. We were now the advance of the Army.

Duane's Bridge was destroyed by the Volunteers. Prince de Joinville says "it saved the Army of the Potomac."[58] (*Error*. Captain Cross & detachment did.[59] G.T.)

[On June 28] We destroyed the Woodbury and Alexander bridge, also Sumner's Upper bridge, so thoroughly as to delay Jackson's command one entire day in crossing the Chickahominy.[60]

New Bridge and Grapevine bridge are old local names.

I recollect Thayer saying as we listened to the fighting at the close of the battle of Gaines's Mill,[61] while Jackson was making the most of daylight, that "our men don't fight as well as they do." Somehow we felt so, and I owe it to McClellan's making a single division stand the brunt of the attack. Porter held his line until night, as he was expected to do, and then retired untouched. They made a most stubborn defense, and unaided to any material extent.[62]

And in regard to this matter, I do not believe in all the after fighting of the war, men ever stood up against such odds as Casey's and Couch's Divisions at Fair Oaks,[63] and under such unexampled and discouraging circumstances. I have talked since with a Confederate who was in that fight, and he told me "they expected to carry the line in one charge, and it took them four hours, and there was no such thing as calling a roll that night."

I don't believe the Army of the Potomac was ever more possessed of downright dogged fighting qualities than in 1861. It was "from Bunker Hill."

The fighting on the Retreat was out in the open field, real stand up fighting. And as different divisions, one after the other, held the rear, no difference could be seen in their fighting qualities. The Confederates never attacked in a bolder or more determined manner; and one of them who was in Pickett's Division at Gettysburg and taken prisoner there wounded, said to me, "Malvern Hill was the hardest battle he was ever in." And at this battle the army felt that it could fight anything, and I never, in all my experience afterwards saw the army so disgusted and discouraged as when we turned back on Malvern Hill.[64]

I remember McClellan riding along and calling out "Porter is driving them." We were where we could see more of the army than other troops—and the grand idea that held them up to their work was that McClellan *had fooled them, and we were going in by the left.* Our men were just as capable of fighting as before, and their stamina would have showed in a next day's advance against Lee's forces who had not captured the Army of the Potomac. It was too bad, we should have stayed there a couple of days anyway.

We went out until the sound of the battle [of Malvern Hill] was away to our left; we were near the forks of the road, and loaded and drew up in line of battle across the road. Lieutenant Babcock posted a picket at the junction. Citizens looking like scouts passed us, but were not arrested or detained. After laying there an hour or so we marched back to a good position, about ———— miles from Haxall's Landing. General Heintzelman[65] was there and was very earnest that we "should slash the woods until they were absolutely impenetrable."[66] This was done; a couple or so of pieces of artillery were in position supported by some Volunteer Infantry; I admired very much the business-like way in which they got ready for work. I do not know as they were attacked, as we left as soon as our work was done. We slashed in the usual way, but timber was slashed the way Lieutenant Turtle mentions at Yorktown, to unveil the batteries when done. Our slashing is shown on the Battle Field Maps.

After this severe day's work, the march towards Harrison's Landing that night was a great trial. Every one would have fought rather than marched. It was terrible; I slept as I marched, and so did others.

I believe the period of greatest despondency in the history of the Army of the Potomac was occasioned by leaving Malvern Hill. We should have stayed there at least two or three days and made a bluff attack or advance on Petersburg; one may be whipped but can still brag and bluff.

Once at the gate of Heaven there knocked
   A soldier brave and true,
And soon the ponderous gate unlocked,
   An angel passed him through;
Few words were said in gentle tone,
   The heights of Paradise still,
"A friend," he said, "and all alone."–
   The countersign was "Malvern Hill."

Warren Lee Goss who was left aside at Savage Station and taken prisoner had a short conversation with Stonewall Jackson on that occasion.[67] He said he [Jackson] looked somewhat like our Captain Cross, especially the lower part of his face. Jackson was of a sandy complexion while Cross had a dark full beard, but the contour of his face and head certainly resembled Jackson—and, Jackson was no braver or sincere anyway.

Note.

In the *Century Magazine,* during 1884, a series of articles commenced Entitled "Recollections of a Private" by Warren Lee Goss.[68] He was a member of Company B of the Battalion. He wrote a book concerning prison life.[69] He was taken sick at Camp Woodbury and captured at [the] Savage Station battle, and sent to Richmond, and [he] never came back to the Battalion.[70] There were several of the Battalion taken at the same time, and one of them, an "old soldier of Company A," came back very soon having met in Richmond some late officer of the regular army who got him off for "Auld Acquaintance's Sake."[71] Goss gives a number of incidents of Battalion history. "Stonewall" Jackson rode by our camp ground & spoke with Goss.[72]

Lieutenant Charles E. Cross. Cross commanded Company B of the US Engineer Battalion from March 1862 until he was killed on June 5, 1863, while overseeing the construction of a pontoon bridge across the Rappahannock during the Gettysburg Campaign.

Harrison's Point, Va.

July 6, 1862. Sunday.

Going to be a warm day. Well so many great events & changes have transpired since last date so I can only write *Reminiscences of the Retreat.*[73] Well, Friday [June 27] eight of us were detailed to take charge of a parallel in front of Smith's Division.[74] All went as usual till about 9½ o'clock, when the Rebels formed in line of battle and advanced towards our front. I saw their white battle flag,[75] and the famous white horse.[76] General Hancock made the dispositions of troops,[77] and we loaded with the rest and expected soon to be real fighting soldiers; however we afterwards took station at two small bridges in a ravine [in] front of the Redoubt to the east. Artillery firing soon commenced, the shells bursting over us, and I never wish to have an enemy in a more hellish place, we quit [it] soon, occasionally getting behind trees to shield ourselves from the shells; we stopped awhile in the Redoubt, but finally went to our camp. Our camp moved to Savage's Station while I staid behind with a detail at the bridges to destroy them when necessary. The firing on the right had gradually fallen back *towards us*, this was Porter's Division[78] (I cannot minutely describe everything), [and] that night he retreated across the Chickahominy. Such a night I hope to never pass again, wounded men, Oh! I cannot tell it all. Well towards morning, we cut away two bridges (Gen. Woodbury's[79] and one below[80]), and then returned to camp at Savage's (June 28, 1862)! Here we stopped over night, and then next morning went towards the James in perfect order and quietness. On the Retreat we have worked tremendously; making poor roads good, and making abbatis across roads to obstruct the advance of the enemy.[81] Yesterday we had our first rest. I am broke out with little blotches occasioned by severe heat and exercise. The banks of the James are quite interesting, I had a good swim yesterday.

The object of this movement on the part of General McClellan was to avoid a too extensive disposition of his forces, and have a better base of operations, gun-boats and this river; this was impracticable until the surrender of Norfolk. It was not a defeat, but a retreat to obtain a stronger foothold. Great losses have been sustained on both sides—ours the least. I *think*, only *think*, there is some movement in their rear by some of our forces, as they retreated from us as soon as we reached here, not troubling [us] materially. It may be, Pope or *somebody* is hammering away at them at some other point of their lines.[82] I hope so, as I wish this accursed Rebellion to end, not that I care for the fatigue &c., but for the sake of a distracted country. Reinforcements are coming in rapidly, and as forward movement will soon be on the start, Richmond *must* fall!

(Dating from July 1, 1862) Our Battalion now consists of four Companies. Details from each Company making the fourth (Company D). I am among the number so I shall have to bid good by to the Topogs, as I am the only one detached from the old B.

I have a strange feeling, so I will note it down for the fun of the thing. I cannot imagine it will turn out as I feel, but it seems—*That great good news will greet the country, the clash of arms will cease, and it seems as though I shall soon be at my home.** Now this is almost a crazy fantasy at this time, but I never had anything forced itself so upon me: we are not allowed to leave camp on any pretext, the mules are harnessed and ready to be put into the wagons; we may go forward, or as my prophet spirit says—go on a transport and—go—home. Is this not wild—wild, but I note it down for either a fantasy or a soon to be fact—soon-to-be-fact—says my prophet spirit persistingly still! I cannot understand it.

* Coming to Washington seemed like getting home.[83]

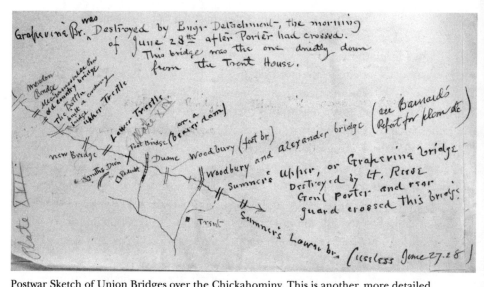

Postwar Sketch of Union Bridges over the Chickahominy. This is another, more detailed sketch of Union bridges over the Chickahominy in the spring and summer of 1862 that Thompson drew after the war. This sketch formed the basis for the map accompanying Thompson's published account of the Engineer Battalion.

Woodbury's Bridge. This small bridge over the Chickahominy River was suitable only for infantry. It was built in early June 1862 by the 15th and 50th New York Volunteer Engineers. Thompson, however, mistakenly labeled the copy of this photograph in his memoirs as Woodbury and Alexander's Bridge (sometimes called simply Alexander's Bridge); this latter bridge, also constructed by the volunteer engineers, was two miles downstream from Woodbury's. LC-DIG-ppmsca-33363, Prints and Photographs Division, Library of Congress, Washington, DC.

Camp Harrison's Landing, Va.

July 11, 1862. Friday.

Rainy. I hardly think the above will come to pass, as we probably shall stay here during the hot months, before we move. We are in a stronger position than before, and it is a wonder to me how McClellan held his position so long on so slender a base as the York Railroad as he did.[84] As I look at things all round, they look *cheering*, I feel more confident than before. Our position here is strongly intrenched and protected by gun boats also. I like Company D well. I feel sort of disagreable to-day, we have been so busy I have not had time to get fixed as I wish, and consequently feel nasty.

Harrison's Landing.

July 25, 1862. Friday.

A fine day for here. I am afflicted with a comforter of Job's,[85] so I am on the Sick Report. I have been very fortunate in the matter of sickness, not being sick since coming on to the Peninsula.

The James is quite a pleasant river, its banks somewhat resembling the upper Hudson, only—only—its water is muddy of a reddish yellow ochre color and you cannot see those beautiful villas and neat cottages so frequent on the Hudson. The view on the river and the scene about the Landing is quite civilized for those who have been in the wilderness of "Before Richmond." The gun-boats ring out "seven bells," &c., sounding quite melodiously.[86] I remember on guard by New Bridge I used to hear bells somewhere in the direction of Richmond at 9 at night. It made me think of old Upton bell. Our camp with considerable labor has been drained so as to be in very good shape; the weather has been dry, cloudy and cool, which is quite refreshing and rejuvenating. Quite a large number of the Battalion are sick, the effects of our Chickahominy affairs. The prevailing complaints are swamp and camp fevers, debility and diarrhea. We have a hospital tent, physician, steward, & nurse now, but our medical department has not been as efficient as it should be until now. The men have been pretty rugged heretofore, and have not really needed medical attendance as they do now, but the effects of their hardships begin to tell on them, and getting to a retreat, they are not up to that plucky point that will ward off disease for a long time out of spunk and spite, but they give up and allow their feelings to have their way. My boils are probably saving me a hospital ticket, I have not had diarrhea to any extent or any pain, cramp, or headache of any kind yet, and have grown fleshy, "fat as a pig." *I am lucky*. In a month we will be quite rugged; many men complain of feeling weak, yet they are not really unwell, we are tired out, that's the story. My feeling, or premonition about going home &c. on the preceding page is a sort of fantasy; we shall stay here until the Army moves, and then we will go with them—unless the Battalion should be so reduced by sickness, &c., it shouldn't pay. Only 105 men were for duty on the Morning Report yesterday![87]

Everything is quiet here, and it is pleasant to be relieved from the never-ending popping of pickets, skirmishing, battles, &c. we have been in lately. It is a real relief, I shall dread the time when it recommences; although *we* shall hear more than we will see, but so much suffering will have to be endured again by our brave soldiers. I am glad to see a policy of energy has been adopted by the government. We cannot carry on a war effectively except on war principles. We have been too goody in our policy. The rebels have not; hence their successful resistance. Our boys are at cooking again same as before Yorktown; they are getting well when they commence to cook. Our very sick men are sent North. Arrangements have been made for exchanging prisoners and wounded, and probably all of our boys left behind at Savage's will fetch up right, after all.

I must note down one thing connected with the Retreat, viz: the feeling of relief, of as though our journey's end was found, when we looked through the foliage and woods and saw the James. Mrs. Hemans, I think, has some poetry about some German soldiers shouting and singing when they saw the flashing Rhine in the distance; so it was with our worn out men.[88] "How many miles to the James?" was the constant inquiry. I was glad myself when I saw the James for sure.* Our boys were quite cheerful and unconcerned, we went tagging along as though nothing was in the wind. It was only croakers and stragglers that dispirited the men. I noticed as a singular fact that those who were wounded and had been in the battles of the Retreat, were *not at all discouraged, but cheerful & hopeful.* Food was short with some, I was offered 25 cents for a cup of Bean Soup, and some were offered that for a hard cracker! Our Cooks gave away good deal of food to them.

* One poor officer stiffened and died on his horse just in sight of the James, a Correspondent said.

Harrison's Landing, Va.

August 1, 1862. Friday.

Rainy yesterday, and muddy and muggy this morning. Last night about midnight, the rebels opened on our shipping from the opposite shore, producing no little excitement in the camps along the shore; some contrabands seeking in "skedaddle" style the backcountry.[89] I am not aware yet how much damage was done, their shells firing wild, it was rather uncomfortable for a while.[90]

Harrison's Landing.

August 5, 1862. Tuesday.

Quite pleasant. The next evening after the affair of August 1st, night, we were turned out late in the afternoon and went down to Westover Landing, where we formed part of a party who embarked on a trio of ferry boats and landed on the other (opposite) side of the river, and destroyed, burned &c., the grounds of a finely situated residence. Harrison's Landing looked from there like a thriving shipping town. I felt a little compunction in cutting down his splendid trees, as I appreciated their beauty &c. This was where one of their batteries was in position, and pieces of their implements were found. Our troops have crossed the river and are fortifying in a very strong and fine position. *Our* Fall campaign work has commenced, we are getting the brush out of the way for the coming hosts of recruits to go to Richmond.[91]

Heavy—very—firing was heard up northward of us this morning for some two hours but has ceased at this time, about 9 o'clock. Got a letter from home. All Right. I have since learned our troops have occupied Malvern Hill.[92]

3

Getting Accustomed to Campaigning

Summer and Fall of 1862

After the army had left Harrisons Landing the Engineer Battalion, assisted by the Volunteer Engineers, built the bridge near the mouth of the Chickahominy. This bridge was about 2,000 feet in length.

The night before the battle of Antietam the Battalion rendered three of the fords of Antietam Creek passable for artillery, by cutting down the banks and paving the bottom with large stones where it was too soft. During the battle the Battalion guarded and kept open these fords. The night after the battle the Battalion, at the request of its commander, was ordered to report to Gen. Porter to act as infantry[1] and in that capacity supported Randall's battery of the First Artillery in the advance to Shephardstown.[2] After the arrival of the army at Harpers Ferry it built one bridge over the Potomac and another over the Shenandoah and was busily engaged in fortifications during the month it remained there. Assisted by the Volunteer Engineers it built a bridge over the Potomac at Berlin.[3]

—LIEUT. TURTLE'S ESSAY

From August 10 to September 25, I copied from [the] journals of Orlando Jackson and others,[4] as my journal was not kept up except in scraps in [a] little notebook.[5]

Sunday. August 10, 1862.

Left Harrison's Landing in Steamer *Metamora* [at] 10 o'clock p.m. Since date of August 5th the Battalion was occupied in taking charge of throwing up works on Coggins Point,[6] the labor being done by "contrabands."

When we (Companies A, C, [and] D; B was left) left Harrison's Landing with three days' rations—leaving knapsacks behind, &c.—we could not imagine where we were going, but we went on board the boat, and I did not know after passing Coggins Point where we were bound.[7] I had thought from several things that something was up, but what it was "Quién Sabe."[8] We were destined however not to touch the dust of the Landing again. We kept on all night, enjoying a delightful ride, the cool breeze seeming like winds from Eden to us.

Monday. August 11, 1862.

Arrived at Hampton. As we passed Newport News we were told that heroes yet lived by the *Congress*, sunk in these famous waters.[9] Hampton wore a more pleasing appearance than it did last spring. The trees with their clothing of green relieved the nakedness of its ruin; and fowl, fish and fruits were in abundance for him who had the "needful." After all our toil we had at last come back to Hampton, we felt a little downcast at the results. Richmond was not taken. A number of barges loaded with Ponton boats gave us an idea of what we were to do. We made rafts of the boats on shore, working without breakfast. When the job was done, Company D went on a tug and went back to Harrison's Landing. What we went for, I have never found out. Companies A & C remained.

Tuesday. August 12, 1862.

Laid all day in stream at Harrison's Landing. Heard that the tents (We had previously been issued Shelters) had been turned over to the Quartermaster;[10] our knapsacks put on board of a barge &c. We amused ourselves as best we could; the gunboats shelled the woods on the opposite shore. In the afternoon a shower came up of a wind, and the Landing and all was lost in the cloud of dust; the wind blew with great violence, vessels dragged anchors, and you could not see fifty feet, and it is as near a Simoom as I ever wish to be in, it was a strange scene.[11] Went up to the wharf at dark, and started away at 12 midnight with orders to anchor when twenty-five miles down the river and await further orders.

Wednesday. August 13, 1862.

In the morning the *Metamora* came past us with Company B aboard, and we were to follow them, and in an hour found ourselves at the mouth of the Chickahominy with the hosts of Ponton Boats and a couple of gun boats (Yankee & ———) to keep us grim company. Companies A & C arrived the day before and unloaded boats and material from barges.

Commenced bridge, two Companies of the 50th New York on one shore and we in the middle and the other shore.[12]

Thursday. August 14, 1862.

Pleasant. Finished bridge in afternoon. The mouth of the Chickahominy is quite a pleasant position, we reveled in melons and hoe cake. At night we went on Picket Guard at our end of the bridge, loading &c., we went to sleep, and that was the amount of it. The bridge is a beauty, 1980 feet long built in tide water. Troops commenced crossing, mostly cavalry.

Friday. August 15, 1862.

Pleasant. Covered the bridge with wheat straw (unthreshed however) and about 10 o'clock a.m. the troops came along almost exhausted having come from Harrison's Landing since 8 o'clock the last evening. Then we *guessed* that some place was being evacuated. Malvern Hill affair, fortifying being feints. Old Gerber arrived with our train, and I shall remember the way he looked, the big fat old (Dutch) veteran driving an ambulance, almost breaking it down, covered with dust and his face beaming with smiles as he recognized the "boys."

Saturday. August 16, 1862.

Pleasant. Remained on the barges. Troops crossing continuously. Took charge of bridge &c.

Sunday. August 17, 1862.

Pleasant. Cleaned up decks, put things to rights. Splendid bathing here. McClellan, Burnside here, Company B boys (a detail) run a boat nearly all the time carrying Generals and Officers to and from the bridge.

Monday. August 18, 1862.

Took up the bridge, commencing about 10 o'clock. Everything went finely, about three hours and a half did it; we had done our part. Harrison's Landing was evacuated, and our advance was at Hampton. At dark we left the scene of our labors, leaving the grim gun boats to protect whatever craft behind. They were cleared for action as we bid good bye to the old Chickahominy, the melon peddlers, and the hoe cake dealers. Anchored 50 miles down the river.

Tuesday. August 19, 1862.

Weighed anchor at light, and arrived at Hampton at 8 o'clock a.m. Remained on board occupied in devouring melons, apples, &c. Left my pocket-book in knapsack, so had to subsist on charity myself, my quarter being spent long before.

Wednesday. August 20, 1862.

At night, 2 o'clock a.m. went on board the *Metamora*, bag and baggage, and in the morning steamed out past the Rip Raps up to the Potomac. I could not but look at the mouth of the York, and think of the time I went there, of the greeting at Yorktown and so on did Fancy go. Arrived at Aquia Creek at 5 o'clock, instead of Washington as some had hoped.

Thursday. August 21, 1862.

Laid in stream. Life on a steamboat when a soldier at best is very disagreable, and we were getting well tired of it. Liquor was to be bought, and nearly all were jolly. I had a good supper on board, and worried time away as best I could. I hate to be on a steamboat, give me marching on land, in dust even for comfort. Two of Company A deserted.[13]

Friday. August 22, 1862.

Went ashore and camped. Moved our Commissaries, &c., a hard job.

Sunday. August 31, 1862.

Went aboard Steamer *Niagara* after breaking camp. Anchored a few miles away from Aquia. Mustered.[14]

Aquia is noted as being the point where the Potomac was blockaded by its batteries.[15] It is an interesting situation, and here it for the first time seemed like home, the crickets chirped by our tent, and the birds were those who, while we were besieging Richmond, were besieging New England fields. It was cool and delightful weather while we camped there. We foraged cornfields and orchards to our hearts' content, and began to feel like ourselves again. It was a custom of Merrill and myself after Retreat and supper to go up where were the remains of a battery (No. 2, I believe).[16] It was a delightful place, you having a lofty and extensive view of the hills and the broad Potomac covered with vessels.

Breaking Camp. According to Thompson, this image, showing a group of soldiers loading a wagon and breaking camp, was a sketch by John B. Geyser of Company D, which Thompson preserved in his postwar memoirs with a photographic reproduction.

We have been occupied in unloading and reloading our wagons, and usual camp duties. We have heard very heavy firing in the direction of Manassas, *gradually going to the right,* the papers giving accounts of severe battles in that vicinity, the rebels victorious, all falling back to Washington.[17] We all felt a little blue at the way all was going. Preparations seem to be made for the evacuation of Fredericksburg, and two citizen refugees on the boat confirmed this; a bright light in that direction seen at early night was the burning of stores, &c., and a heavy sound came from that direction as of an explosion! Well, "it is a long road that has no turning."

Monday. September 1, 1862.
　　Pleasant, as usual. Arrived at Alexandria. River full of craft of high and low degree. Unloaded our wagons, and camped near Fort Ellsworth on a high hill in as hard a rain as ever baptized us on the Peninsula.[18] It was cold and I was on guard in the bargain; the Guard Mount was gone through with as much precision however as though an Italian twilight was smiling on us. The "Corporal of the Guard" was befuddled and made such

ludicrous blunders that we could hardly keep from laughing "right out in meeting."[19] Even in the rain and all we had a merry time of it. It was the hardest night we have passed, it could not be worse.

➤— The Guard Mount September 1st, in the thunder shower, was the last one by Sergeant Gerber while I was in the Battalion. In view of the events at this time, it seems strange we should have been at Aquia Creek; and Captain Duane was on McClellan's staff? Pope may have fought like a rooster without his head, but he kept fighting,[20] and in my humble opinion, should have eternal credit for it. And as for Porter,[21] if Pope had been McClellan, he would have done different, and we might as well have fought Lee at Groveton, as to have marched to Antietam before we could do it. Another thing, my afterwards respected "bunky" Decatur O. Blake, who was in that 2d Manassas battle, was bitter against Porter, and he told me that some of his men went in on their own hook.[22] I know how we felt at Aquia Creek at standing still, but a soldier knows but little outside of his own front. Yet after all Lee had only gained a short interval of freedom of movement to end at Antietam. The idle stay at Harrison's Landing, in that excessive heat, to us was very debilitating, yet were we not as well and strong as Lee's men after their marching and fighting Pope? Pope's "demoralized men" carried Burnside's Bridge at Antietam!

And I will state one thing that shines above all the alleged incapacity of Pope, the disaffection of Porter, the general feeling to "let Pope catch the licking," was the sturdy faithful soldier carrying the rifle in the ranks, and ready to go forward at any command, and from anybody, and if [Irvin] McDowell, [Joseph] Hooker, [Edwin V.] Sumner, or even Pope had led the way towards Lee's army, they would have followed and fought bravely to the last.

Tuesday. September 2, 1862.

The storm cleared away with the morning, and never were the rays of the sun greeted with more fervor than they were that morning. And strange as it may seem, after all hands were well dried and warm, [they] felt actually better for the night's soaking, sick men reported for duty. I have known men who went into the Chickahominy feeling anything like being well enough for the task before, work all night in the water, and after a nap and "dry off" by the fire, the next day feel extremely well! None caught colds, and we are none the worse for our drenching. The operations around [Aquia Creek ?] were rather disheartening, troops came in a miserable style, no order somehow. I must say things looked queer, and we felt queer but didn't say much. We repitched tents in better order, had Dress Parade &c., cool but bracing. We could see the Capitol and strange feelings went through my mind.

Wednesday. September 3, 1862.

Had Reveille at 4 o'clock a.m. Broke camp and marched to Washington, and pitched tents near old Quarters of last winter. Well, some did not come back with us, and although there was no friends to greet me I felt as though we had got home. "Should auld acquaintance &c." No great stir in the city, new troops arriving rapidly.

Sunday. September 7, 1862.

Since last date remained in camp, seeing a little of "civilization," and endeavoring to train up a little more. We must have been a queer looking set when we came down 4½ St. tanned to bronze, and ragged to our decency. We are tough and hearty though. Struck tents at Reveille and marched through Tenallytown, camping some two miles beyond.[23]

✠— After the 2d battle of Bull Run, on our arrival at Washington, we had to guard with loaded rifles Captain Graham's Battery (Regulars) to prevent them deserting, etc.[24] The whole crowd was under arrest; they were perfectly abused, no rations, and allowed no privileges. One of them said, "Well, Jim, this is rather hard treatment for the men who saved the left wing of the army." They were on the extreme left at that battle and had done great execution.

At some battle they were in Captain Graham's horse was killed under him, and they hoped they were rid of him, but he crawled out and halloed out, "Give them a 5 second [fuse], Sergeant!"

This Battery was the best one in the army, but his being a Tartar didn't help it.[25]

Monday. September 8, 1862.

This day marched through Rockville, camping some mile and a half beyond. The weather was warm and sultry, and as we had packed our knapsacks heavier than we ought for rapid marching it came hard on us. Numbers fell out from fatigue; I managed to tough it out. The result was we were allowed to carry only such articles, the rest being sent to Washington, viz: 1 Blanket; 1 Shirt; 1 pair Drawers; 1 pair Socks; Hair Brush & Comb. Everything inspired us with more confidence; there was order and design in the movements. This was quite a pleasant encampment. Milk and Potatoes to be bought, and apple trees to forage.

Thursday. September 11, 1862.

Since last date remained in camp, performing usual duties of camp, and watching the movements of troops.

Broke camp and encamped at Middlebrook. Had a hard march.

Friday. September 12, 1862.

This day marched to Hyattstown, and camped. Went on Sick Report with boil.

Saturday. September 13th, 1862.

Pleasant. Broke camp early. I went behind with the rest of the "lame and halt," but I had to drop behind all; my foot was so lame and painful, it was a hard day's job. I thought I should never reach the camp, which was long after dark. Camped some half mile beyond Monocacy Junction. My walk though painful and tedious was interesting, as the country was very pleasant; the hills though hard to climb up were pleasant to look from, beautiful were often laid before, while beyond towered the Blue Ridge and Sugar Loaf Mountain.

Sunday. September 14th, 1862.

Marched by Frederick. Camped this side of Middletown. I had permission to ride on the wagons. I couldn't walk, and riding was bad enough, Oh! The way Army wagons jar and jounce I shall long remember. At sunset we came in sight of Middletown and the beautiful valley in which it is situated. To us who had grown familiar with the piney Peninsula, it looked like a vale of Eden. In the distance we could see the last part of the battle of South Mountain.[26]

Army Wagon.
Rough sketch of a
wagon like the one
Thompson would
have ridden on
September 14, 1862.

✠— At South Mountain a rebel sharpshooter was behind an iron cylinder—part of a horse power machine—when a bullet went through the iron and all and killed him. The bullet passed through two thicknesses of iron at least ¼ inch thick each.[27]

Monday. September 15, 1862.

Went through Middletown and camped in rear of town. At dark the Battalion left, and camped on South Mountain. I was now part and parcel of the train. All the usual scenes and incidents of "After the Battle" were to be seen. Wounded men, Ambulances with their sad burdens, "Grey Backs," brought-in prisoners, &c. We did not see the Battalion again until Saturday, September 21st, and their doings are as follows:

> Tuesday. September 16, 1862. Went through Boonsboro, to Antietam Creek. Made a ford (on the right—Sumner's Corps), working until midnight. Bivouacked back of ford.
>
> Wednesday. September 17, 1862. Remained in position near ford. Battle of Antietam fought.
>
> Thursday. September 18, 1862. Did Nothing.
>
> Friday. September 19, 1862. Went through Sharpsburg.
>
> Saturday. September 20, 1862. Moved farther on one mile to the front. Rejoined wagons and started for Harpers Ferry. Camped just beyond bridge over Antietam Creek.[28]

During this time we moved from South Mountain and parked near Keedysville; the 19th (I think), went farther on, seeing many evidences of the fight, we passing over a portion of it, where Burnside was.

From our position at Keedysville (near McClellan's Head Quarters), we could see a portion of the fight at the centre (right centre).[29] Though some two miles away, we could discern the charges of the rebels on a battery, and their breaking, &c. It was a belch and a roar all day continuously; we could hear the whistle of the shells &c. Why there was no fight on the 18th, when we could have completely whipped them, was owing to a flag of truce.[30] I never was as surprised as when the night came and no battle. The Battalion had a view of nearly the whole, having probably the best position of any on the field. They supported a battery of the Reserve, but was not engaged.*

* Randoll's [Battery]; about ¼ mile across Antietam Creek, left of turnpikes.[31]

While passing through the Gap,[32] many dead rebels were laying then by the side of the road, mostly "young and fair." They had a portion of blanket or some covering over the face; removing this, sometimes you were surprised by a smile yet on the cold features and then horrified by some ghastly wound, and the look of agony, fear still to be seen in their countenance. I looked at none of them, as I could not get out of the wagon.[33] It was a sad sight, and in the woods they could be counted by hundreds. They all had on this gray rough cloth; and the rebel prisoners that we saw were the most worn out, jaded, forlorn men I ever wish to see. I pitied them; it cannot be their own will to be thus warring against their *own* flag.

> On South Mountain we had a late bivouac and in the morning found we were among quite a number of the dead. The "cooks" in the morning had a bother about their "partners." The Corporal had to try quite a number before finding a "live one."

In a work, *General Ambrose E. Burnside and the Ninth Army Corps*, by A. Woodbury, 1867, it is stated that Burnside was tendered the command of the Army of the Potomac about August 1 and again September 1, 1862, but he urged that McClellan had not had a fair chance and would not accept it.[34]

I always feel very heartsick when I read over the accounts of the Battle of Antietam and also some others. General Lee evidently knew the character of McClellan.

McClellan knew that he had all his army up anyway. Lee couldn't have more than his at most, but by the possession of Lee's order No. 191, he [McClellan] knew that his [Lee's] army was divided.[35] Well, as Swinton says, "every success was earned at heavy toll of blood." (as near as I recall it.)[36]

Yet Lee's Maryland campaign was a failure. He came near losing his army, and his line went back to the Rappahannock.

I saw Jackson's troops charge three times from the woods near the Dunker Church, and broke, apparently, from the fire (as I was told) of Graham's battery.[37]

In the afternoon, the Doctor came to camp with the word for "every man to go to the front." I put on my belts and got my rifle and hobbled out when the Doctor said "go back, we don't want you." My impression is, as though it was a critical time and Lee was expected to attack us, and as we would go to the position of the Battalion, it may be that it was thought that our center was threatened; or it might be that our line on the turnpike was to attack, but I think it was the previous reason.

Although Lee's forces were less in number than McClellan's, yet he offered a greater force to the attacking party on every occasion during this battle (*Antietam*) from the fact that, the attacks were not general, but by divisions, or in "driblets."[38] McClellan, by not putting his whole force in at once, gave an assurance to Lee (*it seems to me*) that he was anxious as to his assuming the offensives, and on his (McClellan's) center.

Thus the Army of the Potomac got to feeling that Lee had a greater army, and that attacks upon him should be such, as if unsuccessful, the army would be measurably intact for defense; thus it seems to me, we should never have attacked, and last of all defended by detachments.

If Lee had made an attack upon on our center, in the latter part of the afternoon, *all things considered*, it would have put our lines back to where they were in the morning. (?) Well, it was fought out on the ground and this is an action on paper. (*June 3, 1886.*)

One thing is certain, the U.S. troops fought well, every man—*no* demoralization! This fact has not been noted as it should be.

It seems as if some power held back the United States from success, when there appears to have been no reason for defeat during the early part of the war. Why did we not overwhelm Lee at Antietam? And yet it was a decisive battle in a political point of view, as it led to the Emancipation Proclamation. The time had not come for the 1864 kind of fighting. And in judging Generals of 1861–2–&3 it may be that this should be thought of. Yet victories were won elsewhere, but the battles of the Army of the Potomac were of more consequence in the political situation.

I don't believe the Army of the Potomac ever felt it could be beaten if handled with any degree of judgment or ability, and it was often a comfort to get into close quarters, so it became a matter of simple fighting rather than of strategy.

I consider the organization of the army on the march up to the Antietam battle, by General McClellan, his most noteworthy exploit, but his name was not a necessary talisman of its success.

General McClellan was a good patriotic man; he had an ordeal to pass through that would have swamped others, and he was supported by every officer of the Army of the Potomac under him, to the utmost of their zeal and ability, which cannot be said of later commanders, and they even evidently thought at last, he was the country. The greatest mistake he made was to leave the field, as some others; this country has a heartless way with such as play the martyr. It forgets a man terrible quick. I may be unfair and wrong in this, as he would have done any duty had he been afterwards assigned to it (??).

Sunday. September 21, 1862.

Arrived at Harpers Ferry.[39]

Harpers Ferry, Va.

September 22, 1862. Monday.[40]

A splendid day. Whew! away here! Well, necessity or something obliged McClellan to leave Harrison's Landing; we built a pontoon bridge 2100

Harpers Ferry, Virginia. This photograph shows the remains of the arsenal and the confluence of the Potomac and Shenandoah Rivers. LC-DIG-ppmsca-12547, Prints and Photographs Division, Library of Congress, Washington, DC.

feet long across the mouth of the Chickahominy;[41] stopped awhile at Aquia Creek then awhile at Alexandria; heard the firing of all the great battles before Washington, D.C.; came to Washington; then went to Rockville, then to Frederick; Middletown; Sharpsburg; then here. I am going to get some dates and straighten out my Journal.[42] This for [a] start; I am in 10 months to-day. We are encamped at Sandy Hook, by the [Chesapeake and Ohio] canal.

Sandy Hook, Md.
October 2, 1862. Thursday.
    Sharp shower yesterday afternoon, cloudy this morning; otherwise since last date we have had pleasant weather. The trees are beginning to be touched with the tints of Autumn, and you can hear the loud and ringing

note of the blue jay through their depths, reminding me of other woods with all the associations connected with them.

I have enjoyed myself while here watching the changes produced by the shadows as they lengthen or shorten during the day on the mountain side, or noting with interest the pictorial effects caused by the changing color of the trees; I hope I can stay here until the leaves have all fallen and the days of Autumn are past.

We are encamped down by the canal just this side of Sandy Hook (towards Harpers), and as we are to stop [for] some time, the inventive genius of each one is displayed in arranging his habitation for any emergency the weather may bring; just to my right towers loftily and proudly above the humbler Shelter Tents an iron clad building that enjoys the title of "Monitor," constructed by Artificer Pitcher & Company.[43] "Ours" is quite comfortable while from its door (!) I can see the shadows play about the Loudoun Heights. We can purchase most all the "comforts of life" in venerable Sandy Hook; bread & butter is my chief comfort. A brick building near us is used as a Hospital, Clerk's Office and Guard House, and seeing our "lame, halt and blind" sunning themselves about its precincts you might think you were looking upon some Soldier's Home or Chelsea Hospital.

We have been employed in building Ponton Bridges across the Potomac & Shenandoah mostly since here.[44] There is some prospect of dabbling at Fortification again, things look like it. The President is here.[45]

A few days ago I went up on to Maryland Heights, the view from it towards Harpers Ferry is quite interesting. It is a strong position, the key of the whole country; it commands everything, and while noting its strength the treachery of Colonel Miles was a painful remembrance.[46] Every step in this interesting place reveals fine views. I must note this down as a fine place for artistic rambles. A season could be well spent here. I am learning all I can, although my hands are still, I am storing up all the effects of light and shade, picturesque points, beauty bits I can, either for pleasant remembrance or, if I should take to the brush & pencil, they will help my stock in trade. When I cannot study one thing I will another.

Sandy Hook, Md.
October 10, 1862. Friday.

Cloudy. The most important event that has occurred is the receiving of my box, which was sent from home some week and a half previous to leaving Harrison's Landing. Everything arrived in fine order, and I have regaled myself in real cookies and some splendid Currant Wine for the last day or two. All the Battalion's Express arrived at the same time, and from the consequence of partaking too freely of the contents of certain packages, the guard house has seen distinguished occupants and instead of only two posts we have five, and you have to get a pass to go out of camp except for water and then only fifteen minutes are allowed you; all from a baker's dozen getting "elevated." So the many suffer from the sins of the few. It will wear off in a day or so I think.

Wrote to L. B. Humphrey yesterday and to-day, and for a change have shaved.[47] Sent my daguerreotype home.

Sandy Hook, Md.

October 11, 1862. Saturday.

Cool and rainy. By sacrificing a blanket to put up at the end of our tent we slept warm and dry and can be quite comfortable even in a decent heavy storm as we have it now, boarded and blanketed.

By kindness of Jackson, a nice neighbor of "Ours," I am enabled to post my dates from the time of leaving Harrison's Landing until the present time, and will fill a vacant blank in my notes.[48] I shall write it as a Journal same as this.[49]

Sandy Hook.

October 12, 1862. Sunday.

Cloudy and very cool, almost for snow. Some geese flew last night. Had Inspection this morning as usual Sunday Service; we looked very little like true soldiers; our boots and shoes are growing old, and we have no "cleaning kit."

Well, old Journal, we must part; and it is like parting from an old friend to part with thee. You that I have carried from Fort Independence in breezy Boston Harbor to West Point, then to Washington, thence the rudest tramp of all the "Peninsula," and now here again where once you were before. These preceding pages some were written amid the wild mirth of West Point, others in that little room in "Washington Quarters," and not a few written when the sound of strife was in the air, some by the campfire, in the Sibley by deadly Chickahominy, at Harrison's Landing on the James, and here in famous Harpers Ferry are scribbled the *last* few lines.

When weary I have found cheerfulness in the old pages and been charged by its old stories. In them I see that I yet love old time pleasures of art and literature, and love dearer than ever the glorious "New England," the home of the free. There are other thoughts in my mind to note down here, but as to an old faithful friend, I say at last *Good Bye*.

N.B. Firing heard down towards Leesburg, 10 o'clock, a.m.[50]

Sandy Hook, Md.
October 12, 1862. Sunday.[51]
Cool and cloudy. Closed up my old Journal to-day, and here commence another; my fortunes and a book are again united, whither we will go, *fate*—if such thing be—alone can tell, but I trust our relations will be of a pleasant and agreable character. Well, as Young remarks:
"Fresh hopes are hourly sown in furrowed brows."[52]
So here goes for ill or well.

Near Pleasant Valley, Md.
October 15, 1862. Wednesday.
A great disposition to rain seems to be in the mind of the weather. Since last date it has been drizzly and drazzly by turns. Yesterday at noon we *broke* camp rather than *struck* camp from the amount of board-work about our tents to make them comfortable, rendering a considerably amount of breaking necessary; our boards were carried for us to our present camp, a mile and some over from Sandy Hook towards Pleasant Valley. The appearance of the country is almost as though we were encamped back of

Army Shoes.
Rough sketch of
a pair of soldier's
shoes.

Harpers Ferry instead of here as two heights towards the east are perfect counterparts on a humbler scale of old Loudoun and Maryland Heights. I was on guard day before yesterday on the Shenandoah Ponton Bridge; it was rainy and dismal; still I made a most successful sketch of the view down the river from the bridge.

Near Pleasant Valley, Md.

October 17, 1862. Friday.

Pleasant to-day, but stormy last night. We have "ours" and Rue's & Company's tents arranged so that by spreading a blanket across the interval between them,[53] they make a comfortable and cosy retreat from the storm; after the first mist not a drop troubled us and we slept like kings.

We are engaged principally in cooking "little luxuries" and Battalion drill. I have taken sketches and if I had an eye for my drill as I have for the bits of picturesque about me it might be perhaps better for me. The Battalion is in pretty good humor to-night, a chap over the street is "coming Forrest" in great style, singing comes from up towards the cook-house,

Charles H. Rue of
Company D.

and were it not for the assistant cook (Fernald) detailing to my "bunky" (Rand) with great volubility his experiences while a "stout, brown country boy" in New York, I might write a better and longer story.[54]

Near Pleasant Valley, Md.
October 20, 1862. Monday.

Real Autumn weather when it smacks of winter. It is really cool nights and particularly in the morning. How it takes hold of the Southern troops cannot be known, but it must severely.

Near Pleasant Valley, Md.
October 22, 1862. Wednesday.

Very windy, but warmer. The weather much resembles that of New England. I meant to write more above, but "Turn out Garrison Police" tipped my cup of intention over entirely. 20th I was on pass and went over to the Ferry and bought some shirts, so now I am "broke." I went over towards Balinor and it is quite a pleasant place back of the town; the more I see of this town and its surroundings the more I find to see; it is the most interesting place I was ever in. At night (20th), the Battalion was particularly "gay." I enjoyed myself with Currier & Beahn—old Topogs—singing.[55] Bobby has the Banjo he and Thayer nearly finished before leaving for the Peninsula, and after a long time of silence it now charms away the evenings in this wild domain.[56] Up in Company A they had a grand dance, Sergeant Walsh playing the violin.[57] We are all in good health and cheerful humor, may it continue.

Yesterday I was on "Garrison Police" and never had a police such a day of it. We buried a horse, then lugged beef, fixed up the Commissary tent *once* [and] the Officers' *twice*, from the wind blowing them over, &c. Retreat brought us relief at last.

We are getting accustomed to campaigning; we can cook for ourselves quite nicely, with crackers &c., making good dishes. My neighbor Wight— clerk of the Company, a little man of once good fair fortune and of fine education, a wee bit conceited though—has his noted Restaurant in full operation, and the epicure has some little dish at every meal;[58] before Reveille he is up and alert stirring up some compound that will reappear after its baptism of fire in a very eatable and fascinating, winning way; I would take his opinion of cooking above any one's else I know of, and was highly elated when he complemented a Make-Up Soup of mine yesterday, and he in return for my honoring his opinion so much gave me [a] pinch or so of Cinnamon to give a flavor to my boiled rations of rice—reciprocated courtesy you know between *artistes* of the gridiron! ahem!

Camp near Sandy Hook.
October 26, 1862. Sunday.

Chilly and rainy; rather dismal in-doors (?) but I received a letter from mother last night, so I am amusing myself by answering it to-day. During the last three days we have been occupied in building a Ponton Bridge across the Potomac at Berlin, near the piers of the destroyed bridge. It is some 12 or 1300 feet long (61 Boats) It was quite a walk for us, it being some five miles from here.[59]

In consequence of a late order of the War Department (October 9, 1862) authorizing the enlistment of Volunteers in the Regulars, our camp has presented a busy appearance;[60] the press was so great I figured as clerk yesterday afternoon—I am making a nice looking page, surely—Our Battalion will probably be filled up to its proper strength.[61] I hope they will select only good men; I think they will. The "old hands" are almost lost amid the throng of new comers, you have to hunt for them. So it goes, those we like, the things we love are noiselessly spirited away from us [in] the hurrying of events. Happy greetings inevitably end at last in that old familiar "Good Bye." So ends this.

Camp near Sandy Hook.
October 28, 1862. Tuesday.

Cold last night, fine to-day, and going to be cold to-night. Heavy frost this morning. On Guard to-day, and was read off to-night at Company Parade as Acting Corporal. I hope I can creditably fill the position. The filling up of the companies renders it necessary, and many of the "old hands" are consequently receiving promotion. If I should be made Full Corporal, it would not be from hanging round the Sergeant, or ——— for promotion, but from endeavoring to do my duty to the best of my ability and also to be a credit to the Company I was in, &c.

Recruiting is under some restrictions by a recent order by McClellan which renders the system much more business like and systematic than before which threatened, by the method adopted, to disorganize the whole army.[62] When I heard the Order of the War Department I feared that that might be the result, both from reducing the volunteers, and breaking up the drill and discipline of the Regulars.

✦— Captain Babcock took occasion to compliment the appearance of the "old hands."[63] I was even counted as a veteran then.

Camp near Sandy Hook.
November 2, 1862. Sunday.

A delightful day. Had an Inspection to-day, and the "old hands" were complimented for their good appearance; the "*new* hands" not having any arms as yet. Rue and myself went "persimmoning" after morning service, and had splendid good luck in finding the ripe fruit. We followed up as fine and interesting a mountain brook as I ever saw. But as I looked on its beauties, now somber or cheery as either solemn hemlock or sunny Maple predominated, one regret was with me after all, that if my mother could be there, how perfect my happiness would be. What a lesson is learned by the brook, it sings as sweetly whether in sunshine or shadow, so should we. I have received two letters lately from mother complaining of an unwell turn, and even though she is improving I am somewhat depressed to-night while thinking of her being alone in the house with

" . . . nothing to cheer her
But the whistling wind near her." T.

Of course she thinks of me when the wind is out or there is rumor of battle, and how lonely, yet how brave to bear it all she must be.

If life is mine, I have surely one overpowering grief in sad anticipation, and it will be when I shall say "Mother," and there will be no one on this broad earth to answer; when I shall see—for the last time—those beloved features cold and still in death; those lips that have taught me the better way to move in speech to me no more, those eyes to look on me never again. Oh! my mother, my dearest mother would that we might die together![64]

Let me put here in this rude way my tribute to her, for I believe never a son loved a mother so well as me. Our relations have been so peculiar from certain circumstances that we have been more united from our misfortunes, and we have shared their toils together,[65] her success was my pride, my advancement her glory. Her tastes accord with mine, no company so pleasant as hers, no evening has ever passed remembered for its pleasantness but she was a participant. In times past when on the stage—a boarding-school actor—I thought not of the praise or plaudits of the audience, but how cherished was the few words "You did finely," from my mother, when back from the theatre. In anything I ever done, I never thought of my own success as a matter of personal pride but as something that would make her more happy. And I shall endeavor to leave the army as good as I entered half for the sake of my mother. She is the centre of my thoughts, her welfare my only care, though the storm beat rude against me or the winter sleet chill me through, my heart still keeps warm if I know the storm affects not her; and strange for human nature to believe, my only fear of death or better the dread of it consists in the thought of how it would affect my mother, how severe the shock would come to her. Life would be a sad and dreary lapse of time, then worldly existence would be without one charm or ray of pleasantness. Should she pass away, I should feel as though the brightest star had sunk here to rise to me at last again in heaven. We live for one another, Oh! if I could sit down in the old kitchen and talk to her.

> "Backward, turn backward Oh! Time in your flight
> Make me a child again just for to-night"
>
> F. Percy.[66]

Candles are rather scarce and I have extemporized a light with pork fat and a wick, a lamp that has been used a long time, and one that made the long Arctic night pass away in comparative cheerfulness to Kane and his coadjutors.[67] Mine does well, this is written by it; and of course it must be good. I believe we move too-morrow at 12 noon, so we will bid Good-Bye to Harpers Ferry for the second time. Well, I and Rue built a fire-place yesterday and I thought we would. We have heard cannonading yesterday and to-day, and I understand we have possession of Thoroughfare Gap. A general Advance is being made from this quarter.

First call for Tattoo, Good Night.

We Are for Fredericksburg

Under Burnside, November 1862–February 1863

The night before the battle of Fredericksburg the Battalion threw a bridge below the city by successive boats, without an infantry support on the opposite shore, at what was afterwards known as "Franklins Crossing."

—LIEUT. TURTLE'S ESSAY

On the March (Towards Strasburg).
November 5, 1862. Wednesday.

Fine cool weather, prospect of rain in a few days. November 3d at noon we broke camp and went down the canal and over [the] Berlin Ponton Bridge and encamped some mile beyond. I had got rather tired of our long stay at Sandy Hook & vicinity although we had everything comfortable and agreable; we wanted to move on. My old box that was sent to me from home and from its associations &c. was the only thing I rather hated to leave, it is strange how like some fruit and delicate vine of the forest our heart will twine around even a rude and plain object. We had a comfortable night of it; four of us (Geyser 1st,[1] Rue, Rand and myself) put our four pieces together and with end pieces we sleep as warm as pigs in "our 'Otel" on confiscated hay and straw.[2] To-day after comfortable though rapid marching we can see two peaks of the mountain range looming up before near which they say lies the town of Strasburg.* I have always looked upon the Valley of Virginia as a sort of land of enchantment, both from its noted beauty and from the varied fortunes of friends and foes within its limits. I had often thought if I could campaign it in the Valley I should be happy, even if it should be one of hardship. I am writing this by the light of a candle stuck in a bayonet which is stuck in the ground, sir.

The Berlin Pontoon Bridge. The pontoon bridge across the Potomac at Berlin (today Brunswick), Maryland, which Thompson mentioned in his November 5, 1862, journal entry. On the right are the remains of the bridge destroyed by Confederate forces in 1861. LC-DIG-cwpb-00274, Prints and Photographs Division, Library of Congress, Washington, DC.

"We" had a pork-stew for supper, and are passing the evening splendidly. rrrrrr goes Tattoo.

⊁— * Not Strasburg. G.T.

Towards Manassas Gap (Rectortown).
November 6, 1862. Thursday.

Cool and cloudy. We struck tents early and about 12 o'clock noon encamped in a piece of woods quite near McClellan's Head Quarters, so here we stop till Head Quarters move again. The country we have passed through resembles New England somewhat, and has the appearance of being long settled, judging from the woods, which are in tracts of five acres and upwards, perfectly clear of underbrush, very pleasing to see. The wood is principally oak, chestnut and walnut. On the march at a "Rest," the boys would pick up quite a quantity of nuts and a great cracking soon issued.

I have found it comparatively difficult to find out where we were when moving through a new country to us, citizens are scarce, and no one knows anything; "Came here yesterday" is often the reply to an inquiry as to the distance, name, or position of a place. So it was on the Peninsula and as bad here; yesterday I wrote we were going "towards Strasburg," so we were, only Strasburg is some ways on yet and we are close to *Rectortown*, and Manassas Gap is ahead some eight miles. As for news, I understand the rebels hold Manassas Gap, and a train of cars have come through from Alexandria a little while ago. "All seems lovely and the goose hangs high," as the tailor said when on a spree, so say we. "We" have a cosy tent sleeping on a variegated couch of forest leaves, and the wind as it stirs the trees sounds like the sea.

Beyond Salem, Va.
November 7, 1862. Friday.

Snowing. Encamped about a mile beyond "imperial" Salem, which consists of some baker's dozen of houses, and a miserable church. Quite pleasant to hear the cars. Rand goeth into the kitchen and Rue becomes my "bunky." Comfortable in tent though it does storm.

Warrenton, Va.

November 11, 1862. Tuesday.

Been quite cold and windy since last date, but has moderated somewhat but is cold o' nights. Rue was on guard and I came near freezing this morning. We arrived at this place November 8th, and encamped back of the town, which is quite a pretentious (southern) city with a fine hotel and lofty Court House and many pleasant residences. There is an air of desolation about it at present, yellow flags yet flying from what were (and are) rebel hospitals.[3] In a grave yard between us and the town is nearly full of graves of rebel soldiers, and [they] are frequently decorated with a wreath of "Pruntelles," the spirit of the town being intensely "Secesh."[4] I was on Guard Sunday, and Geyser and myself went "on Pass" Monday, and we were reminded of this by a couple of young ladies and two gentlemen (?) on a porch commenting on and laughing heartily at our officers as they might pass by, and another with black curls—quite pretty—went by us with a score of wreaths on her arm to decorate and adorn some grave of a soldier taking his rest. Our soldiers take very little notice of such demonstrations; quite a number of shop-keepers took both Confederate and Federal money.

The country we have passed through is mountainous and quite interesting, but there is here, as elsewhere we have been, a lack of enterprise and thrift; the land appears worn out. The houses are mostly built of logs with the interstices filled with strips of wood and made tight with mortar. We remained in camp here since arriving here, the principal topics of talk being our prospects of seeing the Chickahominy again and the appointment of General Burnside in place of "our Georgy," who is going where,* we cannot tell, our camp being in want of a newspaper. All the soldiers are rather displeased with this, although they have great confidence in "old Burny."[5]

* Report at Trenton, New Jersey, and await orders.

To-day has been a profitless one comparatively speaking, I being occupied mostly in drumming up the "Garrison Police." For dinner "we" had a bean-stew. Geyser and myself—mostly G.—cooking, and with our dinner of rice &c. we had a tremendous belly on, and I laid down and slept off my gormandizing. I hear no news, although I hear cannonading plenty towards the front. I wish success to our arms of course, "we" always drink "To our third Campaign." Should our Battalion get a flag we could put on

"Peninsula," "Maryland," [and] "The Valley of Virginia" with a good grace and propriety. Geyser has come puffing in for a "layout," so Good Bye.

✠— The farewell of McClellan to his generals at the Hotel at Warrenton made quite a scene. Vogel said that it was very affecting. I did not witness it.

I think that the graves were particularly attended to when we were around, but we thought the more of them anyway.

Warrenton, Va.
November 15, 1862. Saturday.
Cool but pleasant. Since last date we have gone through the usual camp duties. Policing, Drilling &c. Loafing mostly. Warrenton is busy with business and crammed with Supply Trains. Day of Company B died yesterday.[6] General health of the men tip-top, appetites huge.

Warrenton, Va.
November 15, 1862. Saturday.[7]
Pleasant to-day. Cool tonight. I have taken it into my head to sketch initial letters &c. when I feel like it of anything that will remind me of soldier life, and I feel so like it, that I have gone and made two entries to-day before I thought. A knapsack packed and haversack and canteen embellishes the first, and a "slush light" of pork fat and a wick the subject of the second, a substitute for candles, which it does finely and takes the raw edge off the air with its warmth.

Received a letter from S. P. and mother.[8] She is *well again.* I believe we move too-morrow, perhaps for winter quarters, or—"Mac" is to take command of some expedition and we go with him to some point farther south; it's all guess anyway. I have an idea that garrison life will be a little monstrous to us after life in the field so long; but let it go as it will I hardly care. Since we have recruited up perhaps in the spring the Battalion will be divided up. *Quién Sabe.* Read off as Artificer to-day.[9]

Engineer Knapsack. This is the first sketch Thompson mentioned in his November 15, 1862, journal entry. It shows a packed knapsack, haversack, and canteen.

Slush Light. This is the second sketch Thompson described in his November 15, 1862 entry, showing a soldier's "slush light."

Warrenton, Va.

November 16, 1862. Sunday.

Raw and chilly. Did not move to-day, but probably will too-morrow. The most note-worthy item is the arrest of our former Captain, J. C. Duane on "Mac's" Staff at Trenton. What for, I, nor anybody else knows. "Old Jimmy" is jugged. I imagine him sputtering away in his quick nervous way at it. Most probably he expressed his feelings too freely about McClellan's removal.[10] He is a first class Engineer. I cannot but think that [there is] something behind all McClellan's military faults that led to his removal; I fear he is a little Napoleonic in his ambitions. I have not done anything to-day, laying round, "fat, ragged and lazy." No Inspection. Lieutenants Babcock & Suter to report somewhere.[11] I am writing this from a sense of duty.

I don't know whether in my old Journal I ever mentioned a woman we met on the Peninsula following the army, I think the 4th (*8th? 14th?*) Regular Infantry; she was formerly an actress, and I often used to see her at Camp Lincoln washing and singing by the spring. She wore the Bloomer costume and appeared very neat and lady-like.[12] Well, she was through the camp towards night, fresh from the town, with hoops and long gown looking after a son of hers. Such is the love of a mother. Her name, I understand, is Nellie Crampton. Some of the men have seen her act, I believe.[13]

Catlett's Station (Weaverville), Va.

November 17, 1862. Monday.

"Cloudy, but warm during day. Broke camp early and encamped to-night at Catlett's Station, raining. Town consists of a depot, two or three houses and a mill. Writing this by a camp-fire. Can't guess where we are going."

When I cannot write in ink, I take down a note of our position &c. like the above and such will be known by being quoted, and are copied whenever good opportunity offers. We had some delay getting out of Warrenton on account of the numerous trains, and to get out of the rain some of us went into a lawyer's office, quite a building big as a Yankee school house, evidently used as a rebel hospital. A number of sketches &c. were on the wall. One was a profile drawn quite a number of times. I have not got it exactly correct, but one other scrawl is of more consequence, as the opinion of a southern soldier of the causes &c. of the war. viz.

Portrait of Jno A. Harrington, 4th Texas, Company E. Thompson's sketch copy of a self-portrait of Jonathon A. Harrington, Company E, 4th Texas, which Thompson found with many others on the wall of a former Confederate hospital, as reported in his November 17, 1862, entry.

"TEXAS. General John B. Hood our guide we whip the Blue yanks on all sides. Go it yanks you for Negroes we for our rights and the Constitution."

Quite a number of stars &c. round the room.

Near Garrisonville, Va.

November 18, 1862. Tuesday.

"Cloudy and drizzly. Marched to-day, and are encamped in a most interesting situation, just out of a by-road. It being an opening in some pine, a most secluded 'Forty-Thieves,' guerilla proof camp imaginable, with a fine little creek near by. Lieutenant Cross is a fine officer on a march, a man of good judgment and knowledge.[14] The country along back resembles that by Fairfax Court House, "ills and 'ollers,' with oak, walnut &c., mostly pine at present; we are probably in the transition country where the trees change from those of northern Virginia to southern. Clerk Wight glories in a candle by which I am writing. Had charge of Company Police, all the boys pretty fatigued by our march of a good sixteen miles. Sprinkling. *Guess* we are for Fredericksburg."

Stafford Court House, Va.

November 19, 1862. Wednesday.

Cloudy and drizzly, rainy too at times. A short march to-day. From a sojourn as it were on by roads and in the wilderness, we are now in amongst the "sojers," as thick as thick could be. We almost think we are in the Peninsula by the sandy soil and pines. We have a blazing fire of pitch pine logs by the light of which I am writing in my shirt-sleeves while it is drizzling without.

Near Falmouth, Va.
November 20, 1862. Thursday.

Moved and encamped in a drizzly rain about one mile and three quarters from Falmouth, opposite Fredericksburg on the Rappahannock. Went on Corporal of the Guard. Had a hard day's march on account of the mud &c. in the road. Virginia is the ———.

Near Falmouth, Va.
November 21, 1862. Friday.

Miserably rainy, spent a wretched night and day on guard, cold and wet to perfection. I have made a slush lamp to write by, and am tired and fretty. I cannot but think where I was a year [ago] to-night at home, when I sang at two weddings on time-honored Thanksgiving day, amid all the warmth and light of that mirthful time. Well, here I am in a Shelter tent scribbling away by the light of a slush-lamp in 'ole Virginia. Any quantity

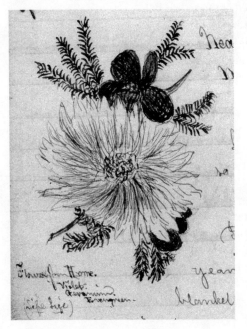

Flowers from Home.
This is the sketch
Thompson made on
November 22, 1862,
of a small group of
flowers that had been
sent to him from home,
probably by his mother.

of turnips have come to camp under protecting arms: and of course I have a large *physique* in some points. Good Night, good bye.

We passed through the following towns on the way to Falmouth, viz— Piedmont; Berlin; Lovettsville; Wheatland; Snickerville; Upperville; Rectortown; Salem; Warrenton; Weaverville; Stafford Court House.

Near Falmouth.
November 22, 1862. Saturday.

Cool but sunny. Felt rather disagreable to-day, have a cold, but feel better to-night. Received a letter from mother, all right at home, therefore so am I, all right. Saw Adams, wagon-master.

Well, no more saying "I wish I was where I was a year ago to-night or to-day," for a year ago at this time I was a "raw recruit from the country," looking ruefully at my blanket and Greatcoat and thinking while I heard the wind whistling round Fort Independence how I should make a comfortable bed in the slat bunk by the stove, and how differently I am situated even now; "a poor soldier boy far away from his home," well, only two years more, and I hope I can leave as I could if I were discharged to-night.

I have sketched above a little group of home flowers [see "Flowers from Home"], sent in a letter to me—

> Sweet flowers! I've often dreamed of those dear hills,
> Or closed my eyes in mournful revery,
> And deemed myself among their lovely precincts;
> Within whose shade and wilderness ye grew.
> That was but an airy dream, a memory,
> Oh! a pleasant reality and thou,
> Of stuff material, of substance real.
> I share the perfume you have lavished
> On the breeze which, while gazing on you
> I seem to hear, stirring the woods to song.
> You are a portion of that so dear to me,
> The soil, my childhood feet did walk upon;
> Then like some gentle spirit bring to mind
> The thoughts, the dreams of hoping boyhood days.
> Sweet flowers! Forth from that peaceful vale I went
> —How short the time, how soon it's passed away—

And many scenes of fair as thine I've seen.
But often while I then enraptured gazed
When rosy rays of setting sun
Illumined each hill and mountain height
And mellow shadows then betokened night
While from some distant plain I heard the sounds
Of noisy camp or bugles clearly blown;
I turned aside from all to gather flowers,
Like you and those that grew so fair at home,
And closely holding them as something dear,
I've quaffed their perfume sweet and dreamed again
'Till silvery moon held sway o'er vale and height
And in my hand the flowers wilted lay.
   Fair pleasant days and long to loving friend
Who thus remembered me; and gentle flowers
May thy successors ever reign supreme
Within New England's vale and vernal bowers.

                                    (November 14, 1862.)

Near Falmouth.
November 23, 24, 25, 1862. Sunday, Monday, Tuesday.

Cool, but pleasant. During this time, we have passed the time in usual manner. Movements of troops indicate some important movement, though I think "Burny" has either found Fredericksburg a hard nut to crack, or he is only to draw their forces here and amuse them to ensure success to some other movement. November 24th, we were detailed off in parties for the purpose of building a bridge across the Rappahannock during the night. We expected to be called out at night about 9 o'clock. We did not go out however, for some reason or other and neither did we last night, which was fortunate as it rained.[15] The rebels hold the opposite side of the river, and the pleasantness of building a bridge under such circumstances may be questioned.

Near Falmouth, Va.
November 29, 1862. Saturday.

Cool, with a good prospect—of snow. Yesterday (28th) moved from former camp and settled near General Burnside's Head Quarters, two miles and some over to Fredericksburg, and about five miles distant from Belle

Plain on Potomac Creek. We are in a sheltered situation among the pines, a noble group of oak however shelters our third rate spring. A real mania is among the men for building semi-log huts, both from the more room attained and the convenience of material. "We" raised "ours" a little ambitiously by three logs round, which gives us the best tent yet. All the day has the sound of the axe and saw has been heard fashioning the logs into the desired lengths and shapes. Fire-places are no longer among the novelties, but send their columner compliments to the air with a rush. From the number of camp-fires, smoke is omnipresent, it steals into the most secure retreat and scaldeth the eyes, it botherith excessively in cooking, it driveth you to the fartherest recesses of the tent and it is there, it cometh out on the Parade and blindeth and stifleth the soldiers, and exulteth when you rush frantic into the distance and are freezing by the chilly blasts of the night, at which it rolleth in mirth and curls itself in all the evolutions of joy. "G. ———— smoke."

One of those incidents occurred just before Retreat which remind the soldier that death is near, and from the solemnity of it all cannot but impress us all, viz., a soldier's burial. The sweet melancholy of "Dead March in Saul" lends a sadness to all;[16] some will not be buried so well. Rest, soldier rest.

Near Falmouth, Va.
December 1, 1862. Monday.

Cloudy, and sorter rainy and sorter not, at least it is real dreary and dismal November weather. To-day at home would enter in a season of sport and mirth, sleigh-bells, skating, coasting, dances and the more quiet joys of the social meeting, but here I suppose it will introduce us to a sublime and pleasant object to contemplate—mud. I wish we might go into good winter quarters and have a little show of civilized life, for I do not anticipate a pleasant time of it in the field, although "we" could make ourselves quite comfortable if we knew for a certainty that it was "stay for sure." The mania for building still holds its sway and residences are rapidly going up, I suppose land will soon increase in value. It is a queer sight to see the camp at present; the eye falls on as varied designs as could well be imagined, chimneys of barrel and board, and mud and sticks raise their odd proportions in proud disdain over the humbler camp-fire though the smoke curling forth from [them] is suggestive of [a] pleasant home with its cheerful fireplace. Too-morrow I mean to sketch some of them.

Our Front Door and Fire-Place. Rough sketch showing the entry and fireplace of Thompson's tent in early December 1862.

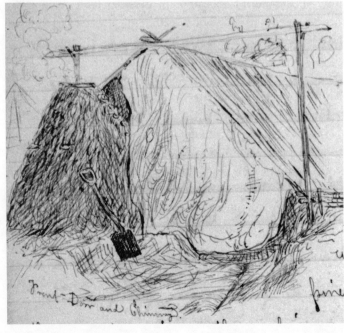

Front Door and Chimney. Another rough sketch showing a different tent's entry with another style of chimney from about the same time as "Our Front Door and Fire-Place."

"We" conferred with each other to-night on the design &c. of a winter residence, and a "Rue des Geyser" may arise yet from the foggy design of our "Castle in Spain." On Guard (Corporal) last night, to-day feel better. No news, no nothing; something must be in the wind, for it blows mighty queer about old Fredericksburg.

Near Falmouth, Va.
December 5, 1862. Friday.

Raining. December 2d, 3d, & 4th. The weather being quite pleasant. The 3d parked some Ponton boats beyond Head Quarters. It seemed very pleasant (?) to handle the old beauties again. The 4th was eventful from the building of our chimney and attendant fireplace, which is a fine success, so we are free from that nuisance—King Smoke. We have quite a comfortable house now. I think we can dignify it with the title of home even. I hear that Miller is dead—an old Topog.[17] So they go. He was a good soldier, but not of cheerful enough temperament for this kind of life. We drill Battalion drill each morning, and that with usual camp duties makes up our routine of duty.

To pass time away I sketch when anything of interest presents itself, and "putter" round the tent, clean my brasses, give my rifle a rub. Idleness is the devil's prime minister, and I believe many of the petty forms and duties of soldiering are instituted just to occupy the time. Garrison life would be complete Indolence without them.

Rumor has it that Burnside is relieved, and "fighting Joe Hooker" takes the position.[18] What we are stopping here for I cannot really see, waiting to see if the South will give in, perhaps; or some such "bosh." I like the President's Message.[19] The late Democratic triumphs are to affect matters one way or the other I believe.[20] Wait, that we may see.

⊁— From the number of regular officers and regular organizations in it, the Army of the Potomac had more of the characteristics of a regular army than any other of the war. The Volunteers drilled by the regular army sergeants become their sharpest rivals in excellence and steadiness. And from the fact that acquaintances were in both regular and volunteer service, such rivalry among them was never more than is beneficial in any army, for the file of the regular army had won the first honor by their unquestioning loyalty to their oath and Flag, un-influenced by either promises of commissions or elevation. Between Regular and Volunteer Officers the feeling was sharper. This rivalry in drill was most beneficial in this respect, that it checked the feeling, which is the bane of volunteer organizations in such a national emer-gency, that "*we didn't come out to drill, we came out to fight.*" The file of the regular army can always be relied upon to a man in loyalty, and it should be sufficient in numbers to have a nucleus of well drilled Non-Commissioned Officers and men to be drill masters and models in such a time. I know we emulated the old soldiers in Company A and worried them to drill us outside of drill hours, something utterly incomprehensible to them, but characteristic, undoubtedly, of the volunteers as well.

And with the one exception of the West Point Cadets, I have never seen as good drill as our Battalion at Falmouth, 1862. General Officers never could pass without stopping for a long time to watch the movements.

Near Falmouth, Va.
December 10, 1862. Wednesday.

Cool. With snow on the ground. Snow fell December 5th, night. It seems like home weather to see snow, and I can but think of skating, coasting, and the girls that graced the joys of the winter's time. Oh! how beautiful were the pines and cedars with the fleecy snow bending them gracefully down, their obeisance to the old crusty—King Winter.

> Oh! there are some whom joys of home and hall entice,
>   And charms of the wild wild rout,
> But give to me a winter's night, on the glittering ice,
>   When the moon and stars are out.   T.

We pass the time very pleasantly in our retreat, and Tattoo often finds us in the midst of a grand talk, and we wonder where the evening has gone. Time flies with us, it is "Come day, go day."

House-building still continues in operation, and the day is vexed with the sounds of labor, the axe is in full operation from "early morn till dewy even." A photographic view of "*our alley*" would be interesting; all manner of chimneys, huts, semi-log houses and tents tower up in haughty loftiness

of their few feet, and are indeed worthy of a Commission of Investigation
and Report.

Near Falmouth, Va.
December 12, 1862. Friday.

A splendid day, like the coming of Spring with the birds singing.
Nothing doing to-day, but yesterday, Oh! my. Now for the doings of yesterday the 11th.

We after having been detailed off in parties at Parade, got one day's
rations and took a look at our ammunition and pieces, which we were to
take with us and ———.

Near Falmouth, Va.
December 13, 1862. Saturday.

Fine to-day. Wrote, to mother this morning and wrote therein an account of our 11th day's work, and will not write a detailed memorandum
of it here. I did not finish the above yesterday, as I washed up my clothes.
The 11th, we built a bridge over the Rappahannock, some five miles below Fredericksburg.[21] We were attacked once by the rebels, but they were
soon repulsed by our batteries and pickets. None of "*us*" hurt.

Heavy firing has opened (*10 o'clock*) on the left, I should wonder if we
had a battle to-day or too-morrow. Rue is on Guard down to our bridge to-
day. I must hang my clothes out to dry, so Good luck to our side.

>— [Editor's Note: In his memoirs, Thompson directed the reader
to pages 291 to 297 of George F. Noyes, *The Bivouac and the Battlefield;
Or, Campaign Sketches in Virginia and Maryland* (New York: Harper &
Brothers, 1864), perhaps because his own letter describing events
along the Rappahannock to his mother did not survive.[22] While
Thompson did not reproduce these pages in his memoirs, they
contain an account of the bridging of the Rappahannock before
Fredericksburg on December 11, 1862, by the Engineer Battalion
and the 15th New York Volunteer Engineers. Because pages 291 to
293 of Noyes's book describe the Engineer Battalion's services that
day, and to reflect Thompson's intent, that limited section is reproduced here.]

"Thursday, *December 11th*. Our entire army was now filling the woods
and fields skirting the Rappahannock, and stood grimly face to face

Pontoon Bridges at Franklin's Crossing. The pontoon bridges across the Rappahannock built by the Engineer Battalion below Fredericksburg. LC-DIG-ppmsca-12553, Prints and Photographs Division, Library of Congress, Washington, DC.

with the enemy. But the river must be crossed before the desperate storming of the Fredericksburg Heights was possible, and the laying the pontoon bridges was the first thing in order.

"Our own, the 1st corps, under command of General [John F.] Reynolds, and the 6th, under General [William F.] Smith, constituted the left grand division, commanded by General [William B.] Franklin, and the spot selected for its crossing was some three miles below the city, where, beyond the rather steep bank, spread out a broad plain toward the rebel heights. Here early in the day the pontoons were brought down to the river's brink, and while our leading brigades looked on with almost breathless suspense, and the long line of our gunners on the heights overlooking the river stood ready to open fire at the least hostile demonstration, the laying of the two bridges was at once commenced—the one by the 15th New York Engineers, and the other by the United States Engineers.[23] The work is simple enough, but I can conceive of no duty demanding more true courage. In the charge even of a forlorn hope, every man, as he grasps his musket, is fired by the common enthusiasm, lifted on the wave of a common excitement, feels to the tips of his finger-ends the martial inspiration; but this duty had in itself no warlike incitement—none of the fervid intoxication of a desperate charge; these men were for the nonce not warriors, but bridge-builders, grasping not the musket, but the hammer; not borne forward in a rush of excited valor, but penned up in narrow boats, from which neither advance nor retreat was possible. Every plank they laid brought them, living targets, closer and closer to the rebel sharpshooters, now coolly sighting each his man from the rifle-pits on the other side.

"But there was no hesitation. The boats were floated out into the stream; each in turn was brought into place; coolly and systematically the engineers united it to the rest with girders, upon which, one by one, they laid down the plank. Nearer and nearer to the opposite bank grow the floating causeways; already they are more than half way across; the anxious thousands watching so eagerly the operations are already beginning to breathe more freely; the silence and suspense are awful, when suddenly a line of fire fringes the rebel rifle-pits, and volley after volley from the rebel sharpshooters is poured upon the courageous workmen. Some are wounded; all fall at once into the bottom of their pontoons, where they are partially protected; and now our artillery posted on the heights sweeps the opposite plain with grape and canister. These terrific discharges soon make every rifle-pit too hot for its occupants, and finally drive every rebel out of his hiding-place. Once more the heroic workmen resume their task of peril, the last boat is floated to its place, the last girder spans from boat to shore; and as the foremost engineer leaps upon the bank, one long, loud, enthusiastic cheer relieves the pent-up excitement of ten thousand spectators, and renders to these brave men the homage of their applauding comrades."

I saw the last charge on the "stonewall," just at dusk [on December 13, 1862]. My feelings were in reversed contrast to what they were when I saw the 6th Corps carry it, at [the] Chancellorsville battle [on May 3, 1863].[24]

I remember a feeling we had that things seemed to lag on the left. We had the bridge down ready for crossing of troops early in the forenoon but none crossed until evening.

Near Falmouth, Va.
December 14, 1862. Sunday.

Warm and spring-like. Yesterday afternoon we, Company D, took one day's ration and went down to our bridge to be in readiness to repair any misfortune to the bridge, and remained over night returning at noon to-day. Our forces had a severe battle yesterday, far greater than Antietam.[25] From our position we could see the batteries firing on each side, and the fighting beyond the town. I think our forces have advanced comparatively little, as the rebels when our troops crossed the river fell back to a fortified range of hills back of the city, which they still hold. Our troops fought with unexampled bravery; the right however were drove back twice but held the ground again at dark. To-day all is comparatively quiet, no attack on our side being made before our leaving. The rebel batteries on the left took positions farther back on a range of wooded hills.

Where we built the bridges, an old slave woman who had come from "over thar" told me, was Mr. Alfred Burnett's place. The [dot] in the sketch from memory is where the horseman came down and reined in his horse while we shot at him [See "Vicinity of Fredericksburg, Va."]. I have understood he was badly wounded and afterwards died.

Near Falmouth, Va.
December 15, 1862. Monday.

Warm and breezy. Nothing doing to-day in camp. No news from the front of any consequence, we hear the firing at intervals of artillery and rifle, like cat and dog. Received a letter from mother with her portrait therein, she is looking quite well. I had a grand mending time on my pants which are attacked with a general debility, but now glory in two big patches—somewhere. The ground has been soft and muddy, but the wind is drying it up.

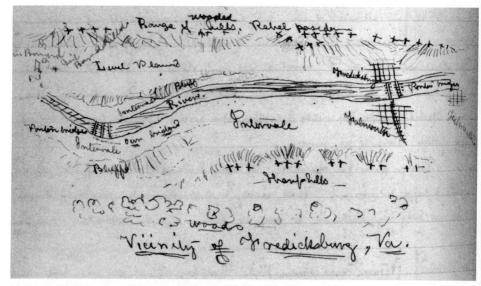

Vicinity of Fredericksburg, Va. Thompson's sketch of the area around Fredericksburg in late 1862 that also displays one of his frequent misspellings of that town's name.

Alfred Burnett's Place. Sketch of Alfred Burnett's home near where the Engineer Battalion laid its pontoon bridges at Franklin's Crossing before Fredericksburg (the bridges appear in the foreground).

Near Falmouth, Va.

December 17, 1862. Wednesday.

Cool with a promising prospect of snow. All quiet along the lines, but our lines have changed. Thus I tell you. Monday night (December 15th, 1862) we went to rest as usual, but it was one of those nights to me when the air is full of warning and ominous meanings, when you conjure up all manner of things evil to happen. I believe I am subject to such impressions. So in accord with my impressions, I was not surprised in our being woke up at 12 o'clock [midnight] quite unexpectedly to all concerned, and marched away for the bridges with arms and one day's rations. What occasioned this movement *we* could not imagine, but after passing Head Quarters the multitude of troops we encountered told us that the army was *coming back across the river*, and we knew what our duty was very well.[26]

And after the troops were all over, we took up our bridge at light of morning, and occupied ourselves till noon in loading up our material on wagons, and at 2 o'clock we left the place that was lately the scene of conflict and contention, to the only sound of the gurgling and the movements of the lonely picket. It was as mean a job as we ever were engaged in, it raining towards morning severely, making it very muddy and disagreable. The Artillery protected us effectually and we were not troubled by the enemy. As a Retreat, or whatever you call it, it was most admirably accomplished, and its secrecy was characteristic of Burnside.

So closes up this movement, and it was rather a *reconnaissance in force* or a—failure. It may be a feint to draw troops from some other point to ensure success to another movement at Richmond. We took prisoners on Saturday who ate breakfast in Richmond;[27] their position was very strong and they had a force of some 200,000 men most probable.[28] All the troops have gone to their old camps, and everything goes on the same as if no such thing had happened, except that some are not here!

Near Falmouth, Va.

December 20, 1862. Saturday.

Cool as blue winter, ground frozen. Colder than at any time in Washington last winter. The "cold chilly winds of December" are in fine operation this morning. I am writing this in a semi-recumbent position with my extremities wrapped in blankets, while Rue and Geyser 2 are playing checkers (Draughts) by the fire-place,[29] which a moment ago caught fire, and we had a grand spattering time to extinguish, and as a precaution went to the spring and filled our canteens (4), and I was disagreably apprized of the chilliness of the weather. It is re-markably cold. We are engaged in building a long shelter for our animals of boughs &c.

Near Falmouth, Va.
December 23, 1862. Tuesday.

Warm and pleasant as spring. Since last date the weather has moderated to the present genial temperature. Log-house building is at fever heat; it looks a little like a *stay* so the why of it. It is a little amusing to see how we approach the ways of civilization. We are trading house-lots, and talk gravely the advantages of such and such a situation like old real-estate speculators. We have negotiated with Church, a neighbor of ours, for his lot when Jackson and Coolidge "move out" so he can "move in," so by day after too-morrow "we" will have a "raising."[30]

The system of "bunkies" is worthy of notice. Bunky is your chum, your adopted friend; if you quarrel, or have a mutual dislike, just say "Good Bye," that breaks up all your business relations and friendship and you can pick up another with all the facility a Free-Coverte could possibly wish.[31] Of course there are numerous trials and tribulations attending it all, your "bunky" may have some one disagreable habit, which you must be charitable with and endure, as many a married man passes by many a whim of a capricious wife. A man with no "bunky" is just as much of an oddity as an old bachelor or old maid in civilized society. I saw [Austin T.] Hartshorn of Company B puttering around his hermitage, and I could but be reminded of many a *solitaire* and "old bach" by his lonely appearance, with no one to sing to him or cheer his pathway with the sunlight of her eye. Oh! let one describe the Joys of "bunkies," when you go on guard or are out in the storm, there is somebody at "home!" to pile on the wood and enquire after your welfare when you return, or if both are on dangerous duty there is somebody to look after and have an interest in your welfare. Some bunkies are drawn together by strange sympathies, some financially, some by similar tastes, others because "he is a good fellow," and some, just as I do outside, unite as a matter of policy and ambition. I have never seen more troubled men than those who have "had a bunkey leave," and come into a dreamy looking camp ground on a cold night. Just think of it, and nothing will compare with it but a loving husband coming home and finding his wife "gone a visiting;" and with what a thoughtful,

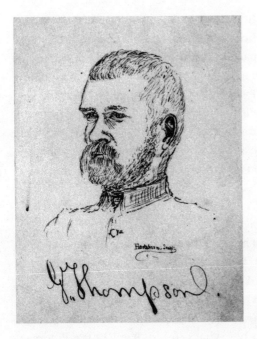

G. Thompson, 1862. A sketch of
Thompson by Austin T. Hartshorn
of Company B.

delightfully contemplative air he views the cup-board but whose resources
are valueless to him, they will not assume the winning form of flap-jacks,
hot biscuits, or the glorious aroma of rich coffee, except under the mag-
ical sorcery of his "better half," who is far awa', and he contents himself
with bread and milk, crusty bread at that.

Camp near Falmouth, Va.
December 30, 1862. Tuesday.
    Cloudy, with prospect of rain, and it is pattering away on our Shelter
roof even now at 5½ o'clock. Since last date we have built a new house,
and the old one exists only in memory. It is quite commodious, two tier of
bunks, big fire-place, &c., in enchanting profusion. Yesterday I went "On
Pass," and amused myself by going to the front by Fredericksburg then
along the river's bank up to the dingy town of Falmouth. It is a strange
and interesting spectacle to walk along the river's bank in front of our own
pickets and see rebel pickets on the other side of the stream, all quiet, all
apparently peaceful as though war had never put forth his hand and called
up his hellish Passions. The church clock struck three while there, and I

shall never forget the night when we went down to put down the bridge and heard it chime two, Oh! how solemn it sounded through the night, all calm, all still, the sentinel paced his round unconscious of the preparations, the moon shone down as bright and fair as ever, but too-morrow, Ah! what a morrow came, and yesterday I sat along with our pickets and there lay the town as quiet as before, only war had been through its streets.

Falmouth is a dingy, dirty forlorn little place with a destroyed bridge. I wonder how it will seem to see a town with everything in order, neatness and repair. My eyes have become accustomed to ruin and desolation.

Near Falmouth, Va.
December 31, 1862. Wednesday.

Cooler, but no rain as yet. The air is sharp and chilly. I feel a little in the dumps, not from ill-health, but from the dull weather and the rather dubious look here. When I looked on those batteries one above another the other day I thought we had a Sebastopol there.[32] Our other "try" was a failure, where will we try next. *Quién Sabe?* I think the troops are a little disheartened, why would they not be? What can the "Army of the Potomac" boast of in the way of results, nothing but decimated ranks; tattered banners, "*nothing more.*" It's the bravest army yet, but I believe no Union army will ever be successful in Virginia; it is too near Washington's, they will have too many assistant generals in that city.

Well, to-night is the last night of 1862. This time a year ago, I was dashing past Framingham, twelve miles of home over which I saw my mother's star, the evening star shining. New Year's night we came to West Point, thence to Washington, where we passed through the trial and tribulation of drill &c., then through the Peninsula, through Maryland, Valley of Virginia, and Fredericksburg, are on our scroll of fame. I have heard the firing of these battles and those marked with a * I've seen. *Yorktown;* *Williamsburg; Hanover Court House; Fair Oaks; Seven Days Fight; 2d Attack on Malvern Hill; Pope's Battles; South Mountain;* *Antietam;* *Fredericksburg.** So I can say I am somewhat an old soldier. Oh! tell Oh! Time what the next year will bring forth; we must wait; but let us drink health to the new year in the goblet of Hope.

I have nothing to look back upon with regret, I have treated all well; and I am more experienced, I think less of the world's good, there is comfort and happiness in a log hut, *or* beneath the starry vault of heaven. I believe more than ever in the lesson taught by Paul Akers's beautiful statue of "The Pearl Diver," that we can hold but an empty shell when the last great change shall come.[33] I am a better artist, and I trust a better writer. If life is granted me, when I doff the blue I shall spend many an hour and day in an artistic vagabond way among the mountain under the canvass.

⟩— The Army of the Potomac was never so "down in the mouth" that it was not ready to try again; at this date I expect we began to realize that it was not to be settled by one decisive battle, but a good many. Our disasters were magnified and our successes belittled.

Camp near Falmouth, Va.
January 2, 1863. Friday.
Pleasant to-day and magnificent yesterday; so much so indeed with its blandishments of two rations of whiskey, baked beans, duff, and 'lasses, apple sauce and pork, beef *a la mode* that I did not write as I like a good boy should have done, but I painted a bit of a picture in India Ink; in the evening with a full belly and a *samather* of mountain dew all hands had a jolly time of it, two or three in the Guard House of course, by morning. Many a toast was drank to the New Year, and many to a one whose name was not spoken, and a heartfelt one "to those who are not here."
"Touch us gently Time, gently Time."[34]

Camp near Falmouth, Va.
January 10, 1863. Saturday.
Raining. All goes as usual. Night before last, I believe, some three to five balloons (red) went over. Drill Skirmishing forenoons. Five or so of the Battalion are practicing and becoming familiar with Topographical Drawing. [William H.] Foss (Company C) and myself are Quad*rats* together, we went out this morning to get our Bases! but it came on evening, so our Quadrilateral occupations gone.

Camp near Falmouth, Va.
January 13, 1863. Tuesday.
Pleasant. All is lovely &c. Succeeded quite well in Topoging it.[35] "Very good." Finished up an India Ink picture of "The Retreat across the Rappahannock," Franklin's Corps re-crossing on our left (over our

bridge). I understand we are going out on fatigue too-morrow with one day's rations. Wonder what to do. Don't care much. Have flour issued occasionally, and to-day "We" regaled on Flap-Jacks. Rue cooking, with his face glowing with delight and gratification, as he alternately and successively landed them on Geyser and mine's plates. Received letters from S. P. [Lillie] and mother. Were paid Sunday, $51.50. Don't know what do with the trash, it is a real case, I now experience the unhappiness of much wealth, "uneasy lies the head that wears the crown."[36] I am afraid I shall be uneasy from those baker's dozen of fritters, and that extra soup, barring the coffee, and that apple that Hartshorn gave me, besides—"Much corn, much care."

Camp near Falmouth, Va.
January 16, 1863. Friday.

Stormy. Heavy rain last night, prospect of clearing away. The 14th instant went down to Belle Plain and loaded up Boat-Train, taking them out of the water. It was a real holiday excursion for us, all being full of strength and frolic. The Topographical features of this section of country are quite interesting, sharp hills and gullies, while Belle Plain is a broad intervale environed by hills, bordering Potomac Creek.

Sutlers suffered as, must it be said, roguery prevailed.[37] Sutlers are regarded as the legitimate prey of soldiers. You would see a box put by stealthy hands back of a wagon and from all parts in a most miraculous and surprising manner would light like flies on the box, heels over head *ad libitum*,[38] and when its contents had disappeared, all in its once fascinating vicinity had vanished, nothing but a lonely empty box greeted your vision, and "none so poor as to do it reverence." Cheese, barrels of cake left for parts unknown to sutler, and empty ones substituted under his very nose. Oh! where is the "Reformed" that will narrate to curious citizens (sutlers included) how the thing was accomplished. Some got whiskey ($2.00 a bottle) and didn't get home in a very soldierlike manner.

Yesterday out Topog-ing it, wind blowing like fun to it, but perplexing to us. While out, had the infinite pleasure of seeing the beauteous Pontons "going to the river," the boys said. There may be a big time around these parts in a while or so. One of Company B has been measuring the rise and fall of the river of late. I understand Currier (a Topog), and his bunky Perkins have taken French leave.[39]

Near Falmouth, Va.
January 18, 1863. Sunday.

Cold; ground froze, last night the coldest yet. On Guard to-day. Read off on Company parade (the 17th instant) as Full Corporal, and have my "sheepskin," a miserable thing to lug round, being quite large.[40] Many rumors prevail and vague pre-guessings &c. All seem to indicate a move *forward*, where—I, nor Madam Rumor knows. We hear of large quantities of *corduroy* stuff being hauled secretly "to where the bridge is going out." When the men see the Pontons moving they began to sniff the wind in anticipation of some work to follow. But to tell the truth I have seen nothing extraordinary yet, nothing apart from ordinary army movements. I heard (!) we were going to put out a bridge too-night? Whew! Still I think we should do something here to keep the rebel forces, either by feinted or actual attack, or we may find them gone from here to reappear in great force and overwhelm some portion of our great army. I feel sleepy and dull as I did not sleep a wink during my twenty-four; I am a regular species of owl. The trials of a civilized house are beginning to force their unwelcome presence upon us, Oh! shall I say it, "we've got rats in our house." My old hat for a cat!!

Sunday evening, well I Never was addicted to courting, so I have no desire to wend my way to the cot my ——— lived (it's really astonishing with what self-complacency I write the above), but I would like to go down to a Conference Meeting in the familiar Vestry and hear some hearty, kindly exhortations and some good old hymns; I fear I should have a lonely feeling to come back to the tented field. Well, this will not last always. Life, if my possession two years from now, will be a field of different action than once contemplated. I am learning more than ever before to be happy in yourself, and let the world with its tinseled fame and empty pleasure get along without my assistance.

Camp near Falmouth, Va.
January 23, 1863. Friday.

Cleared away pleasantly. I am in a hurry, so must content myself with bare notes.[41] *Tuesday* morning (20th) started, off with two days' (1½) rations and took our boat trains up to the extreme right, ground froze when we started, commenced raining that night, great labor to get teams along, cold winds and rain, no blankets, suffered, from cold, an awful night. *Wednesday* (21st), Boats separated, stuck here and there on the road, bivouacked in pines. *Thursday* (22d), staid in our bivouac, made bough houses &c. to be comfortable. Slept on ground as best we could. *Friday* (23d), came home in forenoon, fagged out, ugly and everything else, so ends "Ambrose E. Burnside's Four Days' bloodless Campaign" as far as I know, the elements were against us. We are to go away too-morrow with three days' rations, blankets &c., either to get our boats back, or— perhaps—we are to move against *their left?* Quién Sabe! It may be a grand movement yet, anyway it bids to be fair weather, so I hope on yet. I feel very well, am not quite played out. Got a letter from mother, her eyes being sore, going to write home, so only haste here. It beat the Peninsula (The rebs put up a board opposite Falmouth with "Burnside's mud scrape." on it!)

>+— On "Burnside's mud scrape," some of the pontons were stuck solid and the mules were hitched to the whole, and to prevent them [from] eating the boats in their hunger, they were fed soft prime fence rails for several days—it was all they had to eat—and whenever that occurred, it looked as though a saw-mill had once been there.

Camp near Falmouth, Va.
January 26, 1863. Monday.
    Pleasant. Saturday morn (January 24) went away and came home yester-day afternoon, *all* we did was to park the boats and get tired out. Nearly a whole Company in all sick with colds &c. Well myself of course!

Camp near Falmouth, Va.
January 27, 1863. Tuesday.
    Raining. Writing letters to-day. We hear that George B. is back again to us.[42] I have nothing against Burnside, but would be pleased with the change after all. I don't know why. Anyway the band are playing at Head Quarters "Should auld acquaintance be forgot, &c."

>+— (January 27, 1863) That McClellan would be called to take once more the command of the Army of the Potomac was promulgated by his partisans almost to Lee's surrender. "McClellan's War," and that the Army of the Potomac never was a success except for the organiza-tion which he gave to it, turned up at regular intervals.

Gilbert Thompson, early 1863.
John B. Geyser's January 30,
1863, sketch of Thompson.

Camp near Falmouth, Va.
February 2, 1863. Monday.
  Pleasant. Since last date.
  (My Mother's Gold ring parted the golden circle of life this day.)[43]

5

Camp Life Here Is Quite Pleasant

February–April 1863

During the winter the Battalion was engaged upon the defenses of Potomac Creek, Brooks Station and Aquia Creek.

—LIEUT. TURTLE'S ESSAY

Camp near Falmouth, Va.

February 18, 1863. Wednesday.

Raining. Since last date have been engaged in Topog-ing it down at Aquia Creek and working up the map at the present camp. We started away February 3d, thus the why of the very pleasing and voluminous entry above.[1] We had a grand time—detached service you know. I made some entries in a note book which I copy.

"Aquia Creek, February 3. Off at 12:30, five days' rations, to go Topoging it at Aquia Creek. Went on cars to about one mile of Landing.[2] Encamped in a sheltered position at "Red River tavern," as one of our Western boys jocosely calls it. Sergeant [James C.] Wilson, Company C, in charge; twelve or so in all."

"February 4. Cold, but quite pleasant. Wind blowing sharp and keen. Surveyed; Foss, Wheeler and myself, road from "Ruins," past "Lowry" to its joining to the Stafford County road."[3]

"February 5. Dubious look in morning, finally ending in snowing us in about 12. Camp life here is quite pleasant. To-night the snow is turning into rain and the water is going under us, but a rubber makes all right. Sergeant Wilson is a fine man in charge of a party. Well it has been a round about road since leaving home last summer."

✈— Returned February 11, to main camp.

The Topography of Aquia Creek and vicinity is quite interesting, and makes a very effective map. It is for Engineer Head Quarters of the Army of the Potomac. Wrote home to-day, the first time I have had an opportunity so busy have we been in making the map. It satisfies quite well. Below is an inscription near the railroad on our first day's survey. It was an ordinary table tablet, mossy and old.

Here is interred the Body of
   MARGARET, the wife of
PETER HEDGEMAN,
   of Stafford County Gentleman:
   and daughter of
John *Mauzy*, Gentleman deceased.
   She was married
the 21st Day of September, A.D. 1725
   and had by Him nine Children.
of which three Sons only survived Her.
   As she was a Woman
of great *Virtue* and *Goodness*.
   She was beloved.
and dyed much lamented
(by all who had the Happiness
   of her acquaintance)
on the 16th Day of January, A.D. 1754
   in the 52d Year of Her age.
   Conjux Dolores.
   H.M.P.

The rumor of General McClellan coming back resulted in the true fact that General Joseph Hooker is in charge of the Army.[4] I have an idea he will prove an able officer, at least he seems to take hold with an understanding and energy. He has ordered soft bread to be issued at times. The Potomac Army has been poorly treated, and Joseph Hooker can win the boys to him not by soft words and Napoleonic Proclamations, but by soft bread and little trifling privileges a soldier appreciates.

Camp near Falmouth, Va.

February 20, 1863. Friday.

Windy. Very pleasant indeed this forenoon. The end of the late dreary having come at last, and the sun is shining cheerily on all while the birds are having a grand revelry. Poor things they must miss the woods once so numerous but now among the things that were. As the shores of the Narragansett were shorn of their woodland beauty by the British soldiery in Revolutionary times so falleth the southern pine before the axe of the Federal soldier here. Our camp which was sheltered by thick woods from the searching winds from nearly every quarter takes a bout from them all now. We have to go quite a distance already for wood; and as John G. has the rheumatism and Rue [is] away, I was "heaver and drawer of water" to a painful degree.[5] When we first came here nothing but the best of hickory and driest of cedar was worthy to warm the toes of the Right Honorable Four, but finally we condescended to pine as fuel and now are glad to chop off the stumps we so wastefully left in the days of our luxury and pride. I can appreciate most keenly the possession of these woods, inferior though they be to Northern forests, when I think of woods that have delighted my eye in days ago with their early Spring beauty or solemn magnificence of Autumn being destroyed in a similar manner. Oh! War, thou tramplest on the tenderest affections of man, within thy presence purity and innocence are outlawed while shameless obscenity sits at thy right hand, the old man sees the toil of years and the pride of his heart pass away to nothingness and ruin, a whole life's toil, which has furrowed his brow and sprinkled his hair with gray in obtaining are gone leaving nothing behind to mark the taste and energy of their designer and possessor. I only hope and pray that war may never show his horrid front in New England, the Switzerland of America.

I have nothing to do to-day, but will in a day or so as the Sergeant is off surveying and I shall have enough to do when he returns by finishing up the map.[6] I hardly know what to do with myself. I understand the system of Furloughs is countermanded, from the large numbers who do not return within the time specified, but rather prefer to be branded as "Deserters." Thus many good men are denied a pleasure which they are entitled to, by the wrong doing of others, and [it] determines me never to put myself in a position unless some good can counterbalance, or honorable necessity oblige as at present, where *my* pleasure, my *life's* happiness is at the mercy of the good or evil doing of others. It is magnanimous to suffer a wrong imputed to you [rather] than another, whose shoulders are less broad than your own, but it don't pay. It is a claim that few justly have on you. Though the saying "Take care of Number One," is intensely selfish, yet remember Number One is a gift of God, the capital wherewith to bring happiness to your own heart and those that affection brings about you.

Camp near Falmouth, Va.
February 22, 1863. Saturday.

Pleasant, but growing cold and cloudy by Tattoo. More Snow. No certainty of good weather now. It is towards a year since we made our first campaign, quite a while to be in the field. Nothing being done to-day. Sergeant W. not yet back so I am resting my weary eyes after my previous night's work. Salutes were fired from the gunboats and the army.

Shorn Greatness. Thompson's rough sketch illustrating the destruction to the local environment caused by an army in camp.

Sole Survivor. Another rough sketch depicting the effects of an encamped army on the local environment, though this one projects a small ray of hope that not quite everything will be destroyed or consumed.

Camp near Falmouth, Va.

February 23, 1863. Sunday, morning.

Snowing tremenjously. It commenced last night at Tattoo and continued ever since in a most heartless manner. John G. amused himself during the night at regular intervals, in pounding the snow from the tent which threatened to cave completely in upon us, and by the early morning light the first object that arrested my attention was John the undaunted shoveling snow out of his bed through the door, it having drifted badly; for us, Rue and I were in the lower bunk and escaped. Our tent looks beautiful, snow clinging to each crevice and the floor, once earthen, now *mudden.* I am writing perched on one stool while my left and right legs are respectively resting on two others, while Rue and John have taken refuge in bed. We had not the faintest murmur of Reveille this morning, and "Inspection at ten" will happen some other Sunday. All business of camp is suspended, except Company and Garrison Police, and the sentinels wallowing through the drifting snow. Sergeant Wilson came in awhile ago with a roll under his arm like Rip Van Winkle woke up from sleep, the last two days were full of good things to him, as their pleasantness enabled him to complete the survey entire. So when I can work, I shall have something to do. I am in fifteen months to-day.

A battery near us moved away yesterday and proved the old adage "it's an ill wind that blows nobody any good," as we soon were lugging to our domicils the timber of their houses for our own comfort.

As I am sitting here in this miserable den, though it is elegance for soldiers, I think once and awhile of a certain cosy parlor where many a Sunday like this I have read and written in undisturbed by the elements without. Yes, I would like to be there to-day, I know of old pictures I would look over again and some books I would peruse once more. But Life is not made up of ease and quietness; Achievement is not ease but sturdy endeavor, we must brave the storm, we must toil, we must meet and overcome obstacles if we would be men; manhood is not matured in cosy parlors and drawing-rooms, but out upon the sea, in the wilderness, in the mines.

"Life is real, life is earnest
   In the battle-field of life
Be not like dumb, driven cattle
   Be a hero in the strife."[7]

Camp near Falmouth, Va.
February 28, 1863. Saturday.

Not raining, but cloudy and dubious. Have finished the map, which is very well liked at Head Quarters, "done better than was expected or desired." A good way to commence by doing work too well.

The 24th was memorable as the occasion of George Draper, of *Hopedale,*[8] calling on me.* It was good as a furlough to see his familiar face and to hear him hopefully discuss the prospects of a successful termination of the war. I could not realize I was talking with one of my neighbors as it were. He was lately at Newport News to see the 36th Massachusetts, the 9th Corps being there; William Draper, his son and a schoolmate of mine whose diagrams in Geometry I used to draw for him, being Captain in a Company from Milford in that Regiment. I regret that I could not see him longer, but I understand furloughs can be procured for 30 days so I may yet go home and see them all.

* I sent my broken ring home to mother by him.[9]

The snow furnished a great deal of sport to the boys while it lasted. Being busy I could not indulge, but while ——— I got Charlie to narrate the incidents of their many forays at snowballing.[10] All about C & D taking the Fort of A & B then getting drove off, then being reinforced, taking it again and capturing their colors (said colors being an old cap), and the many hand to hand encounters, taking prisoners and paroling them, &c. Our tent was a very good position and was therefore accidently the mark of many a snowy missile; it was a little troublesome, at which I hoisted a yellow handkerchief of mine as a hospital flag which was respected by the parties in a very honorable manner.

All goes as usual in camp. Detachments are away at Aquia Creek, Brooks Station, [and] Potomac Run superintending Field Fortifications, and they seem to be made for the purpose of protecting the railroad.[11] I hardly think we shall retreat from this position. I understand that Norfolk is threatened. I believe the rebels will be moving somewhere, the quiet since the battle of Murfreesboro will be disturbed;[12] there will be great sounds about Vicksburg, a wondrous commotion about Charleston and Savannah, perhaps the Rappahannock will be lost in the cloud of battle. Is it too much to think that we hear above it all the clear singing voice of Freedom as she holds aloft the Flag of our Fathers and shouteth that the nations may hear, the slave may hear from the jungle where he has fled, the dying soldier as he feels life's current ebbing away. "Victory!"

Muster to-day, hope we get paid off soon, dead broke.

"Taking of the fort," subject for a picture, boys snowballing &c.

✈— When Mr. George Draper came to see me, he had with [him] a Captain Johnson of the Volunteers. They first went to the officers' quarters, and at that time I was drawing on maps in their mess tent. Captain Reese sent for me, and Mr. Draper, before them all, began talking with me about my opinions of the war, etc. Of course I was unknown to him, in just the right place to give my opinions about the conduct of the war, etc. I did say that "all we (the soldiers) wanted was a good commanding general, that we were willing and ready to do our part." I diplomatically got him out to see my drawing and talked more freely. He went around the camp with me, and went in my tent and had a chat with Rue and Geyser, and was encouraging in his talk to us.[13]

August 1, 1892. I still remember his visit with pleasure.

I called on Gilbert Thompson, who has been made a Corporal in the Regular Engineer Corps, and found him busy drawing a plan of the surrounding country, showing all the hills and ravines. I found him well and hearty, and if his life is spared he will yet do honor to the town that sent him to the field.

George Draper
From Letter in *Milford Journal*, March 14, 1863.[14]

Camp near Falmouth, Va.
March 2, 1863. Monday.

A beautiful day, mild and agreable, cooler to-night. Been to work on map, Potomac Run, quite good. Like this work very well. No great news yet, Long Roll was heard last night in a number of places, probably as a test.[15] Somehow I feel as though some one was ahold of matters. I hope so. All we want is a good substantial victory.

We have been now a year in the field, yesterday a year ago, we came from Harpers Ferry. I will note down a little incident which occurred to

Playing Chess.
Thompson's sketch of
soldiers playing chess
in camp illustrates an
activity that seems to
have become popular
among Thompson and
his friends in the winter
and spring of 1863.

me there.[16] After General McClellan's and Banks's Staff had passed along
the bridge, not yet quite completed, I went back and brought back a claw
balk to finish with; it was very heavy and I was so tired I could hardly get it
from my shoulder when a tall man in a citizen's clothes stepped forward
and helped it from my shoulders. The citizen was Prince de Joinville.

Camp near Falmouth, Va.
March 4, 1863. Wednesday.
    Cool and blustering. Northern April weather with a rude way of March
about it. At work mapping as usual. All quiet. We have quite a *furor* on
Chess Playing; Vogel starting it. John G. has made some portrait chess,
Caucasian and Ethiopian, and are quite fine in their way. I like the game
very much, a grand game for soldiers.

Camp near Falmouth, Va.

March 12, 1863. Thursday.

   Usual blustering weather, raining nights and all sorts of indiscretions. Been at usual employment of mapping, going to keep at it until further orders. My work suits very well. Applied for a furlough to-day, I am [in] no great hurry about it, the Lieutenant (Cross) said "Well, I don't know as I can let you go home this spring, if the weather is good." I am so un-fortunate (?) always thus to be needed, my services are always found to be needed when I want to have a holiday, it's "I can't spare you" always. "Nobody can take your place." Well, I mean when I am finally discharged they will miss me when I go and like me back again. John Geyser went away to the hospital to-day; he [is] troubled with rheumatism quite badly; he may be discharged for disability.[17] Jake (Geyser) came from Aquia yesterday, the field fortifications being completed. Wrote to Louisa H. yesterday.[18]

George L. Cobb of
Company B.

Worked in Officers' Mess Tent to-day, as I have at times before. Heard some heavy guns yesterday, some to-day, nearer by. We shall be on the move when good even weather, if such thing can be. [George L.] Cobb (Company B) reported to the Lieutenant: "the water in the river 1' higher than in January;" when they go to measuring the heighth of the water I begin to smell a rat, that's what they did before the first scrape, before the second, and they are noting it now.[19] Joe H. is a live man.

Camp near Falmouth, Va.
March 15, 1863. Sunday.

Cold. Wind, N.E. Blustering and stormy at intervals of hail and rain. It Lightens and thunders occasionally to-night; it did also some nights ago. There is something pleasant in the sound of it, as though Winter was breaking up; his icy castles are passing away with a great sound; flowers will bloom again and the singing of the summer-birds be heard. It has been very dull to-day indeed, with only the excitement of Inspection, at which we nearly froze. I have done but little, the present page being the bigger job of the day, excepting a dozen pages of *The Chronicles of the Canongate*.[20]

I will here record a little incident of soldier life, as I mean to along, as I think of them if not recorded heretofore. When we lay at the mouth of the Chickahominy, on the old barges, after a hard day's work which had put the finishing touch to the bridge, and as we sat on the upper deck we could hear the ceaseless tramping of Infantry, and occasionally the heavier stamp of the Cavalry as they moved over the bridge.[21] We amused ourselves in singing songs, which the gunboatmen applauded near us. Some one suggested "Auld Lang Syne," a favorite air of ours, and we had just almost commenced it, when one said, "I wouldn't sing that, it'll make that officer feel bad, one of them died yesterday and his body was sent away to-day." We didn't sing it, for indeed it would have sounded sad to the one who was left behind.

Camp near Falmouth, Va.
March 16, 1863. Monday.

Hailed last night, considerably, ¾". Pleasant in afternoon and thawing. Saw a Robin Red-breast, wonder if she's the lady that used to make lodgings in my apple-tree and hook cherries?

Oh! hear the breeze on yonder hill
Hear the warblings, clear and shrill
Of merry birds whose song doth cheer,
Telling us that Spring is coming near.

Camp (As Usual).
March 17, 1863. Tuesday.

Pleasant. Practised shading maps with India Ink wash. It looks tolerable; I prefer the pens, it gives a more lifelike appearance, though the wash is pleasant and easy for the eyes, and you can express a country quicker if need be with it than the former, and much neater.

Heavy firing heard to-day, apparently back of Fredericksburg, but probably up the river; it indicated quite a skirmish; in fact since Joseph has been in command, firing somewhere has been heard all the time; he will be an active and enterprising officer. I have asked old veterans, who have fought beside him, what they thought &c., and they shrugged their shoulders at the work before them and said it would be "Kill or Cure." The camp is in quite a *fudge* "old R—— is back!"[22]

Camp near Falmouth, Va.
March 18, 1863. Wednesday.

Pleasant. Brisk breeze from N.E. Washed to-day, wrote two letters, to R. G. T.; M. M. J.;[23] and got none in the mail.

Did not work on maps, it is a little dull work experimenting and practicing. In evening called in to Corporal Sweetland, he is going on furlough to Boston—10 days—had a noisy sing as usual.[24]

Heavy firing heard at times to-day; understand that of yesterday was an attack of ours on Stuart's cavalry,[25] routing them badly.*

* *Kelly's Ford.* Our forces crossed the river even, driving the Rebel's Cavalry back with sabres only.[26]

Camp near Falmouth, Va.
March 19, 1863. Thursday.

Pleasant. Wind from N.E., prospect of snow at night. At work on map of Aquia Creek, *wash.* Quite pleasant to have a job on hand. Went to Vogel's and read off games from a standard work on Chess, very interesting and instructive.

I have noticed that old soldiers have invariably one little pet vanity, and it is of such similarity that it is worthy of notice, and withal quite amusing. *Uncle* Charley's is the prominent display of a white handkerchief from his breast pocket,[27] and I have seen an old mustachois with a dainty ladies riding whip in one of his huge boots, some are fond of lilac and drab kid gloves; as though they handled the sword with a gentle way and united the extremes of courage and gentleness;

> His voice, in battle heard so clear above it all
> > Was soft and sweet in the court and hall;
> And none were strong enough and brave within the land
> > To dare the grasp of his velvet hand.

Camp near Falmouth, Va.
March 20, 1863. Friday.

Storming. Snowing slightly in the day, considerable towards morn and during night. Wind N.E. Worked on map, looks well so far. Received letters from Mother; S. P. [Lillie]. They are passing away at home, some three of the standbys there are in failing health. One, an old man, another a young girl I used to dance with, going too, [and] the other a lady friend of my mother's.[28]

Camp near Falmouth, Va.
March 22, 1863. Saturday.

Disagreable day. Snowing slightly. Wind N.E. Mapping, looks finely—wash. Rumor has it that one or two Companies of the Battalion are going away. Captain Reese is our Commanding Officer.[29] He is not liked by the men; a strict disciplinarian, and a little prone to get you into trouble if possible; but it cannot be denied but he made good sentinels of us at Washington. He always treated me well.

Twenty-four to-day. I suppose mother has been thinking of me more than ever this birth-day. I trust [the] next, one year's day from now, I shall be as good; strong and well. Taking all things into consideration I am ahead, and more than all I have been in *one* good solid year out of the three, sure and too-morrow makes out sixteen months out of thirty-six; twenty more. I thank my stars over and over that I enlisted when I did, it was a good move considering the Conscription Act,[30] and that you must enlist for 5 years now instead of three as heretofore.[31]

Camp near Falmouth, Va.
March 22, 1863. Sunday.

Foggy and chilly in morning, sunny and pleasant in afternoon. Inspected at 9. Puttered a little on map. A little dull. Drill three hours a day, and Ponton drill.

Camp near Falmouth, Va.
March 23, 1863. Monday.

Pleasant and warm, cloudy towards night. Horribly dull. C & D off towards Belle Plain to go Ponton Drilling. Finished map, "Very Good."

Camp near Falmouth, Va.
March 24, 1863. Tuesday.

Cloudy, raining towards and during night. Warm. Frogs peeping, the sound of which forcibly reminds one that Spring is well over the threshold. Fussed around, felt stupid, played chequers and chess in afternoon and evening. Beat Pedrick 2 out of 3, and—him once.[32] At Chess I did very well, not getting beat, but they played poor. I like Chess more and more, it is indeed a royal game. Heard by Jake G. from John G. last night; is at Armory Hospital, Washington, D.C.[33] Comfortable.

The day of the battle of Gaines's Mill, a party of us went out front of Smith's Division to take charge of a parallel.[34] It was a splendid morning, everything so beautiful, the sun rising with unusual splendor, and I shall not soon forget the impression a remark by Thayer made upon my mind at the time; said he "that's the sun of Austerlitz!"[35]

That day and its night were great times to me, as that night we destroyed the bridge after Porter had assembled his shattered brigades on the south side of the Chickahominy.[36]

Camp near Falmouth, Va.
March 28, 1863. Saturday.

Rainy. Wind N.E. in morning, S.W. at late afternoon, probably clear away by too-morrow. Played Chess, and attempted to trace a map for Captain Reese, but it dripped in so badly at the officers tent I had to give it up for the present.

I was reported for Company duty the 26th instant, and went on Guard at Potomac Creek where the Battalion drills. The forenoon of the 26th

Guard House. Rough sketch of a guard house along Potomac Creek.

was stormy, wind N.E. It cleared up in afternoon and I had a good tour. It is quite a pleasant place, I made a couple of sketches, fired my rifle some to get its range &c.; I made some good shots. Came home Friday morning (27th), yesterday, being a delightful day, wind S.W. While going down, a number of German batterymen passed us on horseback carrying feed rations on their horses' backs instead of wagons. They were singing some German air with their clear musical voices, and there was something about it that was romantic as they came along making the woods ring with their song. If I mistake not they are the same Battery men who at "Camp near New Bridge, Va." used to delight us with their rending of sacred music.[37]

I must note down a little reminiscence of campaiging, for fear I lose it.[38] When we took up "Woodbury's Bridge" on the Chickahominy,[39] after Porter had crossed, a medium sized dog came along with the troops, them mostly stragglers—and he had lost half of one of his forelegs, the left I think, by a piece of shell; the poor fellow got along the best he could, and if I ever pitied anything, I did him; it appealed to my feelings even more than the wounded men, he was innocent of it all, blind affection had led him to the field with his master or favorite Regiment or Company, as dogs love soldiers, I have a page to write yet about "Jeff"* *our* dog—and there he was badly hurt. He was faint with loss of blood and would tumble down on his side, but yet he was in good spirits and would hop toward us when we whistled to him; we tried to pick up a rag amongst us to bind on to it, but we were not so rugged then as we were afterwards, and we could not help him. He went over the bridge, and I supposed [he] died afterwards, but what was my surprise, in going up to Maryland to see a medium sized, shaggy dog hopping along with a battery with his fore leg gone, the *very same dog* that we saw on the bridge that morning![40]

* He [Jeff the dog] probably staid back at Packard's, at Falmouth when we moved, there being a very attractive specimen of the opposite sex at that gentle residence.

I received a letter last evening from mother. She is not well at all, her eyes are very bad and I fear her general health is not good; she is getting old and cannot ward off disease as she was wont to do. And for the only time and first I now wish I was out of the army and at home to take care of and look after *her*, for however kind friends may be, I would be better. I am afraid we shall never enjoy "our good time together" that we have written about to each other that we were to have "by and by when I am out of the service;" I can't bear to think of it for a moment, but such a grief I shall have sometime to bear in time, but oh! I hope we can taste the joy of being some days together yet. "Fly swifter round / ye wheels of time."[41] She has had a life so far of grief, trouble, and care, and I have labored in the hope that sometime before she was too far advanced in years, she could realize some of the sweets of life. This desire of my ambition may be dashed from me.

She can write herself yet, and I am glad to see her familiar hand, even though it shows it is written under difficulty. A throng of memories came rushing over me when I read her "don't worry dear" at the close and I could not keep back the tears, they would come, for the first time since a soldier. I hope, I hope.

A rather amusing incident occurred when I was up to the Officers' Tent. I hung up my Great coat by the door, and Lieutenant Gillespie came and took it, mistaking it for his, which hung near by, pretty soon he came back and took his own with "I guess this is mine," when he returned to their tent, a great laugh ensued.[42]

A year ago yesterday morning Our Battalion went to the Peninsula, and it was just such a morning again, frosty, clear and still, the sun rising gloriously. I remember saying as they moved down the river "there goes the Spanish Armada," I hardly thought at the time it was so true a letter.

Camp near Falmouth, Va.
March 29, 1863. Sunday.

Cold with searching wind from N.W. Clear, with heavy clouds, wind probably from the mountains. Inspections as usual. Wrote to mother. Passed quite a cosy day with a cheerful fire. Jake had a little indisposition but Rue and myself made him some hot drink, and I got him excused from Tattoo. Hope I will be treated as well. Grant and Sweetland got home from furloughs, had a good time,[43] Massachusetts folks all well, and a lot of grass widows![44]

Camp near Falmouth, Va.
March 31, 1863. Tuesday.

Monday, 30th instant, weather was rather cool but pleasant. Shot at Target. D made better shots than C. Out of a volley of thirty-nine pieces, we put thirty-two in the target, four of which were in the bull's eye. Pleasant before Tattoo, but this morning found us with quite a fall of snow; and the day was quite unpleasant but it cleared away before Tattoo. Wind from N. March 1st was pleasant, but only to get in position, for he has reminded us constantly of his presence since. Traced a "map of part of Eastern Virginia" for Captain Reese; I had to hurry on it, and it shows great haste.

Received letters from Lizzie B. H. & L. H.[45] Monday evening. Good ones.

Camp near Falmouth, Va.
April 1, 1863. Wednesday.

Clear and cold, wind N.W. Snow is nearly gone. C & D on Ponton Drill this morning. Finished Map. I remain at home as I have the delight of a tour of Guard Duty to-night. Firing heard occasionally towards the right. I have just summed up the weather report for March. Out of twenty days accounted for, 7 Pleasant, 7 Medium, 6 Stormy. The cold winds are from N.E. & N.W. Wind from S.W. [is] genial and mild.

Camp near Falmouth, Va.
April 8, 1863. Wednesday.

Prospect of a storm. Cloudy and cool, Wind N.W. this morning. Heavy snow the 5th instant, that is about 3"! Before the storm we had fine weather with a good drying wind from S.W., I believe. Since the 5th had medium weather. All gone as usual except the 6th, when we went out back of Falmouth and cleared up a large field for the purpose of Review. The

Cavalry were reviewed while we were out. I saw Major General Sickles and *wife*,[46] I understand the President was present, I have never seen him yet. Ponton Drill yesterday. I had a little chat with a citizen while out [on] the 6th; he has a farm of royal proportions—900 acres, had some thousand cords of wood standing engaged at $8 @ cord, burned up now by our boys. Thought we would not have good weather until May, as we had a very open winter and consequently a backward Spring. Finished up a letter for mother yesterday. She is no better. Wrote to L. A.[47]

By the permission of Captain Reese, we went over and witnessed the Review of the 3rd & 6th Corps Infantry by the President, who was accompanied by two of his boys and Halleck, with all Hooker's Staff.[48] The Lancers did escort duty. I saw them all. It was a fine sight and the bristling bayonets appeared like fog rising from the sea. When I reflected all that mass of men was but as [a] tithe of what are enrolled for the Union, and when just across the river was an equally numerous one, of our own blood and kin, I then realized what a mighty nation we might be. The rebels of course could see it all, and I wonder what their feelings were on beholding it.

The President was in citizen's clothes, and wore a chimney top, a little on the back of his head too. He rode quite well, but a little bent forward not like our officers of course. In fact the best riders I have seen were regular Cavalrymen. I never shall care to go to a Circus to be astonished by feats of horsemanship, I have seen better here through stumps, even ditches, everywhere; genuine riding. I felt a little proud of being one of "Abraham's boys," adopted anyway.

✠— I saw President Lincoln twice. The first time on the occasion of this review, and the second at General Meade's Head Quarters in the spring of 1865. He then rode over to where there were some rebel prisoners and I understand addressed a few kindly words to them. He had rather an awkward appearance on horseback, owing more than anything else to his wearing his "stovepipe" on the back of his head, but at the same time he had what we might call a "good grip" with his legs, and evidently would have been a tough customer to throw. He rode a strong horse of good spirit each time.

Camp near Falmouth, Va.
April 10, 1863. Friday.

Delightful. Wind S.W. Yesterday was pleasant though cool, wind N.W. roaring round to S.W. at noon to-day. I think we will have a storm, as it is hazy to-night with light fleecy clouds. Came off Guard to-night at Retreat; and if there is any military duty I hate, it is this. I had rather walk post [at] night along thick and thin than be 1st Corporal of the Guard.[49] I actually dread it. We had Inspection Muster to-day to find the actual number of men, &c. The Battalion made a fine appearance. The note-worthy incident of the day is the receiving of our color—a fine silk Regular Flag. Company D doing escort duty to the color-guard. Sergeant Carney, color sergeant.[50] Long may it wave.

Our Flag. One of the rare color, ink sketches found in Thompson's journal, this one depicts the battalion standard that contained the three-turreted engineer castle and the Corps of Engineers' motto, "Essayons" (or "Let Us Try") in gold on a red field.

Camp near Falmouth, Va.

April 11, 1863. Saturday.

Like New England's best Spring days, only with a lively breeze from the
S.W. which is drying up mud with great rapidity; it is even quite dusty;
hazy. Drilled Battalion Drill in forenoon, after which went out on fatigue
duty; our party making a kind of trestle, hewn. Got three letters last evening from mother, R. G. T., G. H. Y.[51]

Camp near Falmouth, Va.

April 12, 1863. Sunday.

Very pleasant, warm even to sultriness, wind S.W. getting into N.W. at
evening when it commenced lightly raining. We had Inspections as usual.

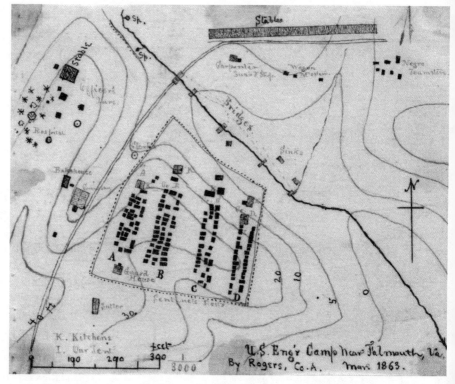

US Engineer Camp near Falmouth, Va. Another sketch originally done
in color, this one by George Rogers of Company A, shows the position
and layout of the battalion's camp at Falmouth in the spring of 1863.

The Battalion looks well; Captain Reese is putting in force a rigorous and "up to the mark" rule. Which is a good thing for us. I see by the papers, Major J. C. Duane is ordered to take command of the Battalion, a Captain & Lieutenant to be assigned to each Company.[52] Captain Charles W. Turnbull, *who enlisted me*, and Lieutenant Gillespie are assigned to D.[53] The Cavalry in large force I understand are going out this morning with eight days' rations.[54] And some say, "The Army of the Potomac will be out of Virginia in fifteen days." Whew!

Camp near Falmouth, Va.
April 13, 1863. Monday.
    A Fine day, cool. Wind N.W. On Company Police. Fixed up Topographical Materials for Reese. Have orders to be in readiness to move at any moment. Signing Pay Roll also. We shall probably be again in the field soon. Well, we have had a good winter of it, taking it all in all.

Hooker Goes on His Own Hook

The Chancellorsville Campaign, April–May 1863

---

*At Chancellorsville the Battalion threw a bridge at Franklins Crossing.
The boats were massed the morning before, one mile from the river, in
a pine forest. At night they were dismounted and carried by infantry
to the crossing, without the enemy being aware of the movement until
the boats were actually in the water. The Engineer Battalion and the
15th N.Y. Volunteer Engineers ferried the infantry across in the face of
musketry fire from the breastworks on the opposite bank. The Engineer
Battalion afterwards built the first bridge, 390 feet in length, in an
hour and ten minutes, and had from this till the close of the battle two
bridges in charge, moving them during the battle from the Franklin
Crossing to Fredericksburg, where they were laid and communication
at that point kept up. After the battle there was not time to dismantle
them in the usual manner, and the method by conversion had to be
resorted to.[1] The material was removed noiselessly, the men taking off
their shoes. The last plank had scarcely been removed when the enemy
appeared on the opposite bank.*

—LIEUT. TURTLE'S ESSAY

Camp near Falmouth, Va.
April 14, 1863. Tuesday.

Pleasant. Wind S.E. at evening, and cloudy, looks dubious for the next
two or three days if I understand the weather. Nothing extraordinary to-
day except being astonished at the bulk of eight rations, "three to be carried in haversack, five in knapsack." Lively marching is evidently before us
somewhere. All our extra clothes are turned over to the Quartermaster at
Aquia Creek, so after we have eat up our eight days' "feed," we will have a

light load. Hooker evidently deems it necessary to the success of this move that we go unencumbered, and we must dispense with our comforts and conquer and endure. Oh! may we be successful. I know of no troops going out to-day; some are to move too-morrow. I hardly think we will move unless Head Quarters do, unless we have a job to do. I traced a Map for Captain Reese this day, of roads south of the Rappahannock.

An odd thing about the tented field is the fact "that walls have ears." I have heard a joke go from tent to tent, and awhile ago as [Alonzo] Rice of B, was playing a fine air on his flute, it was encored by the denizens of three separate tents with hearty "Bravos," which he kindly consented. Another curious fact is when it is storming all hands commence singing; why, I can't tell. Sent a letter to mother, this morning I consigned my received letters to the flames. I hated rather to do it, but I can't carry them. Our Camp is near the residence of Packard.

⊁— On the occasion of the Chancellorsville and Mine Run movements, we carried eight days' rations, and lived eight days on them also. I weighed then about 125 lbs. and must have marched with about half of my own weight. Such a thing is practicable if men are marched with judgment.

Alonzo G. Rice of Company B.

Camp near Falmouth, Va.

April 15, 1863. Wednesday.

Unpleasant, with a driving N.E. storm. All up in a huddle, Rue slightly indisposed, I've got a headache, Jake is so-so. I just beat him a game of chess, a good game, too, got him crowded so he never got easy; just ate a fine soup, and feel quite happy, despite the cold water occasionally thrown by the besieged tents upon me, though once and awhile, I say something not very complimentary to Virginia and the weather in particular; I pity the Cavalry.[2] The storm is increasing, holy murthers!

Camp near Falmouth, Va.

April 16, 1863. Thursday.

Unpleasant most of the day. Wind changeable. N.W., S.E., N.E., sun out in forenoon. Drilled Battalion drill, in morning. Laid abed in afternoon and slept off headache. All as usual. Commenced on our eight days' rations. The army will move when fair weather comes. It seems like those long storms we used to experience on the Peninsula, at Yorktown. We were paid the 15th instant, I had $76.40 to cheer my heart with. Money here does not have the apparent value it does at home, for you are not obliged to buy anything, all is furnished you, none of those everyday necessities that at home put an additional value upon the needful; so it is with me. I sent a letter to mother the 15th, with a $20. Played a very tough game of chess with Rue, lost my Queen the first of the game but won another with a pawn, I beat!

Camp near Falmouth, Va.

April 21, 1863. Tuesday.

North East Storm. Very dull to-day; no drill on account of weather; all the excitement I have had was the turning out of Company Police for their duties and going with them for a load of wood with the usual fuss of mules and negro drivers. I have seen very few good negro drivers, the best are white, although George Draper said they were excellent at the West, but it must be those who have been sometime free and have consequently more intelligence; ours are often contrabands who are often stupid, although they are generally good natured and willing.

Evening. Company B went out on fatigue duty this afternoon taking tools along. I should judge from what I hear that we are going to move;

Brigadier General Henry
W. Benham. Benham
commanded the Engineer
Brigade composed of the
15th New York Volunteer
Engineers, the 50th New
York Volunteer Engineers,
and, on occasion, the US
Engineer Battalion. The
photograph that Thompson
collected in his memoir
was an older one, showing
Benham after the war, but
this photograph depicts
Benham as he looked when
Thompson served with the
Engineer Brigade. LC-
DIG-cwpb-06248, Prints
and Photographs Division,
Library of Congress,
Washington, DC.

we are going to build a bridge to-night or too-morrow night. Also that we
are brigaded with the Engineer Brigade (Volunteers)[3] all under command
of General Benham of James Island notoriety.[4] I cannot but think of the
difference of officers in command when we started out last spring, then
McClellan now Hooker &c. I think somehow we will have a *wonky* time
of it this summer, our endurance and pluck will be well tried; may we go
through it well.

The Cavalry crossed at Kelly's Ford and are gone—Quién Sabe. Been
reading Russell's "Diary" not so bad a man after all.[5] Clearing away at
Tattoo. We have a boat-train.

Camp near Falmouth, Va.

April 22, 1863. Wednesday.

Cloudy and cool. Wind N.E. in morning. No one allowed to leave camp. No drill. I feel indisposed to do anything, yet want to be about something. Seventeen months in to-day.

After Taps. Cloudy but no prospect of storm. Went on fatigue party, down towards the place where we put out the old bridge.[6] A movement is undeniably on foot. The boat train is parked about two miles back from the river, mules unhitched but with harness on. We fixed up the road and took three loads of corduroy down to a point at the left of Stafford Heights, on the Riverside road, just back of where the old bridge was;[7] to be used probably, in constructing a bridge over a gully there. I am pleased to see that everything is ready, roads put in shape, gullies filled up, bad places corduroyed; we have been very slack in this point before, on Burnside's "*mud trip*" not a motion of work was done to clear the way, so we stuck and stuck 'till we stuck fast! Hooker goes on his *own* hook. We are detailed off into parties &c. at Tattoo, for the bridge when it is to be built; I am in the chess party, and if infantry are to be taken across before the bridge is built [I] am to be in the boat party too. The bridge is to be constructed by conversion in four sections, A (1), B (2), C (3), D (4); a good way.[8] General Benham said to our officers that "our bridge would be the first one built and other men will be working beside you, but I wanted you should do the *best* you can." I think it is quite a compliment to us, to be assigned to building the first bridge, for it must be done at the time appointed, and they rely on us. We built ours first before,[9] the 15th [New York] near us did not have the heart to go again to work on theirs after the attack.[10] May we equal what is expected of us; I am honestly really pleased that something is to be attempted, and I *feel* as though we shall *succeed*, and although weal and woe may come to me I am *waiting* to be away.

It is pattering away on the tent in spite of my prophesying, it is nothing but a shower. The roads are in good condition now, quite hard and firm, the last storm really improving them; well, Good Night—somebody.

Camp near Falmouth, Va.

April 23, 1863. Thursday.

Rained all night and raining now, the stars could be seen when I turned in. We were told at Reveille that we [would] probably be called on to-night, but the rain may suspend operations, though I think it will not hurt the roads much. Detailed for Bridge Train Guard, a miserable prospect, raining like fun.

Camp near Falmouth, Va.
April 26, 1863. Sunday.

Delightful with a lively cool wind from N.W. Yesterday was as fine. Had poor tour of Guard duty as I expected, it storming all our term, clearing yesterday morn. We had charge of Boat Train and two residences* to prevent communication. Lights were displayed back and forth past the front windows at night which looked a little suspicious and we reported it. The storm has undoubtedly delayed the intended movement, although the roads are as good to-day as you would wish. These N.W. winds dry up the moisture very rapidly from the ground; dust is flying to-day.

* Captain Sands's.[11]

One of the rumors and humor about our tent yesterday was that the President came here and asked Hooker "where he was going to move?" H.—— replied "Only two know that; one is God Almighty and the other Joe Hooker!" A tip-top and characteristic *bon mot* even if not true.

Inspection as usual. Went over to the Photographist at Head Quarters and had a "Group" taken of five us "Old Topogs," Ames, Slater, Higgins, Fickett and myself; and had a fine picture.

Although the army does not move yet the things of Nature come each in their season and depart at the appointed time. Anemones are in bloom with the blue Violet and its relation a tiny thing like our white one at home. The fresh springing grass is enlivening the landscape with its brilliant hue, the full blooming peach trees contrast finely with the neutral tints of the woodland; the shrubs and trees are starting into life. I wonder where we will be when summer is in full reign, when Autumn comes so peerless in her beauty; and then when snow birds are chirping amongst the flying snow.

When I was on Guard I slept in a negro shanty—*up stairs*! and I never had anything sound so queer as to hear folks *over head*, it is the first time I have slept in a house (?) since leaving Washington for the Peninsula.

Mariner S. Fickett of Company B.

Camp near Falmouth, Va.
April 27, 1863. Monday.

Warm; with wind S.W. The warmth of the day was quite enervating. Drilled Battalion Drill; and had a *grand* Policing time all round the camp, "by order," I guess, as there are cleansing fires in all direction. On Police. Had a busy day of it. No news of any consequence, only the rumor that troops were to cross at Kelly's Ford this morning. The army is in good order, men look well, animals in fine condition; truly, we have a better, more soldierlike army than last Spring; we ought to do up a good job by Autumn, when I think there will be hard fighting at last. We have a triple Yorktown to encounter at the onset, but we can surmount it by energy and bravery; Hooker has those qualities I believe. I think he will be a man that will seize upon opportunities in a manner most provoking to those who present them. I fondly hope this campaign will be in bright contrast to the one of McClellan's. I have always in my Journal written admiringly of him, I was neutral when there were those that were very pointed in their admiration or dislike. But the "Congressional Report on the Conduct of the War" reveals some unmistakable facts that are not flattering to McClellan.[12] How fair they are and unprejudiced I shall not decide, but we common soldiers wondered why we sat down and played Engineer before Yorktown, why we let the final victory go as it did, and the spirit of the army was kept up by the idea that this was the great move referred to in his Napoleonic *bulletins,* and that *while our right drew the enemy from Richmond our left would go into the city,* &c.[13]

[John] Bishop of C came in and so talking took the place of writing. It is really dull, perhaps because I am in expectation.

Camp near Falmouth, Va.
April 28, 1863. Tuesday.

Cloudy this morning, a storm ahead, wind S.W. Cooler. This morning early was delightful, a little cool, but *just* such a time for a lively horseback ride through the country or a row in a dory towards Two Penny Loaf at Cape Ann; but the reality is that I am for bridge guard to-night. I understand Head Quarters is to move and for a surety that our cooks are to prepare three days' rations.

Camp near Falmouth, Va.
April 29, 1863. Wednesday.

Cloudy, warm and even sultry. I am for bridge Guard again to-night so cannot go into particulars at present, suffice to say we put a bridge across the Rappahannock completing it about 7 o'clock a.m., putting men across at first.[14] None of us were hurt in the least, our boats reached the other shore first, and finished our bridge. To his dishonor General Benham was tumbling *drunk!*

I was generally useful. Went with train until the constructing [of the] bridge, when I took the vacant place of a balk-lasher the last two-thirds.[15] Feel well. Hope we succeed; troops are cheerful; no movement of any consequence so far.

✈— The bridge was thrown the morning of the 29th. Shibley and myself took the place of two lashers in the first boat who were disabled, I do not recollect how.[16] Lieutenant Gillespie called on us "Will you take the place, etc?" we being Non-Coms. I saw a sharpshooter firing at us as rapidly as he could, but although he spattered the water over me, he fortunately did not hit; it is a singular sensation to see a man shoot at you, especially in the bow of a boat, without even the poor opportunity of returning it.

I believe I must be mistaken about General Benham being drunk; his face was bloody, and I have seen he was wounded, some said it was where he fell on a stump! He was excited and exposed himself with the rest, and was everywhere, and where there was a hitch of any kind he started it moving. It was quite hot awhile as they kept up a fire on us to the last chance. The General gained my respect in that he attended to details and the whole undertaking was successful and promptly finished.[17]

I had charge of the abutment boat which was left on the wagon and drawn by mules, and I had an anxious time until I had it at the rivers edge; the abutment boat had its fixtures all lashed. When I started down the steep hill to the main flat, I was wringing my hands to discover there was no good lock for the wheels; I ran a rail through the wheels, and feared it would break, and a stampede would have spoilt the whole.

Camp near Falmouth, Va.
May 1, 1863. Friday.
Warm, quite so; good clear weather, very foggy this morning. Was on Bridge Guard yesterday and night before. Am well. We are packed up ready to move with five days' rations. Now I will go back and tell the story of the last few days; I have kept notes along and will fill up the rest.

The 28th I went down to the Train on Guard; the weather being cloudy and raining, but warm. About 3:30 p.m., mule teams came and hitched on to the Boats and material wagons. The 6th Corps now passed along to the Left; General Benham made us a call; he is a large stout man with a full face, whiskers gray and shaved under the chin, with a bluff odd manner which you would remember if you see him but five minutes, and one of the old school soldier style, exceedingly liable to get *mulfathomed* with drink, yet attending to his business in a most particular manner. All the troops are in good spirits, "have an idea we will get a little [of] the best of them this time" said a Volunteer to me, which is what they all say. I was never so pleased with a forward movement as this, "perfectly happy." 6:30 p.m., Troops all collected along with Pontons beyond Captain Sands's; misty and cloudy, but not dank and heavy. Just the night for such work. As we left our old station at Captain Sands's, one of his little boys bid me "Good Bye" quite affectionately; it seemed quite like civilization, it was a new sensation. Poor innocent boy, pitying us, when we were glad to go on.

In an hour or so we moved on from home about a mile farther, and a mile or so from the river; here a number of boats were taken from the wagons and were drawn by hand down to the river's edge just below Deep Run where we put the bridge out before.[18] This operation was a little disheartening to *us*, both from the dull listless way the Volunteers worked and the noise they made, for this was the great thing to be done, to get the troops to the river unknown, unheard and unseen. I could but think of the night when *we* on [the] Chickahominy unloaded boats and material, launched the boats into and took them down the stream, between ours and their pickets not twenty paces apart, and were not discovered! Our Guard was returned back to their own Companies by this time. General Benham was everywhere, ubiquitous, Johnson of our Company amuses us with imitations of him, viz: "O-h! my God! Sh—— up boys, make less noise! I don't want you killed, &c."[19] He did not trouble us much; I heard him say "the regulars can take of themselves." I was with the abutment boats drawn by mules. At 4:30 a.m. we had got nearly to the river at the right of the place of building. We had intimation that they were just to cross with the boats, some of us were laying on the ground asleep, the mules were just drooping their long ears to pleasant dreams, the drivers were snoring in full accord, some on the tramways of the wagons just back of the mules, when suddenly a line of flame shot off [in] the indistinct distance with the crash of the returning volley; at this there ensued one of the wildest scenes of confusion I never hope to witness again; the plain was nothing but flying wagons drawn by the perfectly frantic mules (cutting figure 8s, 3s, &c.!), some were loose of the wagon dragging perhaps one of their own kind, the men about them were running this way and that to keep from being run over; to those who woke up at this moment it must have [been] like going from Eden to Pandemonium; we arranged the teams as soon as possible and then stacked our arms and went to the river. The boats were now plying to and fro taking troops across, a most interesting and beautiful spectacle. We could hear the Officers giving orders to Skirmishers, &c.; there was no firing however after the first firings. The loaded boats of material now came down and bridges were commenced as quickly as possible; we had ours across in 40 minutes at most; ours was first built! then the 15th [New York] completed theirs, say 45 minutes after, it was now 7 o'clock a.m. and we had established ourselves in our position. The 50th New York Engineers then constructed another, making three in all. (A surgeon made his station under the bank at the farther end of our bridge.)

Those who witnessed the first crossing of the boats say it was a splendid sight; the boats were all ready to start, clear of the bank; all was still, no sounds but those of insects and the river as it gurgled against the boats; at the word they are away and disappear in the mist; a flash and a roar of musketry, then a light cheer and you hear them going up, up the hill, then back come the boats with only the sturdy rowers in them, with some prisoners and those who were wounded. Our boats were not fired upon until they reached the opposite shore, and none were wounded until they ascended the banks. Some were wounded on this side, one was hit right by us; we were in more danger than the boatmen.

This was a daring exploit and smacks a little of brilliancy too; it was evidently a complete surprise, as [there was] nothing but an ordinary picket guard; we took two or three prisoners including one of the officers. Had they known of it they could have made a formidable resistance. General Benham by this time was tumbling and shamefully drunk;* he had got a bad looking eye from some tumble, it is related he asked the man's name that picked him up and told him he would *promote him!* Jake was lugging away at a balk and smoking to help the matter, Benham hailed him "You can't lift it; you can't lift it; you smoke too heavy a pipe!" He does! It evidently gratified him to see us work, he only told us to "work away my castle-boys!" never finding fault. After completing the bridge and leaving a guard we returned home by 2 p.m. None of us were hurt, which good fortune, I trust, will ever be with us.

✈— * See note about General Benham a few pages previous.

The 50th New York put one across nearly three-quarters of a mile below us, and were attacked and sustained some loss; they did not put men across at first. I heard they could not get the troops to go across to their shore, thus their loss. I don't know how many were lost among the troops at either place.[20]

All was quiet the night of the 30th; we were on the lookout for fire-rafts, torpedoes and such-like amiable articles, ours being the uppermost— No. 1.[21] Dunham fished out a minnie sloop, used by the pickets of both parties for trading purposes.*[22] It is quite neatly constructed of white wood, about 15" long by 5" wide, 3" deep, about. On the hull was written in pencil "John Butternut, 24 Va Co K." A place was dug out in the centre for baggage and ballasted by bullets nailed to the bottom, fastened with wooden pins elsewhere. A sketch on the preceding page is of her [see "The Rappahannock Blockade Runner"].

⤞— * December 15, 1907. I gave this boat to E. B. Hosmer [of] Company C, who was going home, to Lynn, Massachusetts, on a furlough.[23] I do not know whether he has it or not.

An Order was read to the troops from Hooker that he had turned their flanks, was in their rear, captured 17 pieces of artillery, 10,000 prisoners, &c., whereat they cheered hugely. There was some firing by the lower bridge when we came home at 4:30 p.m. We laid out a parallel by our bridge last evening which was finished during the night. From *it* you

The Rappahannock Blockade Runner. Thompson's rough, small sketch of the "Rappahannock Blockade Runner" that he described in his May 1, 1863, journal entry.

Gilbert Thompson, a la Napleonime. Another sketch of Thompson, this one by John B. Geyser from December 1862, showing him with the distinctive facial hair that Thompson described toward the end of his May 1, 1863, journal entry.

have a splendid view of Fredericksburg, Stafford Heights &c.; from the latter is also a fine landscape view. I saw the balloon away to the rear of Fredericksburg almost. Were mustered, so ended that day and at night for a luxury slept in our bunk, quite agreable after two nights on the ground.

Well, if I were at home, I might *be* having a merry time at a May day Festival.

12 noon. Firing heard on the right.

8 o'clock p.m. Firing yet, on the right, quite heavy awhile ago. Rumor has it that Stoneman and Slocum are killed.[24] Heintzelman with the 8th Corps and Keyes are coming up from Yorktown destroying railroads, &c.;[25] Hooker is in good Spirits. All quiet on the Left. "Enough for to-day." It is pleasant this evening, genial with bright moonlight! Shaved to-day, *a la Napleonime.*[26] Quite warm during the day. Sergeants Yagier and McGee of C have received commissions in the 5th New Hampshire Volunteers.[27] Wouldn't take a 1st Lieutenancy in place of my present position.

✄— [Editor's Note: The following newspapers clippings were pasted into the memoir section of Thompson's journal.]

An Eye-Witness and Part Instigator.[28]

Editor National Tribune: Looking over the Picket Shots Along the Line in The National Tribune recalls a circumstance to which I was an eye-witness and part instigator—that is, one man's desertion from the rebel army. Our corps, the Sixth, was camped at Falmouth, Va., and our picket posts were along the Rappahannock River. This stream of water between the two armies being very narrow, the murderous practice of shooting at one another whenever a head was in sight was abolished. We enjoyed the pleasure of catching rabbits and talking to one another across the stream. We had also a little boat, which was an unlicensed trader between Johnny reb and Yank. At that point right below Fredericksburg we would freight it with sugar and coffee, and put the daily newspaper in the mast. Then the little ship was carried up the stream by a few comrades who were off duty and christened the "Monitor," and when the sail was arranged it started on its trip to the southern shore. We knew when the Johnnies received the cargo by the rebel yell of thanks that echoed back to us. The rebels would return it the same day or perhaps the next laden with tobacco and one of their newspapers, with its name changed to the "Merrimack." Our squad was on picket there for a week or more and one day the Louisiana Tigers being on duty opposite our posts, a member of the Tigers named Lynch, a powerful, big Irishman, over six feet in height, and I got into a conversation about what would be done with him if he deserted and swam over to our side. He had implicit faith in "The Boston Pilot," so I got a copy of that paper and sent it over to him, and after he had read it he called over to me and said that when he came to his post the next morning at 2 o'clock he would swim over. He stated that his gun would be thrown into the river first, then his cartridge box, then "meself, and look out for me when you hear these signals." I was lying on the pebbled shore, wide awake, and heard the signals distinctly. Comrade Henry Lane was walking his beat. I asked him if he heard anything fall in the water on the other side. He said he did not. "Well," said I, "Lane, Lynch is on his way over. Let us walk down a piece and watch for him." We had gone but a short distance when we discovered Lynch puffing like a porpoise. Lane was a six-footer and he waded in the water when Lynch was about to sink, got a grip on his hair, and helped him to dry land and freedom.[29] We had his uniform taken off, built a rousing fire, made him a big tin of hot coffee, gave him our blankets to cover him while we dried his clothing and shortly after daylight I sent a guard with him to Gen. Nelson's quarters.[30]

In his conversation with me Lynch remarked that had he had some kind of a boat he could have gotten all the Tigers over that morning. If Mr. Lynch is living and reads this I would be pleased to hear from him.—Thos. J. McGrath. Sixth Corps. Wilkinsburg, Pa.

On the Rappahannock.[31]

At a recent meeting of Admiral Foote Post, Hartford, Conn., Frank Hartung, 27th Conn., told of the experiences on picket on the Rappahannock in the Spring of 1863. The pickets were within 200 feet of each other on the opposite banks of the river, and amused themselves by sailing across the stream little boats with pieces of paper for sails, on which a letter would be scrawled. One letter received by Comrade Hartung read:

"Gents: We send you a late paper and some tobacco. Send us a late paper and some coffee in return, and tell us what is the matter with Joe Hooker, that he won't let you all boat with us. Joe, I think, he is a little too meddlesome to do well. Tell him if he will send me a late paper I will marry his aunt and dance at his funeral this Summer. It has been so long since we got a Yankee paper we are getting entirely behind the times.

"So be good boys, and don't play too much in the branch.—L. H. Wilkes, Company H, 17th Miss."

Your Festival and Ours.

Go wreathe your crown for May-day Queen,
    Of sweet and early flowers;
While we, beneath the "stars" that gleam,
    Must bear the battle's powers.

Go dance up the village green,
    To music's lively strain;
But ours to hear the shell's shrill scream,
    And groan of sudden pain.

Oh! let your hearts be free and light,
    And let May-mirth abound;
We go to storm the sullen height
    That hems the city round.

You twine with flowers bright evergreen,
     Rememb'ring winter hours;
Your hearts as choice should deem
     The memory of ours.

(May 1, 1863.)

Camp near Falmouth, Va.

May 2, 1863. Saturday.

Quite warm, wind S.W. Battalion Drill in morning. Our returned Bridge Guard reports that affairs have assumed a more warlike cast today. The rebels advanced on the lowest bridge, but were repulsed as soon as our artillery could operate in our favor. They had quite a sharp artillery duel, and injured one [of] the bridges with shot, afterwards taken up. Several shells came near our bridge, also rebel skirmishers endeavored to annoy us from near Hazel Dell. The pickets are firing in earnest, and quite a number are wounded. At dusk from our drill ground we could see shells bursting in the distance over the heights *back of Fredericksburg*, and could just distinguish the sound of firing, quite a singular spectacle truly.[32] Success is evidently attending our arms, may it be complete. No newspapers to hand. Whiskey given out tonight after Retreat! Last night we met in C's Orderly tent, and had a convivial parting with Sergeants Yagier and McGee till twelve.[33]

Camp near Falmouth, Va.

May 3, 1863. Sunday.

A pleasant day with wind S.W. To-day is to be a great day in '63 history, for *we have taken Fredericksburg, and the heights*.[34] Now for the reminiscences of this day.

I was woke up this morning before Reveille by heavy firing by the city and we had the idea that the rebels were forcing our front. At 8 o'clock, while we were preparing for Inspection, were turned out for fatigue duty under arms. We went down to our bridge, and found that our troops had crossed in large force and occupied the city, and advanced a mile towards the front. We took up our bridge* into rafts and boated them up to the city, to where the canal bridge (McDowell's) was below the railroad bridge. Here we constructed the bridge, in about twenty minutes. At our former position we were annoyed by an (unfilled) shell striking near the bridges, and five or six came quite near us.[35]

* At this time there was heavy firing on the right.

At 12:30 the troops charged the works of the enemy, taking them in seven minutes. I saw the last half of it, and about an hour after all the works were taken and the heights that hem old Fredericksburg around no longer disturb us. We heard the cheers and hurrahs as they swooped upon them *and they heard ours too.* This is the greatest exploit of the war. Joseph Hooker is a genuine hero now among the soldiers, gold at par! After this we went up into the city and filled up the rifle-pits across the principal streets; a quite pretty city it is too. We captured a whole Mississippi Regiment (18th) and some pieces;[36] the prisoners are hardy, stalwart men but have an otherwise poor appearance from their butternutt suits and un-uniform clothing. The railroad bridge is commenced by the bridge builders.[37] We have had a tiresome, exciting day and are weary, so I can write but short sentences. As I look back upon this short campaign resulting so brilliantly, I am impressed with the real military shrewdness, calculation, and you may say persevering audacious *finesse* of our Commander. He has cooly gone to work like a chess-player, taken his positions one after the other and to-day, when the enemy were deceived, puzzled with our movements, by a *coup de main, checkmated* them! I must say that it is in agreable contrast with the timid, vacillating conduct of McClellan; although I once believed him a great general; yet I will remark in connection, that there was something mysterious about his generalship. It remains to be seen if Hooker follows up vigorously, anyway; it sounded mightily like it at dusk, there being firing in the distance. Our troops now occupy the heights and the city, having resigned our former position on the left to the enemy if they want it (!) our pickets extending no farther from the city than Deep Run. How it is on the right, I know not. I went over to Head Quarters awhile ago and saw some prisoners, they were quite cheerful. No News; no papers. With peace to the brave dead, and consolation to those that mourn for them, a Good Night ends at last this eventful day.

Our first bridge was laid just below *Deep* Run, by Bernard's house, instead of Hazell Dell, which is back of the town, dividing the heights.[38]

⊬— Just after Sedgwick carried Marye's Heights, some of the men got a chance to look over the field, and one of them told me he was particularly struck by a noble looking Confederate, dead, behind the famous stonewall, sitting up, and with a smile on his face.

Camp near Falmouth, Va.
May 6, 1863. Wednesday, 8 p.m.

Raining and thundering. I hardly know what to write, but I will try at least to note a few details. Monday forenoon (a pleasant day), there was quite sharp work in the vicinity of the city. About 11 o'clock we were turned out "with arms and sixty rounds" to go to work. I was detailed for guard on the bridge; we went down to our bridge at Fredericksburg city and dug rifle-pits on this side, filling up rebel ones on the other side! It appears that the firing proceeding from the raid of rebel brigade who went between the Division that took the heights (Sedgwick's) and the town.[39] We met large numbers of wounded when going down. *Rumor* (!) has it that Sedgwick had to reinforce Hooker by the desperate manoevre of *cutting through to him*. Anyway the rebels held the heights in small force—no artillery, closing in behind Sedgwick. Late in the afternoon we swung the bridge round, and so resigned Fredericksburg. We (the Guard) staid the night in the rifle-pit by the bank—the Battalion bivouacking on the flat—back. It was a beautiful night, bright moonlight with a heavy fog in the morning. I slept in the rifle-pit on the crest of which the pickets walked. There was a very heavy attack towards the northern part of the city on the heights at dark. We were not disturbed, although we had our pieces loaded for anything that might occur. Nothing was heard during the night, but a little skirmishing on the outskirts of the city, a few discharges of artillery—like Camp Lincoln on the Peninsula—the church bell as it told the hours—by which I posted the Reliefs, and the splashing of fish in the smooth running river.[40] The tide came in and went out again, making me think of Cape Ann. I slept well, except for the toads which hopped indiscriminately on earth and face; I was once woke up by one perched upon my cheek, I just touched him with my finger and he went off to disturb some other watch-worn guard, and I to sleep again.

Early the 5th (Tuesday *morning*) the Battalion came down and dismantled the bridge, carrying it up to the flat. It was a tedious job before breakfast (21 boats on the bridge). Our Guard took charge of material at its new position. The rebels did not get fully into the town until 10 o'clock, then only in straggling parties, who were gathered up by an officer on horse-back, whose summons they obeyed sluggishly. Some of their scouts, *I should judge*, came in before clear daylight. About noon bodies of their troops came along the ridges and heights, to whom the heavy artillery near us (Seven Sisters) sent their uninteresting compliments.[41] They hugged the ravines closer whereat. Towards 2 o'clock a Virginia shower came up, flooding everything and ending in a storm which is baptizing us to-day. Understood Hooker was reinforced by Dix with 40,000.[42] Hope so.

Was relieved from Guard, and Rue and Clarke favored me with a due share of their shelter—they having their blankets—so passed a better night than I expected, rained somewhat all night.[43] Our boys were so fortunate as to appropriate some tents left standing by some Regiment that had gone; so did quite well. It was quite cold; the day being hot.

(6th) This morning (Wind S.E.) the teams and wagons came—whose long coming* had kept us there—and we loaded on the boats and material. I was with a party who went down by Captain Sands's house to load three boats, so did not get home (?), which was sopping wet, until as late as three o'clock, p.m.; my commission was wet, though the *reading* is *good* yet.[44] This book fortunately escaping. As for news I hardly know what to write. We hear Hooker is *this* side of the river and rather worsted;[45] this seems a little incredible as this morning we heard firing in the same old place on the right, if anything nearer the city, and "that's Joe Hooker, don't ye hear him?" I can't say as I feel in good spirits, perhaps because I am weary and tired; but if Hooker is thoroughly whipped this side of the river, I shall be disheartened [if] after all our toil, struggling, loss of life nothing has been accomplished. At least after it all there is one little thing left me yet called Life, the gift of God which I would have willingly returned to him amid the din of battle, if something had been accomplished, but have a selfish gratification that I yet have the boon!

  * The shower of the preceding afternoon has so flooded the country that it was impossible for them to come or me go home; we were weatherbound.

  ✝— July 18, 1886, *Note.* If I may be pardoned a little pride, it is because I could write in May, 1863, these pages of my war journal; no wonder the army of Lee was utterly wore out whipping us.

  And as a side-light, the fact is that General Lee—although throughout the south there was great rejoicing over Hooker's defeat—was greatly depressed, after Chancellorsville.

We had it from some source, rebel prisoners I think (?), that General Lee had one spy whose special duty it was to keep him informed of the movements of the Ponton Boat trains, and also of the Battalion.

I think myself such information would give a better idea of intended or proposed movements than any other, as I never knew of our being used for a feint; when the pontons moved, it assuredly meant business in earnest. Nor when the pulse of the army began to accelerate, it showed first by the mules being hitched up to the ponton boats.[46]

Camp near Falmouth, Va.
May 7, 1863. Thursday, 9 a.m.

Chilly and stormy. Real Yorktown weather, a hard shower then a miserable, cold storm from the N.E. lasting three or four days. Wind N.E. Dismal and cheerless, but thank our stars we have as good a place as this old weather-worn shanty. On Garrison Police. No news yet, I think (and understand) Hooker is yet across the river and intrenched. No firing today so far. I am not disheartened yet, but we have retreated so much, it would be quite unexpected to stick to a position. "Joe" will, if any one. I don't see why we should. The Photographic artist at Head Quarters, who went with the army through the Crimea, said "the taking of the Ponton up to the city" to reconstruct bridges there "was the most risky thing he ever saw done," it was truly, as just this (lower) side of the town they passed in full view of the enemy's batteries.

Camp near Falmouth, Va.
May 8, 1863. Friday, 8 a.m.

Weather ditto, with interest. Wind N.E. The army is all back.[47] Received a letter from Mother and "Abbie" last evening.[48] I shall not attempt to detail any movements of the army except our own and what I see. Our Boat Trains were all ready for another move, and mules were actually hitched on, but were afterwards unhitched; they had orders to go twelve miles below. *Hear* Vicksburg's taken.[49]

Camp near Falmouth, Va.
May 9, 1863. Saturday, 8:30 p.m.

Pleasant and sunny. Wind S.E. It is quite exhilarating to the spirits to see the sun again, and we have improved his smiles by throwing open the tents and letting some of the dampness forth. We also had the delight of a newspaper, the *Washington Chronicle* of to-day. It gives some account of our doings as a whole, also Stoneman's great Cavalry expedition.[50] I have an idea that *Johnny* is troubled, Banks is doing well,[51] Porter has Grand Gulf, "the door to Vicksburg."[52] The troops here are in good spirits and ready to start again. "Joe is all right." I understand Peck, while this late battle was going on, advanced fifteen miles on the Blackwater.[53] Received a nice, clever letter from L. A. ———. The Battalion is putting the train in good order. Hear that some of the train went away with some Cavalry yesterday. We are clearing up very neatly in and about the camp which rather goes against the boys' inclination; I don't think it indicates a stay but to keep us in good trim for work, not get relaxed. Captain Charles N. Turnbull was read off to-night as Commanding Battalion.[54] Bands are playing all round. The rebels have pitched their tents in their old camping places, the balloon rises from its old ascending place, all the same as before apparently, no cannon thundering, all so-so. But Hooker will be moving soon somewhere; we will have a busy summer.

The spy Richardson came into our camp I think the 7th instant with maps &c. to sell, I quizzed him pretty close and he was uncommunicative, showed no energy or spirit except when I said "Hooker was yet across the river," this he denied; he complained of being very tired.[55]

Camp near Falmouth, Va.
May 11, 1863. Monday, 10 a.m.

Hot. ditto yesterday. Battalion drill and fatigue duty yesterday, to-day too probably. Begins to smack of Harrison's Landing. It is hotter than last year this time. Not much wind, S.W., what there is of it. Had the pleasure of reading some *Boston Journals*, and they are full of good news. Hooker's late affair here, although not a decisive victory, has laid bare the rebels' resources and their weakness. *They were reinforced here from Richmond, Suffolk and Charlestown.*[56] They can do this with celerity being on an interior line; but it shows that we have a *superior army* in Virginia and its vicinity than they, plainly. Therefore, our course of action should be to attack simultaneously at all points; in that case, their alternative would be to conquer us by detail. We would be undoubtedly overwhelmed at some points, but in the whole we would surely be successful. There is a chance for some master mind to move the armies in one concerted and systematic action in Virginia and North Carolina. Who will do it? We have seen while the late battle was going on that we drove them from Williamsburg and advanced fifteen miles on the Blackwater,[57] and with 20,000 men could have gobbled up Richmond and all, until they resolved on the alternative of abandoning other parts and retaking it. Oh! I'm quite a general!

Camp near Falmouth, Va.
May, 13, 1863. Wednesday, 8 a.m.
    Hot and sultry. Wind S.W. Hazy, Sprinkling, lightning & thunder at Retreat. Nothing to-day of consequence; Company Drill at 7 o'clock. I was on Guard at Boat Train yesterday, quite warm. Large quantity of flour came in, and we have soft bread issued to-day for supper. Graham, recruit, came; formerly in English army, "Royal Engineers."[58] It is insufferably dull here. I would sleep all the time, if I did not feel so mean after sleeping during the heat. I am glad of even the little military duties to break up the monotony. A few days ago we were full of business, and so it seems dull at present. The green grass of the fields is quite pleasant to see, but I long for some woods to lounge round in, trees being very few and far between by our camp, all is bare and tame, hardly stumps left to mark where woods used to be. In Washington's time it might have been an interesting country, but now you can easily trace the furrows of their old plantations amongst the pines.

Same Camp.
May 15, 1863. Friday.
    Cool last night, wind varying from N.E. & N. Pleasant, though warm, breezy from S.W. Clouding up to-night in the N.W. On Company Police. A grand clearing up time, airing tents, &c., *per order* and building a shade of boughs, &c., along the centre rear of our Company tents; looking well and promising comfort during hot days. We have made a little change in our bunks, making them single, Rue to hang up in a hammock on his own hook. This gives us more room, looking neater and cooler hot nights, which by the way are *very* rare in Virginia. A very commendatory Order was read on Parade from General Benham of the doings of the "Engineer Brigade," of which we are a part. Received a letter from mother, not as encouraging as I should like, she is going to an Eye Infirmary. As a comfort to the sentinels on hot days, sentry boxes of boughs have been made,

Sentry Box. This rough sketch of a sentry box illustrates Thompson's description of them in his May 15, 1863, journal entry.

making quite a pretty appearance. Things look a stay, but I can't really think it. Quién Sabe.

Camp near Falmouth, Va.
May 17, 1863. Sunday.

Quite warm, Wind N.W. which is bringing up showers. For a number of nights it has clouded up at sunset, but was clear the next morning. The dust is very troublesome, giving a dingy look to everything, it sounds like drifting snow outside the tents at times. All quiet. I'm for Guard to-night on Train.

Camp near Falmouth, Va.
May 20, 1863. Wednesday.

Warm. Wind S.W. Pleasant. I am tired, but must write a little. Yesterday, by order, we broke camp by taking down our tents, or rather houses, and filling up and carrying away until nothing but a level place could be seen where once towered in mimic grandeur our residences. It was the maddest day I ever had or ever saw since in the service. We took a *curs*-ory glance at the old walls, took a last minute nap in our cosy bunks, then with growlings, &c., we demolished the old homestead. The arbor had to go too. More than all "We" are no longer a unity. Us four Corporals, Shibley, myself, Cummins,[59] [and] Coolidge, have to go together, so "bunky" and I had to say, "Good Bye," and he is a nice smart, clever, good young man, as I know from public and private acquaintance. Well, "Come day, go day." "Us" have an imitation wall tent with bunks—single ones—each side, not finished yet. All up in a heap. Inspected this morning by some inspecting Officer. Rue has just come in to write with my ink, and it seems a little like "home." I might write a lot but I am too tired, so with a look at a certain "Our Tent," drawn some pages back, I will close up.

P.S. Good news from the South West, from Grant.[60]

Joseph Cummins of
Company D.

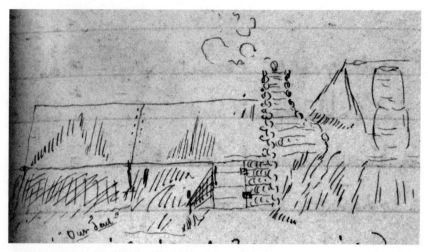

Our Tent, May 1863. This is the sketch of "Our Tent" that Thompson referenced in his May 20, 1863, entry.

Camp near Falmouth, Va.
May 21, 1863. Thursday.

Very warm, and sultry (Wind S.W.). Tired again to-night, and ought to be, received a letter from mother though, quite encouraging too. In forenoon, graded our Parade Ground, a hard and tiresome job, but we made a good job of it, and it has a good appearance. To add to our fun we went on Brigade Review, a dusty job. Our Battalion occupied the centre! I judge a Review to be a very great deal pleasanter to *see* than to be *in* decidedly. Benham reviewed.

Camp near Falmouth, Va.
May 22, 1863. Friday.

Warm as ever. Wind N.W. Comfortable in shade. To-day I'm in eighteen months. It's down hill now, 'tother side of the roof. I am quite agreably situated, Shibley being a mirth provoking chap, but I cannot enjoy my own society as formerly, for a Commissioned or Non-Commissioned Officer has to choose his bunky from his like. I cannot enjoy more liberty and happiness as a private or Artificer than as I am, but something else makes up for that. I can tell better by and by. Ditched round camp and set up stakes for shade. Company Drill in morning. "To *be* sure" woke me early and I had a bath before Reveille. I am indulging in thoughts of green fields, with the perfume of apple-blossoms floating over them, and lemons, pickles and other sour things.

Camp near Falmouth, Va.
May 25, 1863. Monday, 9 a.m.

Cool with a misty storm. Wind N.E. Yesterday was hot, sultry & hazy. On Guard at Trains yesterday. All is quiet as usual. During the past week, Head Quarters have moved to a new position in some pine woods back of us. Our camp is nearly completed, and the aspect of it last evening by candle-light, with its uniform tents, bough awnings, broad, graded Parades had really a delightful and pleasing appearance. Shibley little ailing to-day. I am wishing the time to fly someway now, mother is unwell and I have reached the turning point too. Great news and news from Grant. We are issued Castles and Company letters, so brass is quite conspicuous, some of old Benham's doings (Old Blue Eye).[61] So much more cleaning, that's all.

Soldier's Kitchen. Thompson drew this sketch of a campsite cook spot in the margin of his May 25, 1863, journal entry. In the background are the pontoon boats used by the Engineer Battalion, shown on their wagons.

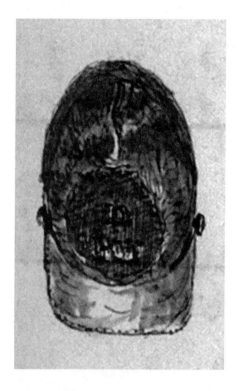

The Brass Castle. This is Thompson's small, rough marginal sketch of a Union kepi with the three-turreted brass Engineer Castle on it that he mentions in his May 25, 1863, journal entry.

Camp near Falmouth, Va.
May 26, 1863. Tuesday, 4 p.m.
Cool in forenoon, clearing away at 2 o'clock. Wind S.E. Commenced Practical Engineering this forenoon, Field Fortification probably, just what we need, wrote to mother.

Camp near Falmouth, Va.
May 27, 1863. Wednesday, 8 p.m.
Pleasant. Usual duties. Drill in morning. Practical Engineering in forenoon. Slept in afternoon, dull again. Great cheering towards Head Quarters.

All We Knew . . . [Was] That a Battle Was Going On

The Gettysburg Campaign, May–July 1863

Capt. Cross, Corps of Engineers, commanding Company B was killed on June 5, while crossing the Rappahannock. It was repeatedly attempted to throw the bridge without dislodging the enemy's skirmishers on the opposite bank. It was found impossible. Forty-five ponton boats were then launched and filled with soldiers, the troops of the Engineer Battalion assisted by the 50th N.Y. Volunteer Engineers taking charge of the boats. Cross was killed in one of these boats. The bridge was built on the afternoon of that day.

"On the transfer of the army to Pennsylvania, a ponton bridge was thrown at the mouth of the Ocoquan and one at Union Mills, twenty miles higher up. When they arrived at Alexandria the ponton boats were towed to Washington and thence up the [Chesapeake and Ohio] canal to Edwards Ferry where a bridge was thrown for the army. During the engagement at Gettysburg, excepting a few men who were detached, the whole Battalion was kept at Westminister to guard the town and to barricade the streets and the roads leading to town against Stewart's Cavalry. On the 6th of July, 1863, a wooden crib bridge, about 150 feet long, was constructed across Antietam Creek near Jones Crossroads."[1]

—LIEUT. TURTLE'S ESSAY

Camp near Falmouth, Va.

May 31, 1863. Sunday.

Quite warm, with brisk wind from S.W. raising a complete dust-storm, which penetrates everything, and men look quite venerable; I saw a chap going down [the] street when the wind lulled who had been asleep, one

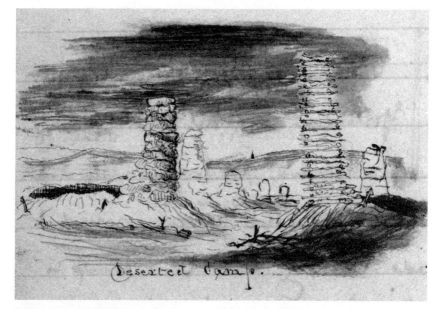

Deserted Camp. This sketch depicts the soldiers' shelter chimneys after their tents had been removed.

side of his head being gray and the other black as a raven. It has been a very disagreable day indeed. It has been trying to rain of late but entirely unsuccessful, dry as ever. It is quite pleasant to-night, quiet with a gentle breeze, moon shining over all. "May-be-s" fly no more, May leaves to-day at 12 midnight. I am not feeling as happy as usual; mother being no better, &c. I hear some of the army have four days' rations; a faint rumor that all hands are going to Aquia; Sergeant [William] Farr has been down laying out additional works. Vicksburg sure to be taken. Our tent resembles a mimic Pompeii.

Camp near Falmouth, Va.
June 3, 1863. Wednesday.

Cloudy, trying to rain; Wind N.W. Have had a little rain since last date, hardly enough to lay the dust, yet making it comparatively comfortable. All jogs along its usual course, our Battery is going up slowly, but well. D Company is small in numbers, so it goes slow. There is not the whit of explanation I would wish; as though they were afraid we would know too much.

Camp near Falmouth, Va.

June 4, 1863. Thursday, 3 p.m.

Quite warm, very little breeze from S.W. We were turned out last night at 1:30 a.m., and had orders to pack up ready to move. We did so, with the exception of not striking tents; Company wagons were loaded and Commissary Stores. After Reveille at 4 a.m. we were told to turn in and rest, which we are doing up to the present time. It was quite startling to be thus turned out after so long a time of quietness here; in fact yesterday, I could but help thinking that it seemed as though there was no such thing as war about. We imagined all sorts of notions when we arrayed ourselves one after the other in the ranks; nothing has happened yet. I hear of no other troops doing thus; with perhaps [the exception of] the 6th Corps. What it means I can't tell; but I think something is up. Vicksburg is stirring up a mess everywhere. Rumor says we are going to the Creek Alexandria; that Lee is menacing Washington, &c. I'm for Camp Guard to-night. We have three days' rations. Rather regret to leave our camp, now completed so nicely; but sometime I can stay and go whither I please. So it goes.

Camp near Falmouth, Va.

June 5, 1863. Friday, 1 p.m.

Warm, hazy during night. Wind S.S.E. Breezy. Had a good night of it, turned out Guard three times only! Officers very particular. The Battalion has just gone off with one day's rations, blankets rolled and arms. Guard remains on. Heard the 15th & 50th [New York Volunteer Engineers'] Train went off in forenoon. Also, that Fredericksburg is evacuated, and our troops are in the city. There was fighting on the right the 3d instant at Stafford Court House. I had rather be with the Company than in camp on Guard.

6 p.m. Prospect of showers, Wind changing to N .W. apparently, now S. Easterly. Cannonading commenced in the same old place about 4 p.m., quite lively for awhile, desultory at present. I should judge a little skirmishing is just going on, none heretofore. *Rumor.* (!) Bridge thrown; no rebs on the Heights; no infantry by the river but Engineers. Anyway there has been firing *from our side at something.*[2]

The band is playing pleasantly at Pleasonton's Head Quarters (Packard's house).[3] Received a letter from Mother, she is really no better; I fear I shall never see her again. Oh! I hope not! Her letter is full of good thoughts, which I shall copy somewhere, leastways keep them in my heart. Been reading *Bleak House* just keeping ahead of Coolidge, who tears off the preceding pages to light [his] pipe with.[4]

Camp near Falmouth, Va.

June 6, 1863. Saturday.

Pleasant, not too warm. Breezy from N.W. Sprinkled a little last evening. To-day I record *Reality*. About 8 o'clock an ambulance came along to our camp with Captain Cross—killed. It seems as if it could not be so. I asked Stevens as I was by No. 3 "What the word was?" he just showed me his hands, red with our brave Captain's blood.[5] Then we heard that others were wounded.[6] Captain Cross was a great favorite with everyone, brave to a fault, a soldier and a gentleman, the boys all gathered round his remains crying, some kissing him. Even now I can't believe it is so, but Company B escorted his remains to the depot, we shall never hear his "Shoulder—*Hrmp*," again.[7] He was shot through the head. Kehoe of A Company was mortally wounded, dying last night. Johnny Carr being the only one [wounded] out of our Company. It was a sad night; and is a sad day. We were relieved this morning; just wrote to mother, and will write somewhere a full account of our yesterday afternoon's work. I feel some tired and sleepy from our two tours of duty. No news to-day, there was some firing on the right. I can't understand this movement at all.

9 p.m. Had a brisk shower from N.W. at Retreat. From our Dress Parade grounds, about as high land as there is about between the city and White Oak Church, with a glass, could not see any troops, camps or anything to indicate any "rebs" on the Heights, except our artillery firing at something. Troops were moving down to Franklin's Crossing during the day, hear the Cavalry have gone to the right. I think Lee is making initiative. The next four weeks will be great in results one way or the other. The shower for a wonder is clearing off clear I think. Good Night.

✠— Captain Cross was shot through the right temple by a sharpshooter, just as he had finished saying "*Come men we must build this bridge!*" and was stepping into the first boat. We had rather it had been any other officer. He was not much of a disciplinarian in the way of catching men, but they would do anything for him.

Camp near Falmouth, Va.

June 7, 1863. Sunday, 8:15 a.m.

Pleasant and cool with a good pure bracing wind from N.W. Clear and splendid like New England. Heard one gun so far. Have one day's ration and blankets rolled to go down to bridge when needed. No Inspection, got all cleaned up. Wounded doing well.

8 p.m. At dinner (1 o'clock) we went down to "Franklin's Crossing," and cut some pickets for running parallel and came home about Retreat. Nothing has happened of any consequence at that place. We have two bridges across. The 6th Corps are down at that point, one [division] across, two as Reserve. The old parallel is leveled and a new one will be probably done to-night farther on to the front, from Bernard's house round to the Deep Run. It seemed a little like Yorktown times to lay out alongside the pickets. I was shown where General Bayard was killed.[8] We could see plenty of "rebs," and papers were exchanged while we were down. A night attack was expected last night. *Rumor* says we are going to the Shenandoah Valley. There is nothing known in Washington about the bridge-building. Papers, like *Jo* in *Bleak House,* "knows nothink." I cannot understand this movement, heard troops were moving towards the right

Our Tent, June 1863. This sketch, another one called "Our Tent," shows the tent Thompson shared with others in June 1863.

to-day. Had a clear, cool New England sunset. A, B, & C were turned out last night to roll blankets and get one day's rations. We slept undisturbed, as I hope we do to-night. Cool.

Camp near Falmouth, Va.
June 8, 1863. Monday.

Cool. Wind N.W. No news. Slept half the day, tried to read *Oxonians, Barnaby Rudge*,[9] couldn't get beyond a chapter, put the finishing touches to an *Atlantic* [*Monthly*]. Companies A, B, & C went out about Retreat with six rounds cartridges in their pockets.

Camp near Falmouth, Va.
June 9, 1863. Tuesday, 9 a.m.

Cool. Wind N.W. Brisk. Pleasant and bracing. The Companies last night (100 total) threw up a rifle pit more advanced than our own of the previous night, near the Bowling Green road. Hear firing towards the right, at some of the fords probably.

Last year at this time we were amusing ourselves in the celestial waters of the Chickahominy. Corporal [Charles E.] Mix of C recently talked [to] a rebel prisoner (5th Louisiana Tigers) who said he knew half of our men, and told all we done there; inquired after Austin, if he died, &c.;[10] thought we were "gay boys," that our "cheek"—daring—saved us many a time; this

Piece of Shell, from Franklin's Crossing. This rough sketch of a shell fragment from Franklin's Crossing is found in the margin of Thompson's June 9, 1863, journal entry.

Regiment being on picket there all summer. It seemed a little odd to hear our own deeds recounted by an enemy.

Account of Building the Bridge.[11]

From what I can learn from all hands, the facts are thus. The Battalion after leaving camp went to Franklin's Crossing. To understand *all* our movements, I will try to describe the lay of the land, &c., by Fredericksburg. The country is made of plateaus of various extent and heighth, steep ascents, ravines and runs. The river flows through an intervale of great extent on which is Fredericksburg. This is bounded by heights on either side, Stafford on this and Salem on the Fredericksburg side. Taking a position of Stafford Heights, your eye compasses the whole. At your right may be seen Fredericksburg, back of which are the famous heights with a wide intervale between, below you is the broad plain with the river winding through it like a trout brook, with steep banks [on] each shore, and were it not for the trees that fringe its shore you could not detect it all; at the foot of the heights is the Riverside road, and on the other is the Bowling Green near a mile from the river. Almost below is Franklin's Crossing with Dr. Bernard's house, now destroyed by fire, even yet showing a degree of substantial elegance not often seen here, it being constructed of stone, and underneath the shade trees that surround it [where] General Bayard was killed. The problem of crossing the river is practicable at any time with the loss of a few lives. As the river runs [along] this edge of the intervale, thus enabling us to have all the protection of our artillery, while on the other side the broad extent of plain, between the river and their heights renders all their artillery null and void comparatively, as it would be only chance shot that could injure the bridge or working-parties. This plain is gently rolling, affording good positions, such as they are, and quite good cover for troops. We have the numerical advantage of 3 to 1, until we cross to attack, then the advantage is all theirs. Thus at anytime the crossing of this river is practicable, while of course it is as disadvantageous for them to cross on us here [See "Vicinity of Fredericksburg, Va." on page 112].

Our boys sheltered themselves behind a little rise by the road until the artillery came and took position on right and left flanking the rebel rifle-pit; when they opened, they went on the double-quick to the river down the bluff amid a shower of bullets, on to the little intervale each side of the river and took shelter, a pitiable one, in a little hollow, just low enough for the bullets to clear them. The boats were driven down and unloaded as quickly as possible, and men, mules and horses were killed and wounded at this job; when a number of boats were unloaded, the Infantry rushed down and filled the boats, which were rowed quickly over and the rifle-pit was carried and the rebs that were in it captured, some Florida Regiment.[12] The fire of our artillery was terrific, so much so that the safest way for those in the rifle-pit was to stay there, which they bravely did. At dark the bridge was completed. Clerk Wight had a bullet through his haversack, "spoiling his strawberries," Bowen had a bullet go between his blouse and side, paralyzing him for the time being.[13] Captain C——— was killed on the bank just as the boats were going in.

Camp near Falmouth, Va.

June 11, 1863. Thursday, 9 p.m.

   Prospect of storm. Wind S.W. warm. All so-so. Hear nothing; Paid to-day, $39.75. Pleasanton's Head Quarters have just moved.

Camp near Falmouth, Va.

June 13, 1863. Saturday, noon.

   Quite warm. Wind N.W. All the Pontons and Material went to Belle Plain yesterday afternoon. Some 28 Gabions were made yesterday after-noon by the Battalion, and were taken away this forenoon somewhere. Farr laid out a Battery Thursday night, at the bridge. We just received orders to have knapsacks packed with exception of blankets. Had Infantry and Engineer drill. (A party mounted the 100 Pounder Parrot, it firing only once.)

Bivouac Occoquan.

June 14, 1863. Sunday, 8 p.m.

   Cool and pleasant. We are at present in one of the most romantic spots imaginable. I am writing by candle-light under an oak-tree, while were I to turn my eyes over my shoulder I should see the little village Occoquan nestling on the opposite hillside almost below me, from which comes to me the familiar sound of moving trains. The spot makes me think of New Hampshire; it is a perfect Eden to us. Oh! how inexpressibly delightful to breathe a pure, untainted air, full with the fragrance of fresh green leaves, blossoming laurel and wild roses. I just came from a splendid bath in the stream, pure spring water, unlimited, free to all. I am hardly myself, although I can [say] truthfully when I look about on the woods "Rich and is himself again."

I will record my notes along.

"June 14th (7 a.m.). Broke camp about 5 o'clock" and marched to the Landing, arriving about 10:30 p.m. Had a hard march, resting really only once. We went a long road to avoid trains. It is the same old joke, we have a Bull Run each year. The main army is moving towards Stafford Court House. Our train got in this morning. We bivouacked north side of railroad. I recognized some of our surveying stations of last winter. "The boys are having a great swim." "9 a.m. Off up river on Ponton raft. Our usual Boat ride. It is cloudy with prospect of rain. Wind N.W. I should judge. The raft is all for bridge construction. It is pleasant to be on water again."

We went up Occoquan River, building a bridge of 17 boats at Occoquan. A pleasant place.

Bivouac Colchester Ferry.
June 15, 1863. Monday.

(Occoquan.) Pleasant. "8 a.m. Quite warm, Trains yet crossing of 12th Corps. No news. We are laying by, with the exception of keeping road in order and bridge. Made a little sketch of river."

(7:30 p.m.) About 10 o'clock a.m. C & D moved down to Colchester Ferry about two miles and built a bridge of 27 boats, assisted by the 50th New York who have left us and we are sole possessors.[14] It is quite a pleasant situation, though not so wild as above. Some wagons, three siege guns and a large number of horses (corral). Our train has crossed above, no news, no noise. It was with no considerable management that the horses were got across without straining the bridge, the most feasible way was to take two oars, and cross them and walk quietly and firmly in front; but the amusing part of it was this; one herd was led off by one solid old battery horse, who though gaunt in limbs, showed his drills. Two men took one oar between them to lead off, when the old veteran put his breast against the oar and resolutely pushed them steadily before, they holding back with all their power. It made a great laugh. I found a line (fish) and tried my luck at the old art; my only reward was a puny fellow, one of the Potomac herring variety I believe. This morning in Occoquan the boys enjoyed a little talk with some ladies and got some roses, quite a rarity for

Colchester Ferry, Va. In the margin near this rough sketch of Colchester Ferry is a comment, added later (perhaps after the war), that "The brother of [James] Jackson who shot [Elmer] Ellsworth lived in this house." Jackson shot Colonel Ellsworth of the 11th New York because the colonel had removed the Confederate Stars and Bars from a hotel in Alexandria, Virginia.

us. A woman's voice has the same pleasant sound after all. The people are Union and have suffered for it.

On Potomac.

June 16, 1863. Tuesday, 6 a.m.

"On Ponton raft bound up river. Last evening about 11 o'clock, we dismantled bridge, making rafts.[15] These were rowed down near the mouth of [the] river and anchored. Our raft being heavily loaded troubled us in coming across flats; we not getting down to anchorage till 1 p.m. Had a great time. This morning at 5 a.m. heaved anchors and attached our fortunes to the *Sylvan Shore*,[16] which I trust will lead to peace and prosperity."

(Alexandria, Va., 4 p.m.) "Bivouacked below Water Street. Got in about 12 o'clock noon. Had a pleasant ride up to this place. We have been indulging in "nice champaign cider," pies, &c., to depletion. Feel a little lived. I can but think of the time we were here before. 9:15 p.m. Received orders to go somewhere. Rumor says we are to report at Georgetown at 6 tomorrow morning and to go up the canal. Men are at work making over the rafts (two abreast)."

On the Chesapeake & Ohio Canal.
June 18, 1863. Thursday.
"Weather hot. Had a gala-day yesterday, all drunk! I wasn't though. Arrived at the locks at Georgetown at daylight and got all the rafts into the canal. Then we stopped till about noon, during this time all was on a "spree," and there ensued a great time, Captain Turnbull being round amongst them, *a la* Harney (I don't believe in fisticuffs).[17] Had a Guard on, but many a sentinel was relieved when he could no longer follow the post, *custodio custodis*.[18] At noon we started again. We kept on at intervals all day and night. The canal is a very interesting work, its banks are picturesque, while through the trees on the left you can see the wild Potomac. I had a busy time of it, as there were not many available hands. I wonder how we got along so well."

On Monocacy River, Noland's Ferry, Va.
June 19, 1863. Friday, 6:30 a.m.
"Arrived here about dark. Had a severe shower yesterday afternoon. A detachment of cavalry are on outpost duty here, and their duty must be arduous. We held ourselves in readiness for anything last night, having

Noland's Ferry, Monocacy River. This sketch depicts the site of the battalion's June 19, 1863, camp near Noland's Ferry on the Monocacy River.

sentinels to each raft. Stormy looking. No news. I judge this is but a rebel cavalry raid. Until we reached here you would not know you were at the seat of war with the exception of a patrol or so. On Guard last night."

11 a.m. We have come ashore and sort-of camped. Boys washing up clothes and resting. I am about fagged out, but I have written up my notes anyway. Understand our Battalion train is here.

On Potomac River, Edward's Ferry, Va.
June 20, 1863. Saturday, 8 p.m.

Gloomy and unpleasant. We returned to this place last night arriving about daylight (3 a.m.) Had a disagreable night of it, raining &c. I was on Guard on rafts, and slept—or rather laid in Guard tent, so kept dry. We had our belts on and arms handy for any emergency, unnecessary though proper. We are at present encamped on shore, in tents. Passed the day fishing for catfish in canal, had an easy guard of it. No news. Understand there are troops on the other side. Don't know what we are to do or where we will do it. Very tired to-night.

Edward's Ferry, Va.
June 21, 1863. Sunday, 7:30 a.m.

Cloudy, but not cool. Last night about two minutes after writing the notes preceding, we were turned out and took our boats through locks into the Potomac, and threw out a bridge. We constructing some, over half, the Engineers of New York 50th, completing [it] at daylight. It consists of 64 Boats, two or three trestles—the latter are unnecessary as boats are as well, but we did not have them.[19] It was a very hard job indeed. We were clean fagged out at daylight. C & D did the work mainly, as A & B reconstructed the rafts at Alexandria. I had some good solid sleep to-day, the first straight lay-out I have had since we started from Falmouth. Heavy firing heard all day on the other side of the river, towards Washington somewhere. I am turned round in regard to north & south.

✠— Captain George H. Mendell, became commanding officer June 21, 1863, and [continued] to August ———, 1864.[20]

Glimpse of Potomac with Ponton Bridge. Sketch showing the Potomac
River through the trees with the pontoon bridge that the battalion had
erected across it in June 1863.

Edward's Ferry, Va.

June 22, 1863. Monday, 6 p.m.

Clear & Pleasant. No news. Done nothing to-day but rest and be easy.
I am in nineteen months to-day. Sent a hurried note to mother. Quite
good fishing in river. Duck (or Goose) Creek is at the farther end of our
bridge.[21]

June 23, 1863. Tuesday.

Pleasant. About 3 p.m. moved camp to the other side of the canal up on
the hills. Hear that Pleasonton has done well.[22] As far as news goes, and
company, you would think you were out in the "free unpolluted country"

they tell about. Threw a small bridge across Goose Creek, half mile from its mouth.

Edward's Ferry, Va.
June 24, 1863. Wednesday, Retreat.

Pleasant. Went on Pass in forenoon. Went out into country and Poolesville, the latter is a lonesome little place. Had a good drink of milk &c. Moved camp farther up hill still, so we are on the top now. Have just a look of Sugar Loaf which seems to the Maryland campaign what the Pyramids are to Napoleon's days in Egypt. Quite a massing of troops has occurred on the Virginia side, and batteries have passed over the bridge towards Poolesville.

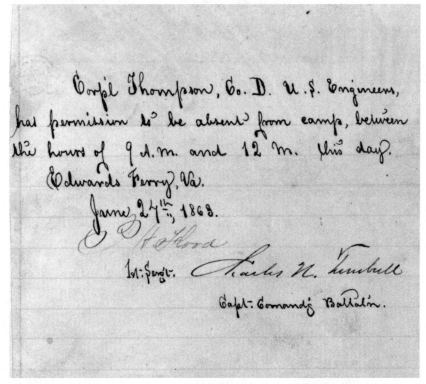

Thompson's Pass. Thompson saved the pass he was granted on June 24, 1863, and preserved it in his recollections. It gave him permission to spend three hours outside camp that day.

✠— One of the orderlies of General Lee told me that the General rode to the summit of Sugar Loaf (?) Mountain and stood there a long time looking towards Washington.

General Lee is the only one of the Rebel commanders that will undoubtedly be regarded with more pity than bitterness for his unfortunate and misguided course. He was a brilliant rather than a great General, and never malignant or fanatical. And the best General of them all.

Edward's Ferry, Va.
June 25, 1863. Thursday, 8 p.m.

Raining. Troops and trains passing all day. The 11th, 12th and others ◊.[23] Before noon we turned out and built a roadway for another bridge. Hear very faintly a rumor that they are now fighting at Harpers Ferry. Lee cannot cross 'well' this side of there. All that concerns me is that canal communication may be kept open so we can manoeuvre our boats, without the tedious labor of loading and unloading. Cummins came yesterday from Washington. Our train is parked at the Navy Yard and they rather expect us to return. The remainder of the 50th is there; I wonder why we cannot go into a little rest *once* in five years or so.

Edward's Ferry, Va.
June 26, 1863. Friday.

Stormy. Infantry and trains passing all day; the rains rendering repair necessary all day. The "Chronicle" has news of Lee being all across the Potomac. I anticipate a busy time the next month at least. Captain Michler came to-night.[24] It seems a little gloomy with the news and rain, but I do not wish to be home, my path of duty is here. A year ago we just commenced quite an active campaign of "Seven Days." General Hooker came along to-day.

Edward's Ferry, Va.
June 27, 1863. Saturday, 4:30 a.m.

Cloudy and misty. Troops are crossing all day, so far. All mud about, our previous rustic life is sadly spoiled by the passing army. Understand our train is all here, I hope so as I would like some cooked food, all we have had cooked was one mess of beans since we left Falmouth. Some one hundred and thirty Ponton wagons are up, so we have a pleasant job ahead; we require 140 at least. Rumor saith we are to go with Head Quarters and the Volunteers take charge of the boats. The newspapers are quite newsy. We shall see how Lee makes out with his grand raid. Sedgwick's Head Quarters are near us. My pants are getting thin, and I am dirty as a vagabond.

Westminster, Md.

July 3, 1863. Friday, noon.

Slightly cloudy, yet pleasant. We are encamped or rather squatted [on] the east side of the town, came here yesterday about 2 o'clock, are rather fatigued with our marches.

"June 27th, 1863. On guard at camp. Bridges taken up. Lower one before dark, upper from 10 p.m. to 1 a.m. All clear."

"June 28th, Sunday. Broke camp at 7:30 p.m. Went to Poolesville where we 'jined' the [Engineer] Brigade, there through Greenfield Mills encamping at Buckeytown. Had a rough old march, no regular rest-at-all." (18 miles.)

"June 29th, 1863, Monday. Broke camp 6 o'clock p.m. Marched to outskirts of Frederick. Unpleasant weather; the sun has not shone since we left Washington on the Army of the Potomac. General Meade in command.[25] Beautiful country."

The 30th we left Frederick at 2 a.m., came past Mt. Pleasant, and stopped beyond Johnsville at Beaver Dam. A fatiguing march. Mustered in just out of Liberty, hope sometime to be mustered into liberty.[26]

July 1st, Wednesday. Came from Beaver Dam to Taneytown, with its splendid residence, I suppose of Chief Justice Taney.[27] Passed through Union Bridge over White Creek. Cloudy and drizzly at times.

"July 2d, 1863, Thursday, 5 p.m. Half Pleasant. Encamped beyond Westminster, a fine place. A big bouncing Dutch girl up here frantically baking cakes in a rush for us."

Westminster, Md.

July 5, 1863. Sunday, 7:30 p.m.

Cloudy, raining early this morning. On guard to-day. Nothing going on. [Company] A has gone on picket somewhere on railroad as C & B have done heretofore. Remained in present camp since last date. Captain Mendell, a too good scholar for practical soldiering, is Commanding

Officer, coming to us at Edward's Ferry—little fussy.[28] Understand we have gained quite substantial victories over Lee. Longstreet being wounded and dying in our lines. Lee is already I think leaving "My Maryland."[29]

While we were resting on Mt. Pleasant—a beautiful place—some troops came along, their band playing "My Maryland," the effect of which was splendid. It was a little of the romantic side of soldier life.

I have slept and "lazed round" since being here; we are not really pleasantly situated; we have good *well* water, but poor show for bathing which we need. I don't fancy a town camp, I had rather be in the woods. The boys are in good spirits, "fooling all round." I have seen a good many "reb." prisoners, they are evidently desperate, one third no shoes, &c., all the color of Virginia mud, their army is but an organized mob. They are in good spirits and talkative.

>+— Perhaps nothing shows more exactly the indifference, or better, the little that a soldier knows of the general condition of affairs during a battle than my records during the greatest battle of the war. Westminster is about eighteen miles from the battlefield. And all we knew from the *roar* of the artillery [was] that a battle was going on.

It has always been a regret that we were not right at [the] Gettysburg battle.* All we knew was the roar of the artillery; it was preeminently a "noisy battle." We were at General Meade's Head Quarters at Taneytown, reporting and camping at, the evening of July 1st, and were sent undoubtedly to Westminster, July 2d, not only to guard the trains and picket the roads, but to be ready to lay out a line of defence, in case the army fell back. This is my opinion, Captain Mendell "had no such instructions" however.**

* We are credited with Gettysburg, "not engaged."

** Letter of November 8, 1887.

A large number of Confederate prisoners were near us, some of them of Jackson's old brigade, one of them said, "they shot Jackson for marching them so like h——l, and they would serve Ewell (?) the same way if he kept on!"[30]

At the battle of Gettysburg went out the last talk of "we are fighting on McClellan's plan," "McClellan's on their rear with 50,000 men," etc., which previously was heard at every battle.

May 4, 1885, I went to [the] Gettysburg Battle-field. The Army of the Potomac fought on a topographical island.

I met a gentleman who was at Westminster when we were, and he said that we were in a very ticklish position, as we were so few in numbers, and not only was Stewart liable to attack, but the prisoners were ten to one of the troops guarding them.[31] He was Adjutant of some New York Regiment. General Buford of the Cavalry was in command there.[32]

I walked over the whole line, and was at the point where Pickett's attack focused, and heard Batchelor describe it, the President was near, General Hunt, Stannard, etc.[33]

Frederick, Md.
July 8, 1863. Friday, 6 a.m.
"Came here from Union Bridge yesterday; the 7th, from Westminster to Union Bridge; the 6th in camp at Westminster. Troops and trains going South Mountain way. Raining. Hard march yesterday; officers are a little queer about that business."

South Mountain, Turner's Gap.
July 9, 1863. Thursday, 6:30 p.m.
Pleasant to-day. Came from Frederick to beyond Middletown where we encamped in a pleasant situation where South Mountain forces its presence upon you, and looking back over your shoulder you can see the town apparently half hid by the rolling fields of wheat. We broke camp early in the rain and a very disagreable necessity it was; and more, we went out towards Monocacy Junction about a mile, then turned back, some *countermarching*; anyway we are relieved (on the 8th) of connection with the Engineer *Brigade* and "old Benham." Glad of the change, going with Head Quarters now. The "famous 7th New York" is to be seen in Frederick.[34] Should like to have stayed awhile near the town; am exceedingly gratified to find since being in Maryland that women yet exist.

To-day we moved late in forenoon from camp and arrived here about 2 p.m. and encamped on the same ground we were towards a year ago on, just after the battle of South Mountain. We are in our old war paths again. Every step reminds us of our "good Captain Cross," who commanded us then. Ammunition trains, artillery going along, the heavy siege pieces have just passed, "the Seven Sisters" as they were called at Fredericksburg.[35] I think Lee is rather worsted, the Potomac is high and he will probably be obliged to give us battle again. May Victory crown our banners as they did at Gettysburg. Vicksburg went under the 4th.[36] Firing commenced towards the front about half an hour ago and continues; the first rumors of the tempest.[37] Am well in spite of rough travel, we having had but one meal of stewed beans and coffee cooked once since leaving Falmouth. Willing to tramp, eat only pork and "Hard tack" if we succeed; the army is in earnest. Had a grand feed this afternoon on lettuce and onion salad, &c.; we have good chances to get some "soft-bread," &c., at very *various* prices. My memory of Maryland will be fair girls waving handkerchiefs and old women asking .50 & 1.00 for a loaf of bread!!

On Antietam Creek, through Benevola, Md.
July 12, 1863. Sunday, 8:30 a.m.

Hazy. "11th. Reveille at 3:30 a.m. Came from South Mountain here (in woods on Beaver Creek, back of Antietam Creek) late the 10th. Built a crib bridge over Creek of four cribs. No news, no fighting." Was tired last night, a tedious job, On Guard &c.

Jones's Cross Roads; 6 miles from Sharpsburg; 6 miles from Boonsboro; 6 miles from Williamsport; 6 miles from Hagerstown; 7:30 p.m. Came to this place in afternoon (to-day), starting about 1 o'clock p.m., crossing our bridge at the ford. Had the usual routine of trials on Train Guard, one wheel came off, one Company wagon tipped over, &c. A very heavy shower came upon the road, all getting thoroughly drenched, yet I feel tip-top for the douche as every one seems to; dear me, if this happened at home, we would change clothes, drink some hot tea, and "get our death of cold" for certain, and talk about our remarkable escape for a fortnight. But I deem the hardships of little account.

I will honestly note that I don't like the duties of a Non-Commissioned Officer, it is a little too much big dog look after little dog, and yet the littlest dog of all! I don't like to be hounding up others, I [would] rather do the work and have that the end of the matter. Well, I mean to do my duty, and have it affect my character as little as possible. I mean not to get surly over it anyway. I would never make a jailer, nor would I need one.

Hear Dix is this way, and lots of rumorous stuff. Saw Sedgwick quite a number of times yesterday; he is rather medium size, solid and stocky, with a round solid head, half growth of full whiskers of auburn gray, plain and homespun in appearance, like some well to do farmer or better railroad conductor, wearing a straw hat, and you would probably mistake him for some guide for his staff instead of its leading character.

Berlin, Md.
July 17, 1863. Friday, 7:30 p.m.

Rainy, shower coming up yesterday afternoon. The 13th, remained at Cross Roads, General Meade went by, Reserve Artillery posted &c. 14th, came to Antietam battle-ground, starting after dinner, hard foolish marching as usual, lived high on bread & milk; 15th, started in morning and arrived at Sandy Hook about 1 o'clock, very severe march, had to fall out—first time; in afternoon went to work on Suspension Bridge repairing, tough; 16th finished repairing Suspension Bridge under Lieutenant Roebling, smart man;[38] received letter from Mr. W. W. Dutcher (dated 8th instant).[39]

"Fly swifter round, ye wheels of time," &c.[40] To-day we came here from Sandy Hook, arriving about 3:30 p.m. Reveille at 2 a.m. too-morrow, whew! Probably stand round until 7 before we do anything.

Berlin, Md.
July 18, 1863. Saturday, 2 p.m.

Pleasant to-day. Reveille at 2 a.m. 2 hours too early, went to work about 5:30 a.m. Built a second bridge (part of it). We move at 4 p.m. to-day.* Just been reading "Fourth July" news in Boston, out of the *Journal*, the Potomac is an interesting river. Well, Good Day.

* Did not go at that time.

The Line of the Rappahannock

Summer and Fall of 1863

On the advance from Centreville after the retreat from the Rappahannock, the Battalion repaired the pike from stone bridge on Bull Run to New Baltimore, removing the old bridges and constructing new ones where necessity required. At the attack on Rappahannock Station it was sent to build a bridge at Kelly's Ford. A bridge was built at this point November 7, under fire.[1] At Jacobs Ford two companies of the Battalion built the bridge, the other two built the bridge at Germania Ford. The Battalion guarded these during the Mine Run campaign.

—LIEUT. TURTLE'S ESSAY

[White Plains, Va.]
[July 24/25, 1863.]

"*Beyond Lovettsville, Va. July 19th*, 1863, Sunday (6:30 a.m.). Broke camp at Berlin 4 a.m. Pleasant. The chief features of this country are the groves of trees, seemingly almost cultivated, being free from brush, and all of good growth. See *Major* Duane.[2] 6:30 p.m. *Weatland, Va*. On Guard. Pleasant section of country. No news. Some large building was burned during night. Our "boys" are not so tender feeling as once. They are getting to be *real* soldiers."

"*Union, Va. July 21st*, Tuesday. With Trains yesterday. Battalion stopped at Union while the train stopped back some four miles, maybe & got through, came up this morning (21 instant)." Got our back mail. Good news. *All Right.*

"*Beyond Middleburg, Va. July 23d, a.m.* The 21st marched through New Lisbon, Philimant to Goose Creek, there commenced corduroy bridge; which we finished the 22d instant and came to this encampment."

"*White Plains, Va. July 24th*, 1863 (a.m.) Arrived here yesterday afternoon from Middlebury, encamped near Dea. Foster's residence. Great
time eating blackberries." Firing heard last evening. Heard whistle of cars.

Resume.

We could soon see the difference of Virginia from "My Maryland," the
ladies' noses have a singular peculiarity of turning up, while the gentlemen—generally retired ones—are quite courtly and sedate. There is nothing to be purchased, it's hard tack, pork & coffee now. Blackberries are
now ripe and in luxurious profusion; our troops also lay their hands on all
that is eatable; poor Piggy is safe no longer, and many a Chauntecler that
once so cheerily heralded the glorious morning now let it herald itself.[3]
Fences disappear, and whole fields of wheat ease the weary limbs of the
brave marchers. Were I so disposed and not so (sort of) tired I would write
more, but I won't. Guard duty with the train is full of almighty (?) interesting scrapes, and every day furnishes some joke or incident, but I cannot
record them all, I must let memory do it. This is the first time I have had

Foraging. This is another photographic reproduction in Thompson's memoirs of a
sketch by John B. Geyser. This one shows soldiers chasing pigs, foraging as Thompson
described in his entry for July 24–25, 1863.

a chance to write herein since the 18th; our officers excepting Captain Reese are green; we generally encamp half a mile from water either in a flat place or on the top of a steep hill.

Warrenton, Va.
July 27, 1863. Monday, 8 a.m.
    Cloudy but warm. Staid at White Plains the 25th, came here in the night of 25th, arriving at 12:30 a.m. 26th Moved camp from bivouac to position back of our former old camp in November 1862. On Guard. Had Parade. An Order read, concerning Reenlisting in the regular service for five years.[4] The town has a pleasanter appearance than last year, the town clock bell sounding very cheerful. From my tent I might almost think it was Milford before me, as the style of the Town-Hall is very much like ours. The association of this place in regard to McClellan's Removal gives rise to many discussion of his vs. others' merits, the old bone of contention. The army may remain here long enough to get our rations, &c., the cars running all right. I hope we will keep moving, so that the enthusiasm that now animates the army will not be allowed to simmer down. Meade's position is now one of greater difficulty than simply to hold gaps and move along under the shadow of Blue Ridge; now comes an open country comparatively, I hope individually we move towards Culpeper, &c., so to see that section of country, and also I think we can effect something by such a movement. Now that Rosecrans is so far advanced, &c., why could not a junction be effected that would amount to something.[5]
    Rations are rather short with us. I refreshed my soul last supper-time with a glorious sunset and my body with only three hard tack—*rare* done. Three roast ones for breakfast, and a drink of water. That is but a trifling inconvenience just for the present. I feel rather tired, as my penmanship indicates.

Warrenton, Va.
July 28, 1863. Tuesday, 10:30 a.m.
    Sunny and Pleasant, we are having a cool summer so far. Dress Parade last evening, hear we are to move to-day. Wrote to Mother and Mr. Dutcher, hearing from him yesterday. Feel more rested.
    Rappahannock Station, 9 p.m. Moved from Warrenton at 1 p.m. and marched to this place, arriving at 8:30 p.m. Experienced quite a heavy

shower during last third of march; train came in loaded with Ponton boats, so at last after all our tramping we come to that miserable river again.[6] "They Say" we shall have a hot time if we attempt putting a bridge across; well, we will see. After some coffee which I trust will equal my expectations, Good Night. We had a splendid sunset; we begin to see the familiar pines again.

Rappahannock Station.
July 30, 1863.
Cloudy and showery during day. No news. Our Train which left us at Beaver Dam, Maryland, arrived to-day at noon, a great shaking of hands of course. Loaded boats, &c., on wagons. Got new cooks (at Warrenton), living well.

Rappahannock Station.
August 2, 1863. Sunday, 7:30 a.m.
Sunny and *some* hot. July 30th night, about half [the] Battalion went away, we understand to Kelly's Ford with some boats, &c. July 31st, night loaded Boats &c., and the morning, early, of August 1st, Company C put dismounted Cavalry (U.S. 2d) across, drove in pickets (or rather true (!) Cavalry videttes), we then threw [a] bridge (7 boats), finishing by 10:30 a.m.[7] General Buford's Cavalry then crossed. Buford is a good sized muscular man, sanguine complexion with mustache, looks generally like B. F. Butler only he *sees* straight.[8] I was interested in the appearance of two of his scouts. Quite hot. On Guard over Bridge Material; the Cavalry advanced to about 1½ miles of Culpeper, and then meeting the Infantry (Reb.) were in turn driven back.[9] *This* morning the 2d Corps crossed over. The Construction Corps are at work on railroad bridge, one of their men deserted last night.[10]

Kelly's Ford on Rappahannock River, Va.
August 3, 1863. Wednesday, 8 p.m.
Hot, singeing hot. Came from Rappahannock Station last night, to this place. Nothing doing of any consequence to-day; some Cavalry came in afternoon. A bridge was thrown here the 31st ultimo. All passed away well. There are none of our troops across of any account. Rifle pits were thrown up to-day by the troops, 12th Corps here. Here (!) we hold Fredericksburg. No news, don't know anything; can't guess what the plans are.

Corduroy Bridge. This sketch of a corduroy bridge over Kelly's Ford on the Rappahannock, dated August 4, 1863, may be the bridge that Thompson described the battalion erecting on July 31.

Kelly's Ford on Rappahannock River, Va.

August 6, 1863. 7 p.m.

Pleasant. Not so hot the last two days. Yesterday constructed Crib bridge across creek (*Marsh*), covering with boards, a hard job. All is about the same except that rifle-pits are thrown up and artillery has taken position on the hills around the ford. Two pieces are in the epaulements near us with the Shelters of the Batteries resting under cover of the work which will break the storm of lead and iron should it come to them. When an army has settled down for even a week in one place, a considerable amount has to be done to put all in a defensive position, bridges are to be made, rifle-pits thrown up, abattis cut to trouble cavalry raiders, and woods cut down that will conceal the approach of an enemy, &c.; no one part of the line must be weaker than another. I think we will occupy the line of the Rappahannock for the present. 30,000 conscripts in Washington I understand, that's what we want, we are not strong enough to advance.

I slept all the afternoon, and am fat, ragged and lazy. A wash in the river is rather a questionable pleasure, as it is so muddy about the banks, you come out after a number of slips and tumbles dirtier than when the so-called bath commenced. I can see why the Southerner resorts to the sea-side in summer, for the waves are pure as a river of Paradise to the Lethean streams of the South.[11] A southern river is like the southern character, at times slow, sluggish and inactive, then rushing on in a whirlwind of overwhelming force and passion, then subsiding again. North Carolina is restive, "Rebellion against rebellion."[12] The end is coming, somebody will have a tumble before long.

Rappahannock Station, Va.
August 9, 1863. Sunday.

Pleasant. Came from Kelly's Ford to this place yesterday afternoon; took up the bridge at Beverly's Ford—thrown yesterday—and put it out again lower down—our Sunday service. Dress Parade.

Rappahannock Station, Va.
August 13, 1863. Thursday, 9 a.m.

A very heavy shower last night; not clear yet. With rare foresight and particularly as Coolidge had done the same—I made me a "bunk" after supper, so unconcernedly let the waters roar and rave. The thunder has a sharp long tremolo sound here. There were quite a number of drenched

Officers' Tents. The battalion officers' tents at Rappahannock Station.

ones this morning, "All hands" were to go in bathing this morning, but it probably is postponed. Since last date nothing of note has occurred. We (Company D) have quite a cosey camp, occupying the side of a residence of considerable circumstance, but now burned, and what few outbuildings are left our enterprising cooks are making over into residences for themselves; and this place thus utterly ruined with its remains of agricultural implements, wagons and carriages lying round is but *one* specimen of the ruin this old State has and will experience as long as the war lasts. Old Virginia has paid dear for the *privilege* of secession. We have Dress Parades. On Guard, the 11th, at upper bridges; the Rappahannock is here a narrow winding stream with quite a swift current, and a hard gravelly bottom, in some places fordable. Here the country is comparatively level each side and does not partake of [the] style by Fredericksburg until you come to Kelly's Ford. Since the army has been here quite a number (10) have been drowned; it is a miserably treacherous river, and the army likes it as well as they did the Chickahominy. A *year ago* we commenced the Ponton bridge at the Chickahominy's mouth.[13]

Rappahannock Station, Va.
August 20, 1863. 10:30 a.m.
  Pleasant; All as usual, only yesterday the bands surpassed themselves, and that with the fact that we have taken all but one bridge and so on, also about two loads of kindling stuff has been cut for something. Don't believe we stay here long. Am Well. Wrote to mother.

Rappahannock Station, Va.
August 24, 1863. Monday.
  Breezy and pleasant. Went to Bealeton Station yesterday, a hot place. No news. On my 22d month!!

Rappahannock Station, Va.
August 31, 1863. Monday.
  Cooler, and quite cold o'nights. Am dying of *ennui*, nothing to do. Mustered in to-day only *seven more*!

Spring House. Sketch of the spring house at Rappahannock Station.

Rappahannock Station, Va.
September 17, 1863. Thursday.

Cloudy and foggy last few days. Since last date dull as usual. Our forces have occupied the country to the Rapidan. On Guard yesterday, at lower bridge, had a busy, anxious time, as the bridge was in bad order and *no material* to repair with. Captain Mendell gave me no assurance of aid and left me to do the best I could, and I really feel that I did honor to myself to get some 700 Army wagons and 10 or 12 Batteries over as well as I did.[14] I blagered Brigadiers, Colonels, Quartermasters, &c. I made them stand round. To-day we finished Block House, other Companies fortifying. We are all done.

Rappahannock Station, Va.
September 25th, 1863. Friday.

Pleasant. The 23d instant left this camp and marched to near Culpeper. The country is level, though hilly about the town. Arrived about 11 a.m.

Yesterday *marched back again!* We went into our old tents again, though they were somewhat disturbed by the Flying Dutchmen (11th Corps [who] were guarding at this point). It seemed quite natural, the old crickets in the trees sounding familiar, every one of them. Coolidge and myself having been counting at times the notes of the crickets per minute and have found that with increased coldness the number of notes per minute decrease, varying from 160–80–60. With a thermometer the data would be interesting.

Culpeper, Va.

September 29, 1863. Tuesday.

Pleasant. Cold o'nights. Back at the old stand where we were the 24th; the 27th came here. The 26th fixed up camp in fine style. I had the bliss of building one certain house and being detailed for Guard did not have even the pleasure of sleeping in it one night, I took the matter as philosophical as possible! but such is soldier-life. All is quiet in this vicinity; we built a bridge while at the [Rappahannock] Station. Our fortifications at that place looking quite formidable. No great prospects of a sharp Fall campaign.

Near Culpeper, Va.

September 30, 1863.

Pleasant, a little warmer nights. Went "On Pass" to view the interesting town of Culpeper, which consists of two main streets, with two churches, one of brick, being quite neat and attractive, both are used as Hospitals, a few of the male gender were to be seen as well as some indifferent specimens of those angels sent to cheer and beguile man in his struggle against the thorns and brambles. Woman must have been considered a doubtful blessing when she accompanied man from the famous garden. I was happy to get back to camp with a bottle of pickles to solace time with and keep the scurvy off another month. All as usual. We pass the time in reading, writing letters, surmising where we will winter, and what we will do when "time is up." We were paid at Rappahannock Station and gambling is predominant—Vogel and Geyser keep up their Chess Head Quarters and the Wight Restaurant flourishes as of yore.[15]

Our camp, though of itself rather poor, has quite a pleasant prospect of the surrounding country, including Culpeper with its spires springing

Signaling. A rough
sketch showing two
signal flags, with
another signal station
in the distance.

above the trees with the Blue Hills and Ridge beyond—what is more
grand than the sweeping line of mountain crest—while at our left is Pony
Mount with its Signal Station; directly in front are General Meade's Head
Quarters, a scattered assemblage of tents of high and low degree.

>+— October 20, 1886. As Geographer, U.S. Geological Survey, and in
charge of the Appalachian Division (extending from the Mississippi
river to the Atlantic Ocean, and from the Pennsylvania line to the
Gulf of Mexico), I camped with one of my parties at the same place,
near Culpeper, Va. Still in the service of U.S. but @ $2500 per annum.
(Pardon this contrast, I would have gone and done my duty in 1861
for nothing.)
    (See reports of the U.S. Geological Survey 1881 to ———.)

Near Culpeper, Va.
October 2, 1863.
    Storming furiously just now, rainy all day. Coolidge "On Guard," dis-
agreeable, can't write any more, tent full of smoke.

Rappahannock Station, Va.
October 11, 1863. Sunday.

Pleasant, but cool. Came to this place last night arriving about 11 p.m. I was on Guard. The boys had just built nice board houses when we left. It was a hard march as we had eight days' rations. Well, "things has changed," we are falling back, and it looks quite likely for a Third Bull Run;[16] and as fighting from this point to Washington is by rule, there will be the usual harassing attacks, &c., and flanking through the Blue Ridge Passes. We'll see. Have had a turn of coffer sickness the last few days, have a cormorant's appetites now. We occupy the old camp, and even the same tent place. More Anon sometime.

Rappahannock Station, Va.
October 12, 1863. Monday.

Real October day, cool and glorious sunshine; the sun of October, there is none like it; let me look back *one year* to-day which is the first date in this book,[17] and I was resting after [the] 1st Maryland [campaign] and watched the trees turn to their gorgeous colors in the Mountain Heights about the Ferry. *Two years* ago a sun like this was ripening the Indian corn that I was husking at Hopedale Farm, next month makes two years.

This morning the troops returned across the river (*other side*) and formed in order of battle, no fighting has occurred in this vicinity, only a few rounds of artillery; heavy firing has however been heard away towards Culpeper, what it means, can't guess, unless Lee himself is flanked instead of Meade, whose strategy is evidently to induce Lee to give battle between the two rivers.[18] Our trains are all back to the rear except Ammunition Trains; the troops have five days' rations now. We have done nothing to-day except fuss round tents and steal away from camp to look at movements across the river; we may have a sojourn again before long in Culpeper. *Quién Sabe?* G.T. 1863.

—✠•✠—

When retreating from Culpeper October 12th, the Cavalry at one time were completely surrounded by the rebels; no alternative was left but to cut their way out. General Custer formed his men in a square, had the bands play, and he leading, with their accompaniment, the whole command in the song of "Rally round the Flag, boys, Rally round the Flag." Then giving his hat to an Orderly, he led the charge which was irresistible.[19] He is

a good sized man, sandy hair and complexion, with an unassuming de-
meanor, and a liking for fun and sport twinkling in his eyes. When I saw
him, he was in neat dress wearing heavy black corduroy pants.[20]

Gottells Station, Weaverville, Va.
October 13, 1863. Tuesday, after sundown.

Fine. Last night, about 2 a.m. we were turned out and packed up ready
to march, then went to Beverly Ford Ponton Bridge which we dismantled
and loaded commencing at daylight; then returned to camp and after
a frugal breakfast left the familiar place arriving here about sundown; a
little weary, cause heavy knapsack, long march, etc.; water scarce here;
we are quite near our old camp of November 17th, 1862. General Head
Quarters are near us.

⊬— October 13, 1863. Marched about 14 miles, camping just across
the run near Catlett's Station.[21]

Near Centreville, Va.
October 14, 1863. Morning.

Cloudy, sprinkling last night. Came through along by [the Orange and
Alexandria] railroad, leaving it at Manassas Junction.*

* We just escaped [the] Bristoe battle.[22] When we reached Centreville
heights we could see the firing; we passed the line of battle, and I shall
always remember what a fine picture the scene would have made with
General Meade for the central figure, he standing out distinct against a
dark western sky, about him a few of the Staff, in front and rear was the
thin blue line of battle, the men laying down; in (extreme) front could be
seen the smoke of the battle.

⊬— October 14, 1863. Marched to Centreville, camped back of the
heights.

Near Centreville, Va.
October 15, 1863. Thursday, afternoon.

Remained at this place all day, heavy firing commenced on the left in
afternoon. No reliable news. Been dull to-day, only the excitement of relieving our limited larder by buying beef and *trimins'*. I regaled on liver;

we have three days more to live on the content of our haversacks. Artificer Hosmer and Private George McMillan not up yet.[23] "Gorgy Mac" where are yee?* The next few days will show the intentions of Lee. Am well. Our camp is near a fine spring on a hill back of the hill on which our works lie. Our Retreat was very fine; "we" just got along.

* The boys got up a fine *canard* that a Regiment of stragglers captured a Battery; and in the run of which dimly seen through the smoke of the conflict could be seen Hosmer and his ponderous "knapsack"—*Mac*— with his gamble-legs throwing themselves with desperate valor against the foe!

Near Centreville, Va.

October 18, 1863.

On Guard yesterday; pleasant; All So-So. Went up to line of Reb. works, fine position—weak on the flanks. Old Tom Leas just come in—a substitute—ha! ha![24] Inspection. Company D built a bridge the 17th of three boats at Blackburn's Ford (on Bull Run).

Grovetown, Va.

October 19, 1863.

Pleasant, though a shower near morning was very disagreable. Came from Centreville to-day. Had eight days' rations & muddy road, thus = tough march. Are near the centre position of our army at 2d Bull Run. One of the men just brought in a human under jaw from woods near by, and such sad mementoes are numberless through the woods. Blake pointed out to me the disposition of the troops and the movements of those two disastrous days.[25] We passed over Cub Run and Bull Run Stone Bridges, famous localities in the annals of the noted "Bloody Ground." I can't imagine what is up, but Lee evidently did not covet an attack on Meade in his position. Our trains are up which left us at Catlett's Station. Feel well after all.

At our first rest, just past the (1861) winter quarters of the Rebels as General Meade came along and Staff, a portion of the 6th Corps who were resting and making coffee left all and rushed in a mass to the road side to see him; it was a pleasant sight and reminded me of the days of little "Mac;" they did not cheer as "old troops" never cheer on ordinary occasions. We followed the Warrenton turnpike to-day.

The Dead at Bull Run and Battle-field of Bull Run. These two almost overlapping images show the Second Bull Run Battlefield in late 1863. The slightly difficult Latin phrase in the top legend reads: *Resquiecat in Pax* [Rest in Peace]!, and the top image depicts the unfinished railroad cut that the rebels used as a ready-made trench on August 29, 1862, while the bottom illustration depicts the field of the second day's action.

✠— I consider that the reputation of General Meade as a soldier will increase with time; one thing [is] certain, he would not fight when Lee desired it, and fought him when he [Lee] would have preferred it otherwise.

Meade was conservative and at the same time could be very daring and aggressive. If he could have commanded an army in the West where he could have been freer, he would have attained a more extended reputation but not a truly great one. Of all the Army of the Potomac commanders he is my preference. When Grant came to the

Army of the Potomac, Meade told him if he knew of one he thought could succeed better than himself not to hesitate, as it was not a time for sentiment.

I have seen the troops cheer him as much as ever McClellan, and he rather avoided [than] encouraged such displays.

Groveton, Va.
October 20, 1863.

Pleasant. In forenoon Battalion was engaged in building and repairing bridges over Bull Run, &c. Had stewed beans for dinner, quite a rarity. The scene of the hardest contested point of the first day's 2d Bull Run is near us. I went over to the spot and made a sketch from near our camp. It is a sad sight, the dead being almost unburied, a little dirt thrown over them just where and as they fell. The rain and decay revealing all. There they lay in the silent sleep of death—unknown—only telling by their nearness to the fatal (unfinished) railroad their bravery and matchless courage; a sadder, more touching sight I don't believe is on the continent.[26] A 14th Brooklyn man told me the course Porter's Division took,[27] and says he, "this is the ground where Porter and his men were accused of not fighting well," and pointing to the graves—if they could be called thus, so thick you can hardly walk between them—"those show whether they did or not!"[28] He found the grave of a comrade of his by his skull—his upper teeth being peculiar. Teams are going at a great rate, like Broadway. Cars going to-night. No news, and worse than all, no letters.

Warrenton, Va.
October 21, 1863.

Pleasant, quite warm even. Came from Groveton to-day. Distance some sixteen miles, and had the usual long stretches, and short rests; I fell out, I couldn't well go any farther, so I rested. Our officers are either *green* and inexperienced, or utterly regardless of our comfort on the march. I hate marching on that account. We came through Gainesville and New Baltimore all the way on the Turnpike.[29] I am in ill humor with anything military to-night. The town seems as of old, bands playing finely, one just finishing "Wood Up" in fine style.

Warrenton, Va.
October 25, 1863.

Pleasant but cool. Wind N.E. Stormy and disagreable yesterday. Have had [a] mean cold, and a turn at Guard Duty. Received eight days' rations of "hard tack," pork, coffee, & sugar, a military necessity, but a great bone and burden, "when my yoke &c."[30] Yesterday hived up in tent and half froze last night; we are on a hill where all the winds buffet us finely making the "boys" talk of how much more time to serve and the slender probabilities of re-enlisting. Thirteen more [months] for me since the 22d instant.

On Cedar Run, Near Auburn, Va.
October 28, 1863.

Pleasant, but cool. Yesterday came here from Warrenton leaving about 9 o'clock a.m. Instead of our former wind-swept hill we are in the cosy precincts of woods in a sunny hollow with a good spring; the woods reminding me of "The Sproutlands" of Hopedale, the soil being rocky. Four of us keep a fire going with stumps and *hard wood, no* pine, with a seat of poles around.

It is dull soldiering at present; we are such old soldiers that nothing less than a *real* battle produces the least sensation of variety; we know all the stories—old & new—the others know; we know where each other came from; and the only topic ventured upon is an unfailing source of interest—the time when each one's service expires, who goes out first, and speculating how, when & where that blissful period will arrive, and our only employment seems now only to be to sit by our fires and note the coming and going of each day until that day of them all shall come. There is only seven of the Topogs in the Battalion now,[31] Lieutenant Eben White lately murdered in Maryland was "one of us."[32] Been drawing a Topographical Map of Rappahannock Station from memory, guesswork, imagination, &c., etc.—tolerably successful. tut-tut-tut-tut goes drummer's tap, so finis for Tattoo.

By Bridge, Near Catlett's Station, Va.
October 30, 1863.

Pleasant, warmer. On Guard to-day. Came here yesterday forenoon. In afternoon went on fatigue, cutting timber for and constructing corduroy bridge over (Cedar) Creek, this being resumed to-day. The destruction of

In the Woods, Among the Leaves. Another of Thompson's rare, color ink sketches; this one is highly detailed and depicts an autumnal scene, though it contains no legend or caption to identify it.

the railroad is complete, every rail and tie being rendered useless by fire.[33]
I believe a mile and a half can be repaired each day; large parties being
on that duty, working night and day. Finished *The Last of the Mohicans* to-
day. We are gradually moving on, and I will note that I think Virginia may
eventually be resigned, and this railroad raid of Lee may be to cover such
movement. We are in the woods among the leaves.

Near Catlett's Station, Va.
October 31, 1863.

Rainy in forenoon; no fatigue duty in morning—quite agreable; cut corduroy in afternoon. Mustered in once more, six more now. From my frequent notes like the one above, one might think that I was homesick, &c. I
am not anxiously waiting for expiration of time; I like camp life—out door

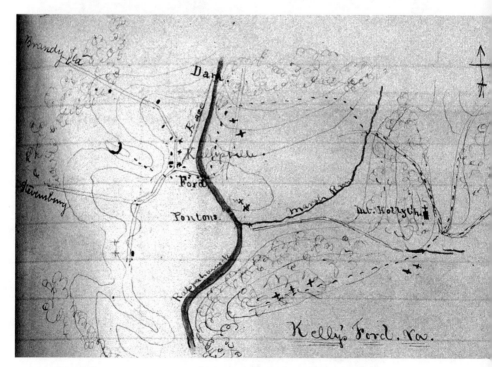

Kelly's Ford, Va. This is the sketch map of Kelly's Ford that Thompson
referenced in his November 12, 1863, journal entry.

life but I don't like *military*, I don't like the idea that is the foundation of military discipline, "You have no business to think," "Obey and not question," &c. It can't be otherwise on duty, but when a drug is nauseous all the wisdom, sophistry, and logic can't make it agreable to the taste. I believe in *military* on duty, off duty then I am for *Equality*; and it is possible, too. Perhaps I shall think otherwise yet. No News. Commenced *The Pioneers*—[James Fenimore] Cooper, like it well so far. Pleasant in afternoon. The wind is sounding among the tree-tops like the sea and casting its leafy spray upon the Shelter, the men are gathered round their fires, talking of this and that and so goes the last day of October 1863 in the camp of the U.S. Engineers.

November 6, 1863.
Move too-morrow to build bridge. I have boat party up stream.

Kelly's Ford, Va.
November 12, 1863. Thursday, 9 a.m.
Very Pleasant this morn. Been very disagreable last few days, windy and cold.

Recapitulation.[34]

The 7th at 1 a.m. had Reveille, left our woodland camp at 4 o'clock with good solid eight days' rations, and at daybreak were well beyond the Junction; at this time the scene was striking and interesting; the roseate tints of morning were seen through the frosty vapor while in the distance apparently below us were the circling and yet blazing fires of deserted camps and bivouacks, and the 1st Connecticut 32s went rumbling by us, all advancing.[35] By long and hard stretches by 12 noon we reached a point near the Church at this place. It was a forced march and a great many of the Battalion fell out from fatigue.

In this little hollow were massed the 1st Division, 3d Corps, and the plan of crossing considering that Confederates held this side of the river can be best understood by the topographical features of this place, which is a perfect *cul de sac* to any force on the east bank; our troops took the course indicated by dotted lines, led off by the U.S. Sharpshooters followed by Artillery [See Thompson's map of "Kelly's Ford, Va."].[36] The 2d North Carolina were thus cut off from retreat almost by our Artillery, some 700 being taken prisoners.[37] Our boys, as *they* (reb) fled across the ford, gallantly dashed after them and drove them away from the Rifle-pit back of the Village and then our crossing was complete. B & C had a bridge down by sunset, A & D finishing one afterwards, we then sought the grateful bivouac on the ground wrapped in our blankets after our *day's* work. At Rappahannock Station the 6th Corps made a fine attack, capturing some considerable number of prisoners, 4 pieces of Artillery, and their Ponton Bridges. Lee evidently expected us to cross mainly at the Station while we came the "possum" and made the real crossing here. It was quite interesting to watch the advance going on the Brandy Station road, and in a few hours the vast mass had disappeared through the woods.

I understand our troops are at Culpeper and our Cavalry have been across the Rapidan. We have been occupied in guarding bridges, &c.

The rebel prisoners looked quite well, most having new clothes of a bluish gray, but they have a white look compared with our ruddy, bronzed fellows. I saw some of their coffee, it being burned wheat, yet being underfed don't hinder good soldiering, I remember the days of Valley Forge, and Natty Bumppo's maxim "that a dog must be gaunt to run well."[38] Smoke is asserting its reign again.

Kelly's Ford, Va.
November 13, 1863. Friday.

Pleasant and mild. Yesterday morning the troops near us (2d Rhode Island) left, thus left the brass Howitzers (12 Pounder), and this afternoon the grim old 32s (4½") under whose protection we have often been, trundled away too, so with the exception of a passing Orderly and the distant drum-calls we are all alone.[39] We move too-morrow; wrote to mother this forenoon, all so-so with me. This candle burns close, so cuts my tale short. Drew some figures for Captain Mendell, go Surveying too-morrow.

Near Culpeper, Va.
November 15, 1863. Sunday.

Rainy last night and forenoon. Battalion broke camp and encamped at Brandy Station, near farm of *J. Minor Botts* whose farm was fenced anew by our army and one sacred. Moved at 1 o'clock p.m. to this place. Surveyed at Mountain Run.[40] Had a pleasant time; passing by Rebel camps with their log huts for winter; I reckon they never felt so keen before as they did when we actually turned *them* "out in the cold," their favorite desire "to be let alone." Firing heard near Raccoon Ford. We are encamped in the front-yard of a fine residence, though deserted, the officers' lights make it seem somewhat homelike, we can see our old camp of September last, and hear the odd sound of dogs barking about the streets of the town, and I should judge they were the only inhabitants too, [in] front of us is Pony Mountain with its flickering signal light nearly all the same as before, only it is real, genuine November. We have some corduroy work to do probably.

(Built two bridges over Mountain Run by Culpeper, Virginia.)

Near Culpeper, Va.
November 22, 1863. Sunday.
Delightful, stormy yesterday. Two years to-day! May the next 22d find me as well. Wrote No. II Shelter Tent Cor. to-day.[41] Am well.

Stevensburg, Va.
November 26, 1863. Wednesday.
Pleasant. The 23d moved here at 3 o'clock. Weather cloudy; Pontons came up with four Companies of 50th New York Engineers and one of 15th at dark, something up.

Reveille at 2:30 a.m. (24th). A & B started out soon after, weather unpropitious, sprinkling. We broke camp at 6 o'clock, went out about 8 miles skirting a plank road (leading to Germanna Ford), then stopped (11 o'clock), and drew to one side of road to allow Artillery & Infantry to pass. None *however* came, and after coffee and persimmon hunting, we returned (3 o'clock) to (this) camp, *without one rest*; all hands cross and ugly—bunky used *bad* English; this morning had to pitch tents in a line which grated again our feelings. A & B went towards Raccoon Ford with 6th Corps; 3d Corps was to go with us, [but I] hear the advance was countermanded by War Department. Fire this noon in West, full yellow moon through clouds, while Pony Mountain on Blue Ridge dimly showed through fog. Lieutenant Gillespie left.[42]

Richardsville, Va.
November 28, 1863. Saturday.
Drizzly. 26th instant, same as 24th, only threw a bridge at Jacob's Ford, Rapidan [River]. On Guard. No trouble. 27th—took up bridge about 10 o'clock a.m., moved with Trains to near Germanna Ford, where A & B

threw a bridge; this morning A & B took up their bridge and moved to this place. The whole town being burnt up last night—one house; we are near a church which is our Guard House. Heavy fight last evening.[43]

✠— The reason of the delay of building the ponton bridge at Jacob's Ford was that a mistake in estimating the width of the river was made or something, and we were *two boats short* and a crib approach had to be made; it was the story of the horse-shoe nail again. Some one should have been put out of the army.[44]

The army was short of boats all-round, needed new lot of boats.

At Germanna Ford two parties started out for forage after dark, one mistook the other for the "Provo's,"[45] and they had a pitched battle in the dark until one of the besieged set up a howl of pain as a stone hit him, when one of the besiegers called out, "Is that you Larry?" When a truce soon followed!

Rapidan, Near Ely's Ford.
November 30, 1863. Monday.

Clear and cool; half froze towards morning. Broke camp yesterday in morning and came here with *Boat* train. Are encamped in a fine growth of pine, reminding of Falmouth times. All well, the only worry being to make our rations accommodate our keen appetites; and the prospect's three-quarter rations too.

Just came in from a "kook out" from camp, the wagon trains are moving back into woods to get into shelter; the news *rumors* seem to indicate that the movement is successful this far—hold Fredericksburg Heights—7 miles of Gordonsville—cut railroad &c. We will see.

Waiting to Do Something

Winter Quarters, December 1863–May 1864

Lieutenant Turtle wrote nothing about the nearly four months the Engineer Battalion spent in winter quarters at Brandy Station, Virginia, from December 1863 until May 1864. Thompson's journal, however, provides a clear window into the lives of the men who fought the war during one of the quieter periods between campaigns.

—EDITOR

Camp near Brandy Station, Va.
December 10, 1863.

Clear & Cool; cold o'nights. The 1st instant went to Germanna Ford, putting down two bridges; the 2d Corps came to the Station, the army having fell back to old *position*, finding the *rebs* in too strong a position to warrant an attack; the consequent loss of life being too great.[1]

We are in a miserable, exposed camp, cold and cheerless reflecting really to the advantage of Captain Mendell's ability to pick out a good camping ground; "old Jimmy" (Major J. C. Duane) on the Peninsula used to aim for a big tree and cornfield; Captain M. (*old Flick*) being late from the Point heaves alongside a big house.[2] The scenery, just here, being quite tame, one straight line will answer for a sketch. The "boys" are building houses at a great rate, "bunky & I" "don't feel like it," and are going to wait, and I rather reckon another advance will be made, the *people* and fat, slick editors cry for *more*!

The Rapidan is a small rapid stream with steep high banks, requiring 6 Boats at Jacob's Ford, 8 at Germanna Ford. The banks are so steep at Jacob's Ford as to be available only for Infantry. Germanna Ford available for all among the service.

Camp near Brandy Station, Va.
December 12, 1863. Saturday.

Drizzly. One of those days that a cosy sit down in a tent or better by a genial fire in a pleasant room seems to be a kind of complete and placid enjoyment; nothing to call you forth into the storm, and the same serving as an excuse for comparative inaction and indolence; wet weather days like this being pleasant to me probably from association of farmer boy days, when a stormy day put a stop to farm labor, and I had a holiday to pursue my inclinations at home; yet should the order come "*Pack up ready to march,*" the rain &c., would be anything but pleasantly spoken of.

To-day if it had not rained, I was intending to make an illustrative sketch of "Soldier Architecture." It is quite interesting and instructive to see the different shapes, styles and designs [that] are in the boys' shanties or tents, in fact no name accurately titles them, being [a] combination of Shelter Tent and whatever material there is handy; the boys call them "houses," so I will title them "Soldier Houses." You can read a man's character in his house here as in civilized life; there is brick and boards from some deserted house & Shelter; John Smith and McCormack and all the ───── take hold of them, J. S. has a nice true house with an anti-smoking chimney, with a little touch at elegance in its finish.[3] McC. gets up a mess of mud and board chimney the size of a Martello Tower, and your mind is carried to the sweet bogs of Ireland and the Dark Ages;[4] you will see the original man with an original chimney "the wonder of the neighborhood" and brick layers either tumbling down or requiring great and frequent repairing; the reader takes the matter philosophically like Diogenes, puts on his great coat, reads, and his hut goeth without a chimney; the Socialist goes six in a tent, the hermit and anchorite alone, the select two in a tent, &c.[5] The rebels have one regular design, probably "by Order," their winter-quarters of '61 the same as those in woods here of '63; there is a lesson to be learned by putting our army's houses, cosmopolitan and varied, with the stiff regular huts of the Confederates. I hope and trust we will be allowed to build as we please, let us suit ourselves in one thing at least.

Four of the boys had to tear down their house yesterday on the charge of taking boards from a barn near camp, and those boards not fit to nail to the barn again, and the four walked past, with a log.[6] Captain Mendell is no favorite with the men, and he ill deserves any kind of respect. Oh! for the days of Charley Cross, a soldier, scholar, and gentleman. Understand we move soon somewhere to winter quarters; we'll see!

Shelter Tent (Ours), December 1863. Rough sketch of the tent shared by
Thompson and three others in December 1863.

Confederate Huts. Thompson's rough sketch of Confederate huts near Kelly's Ford,
Virginia, in late 1863; these may be the same rebel huts that Thompson described in
his December 12, 1863, entry.

Deserted Shelter Tent. This sketch of a deserted shelter tent, dated November 1863, shows the position of the chimney at one end for heat and light, though the tent itself has been removed.

Make Shift. Another rough sketch of a soldier's tent and chimney, showing how they might be connected.

Meek & Lowly. A final tent sketch, depicting a chimney at a slight remove from the tent, which must have been less effective at providing heat but perhaps more effective at preventing the entry of smoke.

Brandy Station, Va.

December 13, 1863. Sunday.

Drizzly yesterday; breezy, warm and balmy to-day. Lazed round to-day, wrote to Dutcher, had a letter from mother to-night, and put in a Memorandum for a furlough; neighbors Graham, formerly of *Royal Engineers*, [and] Pitcher of England had division in the house,[7] Graham a little forcible, *both in* Guard House, and "bunkey" is under arrest for insolence to Sergeant Taylor at that exciting time.[8] No bread is issued at kitchen, borrowed a 25 *Postage* of "bunkey" and ate sugar cakes for supper, "supposed to have two days' bread," saith the Rabbi! at the cook-tent. D Company is getting quarrelsome! and hungry; "Bread! Bread!" In fact had a very peaceable and quiet Sunday of it; Oh! Sergeant Farr complained about the "dirty cooks" in forenoon, ground pow-wow, old "*Brumble*" fumed & fussed, lovely! I can't think of anything else pleasant to write about, only Beahn, "old Topog," is remembering outside about some fisticuffs in B. Oh! descend sweet mantle of Night, and bring peace at last. Mad myself, too, by the by. I'll close! Express boxes come.

D's Cook Tent. A sketch depicting Company D's cook tent in late 1863, showing Culpeper, Virginia, in the distance.

Brandy Station, Va.

December 14, 1863. Monday.

Pleasant in forenoon, Wind S.W. with a little hurricane in p.m. and blowing to-night briskly from N.W., probably be cold too-morrow. Wrote to mother to-day. All hands for a little change were vaccinated; amused myself sketching designs in Journal, like to have had an ache in stomach from eating too many beans, reason why "bunky" don't eat em. Hope we move or do something. Lieutenant Gillespie and Johnny Carr at Knoxville, Tennessee.[9]

Brandy Station, Va.

December 16, 1863. Wednesday.

Pleasant in forenoon, clouding up now, prospect of snow-storm. Have done nothing to-day so far; it is a pity to lose the days of life thus; I want to have each day pass with the record of something done, something accomplished; but a soldier cannot lug books of study, and while waiting to do something, our movements are so uncertain, planning is useless, you have to "*go it blind*" in anything besides real military work; now here we are, those who built houses the first are lucky, if we move too-morrow, those who are building will be unlucky; I and "bunky," are in a plain unadulterated Shelter, been comfortable so far, but for aught I positively know, we may stay until spring right here; last winter actually we never were completely fixed as we intended, all from this uncertainty, which I suppose is unavoidable; I judge the state of affairs here is if Lee lets us alone we will stop and *vice versa*; I understand all Detached Troops and others have gone into winter quarters, yet we have not received the slightest hint what to do. I want two more pieces of Shelter anyway, to build as I wish.

Brandy Station, Va.

December 19, 1863. Saturday.

Stormy the 17 & 18 clearing up (N.–N.E.–N.W. clearing off N.W.); had disagreeable Guard duty the 17th. Built chimney yesterday, a *make shift*, draws finely and adds to our comfort. Wrote to mother to send me a Box. On Garrison Police; understand A is hauling logs to build huts; this is a miserable camp but I had rather be decided than to bother any longer. The weather is cold and windy, N.W.

Brandy Station, Va.

December 20, 1863. Sunday.

Cold but clear, with N.W. wind. Inspection. Went on Pass to 40th New York Volunteers, 1st Division, 3d Corps, dined with Adjutant Sweet (of Milford),[10] felt a little awkward, hands bothered me, shall have to learn all my manners over again. Received a letter from mother, of December 13th, in which occurs this very pretty and poetical sentence, "When I tucked your letter between the lids of your big Bible, I thought it was (indeed) a Holy Bible." Referring to my large Bible where I have put all my letters (unfolded) to better preserve them. My "bunky" Ned Coolidge was broken last night, all the Battalion is sorry, he is on guard to-night;[11] it is only a question of $30 dollars with him; too bad.

Brandy Station, Va.

December 25, 1863. Friday.

Pleasant and Christmas! Oh! what memories of good times come teeming in upon my thoughts. Home and Christmas are almost one to me; today years ago, was the inauguration of the culminating effect and result of all the rehearsals, in aid, trimming with evergreen the old chapel at home; how young declaimers said their "You'd scarce expect &c." mingled with the exercises of those of maturer growth; here to-day—while those at home are enjoying all this, I with others labored on our new quarters, and after "Taps" bunky and I will make a (Condensed) milk punch of our whiskey ration and drink to "Auld Lang Syne," he leaves me too-morrow.[12] I hope some one will at least think of the wanderer to send a sprig of the Christmas tree.

Brandy Station, Va.

December 29, 1863. Tuesday.

Stormy last two days; cleared away to-day. Quite a little thaw occurred of course, and our Company Parade glories in as much *mud* as ever at Falmouth. To-day moved into new house; built according "to Order," four in each hut, two bunks &c., all alike and regularly laid out; "Our"—how often this "Ours" has occurred in my Journal and different ones it includes and means—"Ours" having a good drawing fire-place, a good blessing, two bunks, one above the other; the hut being built of logs, about 5' high

11' long inside, 7' wide; our floor is mud mud—but I and "bunky"—a new one, *Cummins*—Ned and I broke up house-keeping to-day—this "bunky & I" means some one else. I am decently satisfied. The "renowned four" are Shibley, Thompson, Cummins, [and] Blake—now come on old muddy Winter. A Virginia artist should by experience and knowledge represent Winter covered with mud, his locks dripping with chilly dampness rather than icicles and frosty breath.

December 31, 1863. Thursday.

Raining all day, Wind N.E.; attempted to work on Stables in morning but gave it up. Fussed about the tent the rest of the day; it is horribly muddy; a Virginia winter is neither one or the other, I am reminded to-day of a thawing storm of spring at home; our hut has done quite well, our chimney doing finely. "Shib" is on Guard, Blake just out, Cummins and I alone.

We are to have a "general permission day" too-morrow—turkies, oysters, ale, &c.

Received a letter from L. H. to-night, telling of the success of her niece at the "School of Design," New York.[13] Oh! don't I envy such fortunate ones; I will equal thee, I will work for it and I will accomplish my desires. Oh! Nature I adore thee, and no honor to that of sitting a humble disciple in thy grand School of Design transferring THY beauties to canvas; Oh! praises on praises to the glorious art of Painting; but yet I despair almost of ever being a painter, circumstances avant! I must! I will!

Next page comes 1864; and All Hail New Year! December wept to-day for the noble dead of 1863.

Camp near Brandy Station, Va.
January 1, 1864. Friday.

Clear and genial in forenoon; changing to cold with brisk wind from N.W. Blue Ridge capped with snow, looking finely, begetting a heart-longing for the snow-clad hills of home. Worked on Stables as usual, a muddy disagreable job. New Year's passed with us all so-so; except a fine field dinner; *viz*; fricasseed turkey; mashed potatoes; onions and to-night oyster soup; moistened by three jots ale; quite good.

I am but thinking this natal day of the year, what it may bring forth, at least, if well, its November 22d is my last day in the service; but the end of the Rebellion and the inauguration of Peace. The successes of our army and navy,[14] with the significant message of father Abraham are happy omens.[15] Oh! may Peace glorious, successful, *free* untrammeled Peace be the story told by "our Flag" as the last beams of this year's sun illumine its glorious folds.

Brandy Station, Va.
January 2, 1864. Saturday.
   Cold with N.W. wind; clear and pleasant. Out in woods to-day with forty men and ten teams, getting corduroy for Stable; awful wheeling. Quite warm in woods. All froze up all round. Received letters from S. P. [Lillie] and mother; box on the road.

Brandy Station, Va.
January 3, 1864. Sunday.
   Cool but pleasant. Out in woods to-day as usual, I am detailed on the Stable job until it is finished, am excused from Guard Duty while so doing. The boys have had some tough nights of it; we have a new Guard House built which might have been done before, but Captain Mendell is like McClellan, who had to be boxed one side of the head, then cuffed the other, and then only thoroughly woke up to the exigencies of the occasion 'till he had a "regular stunner" spank in the face and eyes.
   I got a little provoked to-day with the men on coming in from work; I want to make it as easy for men as possible, but it is not appreciated, but taken advantage of; I don't believe a single Non-Commissioned Officer ever commenced duty on his warrant but with the best of intentions, but was made "strict and hard on men" from their taking advantage of his leniency and kindness. Good men thus have to suffer for the shirking and growlings of others; I suppose it is so "outside" as here.

Brandy Station, Va.
January 4, 1864. Monday.
   Snow to-day; Wind N.E. Out in woods 15 teams, 53 men. Rumor has that either two or all the Companies are to move. Hope not. No News, all so-so. *Shib* is telling all about Pike's Peak.

Brandy Station, Va.

January 5, 1864. Tuesday.

Pleasant. In woods to-day; had a grand theological pow-wow after supper which has all subsided, and all are writing but Blake who is enjoying a quiet smoke by the fire. There was something in the wind last night, as our teams were drawing rations at the depot as well as the 6th Corps. Ewell is up the valley I understand;[16] perhaps a reconnaissance in force was in view. Anyway a tramp just now would be a little disagreable, especially as our quarters are quite comfortable. The Company Parades are being graded, kitchens constructed, &c., and the regularity of the huts give a substantial character to the camp. Express boxes came, more next time.

Brandy Station, Va.

January 6, 1864. Wednesday.

Cloudy snowy prospect. In woods. Wrote to G. M. & L. H. last night.[17] Shib & Blake on Guard. Drew pants and shoes. All so-so. Our tenting is so arranged we can have lights after Taps which enables us to read & write quite late; a great privilege.

> Dim is the night long, lonely and dreary
>   The fire burns low in the chimney-place wide
>   Strangling the fire with the morn's chill tide
> And weary am I of long communing
>   With thoughts of the past and what may betide.
>
> I am longing for kissing and loving
>   Words, kind and brave my soul needs
>   Smilings, and dotings on me to-night
> How priceless the sound of some woman's laughing.
>   Laughing and singing, how sweet and light
>
> Oh! is there no Mary, some dear darling
>   To twine round my neck, arms soft and white,
> And whisper to me, alone I'm hearing,
>   Cosy, sweet words the heart mansions to light.
>
> Only a vision, awhile to brighten
>   A gleam of golden hair seen but to pain
> While the weakening *sad gray east* doth slowly lighten
>   As we grow stern in heart and march again.

January 6th, 1864.

Brandy Station, Va.
January 7, 1864. Thursday.

Quite cool, a sprinkling of snow just now, at 7 p.m. Out in woods, two days more will see the end of the Stable job. No news. We are in a little village by ourselves with the Quartermasters' Repairing Department—Mendellville is not a rough name, eh!

Brandy Station, Va.
January 11, 1864. Monday.

(8th Pleasant in afternoon; wrote a Shelter Cor. last evening, in woods). On Guard, and a stupid cold time we had of it too. Finished stable Saturday, Photograph came on from New York, quite satisfactory. Corporal Fitzpatrick came to-day.[18]

Brandy Station, Va.
January 12, 1864. Tuesday.

Somewhat cloudy. Thatched Kitchen to-day. Our winter-quarters are yet uncompleted entirely. The Officers' houses yet unfinished, as usual all this is quite interesting to me, as I learn much that is practical. The lack of certain kinds of material and the availability of [others] renders necessary such *modus operandi* as find their prototypes in the days of the colonists and pioneers. Our huts are of uniform style covered with two Shelters, but the cook Houses differ, B has roof of oak shingles, calling in play the skill of a pioneer, to cut and rive them; C has one that reminds you of old times with pine worked into the form of tiles; ours smacks of Ireland being pine-bough thatch laid on "*mud*," solid and rain-proof too; and the camp while in the elevated position "*Charge de Affairs*" on our cook-pot appeared like some mimic town in regularity, only missing the gay equipages of fashion and the places of commerce.

Brandy Station, Va.
January 13, 1864. Wednesday.

Cloudy. Received box from home, all right. Wrote to mother to-night. All so-so. Longstreet back from furlough, all fine up North, quite cold, as indeed it has been here;[19] we have had a colder winter so far than last.

Chief Engineer's Camp, February 1864. This photograph depicts the Army of the Potomac's chief engineer's camp in February 1864. Thompson did not identify all of the individuals in the photograph, but from left to right they are Captain Charles N. Turnbull, Artist A. R. Waud (and possibly an assistant seated in front of him), Captain Nathaniel Michler, two unidentified men, James Daly (Captain Michler's clerk), and Captain Paine. After the war, Thompson noted that "The log hut [in this picture] was Gen'l Michler's, and was a resort by all the officers in the evening for a chat and smoke, it was at one of these 'smokes' that Gen'l Grant remarked that 'Lee's army and not Richmond was the objective point,' and [with] this significant remark, the keynote of the ensuing campaign was passed by almost unnoticed." LC-DIG-cwpb-04050, Prints and Photographs Division, Library of Congress, Washington, DC.

Camp at Brandy Station, Va.
January 14, 1864. Thursday.

Cloudy, and warmer. Puttered round kitchen to-day, dived into Arithmetics, went to Fractions, that is my "start" too-morrow. Had roast duck for dinner, letter from mother to-night, surely I ought to be a happy mortal.

January 15, 1864.

Dived into Fractions and built a little bridge across brook for recreation, threatened to use Shibley's Bootees for Pontons. (14th) Felt a little qualmish about the stomach in afternoon—been eating too many nice things contained in box lately received.

January 16, 1864.

Pleasant; engaged in a little *civil engineering—making sink*. Puzzled over Fractions; it is astonishing how poorly mathematical works are written; I wonder that children do as well; the *why* is neglected entirely. Went in to Bishop's, had a pleasant chat, went to Rice's to hear some music; all so-so.

January 17, 1864.

Pleasant. Inspection and no work. Wrote to M. A. Blunt and mother;[20] received a letter from mother, with notice of the death of *Henrietta Jeanette Munro*, one of my school-friends, one who made the visits of mine to her brother George, the most pleasant of all my holidays.

Thus fade one by one the flowers that have beautified the realm of Friendship, though only to be transformed to pearls on the golden cord of Memory.

Camp near Brandy Station, Va.
January 20, 1864. Wednesday.

Pleasant to-day. The 18 & 19th stormy and chilly. On Guard 19th, Miserable time; received Photographs, sold all, am quite successful in this speculation of mine. Gave the huts a little fixing up, covering the logs with paper and the door with canvas; making a cupboard out of my Express Box, its door rejoicing in the ornament of a quite fine picture "Under the Flag," from *Harper's Weekly*; an old man with a wee darling holding a U.S. Flag over his head, it is an English picture changed, being originally "Under the Mistletoe."

UNDER THE FLAG.—[See Page 54.]

Under the Flag. Though not included with Thompson's journal, this is the image from *Harper's Weekly* that he mentioned in his January 20, 1864, journal entry. According to the caption in the magazine, the illustration was "adapted from an exquisite dmwing [*sic*] by Thomas, a well-known English artist." The caption then explains, as Thompson noted in his journal, that a United States flag was substituted for the mistletoe found in the original. "Under the Flag," *Harper's Weekly* vol. 8, no. 369 (January 23, 1864), 53–54.

Awhile ago I roughly drew a design the features of which I will note here; entitled "Reality & Expectation, or 1864," it being two panels surrounded by appropriate border, surmounted by figures of Fate, Old Time, one panel representing a battle-field: reality—the other a family scene, ships sailing in the distance: expectation.

January 21, 1864.
Leaden clouded weather. Fussed round tent to-day, copied a little manuscript. Grand chat to-night.

January 22, 1864.
Usual weather, warmer. Washed, fried some chef-de-*overs* of buckwheats; received a letter from mother, all well. I have tacked papers over the logs, giving the room quite a cheerful aspect, and when eating I entertain the mind by reading from them, and it would not be a terrible stretch of the imagination to consider myself the host of all the literary characters that ever flourished. Attached Decrials.

Camp at Brandy Station, Va.
January 24, 1864. Sunday.
Breezy and balmy. Held Sunday Service this morning, quite interesting, the first time for two years nearly. Inspection. No duty. Wrote letters.

January 28, 1864.
Very Pleasant indeed the last few days. I cannot realize that it is January. Some thirty of us have organized a Dramatic Club, Captain Mendell encouraging; We'll see.[21] I am of the Orchestra. Received letters from M. A. Blunt, and mother. The former telling me the agreable fact that an old friend of mine,

Married! Oh! I thought the flame of old had fled,
And in Vanishing, leaving but dull gray ashes.
Yet Michael hath blown to life from their depths
A tiny spark of fire, flickering briefly, then gone.
Still by its light I saw her as in other times,
All the same, the old sweet smile and way.
Puff! there forever scatter ye Promethan ashes!

Have made a couple of sketches, "Our Alley," "Our Tent." Captain Mendell wishing me to make a sketch of the camp. Have a diagram to draw for Captain Turnbull.

January 29, 1864.

Cooler, and foggy, prospect of rain. Out in woods cutting corduroy for the Theatre. All progressing finely; Yesterday made some diagrams for

Our Alley, 1864. This sketch probably depicts Company D's tents in the Brandy Station winter quarters.

Camp at Brandy Station, January 1864. Another sketch of the battalion's winter quarters at Brandy Station, Virginia.

Company D Quarters, Brandy Station, March 1864. While this photograph was not part of Thompson's wartime journal or postwar memoir, it provides an excellent comparison to his sketch of his own company's quarters. LC-DIG-ppmsca-33028, Prints and Photographs Division, Library of Congress, Washington, DC.

Captain Turnbull, of a blockhouse, having Sibley Tents on each angle on stockade, serving for a living-place and flankers.

Camp at Brandy Station, Va.
February 1, 1864. Monday.

Clearing away. Puttered on a picture of Interior of hut, half done. Am lonesome to-night. "Shib" kept us interested until 12 last night, telling about the Indians on the Plains, very amusing. He has gone to Catlett's to work on Stockade, such as I drew. Read Scott's "The Lady of the Lake," just been narrating its plot to Blake & Cummins. Am going to read some good letters I have saved up for such occasions, full of genial cheerfulness.

Interior of Winter Quarters, 1864. Thompson's sketch of the interior of his hut at Brandy Station shows the "papers" that he had hung on the walls (see his January 22, 1864, journal entry).

Brandy Station, Va.

February 2, 1864. Tuesday.

Pleasant during day. Hail-storm at Tattoo, accompanied by thunder and lightning; there is something to me very grand and poetical about the first tokens of winter's breaking up; as though nature were shifting the scenes and this the sound thereof. Cummins on Guard, Blake and I confidential.

February 4, 1864. Thursday.

Brisk wind to-day and yesterday. Rich letters, H. G. T.,[22] S. P. [Lillie]. On Guard, rather dull, although a good many characteristic stories were told. A teamster from 2d Division, 6 Corps Head Quarters was caught last night at the Quarter Master's Stables, stealing mules. he was fired at three times, and said "if it hadn't been for the mud he'd got away as twas!" He was a little balmy, and I was not a little amused at his reminiscences of truces, one was this way, "when we got into Alexandria after the Peninsula I went on a spree, and the Colonel ordered me to repair to my Regiment, so I went over to Rockville and didn't catch the Regiment till they was going into that battle there—South Mountain—and the Lieutenant said he had no equipments for me, but I picked up a gun pretty soon, and then a cartridge box and went in, and by G——d when the fight was over I threw the d——d things over a stone-wall and I didn't see the Regiment again till they got to Harpers Ferry." We kept him as the Quarter Master has no such domicil. Quite a number are reenlisting for five years, getting a thirty-day furlough and receiving some $150 bounty.

Brandy Station, Va.
February 5, 1864. Friday.

Pleasant, clouding up at Tattoo. Feel lazy, must physic a little. A & C going on some duty too-morrow, three days' rations, rest in wagons to be gone sometime; a reconnaissance I judge, perhaps across the river. According to all accounts a queer state of affairs exist there, dissatisfaction, &c.; a whole Company came into our lines, officers and all, arms too, and were led to General Head Quarters by a single Cavalryman.[23] The Companies received the order in good spirits, and although to leave these comfortable quarters for a questionable tramp, yet hooting and yelling when the ranks broke, showing that a veteran is out of his element when in quarters. Soldiers have a queer way of expressing pleasure and superficial delight by a sort of falsetto hoot—*Hough O*! like a lot of schoolboys let loose, but when a good solid Hurrah! is heard you may know it comes from the heart. When out in the woods and you wish to "*Break off*" just cry "*Break Off*," then hoot, and it will be taken up one after another, till the whole wood is resounding. The Confederates have a similar yell, or hoot—they never cheer—I shall never forget the *reb* prisoners at Westminster breaking out into such when ordered to "fall in" to go to Baltimore. It made my blood almost run cold, as I have heard it when it meant *blood*, yet there was something wild and inspiring in the sound they taking it up one after the other, with a kind of crescendo and cadence to the refrain as the numbers of voices increased or diminished.

Soldiers are always cheerful, and always following up a pun to its fullest extent, any mistake or *faux pas* is enlarged upon and presented in all its ludicrous phases. A mirth loving fellow starting a joke sees it knocked on to the other like a foot-ball, until some greater will collapses the whole in an unbounded roar of laughter. And when soldiers go along, saying not a word, then the "Knight of the Blue Cap and Button" is completely "played out."

Brandy Station, Va.
February 6, 1864. Saturday.
    Foreboding in forenoon, drizzly in afternoon and raining at Tattoo. A & B went away at 11:30 a.m., and cannonading commenced towards the Rapidan at the same time; mine eyes were gladdened by sight of the Pontons passing over the hills near Head Quarters. I am quite interested in the result of this reconnaissance or whatever it may be. The sound of musketry is quite plain at dusk and now, the artillery having ceased. I am sorry for the boys out in the rain. (Box on the road.)
    Our Camp is on the Ashleigh Plantation.

    ✠— October 20, 1886, I rode out from Culpeper to this old camp ground [at Brandy Station, Virginia]; I had some difficulty in finding it. I had a Confederate map and decided according to it that it was at Captain John Slaughter's house, which was burned down after we left. Dr. Thorn's house is still standing and which confused me. The huts and theatre were all cut up into cord wood for use of the railroad. I suppose I am the only man of the Battalion that ever came back to that camp, and over 22 years after we marched out in 1864.

Brandy Station, Va.
February 8, 1864. Monday.
    Pleasant, cloudy yesterday. The Companies came back about 12 noon pretty well fagged, but jolly. The affair seems to be thus wise; the ————— Division of 3d Corps [and the 3rd] Division of 2d Corps, moved to the Rapidan Saturday morning, one Division crossing, led by General Hayes on foot, they wading, the enemy gradually retiring, the pioneers building a make-shift bridge of trees, &c., they fell back at night;[24] the enemy in full force, shelling the ford (Morton's) effectually. No Ponton bridge was laid; evidently a feint to cover some other movement, our Boats were in full

view and in good range. We'll see! Shib is back on *Pass* to-night, having a good time. Is at Mitchells Station on railroad. On Guard. Dull work.

February 9, 1864. Tuesday.

Pleasant, copied a few tit-bits of heads, I am an artist by nature, I believe. Helped raise rafters to theatre in afternoon. Dress Parade. This page is graced by a laurel flower from Occoquan, one of the lovely places of Virginia. A Massachusetts band played while we were laying the bridge, and never had Music a more fitting Amphitheatre, it sounding magnificently.

The Blue Ridge has a fine and interesting appearance just at present being covered with snow, thus showing them more distinctly, and in a practical point of view being a good study for an artist. Were it not for their range of mountains, the scenery would be very tame indeed. I heard a negro say "he'd gathered corn on one side of the mountains and snow on the other."

Exterior of the Essayons Theatre. This sketch, dated April 1864, shows the outside of the theater built by some members of the Engineer Battalion at Brandy Station in the winter of 1863–1864.

Brandy Station, Va.
February 10, 1864. Wednesday.
Weather pleasant, though cool. Dress Parade, wrote a little on "Shelter Tent Cor.," no. IV. It is a little dull. Received letter from mother.

February 11, 1864. Thursday.
Pleasant, and cool. Started off Shelter Cor. and two letters, slept in afternoon. The re-enlistment men—some over 70 in all—went on their furlough to-day.[25] I had to laugh when Gleason, a smart, capable fellow, though a complete sloven and rag-muffin, told about throwing his shoe after them for good luck, and the cars run over it! rather ominous.[26] They were in high spirits, cheering when they passed in sight of the camp, we being near the railroad by Mr. Stringfellow's house.

February 12, 1864. Friday.
Warmer though hazy at sunset. Dug well in forenoon, in afternoon drew a picture of "Home" from memory, and I am the best pleased with its execution of any I ever done.[27] I saw a Photograph of Mrs. Charlotte Crampton (Wilkinson) as *Lucrezia Borgia*, she was the washerwoman at Camp Lincoln, *Peninsula*;[28] when to hear her pleasant voice, we used to linger by the spring. I have mentioned her in date—November 16, 1862.[29] I saw her at Aquia Creek, also, when we came from the Peninsula; and also, I believe, in Fredericksburg, when Sedgwick took the Heights. Rumor has it that she is intemperate and profane, yet be as it may, she is an interesting character.

Brandy Station, Va.
February 16, 1864. Tuesday.
Blowing like a pack of wolves. On Guard yesterday. Painted a scene for our Theatre—largest sized work of art I ever was engaged upon. Received box from home, rather in poor shape, they open things shamefully at Provost Head Quarters, though mine was probably done on the road. Worst of all an old pitcher which mother had put some pudding in was broken. I am sorry as it was a favorite one of mine; I have a great way of thinking much of such familiar objects from association alone; why, I wouldn't take a mine for my little watch that has done so well since leaving home, and I hope sometime to hear it ticking as of old over the old cat bed at home.

Brandy Station, Va.

February 21, 1864. Sunday.

Pleasant; Inspection; Sunday Service. All so-so. Since last date, one evening in our Theatre, a Mr. Rockwell lectured on "There and There in Europe;" it was quite good, but the best of it all was that it seemed like times at home, and I really felt quite a self-gratification, it was our work and something that is a credit to the Battalion.[30] The stage appeared quite neatly and pretty, my landscape scene standing out finely—stage scenery is very simple, if one knows how. The boys are rehearsing [The] Toodles, which will go quite well I guess.[31] It made me think of old times.

Brandy Station, Va.

February 25, 1864. Thursday.

Very Pleasant. One of those days when you hear the rustle of the wings of the Spring-angel.

The evening of the 22d we had an impromptu "gander dance" at the Theatre.[32] I acted as sort of Manager. We had Cotillions, Schottisches, Polkas, Waltzes. It was a success, all having a grand good time, Captain Mendell kindly postponing Tattoo. No Salutes were heard. The Theatre is now completed, and too-morrow evening, [The] Toodles will be produced, &c. I am only scenic artist. My Violincello not yet arriving;[33] a number of musicians are expected from elsewhere. Received letters from mother and M. A. Blunt, my old boss. I sent my watch away to be cleaned. We are Studying Tactics, with Company Drill. On Guard.

One of the boys caught an owl in the woods, and put him in the Guard House, a queer looking little fellow with his big yellow eyes, a cat-owl I believe. Pendleton calls him Lieutenant Howl! (Lieutenant [Charles W.] Howell of B.)

On my ninth month. An order was read on Parade, about Reenlisting.

Brandy Station, Va.

February 26, 1864. Friday.

Blowing like an insane Boreas, but quiet as a sleeping dove to-night.[34] The event of the day is the opening of the Theatre, &c. [The] Toodles being produced, with songs, &c. The Officers were all in, and also some ladies. All went off well. The scenery looking well. This is a little different from last winter; and it is indeed a credit to the Battalion. All being quite well pleased.

Proscenium. This sketch of the interior of the Essayons Theatre was another of the rare color sketches Thompson made during the war.

➤— Programme at Dedication of Essayons Theatre, Brandy Station, Virginia. February 26, 1864.

[THE] TOODLES.

Toodles .... Zenas Stoddard [Company C].
Charles Fenton ..... George W. Brackett [Company D].
George Acorn .... Orlando Jackson [Company D].
Frank Acorn .... George Kehoe [Company C].
Farmer Acorn .... Charles Sweetland [Company C].
1st Farmer .... Atkins Higgins [Company B].
2d Farmer .... Henry Perkins [Company B].
Lawyer Glib .... Frank E. Beahn [Company B].
Landlord .... John Eldridge [Company C].
Mrs. Toodles .... George Robbins [Company D].
Mary Acord .... John Brown [Company B].

Actors in Costume. Photo of Edwin "Ned" Coolidge and the unit's drummer, ——— Clarke, in costume for a production at the Essayons Theatre. These costumes, however, were not for The Toodles or any of the other productions mentioned in Thompson's journal.

Brandy Station, Va.

February 27, 1864. Saturday.

Pleasant. Paid to-day. The Performance last evening gave good satisfaction; all I cared was the scenery appeared well. Had a dance at Theatre.

March 1, 1864. Tuesday.

Rainy and disagreable, on Guard last night. Had a musical (*extempore*) soireé at Theatre, to try Bass Violin, much pleasure.

➤— March 1, Violincello arrived.

—Journal of Frederick Vogel[35]

March 3, 1864. Thursday.

Pleasant. Company Drill. Theatre Night last evening, very good, *Box &
Cox, William Tell*, [*The*] *Toodles*.[36]

March 4, 1864. Friday.

Cloudy and hazy, all as usual. Recitations. Company Drill, &c.

Camp at Brandy Station, Va.
March 14, 1864. Monday.

Cool winds, dark blue clouds, raw &c. Wrote a huge pile of letters to-day,
practiced some music &c. I have written a musical composition, entitled
"*Retreat from Fredericksburg*," which I am well pleased with, as others. It is a
melancholy wild kind of a piece. Although it is mine I like it better and
better. I have arranged it for five instruments.

Brandy Station, Va.
March 16, 1864. Wednesday.

Quite cool this morning. Last evening we had *Irish Assurance* at the
Theatre.[37] Everything went in a quiet, pleasant manner; the reason of it
being the exclusion of the quartermaster's men (citizens) except those
with Passes. It seemed like some family gathered together, charitable towards error, and warmly praising success. The music was better than before, but I shall *veto* Fritz Vogel's Flute, he plays horrible, spoiling the
rest.[38] My part is liked very well, in fact, I "played all the music," but Jake
does very well, Rice is coming back with *his* flute, then I shall be relieved
of *Directorship*, and be only Assistant. I am writing my Play, *Bag of Gold*, not
thinking of having it acted here but to amuse myself.

Brandy Station, Va.
March 17, 1864. Thursday.

Cooler. Guard. All so-so. Had a grand good letter from mother last
night. Composed a few lines of Poetry, "The Robin of Spring." I am not
satisfied, but here is one verse:

"The woods scarcely stirred with the South wind's breath,
    Nor rustled at all the forest's dead leaves;
For Winter had touched as with hand of death,
    The grass of the fields and withered the trees.

The snow it still lay on the Northern side
  Of distant knoll and wind-swept hill,
And but for the sound of the brook's swol'n tide
  All else to the ear was quiet and still."

"When there lightly beneath my window from his airy soaring,
  A bird came and lit on the hawthorne spray.
His song first was low as though he were mourning
  For comrades of old in summer's bright day;
Then stronger it grew with wild, rich trilling,
  'Till woodland and echoing valley did ring,
While my heart with joy untold was filling,
  As sweetly his song, this Robin of Spring."

Brandy Station, Va.
March 21, 1864. Monday.

Cool. One of those days that are stamped—*good for nothing*—the moment they have existence; too cool—or something—for drill.

This is Birth-day; Twenty-five; I cannot realize I am so old; really I seem no more a man than when I was sixteen; twenty-five—*Tempus Fugit*! Gracious! I have no realization of my situation—only I hope next birthday will find me well and happy, perhaps I may have a more thorough realization of my manly responsibilities.

Brandy Station, Va.
March 22, 1864. Tuesday.

On Guard. Raw and chilly, ending up with a driving snow-storm. Miserable on Guard; a baker's dozen crowding about the fire-place; and too cool to sleep, so the hours dragged heavy, glad I am not on to-night. It reminds me of last February 22d at Falmouth. Just come from a chatty time in Higgins's.

An "old Company A man," came to us to-day—Clancy Collins—a deserter. He is a burly son of Erin, and while absent was one of the Irish Brigade, and we were, of course, treated to a running account of all their battles, &c., quite odd and amusing.[39]

Brandy Station, Va.

March 23, 1864. Wednesday.

Clear and thawing. Was to have a Theatre to-night, but some of the "would-be" actors conceived that stimulus was needed, and one poor mimic is at present amusing himself with a rail on post.[40] I have poor opinion of such, so we had a Dance; but the feature of this day was snow-balling, "we" and C in the afternoon got at it; I would like to tell all the incidents of the brilliant affair; anywise after several ineffectual attempts, we by a little strategic diversion in their rear, made a grand assault and at the first push, drove them half down the streets, then they "stuck," and I thought for awhile we would never start them, but we did, and they broke and run, we yelling at their heels, driving them clear off their own Parade! Those in the tents heard the rumpus and with a little feeling of pride turned out to defend their honor, taking us in the rear, we turned upon them and away back they went, the others now rallied on us, and surrounded we were, and back we went, then retired in good order to our own Parade; the officers looked on, laughing in their sleeve, of course, old "Turny" no doubt admiring his darling D, and I am 25 and recording this, oh! I am yet a boy.[41]

✈— Programme, March 24, 1864.

1. Overture.
2. Song ....George Kehoe.
3. Quintette ...."When Johny comes home."
4. 1st Act. Irish Assurance.
5. Quintette. "Loved ones wait for us."
6. Jig Dance.
7. Quartette. "Fairy Bell."
8. 2nd Act. Irish Assurance.

Brandy Station, Va.

March 25, 1864. Friday.

Stormy, raining huge at present, candle-light. Last evening had a Benefit at Theatre. *Irish Assurance. Limerick Boy*, quite amusing.[42] Such things suit better than heavy pieces. Cleared some $46 @ 25.[43]

The recruits came yesterday, not yet detailed to Companies but billeted round in tents. They are a little queer, but not so much as on the march.

Wrote a scene in *Bag of Gold*, slept in afternoon, have a cold.

It is one of those evenings when you love to draw up to the fire-place at home with friends, and pass the hours in quiet talk; while I shall scribble a little, face into the fire, think of this one and that, mother and home, and listen to the rain as it patters on the tent above me.

Brandy Station, Va.
March 28, 1864. Monday.

Pleasant, but cloudy to-night. No letters—too bad. I am actually in need of a good pleasant letter, though I have no particular expectation of any. On Guard. Practiced music for Theatre in evening. The great topic of conversation, what there is, [is] what shall we do this summer? General Grant is to be with this Army;[44] troops are arriving, 11 & 12th Corps. Quartermaster's men working day and evening; and many other notes of preparation for the coming season as usual.

Brandy Station, Va.
April 3, 1864. Sunday.

Quite pleasant to-day. Inspection in morning, service at Theatre as usual. Arranged some music, that's all.

Brandy Station, Va.
April 5, 1864. Tuesday.

Stormy. Went on Ponton drill yesterday, not amounting to much, we need a Weitzel or Reese to conduct it so to learn anything.[45] We have had quite a number of recruits come lately and all they will learn I will not give much for. I am sorry, but I am not an Engineer officer. This Battalion is not half what it might be in efficiency and character, but I am going out in less than eight months, so what do I care.

The effect of the army's stay here is very apparent in the woods, they being nearly trimmed entirely out; about the Station (Rappahannock Station), it looks about the same only sheared by the axe down to its primal topographical features; a square enclosure with a monument to the memory of our dead, is all that reminds you of the battle there under Sedgwick.[46] All is so-so with us, while other portions of the army are being renovated and thoroughly refitted.

Practised music last evening, although I had a merry headache; four of us. We practiced on a new march, which I have arranged from Piano forte music, "*Soldier's Chorus March*" from Opera of *Faust*, by [Charles]

Gouhnod. A fine thing. Real music in it. I have written an air for "April Day," which pleases me, and others.

Wrote to mother, got some names in my Autograph Book &c. to-day.

Disagreable weather; our winter is all in the Spring; Oh! mud, thou reignest supreme. Received a new Journal from home; So it goes.

Brandy Station Va.

April 9, 1864. Sunday, 9 a.m.

Thank our stars! raining! No Ponton Drill! If we had Weitzel or Reese to drill now, I wouldn't be saying so, but we go to drill, and get out the bridge, and up with it, anyway and anyhow. If it were not for the "old hands," bridges would be built in queer ways.

Thursday evening, the officers had a *recherche* affair at the Theatre, no enlisted man being admitted! it made a little hard feeling, especially the snobbish way they went to work about it, some little disturbances occurred, for which the Battalion has got to "take it"—*forty-five* men! for Camp Guard!! The Theatre is lonely—and gutted now, no more will *ladies* bright grace its boards or heroes of the dramatist stalk and swagger out their little hour of much greatness, no longer will be heard the sweet strains of musical violin and flute through its resounding spaciousness, no more! but when we are gone, it will be but an ignoble stable.

Shadders of my glory, adieux!

The rain is pattering down upon the Shelter just as though [it] loved to do so. Pitch in old Rain, you are a brick to-day.

On Guard yesterday, dull as usual. Received a letter and new Journal from home day before yesterday. And somebody will be reading your pages, old Journal, besides me ere long, and a good deal is recorded here; and I wonder what I shall record in the next. *Quién Sabe.*

Bass Violin and I went down to *Jake's* and immediately soothed our wounded and harried nerves by the sweet strains of "Happy Land," &c., having a quiet little time, playing for our entertainment; may be the last time, as *Orders* have been read to send away all superfluous property, and I hardly think old "Flick" will be so good as to carry our instruments.[47]

Been Reading *Corinne* by *Madame de Stael,* beautiful language, but too much "pensively leaning his head against an antique vase" to suit me.[48] I prefer Lamartine's *Memoirs of Youth* for a sentimental tale.[49] Graziella, methinks I see you now in your father's boat lighting up the heart of the stranger with those wondrous eyes, as you float on the golden waves of the bay of Naples.[50]

"Shib" is Sergeant. All goes so-so. Joe favoring us with quotations and imitations of old Gerber, and occasionally having a grand discussion with me about McClellan for the next President;[51] Skipper Blake favoring the ranche with a huge salt-water mess of Jargon.

7:30 p.m. Raining yet; arranged some variations for amusement; expect our playing is soon over. I reckon the Battalion will be put under strict discipline; rumors that *Non-Comm*'s are not [to] associate with privates, &c., fudge! it may be proper and necessary but that don't make it pleasant. I was not made for ringing folks up to the marks. It is disagreable, and were it not for $20 a month, and prospects, I would as far as peace of mind is concerned, be without rank. But I guess I can slip over seven months more for it quite complacently.

Harmer of Stoneham is just back from furlough and is relating his opinions, &c., to Shib & Blake.[52]

I am writing this just to pass time away, and calm my ruffled breast, and to make words; I'd like to scold somebody; race, run, yell; overplus of animal activity from doing nothing all day I suppose.

Brandy Station, Va.
April 10, 1864. Sunday.

Stormy during day, pleasant in forenoon. Inspection as usual. Lonesome this evening, just went to the Church (!) a Mr. Kirk of Boston, late major 45th Massachusetts, very dull, no girls to come home with so came back to the shanty;[53] Joe has just come from there and is expounding at a great rate to me, which of course I am intently listening to. I was going to write to mother, but Lo! and behold no paper; so content myself with scribbling here and jabbering with Joe about religious matters, all very entertaining to me. We are commencing to surmise and guess what the summer will bring forth; all of which is very positive and conclusive to our understanding. Went up to the theatre that was in afternoon, all is rack and ruin of that portion of its arrangements, the Guard took possession of it last night; I took away a relic in the shape of a bit of flower pattern from one of the wings; Blake has just come in, more reviewing of dogmas and doctrines, all very entertaining to me of course. Awhile ago, I heard the closing hymn up there, and I don't know of anything that touches me in such a peculiar manner as sounds of worship. It makes me think of old times and I seem floating on sweet sounds and pleasant memories. Gently, Time, gently; keep them young and fair, good and true, those companions of times ago; I shall have to commence again in a new world as it were when I go home. Ah! well-a-day, well-a-day.

I have been quite interested in music of late, but I shall have to amuse myself with sketchings, &c., when the instruments are sent away, I have the Violincello for a trifle, and shall send it home to surprise mother; and I trust sometime to draw as sweet strains up North as ever in Ole' Virginia. It is a very nice instrument, and has contributed in a great measure to my enjoyment this winter, and to others also. I have no doubt I think my humble services have been appreciated; Blake and Cummins still *conversing* on religious matters, entertaining as before!

The fields are just tinging with green, the sun seems a little warmer, while the storms have an inclination to partake of the rakish way of thunder-showers, yet the Blue Ridge is mantled with snow, all of which is respectfully submitted.

G. Thompson, *Journalizer*

Brandy Station, Va.

April 12, 1864. Tuesday, Tattoo.

Pleasant in forenoon, clouded up heavy in afternoon. Sprinkling a bit too. On Ponton Drill to-day, river has been very high. Yesterday went to Culpeper, repairing corduroy we put down last Fall, washed away; rode home—(*all hands*) in Quarter-Master's wagons which had been hauling corduroy. Hear the army is to move the 18th, Captain Mendell &c., reconnoitering the Rapidan; usual terrific rifle-pits, hosts of pickets, &c., "*a Cavalryman said so!*" Anyways it looks like leaving soon, already I anticipate bidding good-bye to our shanty for another campaign; I hope we all shall be fortunate, Jake and Fritz Vogel came in to-night and we had a quiet little play, very agreable to me. Paid to-day also. (Lent Rue $10). Usual heavy Guard. Inspection too-morrow at 10 o'clock, *all hands*, I smell a rat; "straws," &c. Blake is snoring already in his bunk, a lot of pine chunks are Burning commendably in the fire-place, Joe at his crotchets, while I am scribbling with Bass Violin at my left—*Taps*—Good Night.[54]

Brandy Station, Va.

April 14, 1864. Thursday, Tattoo.

Pleasant. On Guard—fifteen posts; feel dull. No News. Tent occupied by a surprise party as they say, which entertained me with extempore improvisation, mementos, &c., songs; I gave them the freedom of the house and listened, Coolidge performing on the Violoncello, very pleasant to me, which is to be carried this summer. So I shall not send it home, wrote to mother saying I should. I think I shall give up correspondence, I have to *work* for all the letters I get except mother's.

Rumor saith—two Volunteer Engineer Companies go with each Corps. I hope so, some of our work will be minus, also that D is going away, &c., all fudge.

Feel dull and sleepy, Ponton Drill too-morrow, I suppose. Prospect of storm, rather cool after all.

Brandy Station, Va.

April 15, 1864. Friday, Tattoo.

Dull to-day, prospect of a storm, it pattering away on the tent now; received a letter from mother, I must write to her more frequently. I should not neglect her, who is almost my only Correspondent; I believe I must write a little each day as she does, but writing sir Journal makes it seem double employment. I wrote yesterday to her. Was to send her a box, but as the Bass Violin is to be carried, I have concluded not to. I am a little sorry, as I suppose she has been rather expecting one; and a little incident of that kind would be quite an event in her every day life, but I shall be sending this old companion of mine soon and an Autograph Book, &c., in which are the Autographs of such of the Battalion as I wish to recall, together with their little souvenirs.

The great event of the day is having my haircut, trimming my shaggy whiskers myself, quite an undertaking and artistic operation. No news. Inspection of knapsacks, "as we march," of course the Recruits turned [out] with huge ones, while we "*old*" ones tucked in a blanket or so, enough to call a knapsack, and that's the end of it.

Taps—Good Night Everybody.

Brandy Station, Va.

April 16, 1864. Saturday.

This companion of my campaigns leaves for my former home in Hopedale, Massachusetts, may it find all well, and amuse the good home folks with its contents.

Good Bye,
G. Thompson.[55]

Brandy Station, Va.

April 16, 1864.[56] Saturday, Tattoo.

Showering like neither storm or sunshine, but when the sun rays stem part of the rain—a golden mist. Mailed my old Journal home to-day, and when I remember what tramps that old companion has been with me, I commence this acquaintance with feelings, both pleasant and anxious; if all is well, on some future page I shall date an entry "*At Home.*" Seven months and six days before that happy event. I am now in good health, hopeful, experienced in campaigning life, which blessings I trust will continue. We had a musical *soiree. Essayons Quintette Club.* Vogel, Rice, Mather, Geyser and myself;[57] had a successful and pleasant time; moon shining at Tattoo. *We meet again.*

Brandy Station, Va.

April 17, 1864. Sunday, Tattoo.

Trying to rain, April like; the mountains presenting quite an interesting appearance being mantled with snow, and as the heavy clouds passed over them anon falling like some curtain from the sky behind which the mountain peaks disappeared and reappeared again like the shifting scenes of a Theatre. I have passed the day in a shameless way, doing nothing, but I am feeling that way when I do anything I spoil, so I best float down the stream. Had a Trio Club at *Jake's* (*Geyser*), all nice, shall dream of the sweet sounds we made most probably. Ponton Drill too-morrow, confound it, Taps—Good Night.

Brandy Station, Va.

April 18, 1864. Monday, Tattoo.

Have a poor pen, half headache, half-tired out, half-crucified by some execrable playing by ear by Rice and his musical friend Daly;[58] Oh! I despair "ramping in," a practice only in favor with country-jig players, of a very old pattern, too; it is detestable, I can do it when hard pressed, and very hard too; tinkered some on box for Instruments; get along very well; drilled with canvas boats.

Brandy Station, Va.
April 20, 1864. Wednesday.
On Guard. Dull as usual. Received a letter from mother, 18 days between a letter from me, that is too bad, I am ashamed of myself, indeed. Had a pleasant chat to-night, telling stories, &c. Vogel (*Fritz*) telling some reminiscences in a matchless manner, all studiously perfect, we "Yanks" tell stories as though we had not time, while a German dilates on each theme presented, every plase of incident is fully brought to notice; in fact, just the way for a quiet sit down time; but that is something Americans have not the national ability to enjoy.

Parties are going away too-morrow to fortify along the [Orange and Alexandria] rail-road, I understand. I don't care to go. I shall be well satisfied to be left at camp.

Brandy Station, Va.
April 21, 1864. Thursday.
Pleasant with a few April showers coming down upon me while at work on my great box for Violincello like some airy baptism. Read a pretty love-story out of the *Atlantic*, the "Schoolmaster's Story," finished *Corinne* yesterday on Guard. It "turned out" in a pathetic manner, yet Madame de Stael, with all her art could not make Oswald the husband of her, it was too daring an attempt; she was not a wifely woman. Musical Evening again. Blake away on party. Fritz at Retreat was the Company, as a whole, "*ven they turn out the Company that's me!*"

Brandy Station, Va.
April 22, 1864. Friday, Taps.
Pleasant & warm, prospect of storm at Retreat, moon shining now. Copying music all day, and as I reflect how many aimless days I have spent in the army, I feel as though I were literally wasting one of the choicest things of life—time; but soldiering is two-thirds doing nothing and waiting, but it is better to be copying and arranging music than looking at the

clouds and sleeping. I have a very good selection of instrumental music; it is strange there are no better collections of instrumental music for Trios, Quartettes, and Quintettes; in the *Germania* are found the best.[59] Foster's *Social Orchestra* a very pretentious work—only half a dozen good arrangements are found.[60] The trouble being they take an air, put a Bass part to it intended for a Double Bass in a full Orchestra, a 2d Violin part of monotony itself, good in its place, all these constitute a Trio as found in such works, which *gets along* like a Grenadier, Artilleryman and Cavalryman marching—they are soldiers in a general sense of the word—so are the different parts often hitched together for a Trio. I believe a work carefully arranged with good taste and discrimination of pleasing airs—both secular and Sacred would be a great dissident turn in the amateur musical world at least. The first piece we have is one, the *"Prayer,"* simple, yet arranged in a varied and correct way for three instruments, *Gounod's Soldiers March* is another which I arranged from the Piano music by *Baumbach*, varying the Bass in a few places, to give a better effect;[61] a Piano Bass is different altogether from a Violincello part, yet some would stick it down; *it is Bass*, and of course it is right! Two flutes, smoothly played, 2d Violin, light, with a Violincello can execute in a manner hardly distinguishable from an Organ. I delight in Instrumental music. Some of our absent parties are back for rations, D Company's detachment being at Bull Run bridge, having a good time; so am I. Bunky on Guard.

Bull Run Bridge. Copy of a sketch by Thomas Beddoe, Company C musician, showing Bull Run Bridge with an army wagon and a lone soldier crossing.

To-day commences another milestone turnt, seven months more. It is growing short indeed. Grant was "in town" yesterday, the cars running off the track, obliging him to change cars;* those who saw him speak of his being very easy and unassuming in his way. It is nothing more common than to hear a scraping and thumping along up to the railroad as "one more unfortunate" pursues their wayward career. I saw an engine bottom up below here the other day.

  * he gave a lift at a rail to get the engine on the track.

Brandy Station, Va.
April 23, 1864. Saturday, Tattoo.
  Pleasant, but quite warm, occasioning a very *lazy* feeling. Writing this with my belts on; it is quite pleasant, a brisk breeze blowing and a big round moon shining; finished box, arranged a little music, washed a few articles including myself. *Au Revoir.*

Brandy Station, Va.
April 24, 1864. Sunday.
  Warm, gradually clouding up, raining at Tattoo. Lonesome to-night, in fact, since the detachments have been away, it has been lonesome as a grave yard with the tombstones stole; the few remaining in camp flit about like so many spectres, whisper to each other, and if you meet one on the sidewalk, he seems to avoid you; call out, all sit with head on hands singing some *Doloroso,* perhaps open a door, seeing nothing but a blank therein where always before smiling faces and hearty greetings met you, or find one locked, pass on disappointed, hear a creaking behind you, look back, see a face peering out at you with suspicious glances like some maiden lady at a traveling itinerant. It is raining now and with no sounds of singing or laughing to break the silence, it really seems lonely in camp. Taps will sound soon and the quietness will seem more familiar. Wrote to mother. Had a pleasant Guard; only a "few unfortunates" to walk post &c. Well, Good Night.

Brandy Station, Va.
April 25, 1864. Monday, Taps.
  Rainy-looking, clear during day. Arranged music to-day, "Signal March," quite pleasing, also a little trifle of my own, had a musical soiree in evening,

am a little riled with a few little occurrences from Rice, a very flashy, pretentious performer by ear, (!) he evidently does not like Mather for a leader, or feels that some mistake was made, &c.!

Indulged in buckwheats, butter & pickles to-day; no soft-bread just now; sent a little box by Ruby home, and was made happy by a letter from that same dear spot too. My mother writes the best of any of my correspondents! Among the news is that my *old* Journal has arrived safely home, which I am glad of, as I would hate to lose now that old companion of mine. Some dozen men were discharged to-day, time out, and a very smiling lot of men they were too.[62] Mother wrote me how many days I had to serve, but I have forgotten. I know no news but shall not be surprised some day to leave this abiding place; in fact I just begin to appreciate it now.

Brandy Station, Va.
April 26, 1864. Tuesday, Taps.

Clear, lightning towards the South, there may be some other kind before long. Arranged a Waltz; and rested myself! Went over to Mather's and heard him and Fritz play some Duets by some German (Ruieth), they were delightful, yet they are not of the style to suite the populace (!) and I can't help laughing when I think of the way Robbins—drum major—in here last evening related to me the way Fritz maneuvered in some of his divine moments;[63] imagine F—— before one of the "magnificents," said F—— being a small German with flaxen hair and heavy whiskers of the same hue, usually has a choice meerschaum "just coloring nicely" in his mouth with a thin wreath of smoke curling from its ample bowl, now lying beside an octavo sheet of written old style music—huge lettered Adagios, &c., in glaring perspicuity, yellow with age, and I doubt not a connoisseur could detect the fumes of tobacco and beer gathered in "good old times."[64] F—— prepares by giving his mustache an extra twine to be out of the way of that "high E," now Robbins has it, "F—— clears his throat a bit—then— *one—two—three* 𝄞𝅘𝅥𝅘𝅥 *one—two—three—* 𝄞 then he looks round—with—splendid! magnificent!—lovely!—enchanting!!" I always laugh then.[65]

Brandy Station, Va.
April 28, 1864. Thursday.
Pleasant, though a little cool. On Guard to-day. Wrote to S. P. L., an old Correspondent.[66] The boys are all back again, so it seems like home; it really seeming strange to hear so many voices. Had a musical evening, went quite well, had an admiring audience of two or three towards the last.

Hear Burnside's Corps [of] 50,000 are coming this way.[67]

I must note one little fact; day before yesterday in the fields near us where the army cattle graze there was 6500 head in one drove at once, and it was quite [a] vision of prospective *beef-ala-mode*, &c. Sometimes they stampede, and it is almost hazardous to restrain them, one night I am told, they went 10 miles!

Read Rogers's *Italy*, can't say I am fascinated, yet am pleased;[68] he lacks fire and warmth, he is too exquisitely elegant; give me *Childe Harold* for his painfully polished and subdued lines.[69] I think if he had written on simpler themes and let his natural grace of composition gone a little untamed, his reputation would have been greater and more lasting, but it would have been undignified for a banker of London to write on humbler themes than *Italy, Home Life,* &c. He would have been a royal Burns.[70]

Brandy Station, Va.
April 29, 1864. Friday.
Pleasant. An eventless day, copied a little music, practiced a little, and chatted in the evening. A detail is going away too-morrow. Fritz was in, and we had some choice stories of course.

Brandy Station, Va.
April 30, 1864. Saturday.
Pleasant, though cloudy towards dark and sprinkling. Fatigue to-day, at Rappahannock Station, building stockade, quite heavy work. Made a bit of a sketch; hear the 50th went to Kelly's Ford yesterday to build [a] bridge for Burnside [and] was pointed out his advance, &c. Guess he's about. Saw one real black soldier; hear the Colored Brigade of Burnside's Corps are guarding [the] railroad, relieving the others.[71] I saw a portion of 5th Corps moving to the front, after having been relieved. I hope we will have an ("inevitable") army this time.

Mustered in—three more.

Brandy Station, Va.
May 1, 1864. Sunday.

Pleasant, spent May-day in writing to mother, loafing, washing up clothes, coffee and pork bags for a move. A portion of the 5th Corps moved near here to-day, and are encamped, the 9th Corps relieving them from guarding the railroad. A detail finished the works at the Station, General Meigs is in camp, now Chief of Corps of Engineers, he looks like his portrait. It is something to have Totten's name to a parchment Warrant, if only a Corporal's.[72]

Brandy Station, Va.
May 3, 1864. Tuesday.

Pleasant to-day though cool, yesterday closed up with a terrific dust storm, ending in a shower. On Guard, writing this in the Guard House on the old hut table; this morning at about 8 o'clock, "we"—the Guard and Lieutenant Benyaurd are left behind to bring up the train;[73] some wagons under repair not being finished at the Quarter Master. I shall bunk with Blake, Cummins going it "back." I indeed felt a few regrets on seeing the old hut going to confusion, I was over to get the table and Joe's stool, and a few coals were smouldering in the fire-place, while the picture "Under the Flag" was cheerful as ever, I suppose a certain diminutive Grandmother in spectacles is smiling from the poster wall at home as ever too. I guess we are going to the lower Rapidan, perhaps occupy Fredericksburg Heights, indeed I would like that for awhile. So we begin tent-life again; it seems the last round on the ladder, then good bye U.S. Army.

✈— Battalion marched out May 3 [in the] morning. "3 days' meat, 6 days' coffee and sugar" (Vogel), 30 rounds ammunition.

The train and guard left at 6 p.m. the 3d of May, the Battalion at 8 a.m. same day—camped at Richardsville.

Chief Engineer Joseph G. Totten. This photograph of Chief
Engineer Totten during the Civil War was not included in
Thompson's combined journal and memoir, but his pride
at having Totten's signature on his corporal's warrant seems
to merit its inclusion. LC-DIG-cwpb-05190, Prints and
Photographs Division, Library of Congress, Washington, DC.

Bvt. Brig. Gen'l, and Col. Eng'rs.

Totten's Signature. The signature of Brigadier General (and
Brevet Major General) Joseph G. Totten, Chief Engineer, that
Thompson was so proud to have on his corporal's warrant.

Something Earnest Is Intended

The Overland Campaign, May–June 1864

---

*The Engineer Battalion was engaged, under the direction of Gen.
Duane, as Chief Engineer of the Army of the Potomac, at the Wilderness, Spottsylvania, River Po, North Anna, Cold Harbor and siege
of Petersburg till the surrender of Lee. At the battle of the Wilderness
it acted as infantry, being placed, together with the 50th N.Y. Engineers in line on the right of the 5th Corps, crossing the turnpike to
check the rebel advance. They held their position until the 6th Corps
reformed and took up a new line. At Spottsylvania it was engaged in
the construction of bridges across the Po and also in the construction of
batteries along the line, the greater part of the time under fire. At Cold
Harbor A Company was with the 2d Corps, B Company with the 6th
and the other two with the 9th and 18th Corps engaged in constructing
batteries and advancing our lines during five days and nights, mostly
under fire. A portion of the Battalion attached to the 2d Corps was
engaged in running a mine to blow up the enemy's battery occupying
the crest overlooking Gaines' Mill. The army moved before the mine
was completed. On the night preceding the army's departure from Cold
Harbor, the Battalion fortified a short defensive line running through
the town, to be held by two corps during the flank march of the army.*

*It seems that the extent and value of the services rendered by the
Battalion in the building of the ponton bridge across the James, over
which Grant's army passed, was overlooked or ignored in the reports
of that operation. "When the Battalion reached the river, Gen. Weitzel
was there with several companies of the 1st U.S. Volunteer Engineers,[1]
and nothing was done towards a commencement of a bridge. The boats
with their material were scattered in confusion over the low marshy*

*ground, stretched along the shore, and the officer of volunteers could
not make his men go into the mud and slime to bring the boats ashore.
Gen. Weitzel expressed his gratification to Capt. Mendell (commanding
the Battalion) in warm terms at its arrival. At the word of command to
build the bridge, the detachments, non-commissioned officers leading,
jumped into the mud and water almost to their necks, and by commend-
able but unrewarded zeal and energy succeeded in one hour in building
a bridge abutment 150 feet long, that reached the water proper—it
was then that the volunteer work began. The Battalion was afterwards
transferred to the opposite shore."*

—LIEUT. TURTLE'S ESSAY

Richardsville, Va.

May 4, 1864. Wednesday, 8 a.m.

Pleasant morning. About 5 p.m. left old camp with train, arriving here
at 10:30, quite a brisk walk for green feet. I never felt so lonesome and
forlorn as when going through the camp after the Battalion had left; the
coals kept bright in our fire-place, and when I last looked in, they flick-
ered up, up into a little blaze, as a sort of Good Bye, and if old Mythology
is true, I might deem some Penates or spirt of the hearth smiling at my entrance;[2] it seems as if coals keep bright the longer in a deserted fire-place.
But it seemed the next Good Bye to the last, when I shall leave camp-fires
and army tent-life for good.

It seems natural to be in tents again, though I feel a little awkward.

I understand the Cavalry crossed the Rapidan last night, our Battalion
repaired roads yesterday afternoon.[3] Feel quite well this morning after
all, I will soon be all right, though I dread marching with the rations and
foolish and inconsiderate officers.

Greenwood, Va.

May 5, 1864. Thursday, 6:30 a.m.

Splendid, going to be hot. Left Richardsville Camp at 3 o'clock p.m.
yesterday, arrived here about 11 p.m. Passed over Ponton Bridge built by
50th [at] Culpeper [over] Mine Run. I noticed no trash, dog carts and
so-on among [the] trains, all clear. This is a pretty place!

"*Left* Greenwood at 6 o'clock, made one march, halted. Went with
Captain Mendell to act as guide &c., "*attached to Head Quarters!!*" Saw

Grant, Meade, &c.—*Burnside.* The day's work has been they attacking us, we repelling them and making arrangements &c. still, troops hike [to] Burnside on the Left I think. 6th Corps engaged from 12:30 to 3 p.m., and 5th from 3:30 to dark—hear we go in as skirmishers too-morrow (*perhaps*). I am to act as *First Sergeant* of *D.* All right, but I rather hope not. Guess I'll go and rest a little."

⟩— I was detailed to General Meade's Head Quarters the day of the 5th to act as guide, etc., having a horse. General Meade came up to me and asked "if I had been down the plank road and seen where the 9th corps was." I had not. He, although a brave man, had the peculiarity of being of a tremble with excitement and at the same time his voice was as calm and full as though nothing was going on.

Spotsylvania Wilderness (Near Court House and
   General Headquarters), Va.
May 12, 1864. 8:30 a.m.
   Reveille at 2:30 (this morning), at 5 came here (Near Gayle's House) and camped. We had a decided success at early daybreak, on the Left, capturing 3,000 prisoners and quite a number of pieces of Artillery (20 or 30) and we are cannonading away at a great rate now, following them up probably;[4] this mixed with the rain and thunder make quite a hub-bub; I just saw a "*Reb*" battle flag with fourteen battle names on it, captured this morning, the capturers taking it to Head Quarters. Grant's *cook* (!) says *he*

Greenwood. Sketch of Greenwood, Virginia, where the Engineer Battalion camped May 5, 1864.

is in fine spirits, &c. ha! so we all are. I will copy now the notes I have of previous days' work, &c.

"May 7, 1864. 9:30 a.m. *Yesterday* (May 6th, 1864), about 1:30 a.m. we went out—and threw up rifle-pit in afternoon, lying in rifle-pit *in forenoon*,[5] at sunset the troops on our right broke (4th Heavy Artillery (?)), and we had to slip out actually between Reb & Fed—the Battery men were cool and in good *morale*—our situation was really critical as we had no belts on or guns. I can't note all the little incidents of the affair—the *Rebs* with their *Hi– Hi–* and the Fed officers with their *Halt– Halt–*.[6] We after taking "duds" took *position*—on the left flank of 3d line (I think), in a responsible place. "I can't trust *Vols* there!"* said Griffin (?)[7]—Remained there all night."

* a doubtful remark.

"*This morning* [May 7] at grey—rebs charged our rifle-pits—we occupied day before—highly exciting—were fearfully repulsed.[8] Then moved to Warren's (?) Lacy House[9]—repaired road—About middle of afternoon Burnside's Corps began to mass in the centre; heard Major Draper—an old schoolmate—was wounded badly.[10] At sunset we started on plank road to Fredericksburg, turned to right, a very hard and tedious march."

Remarks. I understand it was at the Lacy House that Stonewall Jackson died, his arm is buried here with a board to note the internment; "*Arm of Stonewall Jackson*," if such be the inscription, it is suggestive.[11]

The 6th was a day of much interest; which culminated in the affair of the evening—the break; we had nearly finished the rifle-pits when it was made; several attacks had been made on our right, at + [on "Wartime Sketch Map of the Wilderness"], and we were all confidence; the woods at this point where we were, could not be penetrated by the sight for more than a rod;[12] just in our front were popping away the skirmishers, and all at once a rebel yell went along the whole front; and I know of nothing so thrilling as that; to hear from behind that tangle of young pine, scrub oak, and a complete curtain at times of dogwood blossoms, yet behind those pearly flowers, and singing pine lurked the enemy unseen; anon you would hear a distant boom and forthwith a shell came crashing through scattering its fragments, then one from the right, we were perfectly enfiladed, and that wild yell going back and forward past our front was strangely fearful, yet I can't say it inspired fear, it was too familiar a sound, "that's the Rebs" was the only note of it, then a brief rattle of rifles on our right commenced, and then we heard the Hi; Hi; of the Rebs, and the "*Halt!* halt!" of our officers; "they have broke;" we soon gathered our tools and walked back to the rifle-pit, the line of troops where we had been swung round in a position for defence, abandoning the rifle-pits we had made; at the rifle-pit stragglers came passing in, and were driven back by the officers and provost Guard; our color guard assisted also and at one time had quite a number round our flag which was the only one flying on that position; we were to support a Battery near [us] but finally bivouacked for the night at [the] second abbatis; about 12 midnight, the enemy made another charge with a howl but were soon shut up; they tried it again in the morning but received a fearful repulse, our artillery doing great execution.

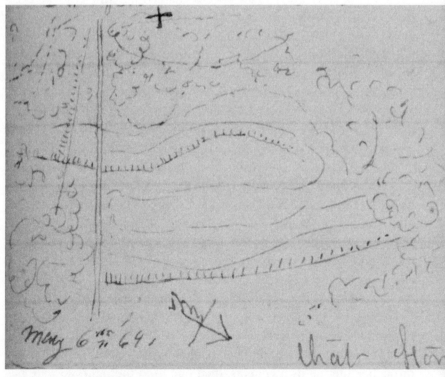

Wartime Sketch Map of the Wilderness. Thompson's rough sketch of the Engineer Battalion's position during the Battle of the Wilderness on May 5–7, 1864. He referenced the position marked on this map with a "+" (along the upper edge of the map, just left of center) in his remarks after his quoted May 7 journal entry.

Rifle Pit. Thompson's rough sketch of the line of rifle pits that the battalion occupied when the Confederates attacked on May 6, 1864, in the Battle of the Wilderness.

Section of Field Rifle-Pit. Generic cross-section of a rifle pit.

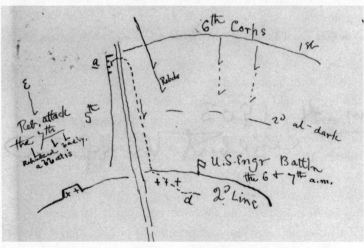

Postwar Sketch Map of the Wilderness. Thompson's postwar sketch of the Engineer Battalion's position during the Battle of the Wilderness on May 5–7, 1864. He references the positions marked on this map in the memoir sections on page 258.

✠— We were at *a* [on "Postwar Sketch Map of the Wilderness"] building intrenchments when the 6th Corps broke the 6th of May.[13] The
5th faced about and would have fired upon us if some of the regulars
who knew us [had not] hollered out who we were. We came to *d*, the
rebs on our left hand and in sight.

We were at *d* when the rebs. made their attack the 7th from about *E*.
They were quickly repulsed.

The firing on Hancock's front the 6th was very heavy.

Note. In 1866, I assisted in surveying this field, and our entrench-
ments at *a* were in good shape then. G.T.

"Engineer troops to the number of about 1,200 had been sent to
General Warren the night of the 5th, and had been placed in his second line. They were now used for constructing intrenchments and
bridges and were not at any time afterward used as infantry,* for it
was difficult to replace such well-instructed, experienced engineer
troops."

* Except at Spotsylvania when we went to Birney, but were not
needed.[14] G.T.

Andrew A. Humphreys, *The Virginia Campaign of '64 and '65; The
Army of the Potomac and the Army of the James*, Campaigns of the Civil
War, Vol. XII (New York: Charles Scribner's Sons, 1883), 42–43.

NOTE. Will it not be found that Lee never or seldom attacked unless he thought he had the advantage, either in position or through
the characteristics of the general opposing him. He undoubtedly
thought the Army of the Potomac was discouraged and demoralized
at Gettysburg. And he refused to attack the position of Centreville
twice![15]

I have often imagined how rosy the prospect would have been for
the "Cause" if the Army of the Potomac could only have been destroyed! This speculation reveals the prominent position of the Army
of the Potomac, and again I am thankful the Wilderness campaign was
fought right straight through as it answered a great many questions
and settled many a false notion. The Army of Northern Virginia and
the Army of the Potomac were two great opposing armies, tenacious

and tough fighters, but wary as to having the advantage. Lee refused to attack at Centreville in 1863 and let us go back in peace after Mine Run, but he had to attack at the Wilderness, as it was his only hope to delay for a year or more the final result by blocking our progress then and there.

Lee held his lines well but he would have given all, if he only could have headed our flank march from the Wilderness to the James River!

"May 8, 1864. Piney Grove Church, Va. Arrived here at sunrise, marched all night, shall probably go to Spotsylvania Court House."

Remarks. Saw the Brick House used as Hooker's Head Quarters at that Battle.[16] It must be a sad looking place in the daytime, a bad smell was all we could judge we were near the field by. It was a tedious march, dusty, so you could hardly breathe. This is called by some "Pine Creek Grove Church" [or] "Tabernacle Church." Grant's Head Quarters were at *Lacy's House,* near which we were during the day. About 5 p.m. a great slashing of timber took place, which must have been cutting a road or abbatis. I know of nothing so earnest sounding to me as cutting timber, it makes me think of the "Seven Days' Battle"; loading pieces for a fight has not half the excitement to me as the former.

☛ I do not know that during the whole war I had such a real feeling of delight and satisfaction as in the night when we came to the road leading to Spotsylvania Court House and turned to the right; then I felt relieved of the nightmare of just remaining at Fredericksburg Heights, but now I knew we were going to "hook on to them," until the end.[17]

"May 9, 1864. Monday. *Yesterday* [May 8]. Hot weather right along. Remained near Piney Grove Creek Church (near Head Quarters), moved with Head Quarters at dark (*old corn-field—~~music for first time~~*). We go with Head Quarters, one day with this Corps or that; the 7th instant, were with the 5th Corps."

"*To-day* [May 9]. D threw up and superintended rifle-pit close by *Hancock's* Head Quarters.*[18] About 2 p.m., troops commenced moving forward on road (*closing in to the 6th*) I judge; we remained completing rifle-pit (abbatis excepted). We then *patrolled* (!) road from 5th to 6th

Todd's Tavern. Thompson's rough sketch of Todd's Tavern, site of the cavalry engagement fought by Major General Philip Sheridan to open the route to Spotsylvania Courthouse for Federal forces on May 7, 1864, and subsequently the headquarters for Hancock's II Corps.

Corps, and we came back to camp. B & C being with 6th Corps throwing up a rifle-pit. General Sedgwick was killed by a sharpshooter near them.** When we came in we saw Grant, Meade & Staff—quite a sight. Head Quarters Band played to-night for first time."

    * Todd's Tavern. This was the scene of Sheridan's Cavalry Fight.[19]

    ** Shib, who was there, says bullets came round everywhere and that it was a chance shot [that] hit him.[20]

    Remarks. When we went up it looked like an approaching fight; the saddest sight I have seen was the body of a man which was burned completely black; near a rail-fence, I only hope he was not burned alive; Oh the horrors of war; the fields are so dry that fire goes with fearful rapidity, and to a severely wounded man sure death, if exposed. I have seen quite a number scorched slightly, but they were not badly [burned]. I heard the same of Chancellorsville. B & C threw up their rifle-pit under musket-fire. I believe Sedgwick was killed by a sharp-shooter. There was heavy firing to our left—the 6th and 3d I think being engaged.

    I shall long remember how touching and finely the music of [the] Head Quarters band sounded after we had come back to the old corn-field; we had lain down, worn-out and tired—hard day all round—Sedgwick killed—and then to hear that sweet and appropriate music the first time since Brandy [Station], I can't describe how it stirred our hearts, we thought of everything and seemed for awhile to pass to a glorious feeling of tearful yet joyous ecstasy. Music I never heard to sound so appropriate and inspiring, as under such circumstances, I remember the night after Antietam with this [remainder of line missing]

"May 10, 1864. After breakfast Battalion went out past Head Quarters—saw Babcock[21]—and took post left of *Warren*'s Head Quarters in pine woods, where B & C were the 9th—that is, *Union Head Quarters**—A & C went out and built crib bridges across the Po, then destroyed them, coming back about noon. At this time affairs began in earnest and lasted until dark, 7:30 p.m. At dark a grand charge was made.[22] Captain Turnbull took us down to the front on his own hook and volunteered to assist in holding the line but we were not wanted. Understand he was reprimanded for it severely by Mendell & Major Duane.[23] I think it would be very poor policy indeed, although I am ready & willing to do my best when the pinch comes. We bivouacked as usual near Warren's Head Quarters, General Head Quarters moving up to this place. Some mail came, and a *hat* was my share."

✈— * I was mistaken in [Union General Head Quarters] being "where B & C were the 9th." They were more to the left.

Remarks. This was a fierce fight in the afternoon. I could see but little from a tree; the fighting seemed to be in an open space between pine woods in an orchard; wounded came past us in a mournful procession, all cheerful and hopeful; one young boy with a bad hand said, "It was hot, but we stood up to them." A captain was buried near us,* a great favorite with his command, and I could but be touched with the feeling of a few of his men who buried him, lion-hearted men too. He died on the field of Honor. Another Captain** died in our Hospital the 6th instant, of Hartford, Connecticut; he told his Sergeant to write to his wife that "he loved her, and wanted she should be good to the boys," so they go down amid the storm of the battle kind and loving, and brave as well, 'tis "the loving are the daring."[24]

* Captain Stone, killed by a shell in the back.[25]

** C. C. Billings, mortally wounded in the thigh.[26]

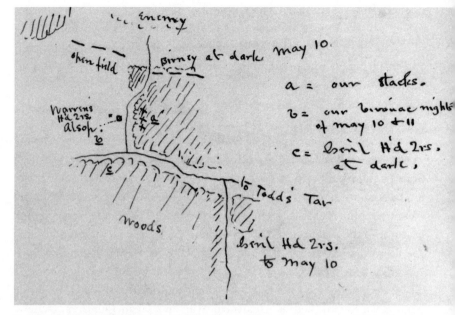

Postwar Sketch Map of Spotsylvania Courthouse. Thompson's postwar sketch of the location of Company D, Engineer Battalion, during the Battle of Spotsylvania Courthouse on May 10, 1864.

It looked a little serious when we went down to the front, but every man was determined to do his best, there was no straggling at all, and I consider it no little praise that not one of our Battalion has been so far in the hands of the Provost Guard.

Gen. Grant passed us just before to take a look at affairs, and a quite exciting period it was, as some Artillery from the front came to get Ammunition, the guns and gunners black with powder smoke, but they were in the best of spirits, and determined. A charge was made at dusk which was successful, and a very quiet night it seemed after the day's din.

"May 11, 1864. *Reveille* late. At 1 p.m. went out and repaired road from Head Quarters to Left Center (?); shower, very bad walking (*home!*) back to former camp (Near General Warren's Head Quarters); very disagreeable."

Remarks. Understood a great change was to be made at 5 p.m., but the shower prevented [it], the road is a complete quicksand, terrible to man and beast; this of course ended in a storm, all Virginia showers do. We were up late drawing rations, and did not get much sleep, our principal charge of ration is in fresh beef which is furnished each night. I like it well, broiling it usually with plenty of salt and pepper. I hear that reb. prisoners almost fight for the salt scattered on the ground where they may be. Bands played in our front, cheering &c., [and] during the night a few shells passed over the camp; unusually quiet along the lines.

At Grant's Head Quarters, Landrum House I think (?).

"May 12, 1864. 7 p.m. At 9 a.m. we went out to where we repaired yesterday; corduroying a long piece; hard fighting all day, a great number of prisoners have been taken with some 42 pieces of Artillery."[27] I have no time or inclination to write more and think I have done well to copy off my pencil notes here;[28] which is the first time I have been able to write in here since the 5th instant, a month it seems too; a great deal is crowded into a few days and even minutes. The day has gone well for us, rainy at times all day. Somebody must wear out by and by, Fed. or Reb. Oh! I have seen fearful things of war the last few days. Still "all Hail to the Stars & Stripes."

Remarks. Reveille at 1:30 a.m., moved at early morning; and the first intimation we had of the morning's work was the wounded coming from the field, and we found out gradually the news, and [as] we came near to [the] bridge we saw a "pile" of graybacks, which was satisfactory of course. The fighting for the rest of the day was very severe, we only holding our position.

>+— *Memorandum.* It is almost impossible to locate our marches during this battle, or series of battles. I judge we camped the 12th near ~~Stevens~~ *Brown.*

Note. December 12, 1887. From Mr. E. C. Barnard, M.S., G.S., who surveyed this summer over this battlefield;[29] he states that Grant's Head Quarters were at the "Brown house"—this then was our camp made the evening of May 12, 1864.

Hancock formed his columns for attack at the open space by the Brown house.[30]

Near Gayle House.
May 13, 1864. Friday, 9:30 a.m.

Rainy all night. Reveille at 2 a.m., left camp at 5:30—marching order—and are building corduroy road at ford over Ny river (so the pickets told me), a small stream with quite a rapid current, fringed with under-brush, white birch, swamp-oak, and about 15 or 20' wide. Saw Burnside, understood Rebs. are falling back in our immediate front; no 8th Corps up yet!

May 14, 1864. Saturday, 7:30 a.m.

Worked on roads until late last night, returning to same camp at General Head Quarters (At Gayle House). Roads are horrible and rainy yet, will it ever stop. Head Quarters moving this morning. Reveille at 2 a.m., moving about 6 a.m.—miserable! I slept in my Shelter and let breakfast go.

(4 p.m.) *In camp.* Head Quarters here (near 9th Corps Hospital), some firing in front. Repaired road as we came along, are near 9th Corps Hospital which we passed yesterday. Clearing away; thanks! Hear the boys calling out "rainbow! rainbow!" I expect hard fighting yet; Lee will fight tooth and nail. The fighting of the 12th was of the most desperate character, it came right to bayonet and butt; both our men and Rebel prisoners unite in saying it beat anything of the war—"it beats Antietam" so they said.[31] It is almost a question of endurance, yet it is better to use up Lee in the field than inside the fortifications of Richmond; something earnest is intended by this campaign, the men are earnest, "we have fooled long enough," yet I can but notice that this army has become so accustomed to retreats that even a slight move is naturally construed into a "fall back;" you hear "Fredericksburg" mentioned as a refuge, but a "fall back" now would be a mortification to every soldier; we have a habit in that respect, but Grant will break it up I hope. A story is going round that "Richmond is taken"; it passes round, but such yarns are old, and with many a dubious shake of the head; it was so, even when a *Head Quarters* "Order" was read that Petersburg, Virginia, was captured,* &c. We fight on and do not hope too much; this must be put down at all hazards.

* We were wrongly informed, the Order not being read to us. Captain Turnbull told [us] through 1st Sergeant Flood.[32]

Near 9th Corps Hospital.*
May 15, 1864. Sunday, 2:30 p.m.

✂— * In the Atlas of the Rebellion there is a map giving the location of the 9th Army Corps Hospital.[33]

Cloudy, occasionally sprinkling, that's all. Eat and sleep is this day's record so far. Head Quarters' Teams have been harnessed all day, but a little rest is agreable, no fighting of any moment to-day. The Band has been playing since noon, sounding finely; field-soldiering would be without one charming feature when music is omitted; and when after a long silence the bands strike up, then it seems as if the critical period had passed and we might let our nerves relax a little; just the wear of mind is not to be despised along with fatigue of body; there is an anxiety, constant and unremitting which wears hard on a man's constitution; but it can't last always; it is now twelve days only since we left Brandy Station, and it seems a month's service. When sleeping, the day's work will mix up with your dreams, taking batteries, being shelled and all manner of contingencies. I shan't long forget the other day (12th instant), a man who was made crazy by a shell's bursting over his head, not making a scratch although it tore his cap away, he was yelling in a fearful way, sometimes with a "Ya-hoo!" that made your blood run cold; that is only one horrid rememberance.*

✠—   * Grant made note of this man—not May 12 but the 10th.

Just been over and seen caissons and guns, captured by Burnside, and they are completely riddled with rifle-balls; the caissons were made in Richmond, Virginia, the gun was U.S. I tore a relic from one of them "L—C—1st Caisson—Pendleton's Battery" they are full of ammunition.[34]

I hear that all the Corps Commanders are at Head Quarters—council of war, perhaps—also, that Joe Hooker is on our Left with 40,000 men[35]— 8th Corps is on the road;[36] hope it is all true. I guess reinforcements are coming.

I wonder if the folks at home are proud of us, appreciate our efforts, and will they deem us worthy of admiration; we deserve it anyway, Oh! I love the "Old Flag," "old Glory" torn and tattered as it may be, it now is pure and clean, the emblem of the Free; those who love it most, are those [who] suffer, die and toil for its perpetuation. I can't express the feelings I always have when beholding it floating either fresh and clean in the peaceful air of home, or torn and rent waving triumphantly above some battlement.

Hear the Cavalry are on a raid, and the railroad is in good operation up to Fredericksburg—only yarns.

Near 9th Corps Hospital.

May 16, 1864. Monday.

Had a straight night's sleep, quiet this morning, and a heavy fog; just finished breakfast—coffee two hard tack—bit of broiled beef; am unwashed thus far, but my blanket is folded; I find it better policy to march on a full stomach than an empty stomach and immaculate complexion; guess I will wash now.

I find a great deal of interest in the affair of the 6th instant;[37] the Captain of the 7th Maine Battery was in agony thinking he might lose his Battery (6 guns), as his men were on fatigue duty and he all alone (with his drivers (?)), and when we took position in front of his Battery, his strength of nerve gave way, & his feelings overcome him, and crying like a child, said he to Perkins (in charge of tools), "I never saw anything like those men laying down their tools and rallying at their stacks, so cool and determined," and said he "I would have died alongside my guns before I would have left them."[38] Rand was the first to commence to rally them. General Griffin says to the Stack Guard "who are you?" "Regular Engineers!" "Captain Mendell's men?" "Yes!" "Well, go in as file-closers and push them up!" But a funny phase was some ministers, I judge, who showed their craft by their "*Now is your appointed time to save your* country!," the boys laughed a little, although they appreciated their example and courage; another saw is this "What Flag is that?" "U.S. Engineers!" "*Rally round the Flag!*" and as soon as they caught sight of it, a great number came up into the rifle-pit. The chief rush was through the hollow on our right; those who saw it said it was as though a storm of wind had burst upon the whole 6th [Corps], and dashed it back like a torrent. General Sedgwick said, "I don't blame them for breaking, but I blame them for not rallying." I hear it commenced on the right and extended to the 5th [Corps] where it stopped. The night of the 5th the Zouaves and regulars fell in promptly, faced to the left and filed to the right and took up a position diagonally across the pike, and we slipped out between their front with the Rebs. and rabble on our left. They fortunately knew who we were and did not fire upon us, and as we had just done a good job, they were a little pleased with us, and we could hear them say "they are all right."

(8:30 p.m.) Quiet all day as a Sunday, except a little cannonading about 4 o'clock. Understand an "Order" has been read to the soldiers congratulating [them] on their success, &c., also that the "outer walls" of Richmond were taken; Atlanta, Georgia, also; and reinforcements have arrived, &c.; it seems too good to be so;[39] fortune & Victory is smiling indeed on our flag.

Wrote to Mother and just afterwards received one from her with [a] portrait and how proud I was of her too; it came in [at] just the opportune moment, I have read it over and over again with one from Abbie D——, too.[40] Good Night—no Tattoo, I am "gay and happy."

Camp near 9th Corps Army Hospital.

May 17, 1864. Tuesday.

9:15 a.m. At this time packed up to march. Have had an excellent *siesta* after a fine breakfast, with the addition of a super soup of Hosmer's get up, a "few of us," going in "snacks"—no firing yet. Read a little in *Good Society* by Mrs. Grey, was thinking of other matters more than the characters shown;[41] a letter I had from home with that portrait; Oh! how sweet is retrospection, as well as the future as we fondly paint it; how much good a nice letter does a soldier; yet I would not really delight to go home just now, I wish to see this out and trust I shall see it come to a successful issue.

(7 p.m.) We marched perhaps two & half miles and camped in a pleasant woods on the "*Anderson Place*," a fine residence near by (¾ mile) of a rebel Senator by that name.[42] Understand the Rebels are retreating, leastwise about 5 & 6 p.m. firing was heard at a great distance to the south of us. Grant has left for Fortress Monroe, I hear yesterday.

This is the first opportunity we have enjoyed of an extensive view, which is fine and really inspiring; I reckon we are indeed "Getting out of the Wilderness."

I have a cosy Shelter as usual, with a big bunch of Swamp Pinks above the "door (!);" it was really pleasant, a band practicing near us helped a little too, then the pleasant breeze and pleasant thoughts made all gay; what a life is that of a soldier; joy and sorrow, despondency and exaltation combined. Fritz came up from the train, rambled all over Marye's Heights. Fuller saw our old Falmouth camp;[43] "Old Jeff" is at Packard's yet, who is well, too.[44] Fredericksburg is one vast Hospital. I must close, as my entry is measured by a deplorable small ration of candle.

Anderson Place.

May 18, 1864. Wednesday, 5 p.m.

Reveille at 2 a.m., a little hazy and warm; marched about 5 a.m. to where we repaired road near Ny river, passing our camp of 16th instant, an attack on the enemy being the order apparently of the day (Grant passed us). We lay there awhile, then marched back, camping near where we were this morning, our previous camp being occupied by 5th Corps Hospitals. As we came back we passed the 6th Corps Hospital Department, in full operation, and there is no denying but all that can be done that is possible for our wounded; I would have liked to investigate more closely, but like much of my sight-seeing while in the army, [it] is on the march, with sweat and dust blinding my eyes.

Our troops were fighting on the Spotsylvania turnpike, with what success I know not, there has been but little firing since noon.[45] Received a letter from mother with some flowers enclosed. It is just commencing to rain but if we are allowed to remain in our Shelter, Blake has just ditched it, and that is one occasion of confidence; we are in the woods.

Anderson Place.

May 19, 1864. Thursday, 9:30 a.m.

A long night's sleep. Reveille at 5 a.m., the affair of yesterday was only a reconnaissance in force, &c., to see if they had left, as I really think they will before long; and we must know the hour almost they commence to do so. Sent a letter to mother, all quiet. Wrote up my *Remarks* and sketched in a few picture notes.[46]

Anderson Place.

May 20, 1864. Friday, 8 a.m.

Pleasant this morning. *On Guard.* Understand the enemy held a portion of the "pike," the trains coming [up] the road near us.[47] I hardly believe such to be the case. Had a pleasant night. A camp of Shelters appears quite interesting and pretty among the trees, with the moon shining down on their white roofs.

(8 p.m.) No Tattoo. About noon a detachment went out with arms to repair road but it was not required. Understand we took more prisoners; a squad passed here of perhaps 300; 2d Connecticut passed here (Heavy Artillery from Fort Albany). Received another letter from mother to-day

Camp in Woods, Anderson Place, May 20, 1864. Thompson's sketch of the battalion's campsite in the woods near Anderson Place in late May 1864.

which is the right kind of cheering to a soldier. Had a great soup for dinner, gave Fritz a bit for taste, he reciprocating with a cut of a hard-tack cake, which from [some] reason always goes by the sobriquet of "d——n son of a b——h!" an awful name for a favorite dish. I can't say what gave it, but that is its name, more properly I suppose a "pork-stew," and as its thickness of ingredients become by ample quantity of material, it [is] a "cake." Oh! gentle ladies behold my fry-pan, my brown kettle, and "look on this and that," and weep.

Made a sketch to-day of camp, &c.

Anderson Place.
May 21, 1864. Saturday.

Reveille at 4 a.m., marched at 8 a.m., delayed on road until we passed Massaponax Church; here the country is very interesting, the Church of brick appeared charming among the trees. We were opposite the same verge of hills as at Anderson's, making me think of some I know quite well. Grant, Meade & Staff passed *us* on the road. We rushed right along, and I was nearly "bushed"; at about 3 p.m. we crossed [the Richmond,

Fredericksburg, and Petersburg] railroad ahead of everything; "all hands"* about Head Quarters organized as an *advance.* Meade's son in charge, I judge,[48] the 1st Massachusetts Cavalry (dismounted) leading, and carried the Bridge (Guiney's).**[49] C & D acting as Reserve to the skirmishers (68th New York). A & B repaired bridge which was set on fire by the enemy—a squad of Cavalry—but was not injured; we lugged knapsacks and rushed and many fell sick, Captain Williams was sunstruck, I was unetched as well;[50] the 3rd Division, 5th Corps ([under Brigadier] General [Samuel W.] Crawford) then came up at late sunset, relieving us, and we returned to Head Quarters completely fagged. Turnbull joked to Crawford, "we have saved you again!" He laughed. Indeed it is queer for General Head Quarters to skirmish for their own advance.[51]

Note. This was near Guiney's Station. A little dainty gave me a rose.

* 114th Pennsylvania (*Zouave*), 1st Massachusetts Cavalry (*advance on bridge*), 68th Pennsylvania, U.S. Engineer Battalion, and other parties around, 8th Pennsylvania Cavalry, &c.

** 9th Virginia Cavalry, small party opposing.

Tyler's Plantation.

May 22, 1864. Sunday.

About noon moved from Guiney's Station to near Bethel Church, George Tyler's plantation (Blenheim Place), a pleasant place.

Guiney's Bridge. Another copy by Thompson of a sketch drawn by Thomas Beddoe of Company C. This one shows Guiney's Bridge, which Thompson often spelled as "Guinea" and which, as he reported in his May 21, 1864, journal entry, was carried by the 1st Massachusetts Cavalry (Dismounted).

Milford Station.

May 23, 1864. Monday.

Marched in morning. Delayed all day until late when we rushed along to Head Quarters near *Carmel Church* (Montague's Home). Heavy firing in front, at sunset.

Jericho Mills on North Anna River.

May 24th, 1864. Tuesday, 9 p.m.

Marched in morning (9:30 a.m.), resting quite awhile at Carmel Church, a brick structure. The Band played to enliven the time; very hot to-day.

Are on South side of North Anna river, crossing Ponton Bridge at large Mill. A Battery [is] in position near us, and we could see our skirmishers about a mile ahead. Have just had a splendid bath. The banks are quite high, steep and rocky with level plateaux on each shore.

Rumor has it that we [have] Hill's Corps surrounded (?). We are going to have a tremendous shower; it has been all round us, but guess we will catch [it] now I guess. I hope for a dry rest, double ditched, and pitched steep. The thunder is very sharp and keen; all quiet along the lines.

Quarles's Mill.

May 25, 1864. Wednesday, 8:30 p.m.

Warm, showers at sunset—a *long* shower brewing I reckon, as usual. It is becoming quite warm a-days now.

Reveille at 2:30 a.m., marched—recrossing river to Quarles's Mill—a sawmill—where we stacked arms then went with tools to ford at Mill, the 50th detachment laying Ponton Bridge—and with them building a military bridge covered with boards over [the North Anna] river, and during day repaired roads &c. Head Quarters came here (at late afternoon), this being about two miles from former place (Jericho Mills).

[William S.] Proutz of D came in to-day from a tramp with Lieutenant Howell on Sheridan's raid;[52] he [saw] several of our old camps near [the] Chickahominy, all looking natural; Duane's Bridge being used by the Confederates for a Bridge, all the other bridges on that river being all repaired now. Dr. Gaines has left; so we hear of our old camping scenes, &c. I saw the recaptured prisoners;[53] also *Sir Percy Wyndham* for one new notoriety to-day;[54] I saw him first when a Colonel going out to the Battle of Williamsburg.[55]

Rather disagreable pitching tent, wind high, and tent sweeping; cooked my coffee in the rain, Oh! I wonder if the good folks at home will ever appreciate our trials, &c.

Quarles's Mill on North Anna River.
May 26, 1864. 6:30 p.m.
Clear and warm, shower on the docket now. Rested in camp. No news. Saw a woman—Rebel prisoner—a real termagant—storing the curious away while stories become too scarce.

⟞ The remains of a woman in Confederate uniform were found between the lines near the Appomattox river;[56] an ex-Confederate soldier told me that a man and his wife went together, she putting on the uniform; General Lee when it came to his knowledge had them detailed so they could be together, I think at his Head Quarters.

Mangohick, Va.
May 27, 1864. 7:30 p.m.
Warm but not disagreable, a little breezy. Reveille at 2 a.m., marched at 4:30 a.m., have had a driving march; going down the river a ways then taking the road to Chesterfield (a Station on the railroad) at Carmel Church, a point of many road junctions; we passed by *Concord Church* (1857), leaving Hanover Court House to our right, arriving about 5 p.m. The bridge we built yesterday was destroyed and when we passed the mill, an Infantry detachment was busy throwing up a rifle-pit, to prevent the passage of the ford by the enemy, our forces having (evidently) entirely abandoned the south bank. A wagon with rations from the train for us has come to grief with Sergeant Turner (a dead beat),[57] and the prospect is dubious. I have filled myself with fried beef and a bean stew, which I picked up—foraged. No noise or news.

This is quite a place, though level and Peninsula like.

On the Peninsula. Bridges, Littlepage's Ford on Pamunkey River.
May 28, 1864. 6 p.m.
Pleasant and cool. Up at 1:30 a.m., marched at 2:45 a.m., passing through the village deriving its name from a man getting drunk in these parts, and was identified to his searching friends by *Man—go—hic.* It was

a beauty morning, pleasant moonlight, we went along at a nice easy jog, and I couldn't hardly realize I was a soldier. Picking a May Apple occasionally (*Swamp cheeses*) and also ripe wild strawberries, a few. Repaired road during day at Ford, Pontons being down, and we camped on the south shore, cloudy now.

I suppose we are on the Peninsula again, and it was with a mingled feeling of triumph and sadness when a colored man told me where that fringe of trees was, there swept the Pamunkey. I thought of old times, old companions and a great many things. We cannot be such a great distance from some of our old camps. We are near "The Golden Farm" (J. B. R——'s house).[58]

The bed of the river is low, fringed with trees, and the country flat with that light, white sandy soil; a splendid collection of springs at the bridge, which is destroyed or swept away; shaded by some magnificent beeches.
I was reminded of "Camp near New Bridge, 1862" by a Magnolia bud.
I understand the remains of J. E. B. Stuart are interred at a large house below. (?)[59]

✝— *Note.* Crossed [the] Pamunkey River 4 miles N.W. of Hanovertown at Huntley's not at Littlepage's Ford. G.T.

Haw's Store, Crane Swamp, French's Plantation.
May 30, 1864. 4 p.m.
Warm, cool at night. Remained in camp yesterday, no news. Moved at 7 this morning, and we encamped on a characteristic dry, piney barren just off the road about four miles from the morning camp. No news. On Guard. All hands have been living on faith and pickings. I made a dinner of parched corn and coffee, saving my bit of beef for supper; beef and coffee for breakfast, "that and that only." Have got along quite well nevertheless; but am overjoyed to see a wagon come just now with rations.

Camp at Crane Swamp, French's Plantation, Near Jones Plantation.
May 31, 1864. Tuesday, 4:30 p.m.
Warm. Remained in camp; we are just at the east point of *Crane Swamp*, on French's Plantation, yet I am not sure. We have excellent water, through a gravelly sub-soil in the swamp, almost dry through. A cavalry fight came off here and a number of rebel cavalry-men are buried here.[60]

A number of make-shift rifle-pits are quite interesting near by, being a few rails laid up, and dirt scooped out with hands and bits of sticks, you seeing the prints of their hands where they had patted down the soil, being just enough to cover a person from rifle bullets.

But oh! we were issued rations and I have lived to-day, a certain portion of my *physique* rounding up in beautiful outline; breakfast, *hard tack*, broiled beef, coffee plenty of; and a kettle of beef soup, with the addition of a few mature peas and great number of embryo peas in tender and delicate pods; I was for awhile when cooking it the embodiment of "Present and Prospective Happiness," lying in my tent, *negligee*, reading a *Harper's Weekly*, anon casting my eyes through an opening underneath the tent, to my pail hung over a slow fire, sputtering and steaming away *so* beautifully. When this is written, a light supper of coffee and hard tack will conclude. A fine bath this morning. Received a letter last evening from mother. Our forces have evidently advanced.

Camp at Gillson Via's Plantation.

June 1, 1864. Wednesday, 3:30 p.m.

Warm, but breezy. Reveille at 5 a.m., moved at 7 a.m. to this place; it is hard to find out where you are. We passed through quite a little settlement (Harris Town) and Totopotomoy Creek, it may boast a great name for aught I know, but no one knew. A darky gave the above name to this arid little desert; though in a little run near here are good springs; we passed rifle-pits and epaulements for artillery made as our forces successively took up their positions; in fact we commenced to besiege Richmond when we crossed the Rapidan; understand we are about four or five miles from Gaines's Mill—don't know for certain. We leave our tents pitched like a fly and are cool as possible.

Camp near Cold Harbor, Va.

June 2, 1864. Thursday, 6 p.m.

Warm, sharp shower, late in afternoon; end in a storm I guess. *Last* evening at 9 p.m., C & D packed up and with tool wagons, went out cross-cut over awful cross-cut, hard corn-fields, clearing an infantry road as we went along. C stopped at *Allen's Mill,** D continued on about a mile, where after corduroying a little (Had to build a large fire to work by), bivouacked (12 midnight); troops were expected to move this way, but none came,[61] and we had an undisturbed and refreshing nap.

Allen's Mill. This sketch, also a copy of one by Thomas Beddoe, Company C, depicts Allen's Mill, where at least part of Company C stopped during the battalion's march on June 1, 1864.

✠—* *Error.* Part of C went to 5th Corps.

At a little farm-house near by (Burnett), I procured milk and some onions, and had a good rare breakfast; then during the day exchanged eggs, &c., for hard tack, they having no flour or bread; the old lady, about forty, was pleasant and accommodating and her dark-eyed daughter of sweet fifteen was a very agreable vision to an intensely bachelor soldier, they being the first of women-kind I have spoken to since we were last in Sandy Hook. We laid and sunned under the shade of scantly leaved pines until about 3 p.m. C came along and joined the Battalion at General Head Quarters (Wood's farm). Understand we are near our old camp of some *two* years ago; well a good many changes have come about and those that are left are not as green as then; I think in coming here we crossed the road we went to Cold or Cole Harbor, the first we have seen of the old warpath. There has been firing every day along and hard fighting last evening (9 p.m.).[62] No reliable news, all rumor, only the 8th Army Corps *is up*!![63]

Camp near Cold Harbor, Wood's Farm.
June 3, 1864. Friday, 6 p.m.
    Rainy in morning, cleared away after noon. Were ready to move, at a moment's notice all day. Remained in camp. Very hard fighting towards Gaines's; successful I judge, took prisoners and artillery; hear all kinds of

stories, of course. We are endeavoring to gain the ridge beyond the little stream that supplies the Mill which is their last good position fronting the Chickahominy; they may give the right, *changing front*, which they must necessarily do if we are entirely successful in forcing this.[64]

I have a fearful and inexorable appetite; I would like just for experiment to see how much it would require to satisfy me for even one hour, every one else is the same sad way; talking of good victuals, &c., I think of Brandy Station with the unlimited means of good living at my disposal which I had an appetite for. Oh! could I recall in reality that bag of Buckwheat never eat up; those chunks of bread thrown to oblivion; I wish I could have only had my present appetite then.

Camp near Cold Harbor, Wood's Farm.

June 4, 1864. Saturday, 9 a.m.

Pleasant. Just as we were drawing fresh beef rations, we ([Company] D) packed up and reported to 18th Corps Head Quarters,[65] and about 10:30 p.m. (night of June 3) received tools and went out to picket line, say 500 yards beyond where arms were stacked; throwing up rifle-pit, and 4-gun sunken Battery, and under fire of a few sharpshooters, whose bullets came right in where I was on Guard at Stacks; a little unpleasant. About this time a terrific charge was made in our immediate front; I almost breathlessly awaited the result which was yielded to our boys after a stubborn attack on their part, then all was quiet and both sides went to usual camp work as though there were no fighting, &c., they fortifying as well as we;[66] and so the night wore away when about *five* (5) a.m. D came in and we after ——ing for some woods, cooked coffee, &c., and then came to camp at old place. The other Companies went out to other points also. Vogel came in after the Company came in—lost his Haversack.

The Company worked like heroes, and one man who was round with Gillmore & Butler said "it beat anything on Morris Island."[67] Saw a few Reb. prisoners coming in belonging to Beauregard's *corps de armee*.[68]

Near General Smith's & Neill's Head Quarters (18th & 2nd Division, 6th Corps).[69]

June 5th, 1864. Sunday, 9:45 a.m.

About 6 p.m. yesterday, D packed up, moved out to this place; at 10:30 p.m. went out and threw up rifle-pit; first tracing it by covering ourselves, then completing it more perfectly; broke off, coming back to Stacks about 2 a.m. to-day. We were in a very exposed position, but a short distance from Reb. lines, a little firing occurred when all was quiet. It is an interesting sight to see how the troops on the extreme live, every Shelter in rear having its barricade against Minnie [Ball] and Shell, every one having his hole. I fell into a dozen of them, both vacant and occupied; in the latter case receiving a delightful Saxon blessing. We are now (10 a.m.) by Smith's Head Quarters and will probably go out again to-night. We were just now rather forced to leave our present position by Neill's Head Quarters as the enemy's Battery made it unpleasant for us; a man was mortally wounded in a passing Regiment near us (*Storms,* 10th New York Heavy Artillery[70]). *Shib* and myself have tented down behind a big pine. Made a bit of a sketch of it for future use.

Near Smith's Head Quarters.

June 6, 1864. Monday, 7 a.m.

Remained in Company camp, clearing away a space for stacks, &c., so have a cosy place.(!) Details were out last night superintending work; I was on Guard; had a pleasant night. I enjoy bivouacking there. The enemy made an attack at dusk, were repulsed.

Near General Smith's Head Quarters.

June 7, 1864. Tuesday, 6:30 a.m.

Pleasant. Out Topoging yesterday, lost hat—saw Herbert Bennett;[71] went down to camp; shelled last evening and this morning about 3 a.m.; it is a little tedious.

Near Smith's Camp.

June 8, 1864. Wednesday.

Pleasant, warm. Surveyed 6th Corps Front *yesterday,* risky work, had Graham & Hayes with me;[72] shot at a Rebel Battle-Flag twice, came nigh it; saw a Flag of Truce operating, interesting. All the Companies came to General Head Quarters Camp. I am tired, sometime I will write the many incidents of the preceding days out. I was on detached duty to Survey. Captain Farquhar asked me my name, perhaps he would like to get my services;[73] anyway it is pleasant to even receive a hint that my services are anywise appreciated. Dug a cover last night. *Conversation.* Where does John stop?[74] *Answer.* In the farther hole!

At General Head Quarters, near Cold Harbor.

June 9, 1864. Thursday, 10 a.m.

Cloudy, warm. On Guard. Feel my creeping dodging work of the 7th in my legs. It seemed strange to be where there was no danger, a fire after dark last night occasioned uneasiness, and the sound of a cannon made me cringe involuntarily—can't help it. Sleep last night done me no good; was in all kinds of bad scrapes; feel tired and relaxed now.

Wood's Farm.

June 10, 1864. Friday, 7 p.m.

Pleasant; nice little breeze. Been engaged in the very agreable process of rejuvenation. Our late diet of pork for a few days is a little unsettling; and will continue; I hope we will have fresh beef and especially if we can cook it ourselves, take it right along, I had rather cook for myself, so had the rest. No news, as usual at the front, as far as I know. I hear less picket firing; understand the railroad is being *destroyed*—which is an odd way of keeping a base of supplies in order.[75] *I guess a great deal* but know nothing. Amused myself working up the "View on the Pamunkey," will make a neat picture.

The 7th while surveying I was bullet-bound in one rifle-pit, over whose crest I was obliged to go to get into another I wished, so I resigned my-self and found a good seat and watched affairs about me, and the birds interested me as much as anything, they commencing to sing in a wild and unnatural, yet gleeful way as the bullets embedded themselves in the trees or cut with a sharp spat the leaves near them; as though experienc-ing the same feeling as humans under fire, neither wanting to stand, lay down or move away, laughing in a queer way as the missiles flew passed; I remember when we skirmished at Guiney's bridge, a little dog who went with our Company and was ahead barking about the bushes, thinking a grand hunting scrape was on the go; Old Jeff used to chase the bullets at Fredericksburg, poor old veteran. One of our cannon fired every half hour last night. Have a good prospect of string-beans for breakfast, a chap and me "going snacks" on some; the lady—Mrs. Wood near by—refusing money because "she couldn't eat money," but took hard tack &c., in ex-change. I found a couple of cotton shawls hid in an old hollow stump, near Smith's Head Quarters. Guard.

View on the Pamunkey.
Thompson's sketch of
the Pamunkey River,
which he worked on at
the camp at Woods Farm
on June 10, 1864.

✠— While surveying the lines at Cold Harbor, under fire, I wrote my
name and Company etc., and put it in my pocket. I was out by myself
and it was close work.

At General Head Quarters, Wood's Farm.
June 11, 1864. Saturday, 7 p.m.
    Pleasant, cool to-night, heavy wind, clouds coming up. Remained in
camp; Details out on fortification. Worked on Sketch, much pleased with
my success. No news. Lincoln nominated for President, glad of it too. The
greatest drawback to our present camp-life is the want of something to
read; "anything to read?" is the question of all hours. Sergeant Turner
came to camp, a great cry of "Who lost the Hard Tack?" was raised (Look
at date, May 27th, 1864).

I am noticing that the heat does not trouble as two years ago here, but Sibleys are not Shelters.

NOTE. When we went from Cold Harbor to the James, we found on the same [some] old dead horses, all heading towards Richmond and with the old stench still lingering like the perfume around a crushed rose!

Charles City Court House.
June 13, 1864. Monday, 9 p.m.

Pleasant. Moved from camp yesterday, passed an old corner of two years ago, crossed railroad, encamped on Moodie's Farm, 15 miles from Malvern Hill. *To-day*, marched at daylight, crossing Chickahominy at Provence Ford (Forge Bridge),[76] having a good rest at Providence Mill.[77] If I'm not mistaken, I can see where we encamped on the "Seven Days";* no firing &c., all quiet so far. The Court House and jail are left, the rest are burned close by. Four miles from Malvern Hill I hear. Writing this by fire.

* Mistake, we were then at Charles City Cross Roads.

Near Fort Powhatan Landing, James River, Weyanoke Landing.
June 15, 1864. Wednesday, 6:30 a.m.

Pleasant morning. Moved from Charles City Court House about noon, arriving middle of afternoon (14th instant). Oh! how fine it was to see ships and steamboats and the old river again. I was a new man again. We are near residence of *Tracy*, a fine place, I ate a modicum of mulberries, &c. After arriving we went down and commenced building Ponton Bridge across river;[78] finished about 11 p.m., we remained there awhile then came up to camp, to be turned out again just when nicely asleep, from a ferry boat running into the bridge, dragging anchors, &c. We "About faced" when on the bridge and came back across &c. Understand there are 98 Boats in Bridge,* with a trestle work some 150' long also. 1960' X 150 = 2010'.[79]

* 100 Boats. I was told 102–4 by 50th men on Guard. 101 says Mendell's Report.[80]

The great event was when the *John A. Warren* came steaming up along and a stentorian voice roared out, "Halloa there! Send a Ponton boat to take General Benham ashore!" Had a Punch & Judy been suddenly revealed, a general laugh could not have been quicker started; soon he came along pleased and fat, with "Hard at it, boys," and the old laugh—a fine little comical sketch could be made of the effect the news produced

Brigadier General John G. Barnard. In the spring of 1864, Barnard was the chief engineer on Ulysses S. Grant's staff; two years previously, he had served as the chief engineer of the Army of the Potomac during the Peninsula Campaign. LC-DIG-cwpb-05400, Prints and Photographs Division, Library of Congress, Washington, DC.

among the semi-amphibious crowd on the other side when some of us crossed over and gave them the news "*Old Benham's come.*" In a bow of a Ponton Boat I saw Duane & Weitzel [and] Grant's son, sitting together,[81] and saw Barnard, Duane, Benham, Weitzel, Mendell in a knot together, quite a galaxy of Engineer talent.[82]

Troops were crossing to the other side by boats yesterday, and Ambulances, Artillery, &c., are crossing on Ponton Bridge at present, the *James is bridged!* Saw the old *Metamora* steamboat, and also the captured rebel ram *Atlanta.*[83] This is indeed a change of base—forced I suppose the carpers will say.

A darkey (slave about here) says the people liked McClellan, he protected their property, &c., but they don't like Grant! quite significant; velvet gloves are laid aside now. This is indeed an interesting movement.

2d Division, 2d Corps Hospital, Towards Petersburg, Va.
June 17th, 1864. Friday, 9 a.m.

Hot. *Yesterday*, marched at 8 a.m., passing Prince George Court House; it was very hot, and I was never so used up as when we arrived here (at Bryant's house), about three miles from Petersburg. I judge our lines to be towards two miles ahead. I saw prisoners (Beauregard's).

The country is more rolling than the Peninsula, long ridges, quite good farms, and many real fine residences. I have noticed corn is principally planted, and some wheat corn, a foot and a half high is usual. All the citizens have left.

Blake made up lay out and all; it was as much as I could do to drink a cup of tea,* sent in a letter from home. I feel decent this morning, only my old yesterday's fatigue hangs on; I hope we remain in camp all day, so I can recuperate. A hospital is made of the house near us; there was heavy firing in our front last night and this morning, while in the distance we can hear the gun boats occasionally. Saw Marshall, looking well.[84] This is the Anniversary of [the] Georgetown spree![85]

—✈— * My mother sent me a little tea in a letter once in awhile for me to use, as we could not get tea except [when] we were sick, and from the hospital stewards.

Remarks (1887). There are some who state that the Wilderness campaign was simply a problem in "hammering," [but] others, notably General A. A. Humphreys, show that it started out with a settled plan, and evidenced (to me) particularly by the construction of ponton boats, etc., for the passage of the James River.

It seems to me that it began the right way to fight the rebel forces down, and with the advantage of numbers at a later date to then resort to a course of worrisome strategy as wearing as killing. That Grant invested Petersburg simply to stretch the enemy's line so to assist Sherman is not satisfactory to me. General Sherman, if he lives long enough will finally believe that his army was necessary to the salvation of the Army of the Potomac.

The miscarriage of the capture of Petersburg in June 1864 is to me still a marvel. If Grant had held Lee at Cold Harbor to capture Petersburg, it would have been better than investing it to assist Sherman. Lee had to face the Army of the Potomac *wherever it went or was*; the second period when strategy could be included in the movements had now arrived; the battle of Cold Harbor was the turning point of the whole campaign and as such is overlooked it seems to me, and after which and inclusive, we should judge the movements in front of Richmond by other principles than the simple one of fighting anyway and anyhow, and which was undoubtedly a correct one up to the Battle of Cold Harbor.

Engaged on Fortification

The Siege of Petersburg, June–December 1864

At Petersburg the duties of the Battalion were of a most extended character. From the moment our army appeared before the town to the evacuation every officer and man was engaged upon the defenses superintending the construction and doing the finer work—the front being more especially favored by them. In addition to the small mine at Fort Steadman, several shafts were dug at Fort Sedgwick,[1] familiarly known as Fort Hell. The shafts were sunk in the outer ditch and were connected with each other and extended to the front.

At 1st Hatchers Run the Battalion held a portion of our lines near the Peebles House.[2] At the 2d Hatchers Run it was sent by Gen. Humphreys to the support of Gen. Miles and placed in line on his right.[3]

It was at all times held in readiness to act as infantry and in every case of emergency was used to strengthen some weak point of the long line held by the army, and "ever evinced that ready spirit for duty in this new sphere that characterized it in its own." The construction, repair and strengthening of our line from the Appomattox to Hatchers Run were under its immediate care.

—LIEUT. TURTLE'S ESSAY

Near Dunn's, *before Petersburg*, in Rebel line of works, Captured by Jordan's.[4]
June 18, 1864. Saturday, evening.

Hot. On Guard. Moved from former camp about [a] mile ahead.

It was a sad spectacle near Hospital yesterday; the uncomplaining wounded; the operations, I looked at a doctor administer the chloroform, but when another began to cut and probe into the flesh, I turned away.

Heavy firing at dusk; I am very anxious about capturing Petersburg.[5] As I lay there with the sentinels pacing near, and the moon shining down, strange fancies would come into my mind; a man comes over from the Hospital [and] wants to know where "Corporal K—— Company C stops, a friend of his is dying." Another wounded man shrieks out once and awhile; a prisoner walking post as punishment tells that "the 2d Corps made another grand charge, driving the Rebs. to h——l and gone," that's the very history to me first-hand;[6] it being chilly towards morning I started a fire at the Guard bivouac, and pretty soon a half-froze wounded man comes over to it, almost hump-backed from a wound in the shoulder, "it was only a scratch, a little worse than he thought," and he cringes a bit with pain and cold; he goes away; I look around and a short stout figure in Zouave uniform has come to the fire, was shot though the mouth, [the bullet] just coming out [in] front of the right ——, commences to tell me, the words coming through the clotted blood in his mouth, how "he laid there until he was cold, and thought he came to ——." I interrupt him by my "All Right; make yourself comfortable," he nods his thanks, and warms himself before my blazing rails. Morning comes and I just take a look at the burying-ground—in the apple-orchard near the house, and only a large pit where those whose souls have passed away during these quiet, mellow moonlight hours are to be laid side by side; one lays close beside, only waiting for the diggers to finish the pit; a man comes from the door-yard and says "There is one more, that we hadn't found," a burly Irishman tosses up a shovel-full of dirt and says "bring him along, I guess we can find room for him;" the size of the pit, some over six feet wide and four feet deep and ten feet long evidently depending on the number found dead in the morning. A little board, at the head, has the name, &c., of the one beneath, written in pencil, sometimes fanciful, and more often plain and rude, with here and there an "*Unknown*." Honor them, cherish their memory, good ones at home! angels remember their graves! for so suffer and pass away those who in the din and smoke of battle seal their fealty to that glorious Flag, the emblem of the highest civilization of the world.

I understand affairs have progressed favorably to-day; we were here in advance of Lee's forces, carrying a line of works near us of great strength.

June 19, 1864. Sunday, Tattoo, 9 p.m.

Warm. Surveying captured Rebel works to-day with Foss & Graham; if they (the works) had been properly manned we never could have taken [them], we only "flanked" them![7] No *great* movements, great cheering at dusk. Been making up for my day's fast—1 Kettle of Coffee; 1 pan [of] fried crackers; 2 daintily fried hard tack; 1 pan (*small*) of fried apples and hard tack to go with and innumerable tit-bits. Total in the raw, 7 hard tack; &c.; no matter about the Total, I'm full and satisfied, with an appetite left to eat numberless pans *full* of sumptuous preparations yet. Oh! that I could only have had this yearning and decided predilection for food at Brandy! Oh! I saw the spires of Petersburg and houses; they (the rebs.) are now in their stronghold; so are my brans (I guess) in my strong hol-d, by the way I feel.[8]

June 20, 1864. Monday, Tattoo.

Surveying; foggy in morning; nights are quite cool; warm during day; some attacks were made last night—feelers; the men are arranging bough shades; raised banks &c. Hat came with a nice letter too; another school-girl married—*M*——, another killed in battle—Eli Ball—just got his commission.[9]

Fried hard tack for supper, eaten out of the pan, on the same principle that whortleberries taste best right from the bush, water fresh from the spring—that "half-perceivable, delicate flavor" otherwise would be unfor-tunately lost, anyway 'twas *harder*! Had *bean-soup* for dinner—eaten at the front—Graham bringing ours out—cooked by our enterprising ration-is-suer—Pitcher—in a vast cauldron confiscated at a house up near here. A wealthy one here.

Near Dunn's, before Petersburg, Va.
June 21, 1864. Tuesday, 9 p.m.

Warm; very foggy mornings. Surveyed; to about 600 yds. of Appomattox River, about size of Rapidan. Some artillery dueling near us—quite near at times! *Taps.*

General Head Quarters, near Jones House.[10]
June 23, 1864. Thursday, 8 p.m.

Hot. Have been wrong on the week-days since the 15th, one day ahead;[11] however, I am on my *fifth* month.

Finished Survey of Rebel Works yesterday by ending up in our Batteries across old rifle-pit in full operation; couldn't get two on right, sharp-shooters the reason. When I got to Head Quarters, they were "up on end" and off, from some partially successful attack of the enemy—Head

Quarters were packed up, and on the road in 15 minutes—quick work indeed. Some apprehension must have been felt, as I was surprised by Artillery poking their black muzzles through the bushes almost in our faces; There was rough work all night. I reported to Captain Michler with Survey Notes, had to hunt him up, "Head Quarters in Saddle";[12] hear that our forces hold one of the southern Railroads;[13] rumor has it Hunter &c. have captured Richmond, which really is not improbable under present circumstances;[14] Anyway it seems to me, if we remain on the left—*progressive* and defensive, Lee must come out and fight *us*; he will soon have—if not now—a Petersburg investment to break, as he once had a Richmond. The defensive works are admirably arranged that I have surveyed—22 Batteries in all, mounting in total—120 Guns—although they are not built for actual service, as our Artillery men would, digging their beautiful slopes and well-proportioned faces into horrid looking merlons and embrasures; all originally being arranged for barbette-guns, scarcely three feet cover for Artillerymen and the rifle-pits hardly better, the interior slope being in most cases natural. In fact, our Batteries in the open-field actually shelled the enemy's batteries completely out; These extend from the Appomattox on the north around the "*Cockade*" city, in all 29 Batteries, I handily surveyed 22 as *they* numbered them and *two* commanding City Point Railroad, and have positioned three, leaving *only* two that I have not seen.[15] A large detail was out building batteries Last evening; came in at daylight.

I am to report too-morrow morning to Captain Michler again, I may have to plot my notes at the Topographical Office at Head Quarters. I won't like that in every respect—I shall feel out of place; what will be, will be. Surveying is extra duty entirely as arranged; Capt. M.—— asked me "if I had a horse?" Good Gracious! Told me at first to remain at the house where Head Quarters were (Jones House) and the Staff had moved, and I *had a horse*, my humble self might have been seen on some unfortunate Rocinante, for the time being a member of Meade's Staff—attached![16] Ahem!

Very heavy cannonading as well as musketry has just opened up on the right; I consider the present position one that may flare up into a hot seething flame at any moment.

Those works were mostly built by colored "free-people" and slaves furnished by planters. I talked with an old colored man who was of decided opinion on some points, though some sixty years old.

Major Nathaniel
Michler, Corps
of Engineers.
Michler served with
the Army of the
Potomac from the
summer of 1863
until the end of
the war overseeing
its Topographical
Department, in
which Thompson
occasionally
worked.

General Head Quarters, near Jones House.
June 25, 1864. Saturday, 8:30 p.m.

Very hot and dry. Water is scarce, mostly procured by sinking holes in
low spots, and is of poor quality, with a bluish tint. The air is full of dust
and smoke. I saw one night a hundred yards away from the road you could
not see ten feet. I feel rather tired to-night, working on my Survey; I would
like such work but it is hard to do one's own cooking, &c., and that beside.
To-day I quit at six, came *home* (!) cooked supper, ate it, then went half
a mile for water—waiting until the box filled—and have just got down
to scribble these hard forced notes. When I came back along, I passed
a horse, he sniffed at the water in my canteen, and I suppose the poor
brute thought, if thinking, "he can go and get it, I must be taken." I would
have loved to have given him all I had, but I stifled down the benevolent
thought, as we have to a great many good feelings to get along in this

world; so I wish young good steed, some day, a full dear stream to drink from, and broad pastures to graze in, all smiling under the genial and loving sun of peaceful days; yes, and I would delight to live again in such scenes, as well; but pony, we must do our duty now, and hope.

One horse ambled into a well for thirst.

It is difficult to even have "a good wash," as I hear the inquiry, "Bill, where did you wash?" "Oh! I found a little *damp dirt* up here a little ways!" I hear no news, nor even camp rumors.

Jones House, before Petersburg, Va.
June 26, 1864. Sunday.

Worked at Head Quarters, very warm, 106° in the tent where we worked; it does not seem to affect me much. A *shadow* of a shower at dusk.

Jones House, before Petersburg, Va.
June 28th, 1864. Tuesday.

Cool, even chilly, from previous hot days. In Topographical Office yesterday, but a shower—light—last evening. And when I came from the Office to camp, it was a novel sensation to have water dropping upon you, with surprise and delight, akin to a savage on seeing a looking-glass, I held up my hands catching the drops, startled by their coolness on my face, that which is so prized, the air is full; it was like the West Indian on first beholding ice; a perfect anomaly to him, so rain had become almost to be to us.

Jones House.
June 29, 1864. Wednesday, 6 a.m.

Very chilly last night, even a fire being a comfort. What weather; broiled and chilled. Felt tired last evening, but cool weather is better for work. The most noticeable features about the camp are the bough shades and bunks, and war discussions up and down the Company Parade, the principal subjects being Grant, Lincoln, occasionally "Mac," and the Rebellion; and there are some men I wish were in the gray, and they might be happy; I despise such carpers. If Lincoln was as much of a tyrant as Jeff. [Davis], if copperheads were driven to the caves and swamps as loyal men of the South [are], we might boast of a united North; a quiet people under a despot's rule does not always indicate unitedness.

When Theilkuhl, *Topog.*, was out yesterday to the front surveying, he was much surprised by a rebel picket asking him "which way West was?"[17] He was lying down in the shade of some bushes, T—— told him, and went on. The reason of it all being that the pickets of both sides had agreed not to fire, a very sensible decision. After the flag of truce was over at Cold Harbor, it was "well, I suppose we must go to firing at each other," but there was none however.

Jones House.
July 3, 1864. Sunday, morning.

A pleasant breeze blowing; but the sun is hot when unmitigated. At work at Topographical Office on Survey—a long job. Two years ago at Harrison's, so it goes. Picket firing quite-brisk during night, more so than in the day time—not so risky I suppose.

Evening. Too-morrow is the glorious Fourth; I wonder what kind of a celebration the Army of the Potomac [will have]; there is a feeling among the men as though there would be a thundering noise—we'll see. I worked in the forenoon, wasted this afternoon.

Just as I was eating my supper of coffee and hard-tack off a cracker-box, the former with a little touch of luxury about it by the addition of some condensed milk, the sun had set and the air was full of a golden atmosphere, Blake was walking up and down [in] front of me, thinking this Sunday evening of his little ones at home, when I heard away in the distance a band playing "Old Hundred," and it sounded as though men were singing with the instruments. I don't know exactly why, but my thoughts were turned to the Sunday evenings at home, my ear lost the sound of the guns by Burnside, hearing instead the devotional hymn of the conference meeting while through the windows of the church came the fragrant breeze laden with gathered perfume from the flower-gardens, and down the street I heard the laughing of girls and children, and the cajoling of the happy mother to her child; so the strains of that band kept me thinking of home, and the tears to almost moisten my eyelids. Band music is the only ameliorating feature of soldier life and their inspiration can never be thoroughly appreciated until heard under the circumstances of active-service; Adam was driven out of Paradise, but Music came with him, and has almost made another Eden of this thorny and stormy world after all.

Issued rations to-night, and there are many features about it of interest.

After issuing, bartering commences, and "who wants coffee for sugar?" "coffee for pork?" "hard tack for your pickles," and at a certain interesting time in our hygienical sanitary experiences, a chap startled the whole Company, by halloaing at the top of his voice, "Who wants to swap beef for anguintum?!"[18] The scarcity of an article determines its value; hard bread being the basis of our operations in trade, as gold [is] in the financial world outside, only this difference, gold is a minor matter beside hard bread, some quoting away above par then worthless as a Confederacy shin-plaster; a ration of pickle to-night—about an inch long—brought three hard tack—a three-days' ration of coffee, twelve [hard tack]—pork @ five, and so on.

Tattoo has just beat. A great number of bands are about here in full blast, and from what I hear—if true—operations Before Petersburg will be of more interest than "All quiet—usual picket-firing." I prophesy that too-morrow a great artillery-battle; sutlers are packing up, trains drawing out, and artillery just covering the fields back of Burnside.

Before Petersburg, Va.
July 5, 1864. Tuesday, Tattoo.

Quite pleasant evening. No rain yet, all dust. Finished Survey Plans, put my name upon them, Captain Mendell wished me to do so. I felt a little proud of them, I must confess. Go for Company duty too-morrow *of course!* The 4th passed away in a very quiet manner. All so-so. Indulged in some lemons and sugar-cakes for supper, took a lunch with the Topogs at Head Quarters for dinner. Soft bread, roast beef (cold), tea, butter, pickles—a lunch! I call three fried hard tack and coffee—a supper! Blake on Guard. Stirring Rumor about camp to give us nightmares—*Ewell going up the Valley*!!![19]

Before Petersburg, Va.
July 7, 1864. Thursday, 5 p.m.

Yesterday engaged on Fortification [in] front of ——— Corps on ——— Road.[20] And was detailed to superintend work upon it during a portion of the night, which I am to do with 5 others until it is completed; remain in camp daytimes; just after I had eaten breakfast, Foss came down for me to go out Surveying (Howell's order!)—I thought I wouldn't go! Sweltered and drowsed during [the day], and wrote a part of a letter to mother. We have had a rare treat—two days' soft bread!* and I indulged in 50 cents worth of butter in consequence. Flies are becoming somewhat numerous and very familiar; I had to transfer the sugar from bag to coffee with all the *finesse* of a young one abstracting the "too much" at supper-table beneath the sharp eyes of a hygienically inclined mother; my butter was a "valley of death."

　　* and "one lemon for two" from the Sanitary!!!!!!!!!![21]

Before Petersburg, Va.

July 9, 1864. Saturday, sunset.

　　Warm, but not extremely oppressive. Yesterday, worked on work, same place; did not get in—by some tom-foolery—until late, and we were fearfully cross—may the angels be charitable and turn their heads the other way. Replotted Survey at Topog. Office; Working there I don't think is good for my *morale*, as I see the difference between an officer, civilian and soldier. Saw some men who live near Milford, and remembered seeing me somewhere; I wasn't aware I was so noticeable as to be seen at home and remembered. It was pleasant indeed; they are going home soon—time out.

　　There is indeed quite a raid into Maryland, the train bridge at Harpers Ferry burned again;[22] but if they can't drive them out at home, I hope they will burn and let them know what war is, without the Army of the Potomac driving them back every year; as Hosmer oddly expresses it, "if they can't drive them back, let their hens get stole!"

　　Declaration. This Rebellion must be put down, if it takes every blamed hen on the farm.

　　　　G. Thompson,

　　　　　　Corporal, U.S. Engineers Troops.

　　　　　　Before Petersburg, Va.

Jones House, before Petersburg, Va.

July 11, 1864. Monday, morning.

　　Yesterday finished plotting about noon; thereby had the afternoon to myself, which I improved by a wash and rest, the first chance I've had since June 19th. The "boys" have dug a quite good well, which makes it much better. I added to our establishment a table, from the debris left by the Battery, which left.

("Waiter, fried hard bread for two, and mind—have 'em well soaked and done brown.") "Put him in a canteen!"

Before Petersburg, Va.
July 14, 1864. Thursday
Hot the last few days. The 11th in afternoon profiled a new work (*Fort Bross*) 200 by 200,[23] under Captain Harwood, our new (Company)

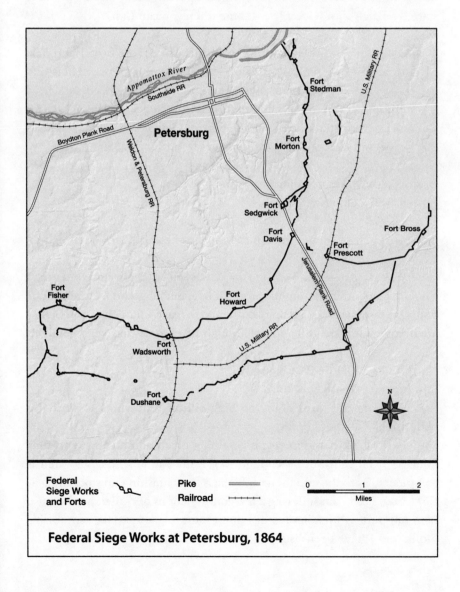

Federal Siege Works at Petersburg, 1864

Commanding Officer.[24] 12th, completed profiling, our detail leaving camp in marching order, joining Battalion at night at General Head Quarters, near old camp of June 17th &c., I judge. *This* morning just completed a twenty-four hour tour of duty on some work;[25] am rather tired; but expect twenty-four hours of rest as well. Had negro soldier details, and they work nobly. We Engineers are in full run of business now. We are camped among the pines; it continues dusty as ever, a foot deep only; "Oh! what dirty children!" When we were leaving camp the 12th, one of the boys started a laugh with "Good Bye—come when you can (kin)."

⊁— I built the rifle-pit connecting this work [Fort Bross] and Fort Howard in one night—I had over 1,000 negro troops.[26] Their officers were excellent men, intelligent and old experienced soldiers. I suppose they were the same that made the attack on the mine, a *fiasco* I never could understand.[27] (One of the colored soldiers—Adam Reed—was the cook of one of my survey parties in 1886.[28])

Norton's Run,* before Petersburg, Va.
July 16, 1864. Saturday, 9 p.m.

⊁— * Left of Dunn's, near Burchartt's, at head of Blackwater Swamp.

Very pleasant to-night. I am on Guard; was out last night superintending rifle-pit. Slept after coming in camp. Of late, details go on for twenty-four hours on distant works. I have had no time to learn what other Companies are doing even. I am well as usual; though I feel somewhat weary to-night.

Norton's Run, before Petersburg, Va.
July 19, 1864. Tuesday, noon.
Raining! and we [are] doing nothing either, a nice time to write if a body felt like it—but I don't.
I feel really tired and sleepy; it is raining nicely and about twenty-four hours of such rain will be enough too; I am a little suspicious when it commences as to the end thereof. Blake is away finishing up stockading at *Fort (Bross)*, and I am suffering a few compunctions of conscience because I am not putting up a bunk, but I don't want to get wet. Jake sent for his Violin and I have been listening to him and Fritz play over some of the

Brandy Station airs, quite pleasant, although this went a little stiffly and no wonder, I have a pair of paws like a fore- and after. The cooks are getting up a dinner. *Au Revoir.*

Norton's Run, before Petersburg, Va.
July 22, 1864. Friday, morning.

Cool and pleasant after late rain. Wrote letter just to mother, probably go out to-night. Yesterday was on a job just to keep us out of camp I judge, and I could but laugh and do now when I think of how Jake got off a saw while at work; he was standing on the parapet of the covered way, fussing and patting with his shovel (making a neat job);[29] he had selected with great care a spot where the umbrageous foliage of a solemn pine threw its shadow, his hat was off, revealing a head with the hair cropped short, a face bronzed, with [a] humorous twinkle in his eye, he stands silent for a moment in deep meditation, grasping his shovel *a la* Metamora and then he spake, in a slow measured way, "During the one hundred and sixty-five days of the siege of Petersburg, the Engineers toiled day and night!"[30] It was exquisitely humorous to me knowing we were then only working to kill time, and to present a big roll of fatigue duty.

I forgot almost—four months more to-day.

Norton's Run, before Petersburg, Va.
July 24, 1864. Sunday, morning.

Cool and pleasant. Yesterday worked on Fort Hell (Sedgwick) (near Chimneys), rather tedious day from 4 a.m. to 11 p.m. for me—a long day.[31] Reckon I will have to-day to myself. Where I work, the pickets are on terms of "Peace," they say, within easy talking distance, and the more I saw of the amicable arrangement the less I could believe my eyes. There is a spring between the lines both parties get water from, and one chap capped the climax by letting me know they cooked in one place on the same fire! (?) We worked quite open, but were not troubled, they fired a few shots at a band, whom kept on however, in spite of their attentive missives. One of our pickets had an accordion and while playing the rebel pickets gathered in quite a knot listening to him. They were busy as bees repairing and making additions to their works, in plain view in knots on the parapets. From what I learn there is really almost a general desire to come into our lines, and they are losing more by desertion than we could kill or wound of them by picket-firing, and with no risk to ourselves, as seldom [as] one of our men deserts. Another story is of one of our men taking a basket of "Sanitary Stuff," and being assured of being protected, called out going over into their rifle-pit, "all hands" feasting on the viands, and after a pleasant chat he returned loaded with tobacco, and whatever they could give him. Another time one of our men having received rations, &c., called over to John what he was to have for supper, potatoes, onions, fresh bread &c. John didn't believe it; Blue back says, "Come over and see then for yourself," and after dark, John came over and "had tea," Blue Back officiating, Johnny returning to tell his comrades of what the "Yanks" had to eat; and if ever we get them started there will be a tremendous struggle among them to fall into our hands. There is a little stunted tree between the lines, a kind of Peace Tree, where they meet in friendly conclave. Their lines goes through a corn-field, which if all is as usual, in time will hide the contending armies by its growth, and its edge is the neutrality line, rye being planted next to it. A Volunteer was telling how, when they first made this "Treaty of Peace," it was to stop firing until after breakfast; well about half an hour after both had finished breakfast, our boys called over, "Halloa! Johny, shall we commence firing?" "No, we won't fire any more!" the pleasure of enjoying a quiet meal being a very pleasant precedent of all day's work.

A rebel brigade was on picket at this place, and one of their captains commanding pickets made arrangements for all of them to come over, if we would not regard them as prisoners and be allowed to take the oath of allegiance and if we agreed three rockets was to be the signal on both sides; the rockets were thrown, but that brigade was relieved about an hour before the time appointed, and men of the relieving [unit] bragged of relieving the other brigade to prevent their "coming over!" A captain of Artillery in one of their works came over, spiking the guns of his Battery before leaving and reported so to Head Quarters, and would stake his life that we could take the work without any trouble. I understand no shots were fired from that work the next day, but the captain's word or risk was not trusted; yet all these, even though they are soldiers' stories, are significant.

In front of Burnside's Corps, it is rattle all the while, on account of the negro troops.[32]

July 24, 1864.[33] Evening.

Cloudy and cool all day, raining now gently on the Shelter. Slept all day, and had I felt in the morning as fresh as I do now, I might have accomplished something, but it took a day's retirement from worldly matters to feel this refreshed.

An officer brought the word "Atlanta is taken, General McPherson was killed in the streets by a citizen." He recruited C Company and it seems like losing one of our own acquaintances.[34]

I have often observed that on the march, when everything seems to conspire to make it disagreable, fun is most predominant, perhaps not of the highest character, a whole Company oftentimes bursting out into a general roar at some apt repartee or mis-fortune or stumble; and I remember on some miserable jobs we have had, when wet, covered with mud, worn out, everybody cross and crabbed, and looking at each other saying nothing, someone would start a laugh with an infantile "I wa-n-t ter guh hum," and I never heard the name mother, father, sister or brother used in this connection, all having a veneration and holy respect for them akin to the memory of brave ones departed.

Still pattering down on the Shelter; all right.

Norton's Run, before Petersburg, Va.
July 25, 1864. Monday, evening.

Cleared away, raining all last night. Our tent, though pitched high, was in good trim and we had a good night's rest after all; rather cool however. Laid abed wrapped in my blanket, reading *Harper's* and altering blouse in addition.

July 26, 1864. Tuesday, Retreat.

Pleasant. Last night was out at work on Battery—done a large amount of reveting, a Brigade for a fatigue party.*[35] All quiet in our front, the Rebel Battery throwing a few shells as usual at the Band. To our right in the lowland could be seen like lightning-bugs of a summer's night, the picket-firing in front of Burnside, sounding not unlike a gang of carpenters laying floor.[36] Occasionally a rebel mortar shell would cut its fiery circle in the air then exploding with an immense burst of flame; their flight being very interesting, they rising to their extreme heights, then pausing a moment before commencing their downward flight, the report of a mortar being dull and heavy. About 3 a.m. a rebel bugler played Reveille opposite us— our Reveille, and he is a fine performer, and to hear him playing just as the gray of morning was seen was no small experience; there is no denying but the history of the rebel army under Lee will ever have a romantic and lasting interest; yet the Army of the Potomac has battled single-handedly with them, and I can't see but to be a "6th Corps man," &c., is as much as to be one of Longstreet's, "Stonewall" Jackson's, [or] Hill's men; in this connection it may be well to remember the exclamation of fiery Longstreet's Corps men at Gettysburg as they made that great charge, "what, the whole Army of the Potomac," and later when their raider's star fortune waned under the glory of the Cross at Fort Stevens.[37]

>+—   * Under Lieutenant Cuyler—a regular brigade, where old rebel lines came into main line.[38]

The 2d Corps is making another erratic movement.[39] I have slept all day, continually growing sleepier. It seems as though some heavier guns opened to-day, shook the bed! considerable firing all day. Seylandt tells me the rebels were at work on theirs so close you could almost see the buttons on their clothes;[40] this is a remarkable feature of this siege; and when a shell is fired by either party, all hands set up a hoot, which sounds oddly enough to be sure.

Norton's Run, before Petersburg, Va.
July 28, 1864. Thursday, evening.
    Warmer. Have slept the last few days during the day, calculating on an evening's work; but have decided not to do so to-day, and probably *shall* go out to-night, although our works are near completed, so we may have a little rest. [Company] A is back, they having been with Burnside (*under Lt. W. H. H. Benyaurd*[41]) since this commenced. A party is building a bough fence about this camp. Smith, our Sutler, was about yesterday so I presume the paymaster is coming—Oh! bird of happy omen.
    The 2d corps I understand reinforced Foster who was driven back, the reinforcement of the 2d turned the tables, however.[42]
    Had a musical evening last night, but it went rather hard—no wonder.
    I have done nothing to amount to anything these last few days, for

which I feel ashamed, yet after such a campaign, and our late heavy labor, so taxing to a person's vitality and *animus*, that a long time must suffice before the life and vigor of the early days of the campaign will return. And when a soldier has no duty, there is no idea on the earth to compare with him. This can be attributed mainly to no inspiring influences about him; good books, lively society, the many phases of trade which to a citizen are sources of recreation and amusement, a soldier is deprived of entirely; an active campaign leaves him exhausted, his nerves, lately strung to their utmost tension, are now utterly relaxed; and he has no disposition to more than make himself comfortable, and sleep away the remaining time; after awhile, when partially recuperated, comes the desire for something to do, and more than all, "something to read," yet there is nothing to do except the sameness of cleaning accoutrements, and good books are rare indeed, and he who was in a whirl of excitement awhile ago is now oppressed with an *ennui* such as fashionables know naught about, so much so, indeed, even an expedition of danger is welcomed with pleasure as a relief. And the severity of the late campaign may be judged, when with all our fatigue duty at night and day work, the army is actually resting. The wear of mind on a campaign is tremendous aside from physical exhaustion. Yet, while on the march any more than a day's rest is an injury rather than a benefit!

Before Petersburg, Va.
July 30, 1864. 6:45 a.m.
Warm. Certain orders round about last evening gave us suspicion that our batteries would open on the city this morning; an old soldier can smell a rat quite soon. The Battalion was routed up about 2 a.m. and except those who had just come in from fatigue and the Guard Detail—I am one of the latter—went out to the front. I rather regret remaining in camp, yet I could not really see much were I out—we'll see. At twenty minutes of five with a roar our batteries opened. I had lain down to sleep awhile, but that was now impossible; I went out to the edge of the woods, passing by the 9th Corps Hospital, everything neat and ready but no patients as yet; I could see but little, and heard no news at all. The most rapid firing seemed to be of the 5th Corps, and a gentle morning breeze was bringing the smoke of the cannons so as to hide almost what might have been seen; the ground fairly shook at times; and the reverberations of the reports surging like a mighty sea of sound among the pines had a grand

effect; when they opened, I believe a light cheer went from the front to City Point; all hands gave a hoot. The firing has now diminished in intensity seeming to be confined to heavy pieces. *Rumor* has it that the explosion of the mines was the signal, three acres* being blown up by one, and also that we charged and took their first line; I do think we hold a portion of their line, and if that be the case they will attempt to retake them if possible. Again our men are in the city. I guess I'll stroll over to the Hospital.[43]

✈— * 120 x 60 feet.[44]

7 o'clock p.m. Shortly after the above was written, artillery firing ceased its vehemence, and when I went up to the Hospital, I could hear the cheers and musketry of some charge sounding like "Wilderness days;" some wounded had come in, and some rebel wounded who were in the mine when it was blown, nearly all were asleep, and a regiment was buried beneath the rubbish, and I was told they inquired "if our men would dig them out?" The explosion of the mine was as though a mountain, and immediately our whole artillery opened while you could count three, and it is evident they did not recover themselves. The 5th did not charge.[45]

At this time disheartening rumors are about camp that our men this afternoon were forced back—Bartlett surrendered his brigade—I hope not, and I shouldn't wonder if the main facts are true.[46]

Again we try—again we fail
Again we fail to reach the goal,
And manly beauty, youth and pride,
Are dashed like paltry sea-weed by the tide
Against the ragged cliffs to be lost.
Still, dash aside the tear and aim again,
Choke the rising spasm and hope again.

Before Petersburg, Va.
August 2, 1864. Evening.

Hot. Since the late attack, all has been quiet along the lines, being quite noticeable, especially the artillery. I hear Butler achieved quite an advantage the same day.[47] Hope some mitigating circumstance will counteract what I deem a disaster. If a feint, it was a dear one; if a genuine attack, it was an unmitigated disaster; although I understand the rebels own they were badly cut up, and our men engaged say the same. The story is, that a rebel General and some of his Staff rode into the work just before it was blown up, and saddled horses were dug out of the ruins. Seylandt, my neighbor—who was "on pass" to-day among those Regiments engaged in the affair, says they could have taken the whole line this side of the river and could have been in Petersburg; and the men are enraged about it.[48] S—— says they "draw it out, and swear," and the soldiers are *generals*, all of them.* I can't understand it; somebody must have lost their nerve. Yet the Order to retire came from Meade, and he may have deemed it impossible to hold it against their second line, but he ought to have known that before. We will see. After the mine exploded, the rebs left the first line completely demoralized!

* Strategy has indeed changed, since M.—attacks the interior instead of salient angle!

I am amusing myself with arranging music today; something to do. Garrison Police duty helped a little. Our men are hygienically-living on "Sanitary stuff," leastways those who can forge Orders!

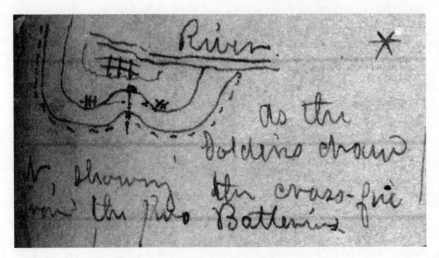

Battle of the Crater. A very rough map Thompson drew in his journal entry for August 2, 1864, to illustrate his understanding of the Battle of the Crater on July 30.

Before Petersburg, Va.

August 3, 1864. Evening

Warm. One of the above "Sanitary Stuff"ers came to grief to-day and now muses over his *crimes* in the Guard House like Dick Turpin in New Gate.[49]

I have had a secret opinion, the real reason of the late *fiasco* is that all our mines did not explode. (*No, there was only one, and it exploded.*)

August 5, 1864. Morning.

Warm; going to be hot. The night of the 3d was out at the [Eighteen] Gun Battery (*Fort Sedgwick*) near the Chimneys with six men "on picket" some fifteen feet under ground.[50] Discovered nothing; this going *gophering*, digging after "rebs." is fun! (?)[51]

A laughable incident occurred yesterday morning on the picket lines; which at this point are about 75 paces apart. A Johny anxious to barter came over and laid some tobacco on the fence to trade for bread, which is the neutral line, being on the Jerusalem Plank Road. Our picket run back to his haversack to get the bread, which time was employed by a worthy of the 50th, who took the tobacco and in lieu thereof put a rusty jack-knife—Johny looked glum at this over in his rifle-pit, and when the picket returned with the bread, he was also highly indignant at our friend, the 50th operation, and to prove his non-complicity with such a foul deed to his business acquaintance on the other side, forthwith puts the loaf of bread on the fence-post and returns! But Oh! what a disappointment was yet in store for John, for just as he [was] commencing to approach the bread, a couple of his officers appeared, and he was obliged to give up the attempt, devouring the bread with his eyes only, and after so doing awhile called out to some of his companions to come and look at the loaf of bread, and when we came away, there sat the loaf on the fence, meek chronicler of Trading between the lines, with half a dozen tall gaunt Johnies looking over at it with mouths watering, while our pickets looked on smiling at the sequel of the trade. The loaf of bread remained there until night when perhaps it answered for supper.

Before Petersburg, Va.

August 10, 1864. Morning.

Pleasant this morning, in fact it is the only pleasant part of the day, on account of the "flies," which are quite numerous; I thank my "body and bones" they are not the McClellan fly of Harrison's [Landing], which bites, probing you in every available place. The torments of to-day are the common house-fly. Occasionally you will be startled by a miniature mine of a cartridge flashing up in some tent, or again set to sneezing by burning pepper to drive away the intruders, then perhaps some one exasperated with them pounds away at the villains with a sledge-stick, nearly destroying house and all in his frantic movements.

All so-so as far as I know, our men are putting up a Battery [in] front of Burnside in a very exposed place, and every party coming in has a hole to show in a hat, a dent in a shoe, "where a spent ball hit," &c. I am glad they have nothing worse to show.[52]

I have been Surveying Works again, and am now engaged in plotting up my notes. I am going to take my time; even slow as I am doing it, I am doing more duty than as though I were on Company duty; they have made some recent promotions among those who "had over six or eight months to serve," thus cutting us lesser men, so I am just staying here awhile, only remaining, and don't have quite the interest I did—three months and twelve days more to stop at this Hotel; Captain Mendell continually forgets himself and calls me "Sergeant," then correcting himself; $14 more a month for three [months] would not be bad, eh?

I must note down something funny which occurred one day when we were going from Culpeper to Rappahannock Station.[53] Captain Turnbull has just rather reprimanded the men for falling out, and ordered that all who wished to "fall out" must ask permission of him; now it was no pleasant undertaking, and to a sick or fatigued person almost impossible to get to him at the head of the Battalion to ask his permission, particularly when the Battalion was moving; the men privately said "d——n humbug" and toiled along; presently Wagon-Master Slagg went by and behind him ambled some stray mule, who all at once set out in a gallop for the head of the column; this could not be lost and some mother-wit bawled out "there goes that mule to ask Captain Turnbull's permission to fall out!" It pleased the Doctor and other officers.

Before Petersburg, Va.
August 10, 1864.[54] Evening.

A little more endurable to-day. Worked on Survey. On Guard at present. No news, only a swarm of rumors flying about camp. O!

A soldier says of a dying comrade "he's gone up;" at first hearing it seems rough and callous-hearted yet there is meaning and Poetry in "*Gone*

A Group of Us. Taken in the late summer of 1864 near Petersburg, this may be the
photograph mentioned by Thompson in his second August 10, 1864, journal entry.
Standing, L to R, are: George H. Brackett (Company D), George H. Kehoe (C),
William B. Lincoln (C), Zenas Stoddard (C), Orlando Jackson (D), Charles E. Mix
(C), John Eldridge (C), George H. Lovejoy (C), Charles W. Sweetland (C), Barnard
Carney (A), Melville C. Grant (C), Jacob H. Putnam (D), George Howland (C),
Alonzo G. Rice (B). Seated, L to R: Charles W. Garvin (B), Isaac C. Winchell (D),
Edwin H. "Ned" Coolidge (D), William Shibley (D), John Coughlin (D), Joseph H.
Rogers (C), Gilbert Thompson (D), Jacob D. Geyser (D), George H. Robbins (D),
Ebenezer B. Hosmer (D). On Ground, L to R: Wendell Phillips Putnam (C),
Abram W. Kimball (B), Robert Kelly (A), John H. Brown (B), Thomas W. Beddoe (C),
Jacob H. Mudgett (B).

Up"—a good title for a picture; a sailor under such circumstances says "Gone Under," not as touching, though truthful.

Have been bothered with a cold. A Group of us had a Photograph, very good, all considered. It is tedious life in camp in daytime, flies—heat—flies—flies—but thank the beauteous Night, then we can enjoy a sleep, the only sound being the locusts sounding their "long-roll" in the pines above—it seems like Autumn; indeed they are sounding her Reveille, and if all is well I may hear "Taps" in cool New England. I hope so.

Before Petersburg, Va.
August 14, 1864. Evening.

Quite pleasant on the whole to-day. I am on Sick Report—first since October 1862—with cold and headache, but better tonight. Yesterday, reorganized camp, changing tents; we changed *"front to rear,"* have a fine tent now. Misfortune never comes singly, Blake is sick! too!

Had orders to be in readiness to march this morning about 9 a.m. Hear Head Quarters are to move too-morrow at 6 a.m. Rebels evacuating our immediate front, going somewhere, &c., there has been fighting Butler's way, the 2d [Corps] perhaps being about. *Quién Sabe?* I think something is in the wind.

Jake brings me a *magnificent rumor*, the enemy made a feint upon our left, and we not regarding that as much attacked them on the right (*ours*), Butler capturing 3,000 prisoners, [and] 8 guns, this all on the 14th day of August, Year of our Lord 1864, and from Head Quarters, ye chronicler anxiously awaits the next reliable contraband. The 2d Corps embarked on transports, went about six miles down the river, then back again.[55] If so, this is my highest idea of strategy, acting as though the enemy know everything you were doing, humbugging spies of the army.

It is quite cool to-night, showers thundering all around.

Before Petersburg, Va.
August 15, 1864. Evening.

Quite a brisk shower last night, some sharp thunder; slept dry though "water was all around;" in consequence it is quite agreable to-day.

The heavens have not fallen, so I judge all is so-so; though I have noticed it is very quiet out to the front, no picket-firing at all, which is a little singular.

Another Group of Engineer Soldiers. This group photograph was not in Thompson's journal or memoir, but it was dated Petersburg in 1864, so it could also be the photograph he mentioned in his second August 10, 1864, entry. Thompson is the leftmost person seated on the ground, and right of him is John Brown (Company B). Seated in the middle row are Charles E. Mix (C) on the extreme left, George H. Kehoe (C) is to Mix's right, and Frederick "Fritz" Vogel (D) is the second seated man from the right. Jacob H. Mudgett (B), is the leftmost person standing. LC-DIG-cwpb-03680, Prints and Photographs Division, Library of Congress, Washington, DC.

Buel Chipman of Company A.

Strange I did not note the fact, but I am a Hundred Day Man from yesterday—99th to-day. Wrote to B. Chipman.[56]

My neighbor Seylandt has a fan arranged to work with his foot to drive away flies, which attracts considerable attention.

August 16, 1864. Sunset.

About 3 o'clock, we experienced a real Peninsula shower, literally pouring in sheets, accompanied by sharp lightning and heavy thunder. Magnificent heavy clouds to-day; out "Topoging" the Redoubt D Company built (*Fort Bross*).[57] Have had an early day and meant to, sir! I guess all the rumors came from the 9th Corps relieving the 5th—the 10th relieving the 9th, all moving by the "left flank." Therefore the 9th is all of the Army of the Potomac at the front. Rumor has it that Meade is going to take the whole Army of the Potomac somewhere else.[58] We'll see.

Before Petersburg, Va.

August 18, 1864. Thursday, 7 p.m.

Cool and cloudy. *Yesterday* worked on Survey, a light shower at sunset. About midnight the enemy opened with artillery, rousing us all effectually, and revealed a scene remarkable for its naturalness of &c.'s; our guns soon responded making a din equal (being at night) of the other affair; no damage was sustained as I learn; it continuing until day-break. It was a little singular to hear the familiar sound of picket-firing continuing the even tenor of its way amid it all; and by that we gauged the whole affair. A & B were out early on fatigue, and Kelly of A, was hit in the knee with a Minnie [ball], rendering amputation necessary.[59] He was a fine looking fellow; too bad indeed, but we have been lucky. C & D out to-night.

Employed myself *to-day* on Survey as usual. Am to do a little job for Major Michler. And on an errand connected with it, went on horseback—poor nag half teased to distraction with flies—to 9th Corps Head Quarters, at ——— house, a quite respectable and pretentious residence, even now giving evidence of being quite well furnished, it is surrounded by some fine box wood hedges, having an odd appearance; and although the *family* (!) had just "moved in" you would hardly realize you were at a Corps Head Quarters, no bustle, all so-so, the clicking of the telegraph on a little table in the Adjutant General's office, with the uniforms only reminded you of the fact.

For a *rara avis* I saw a kitten, and chased her into a little frolic after a straw, which took her fancy as much as though my tent was a cosy room, full of light and many children.[60] I could but be guessing what home her ancestor—who is an inhabitant of camp, I understand—makes even more pleasant by her attractive ways; and as her darlingest was tumbling round on my knapsack; I was thinking of how odd it seemed for her to be there, as much out of place as somewhere on the march, a lady's lap-dog was the only living creature left in that vicinity, and I could but pity the delicate little fellow, shivering in the unusual cold to him, and knowing, too, what a future lot was his.

Before Petersburg, Va.
August 20, 1864. 8 p.m.

Rainy, about 3 it poured. Am on Survey Work, can't work when it rains, so get along slow—I don't care! Warren the 18th moved to the left and took up without much opposition a point on the Weldon Railroad taking some prisoners. It must have been a little surprising to John who in dead earnest went to cannonading us to see if we had gone, then find us on their flank.[61]

Before Petersburg, Va.

August 23, 1864. 7 a.m.

Shower last evening, pleasant yesterday; cloudy and stormy like this morning. The 21st the rebels attacked Warren but were repulsed with very heavy loss indeed; I saw some prisoners at Head Quarters; they seemed somewhat downcast and mortified, and were talking among themselves about the affair. Yesterday morning (22d), the rebels had retired from Warren's front, and could not be found. The 5th Corps were bringing their dead left on the field (1,100). It appears a little singular to me that they should resign that railroad thus; a little significant I think.[62]

All is so-so. I am on Topog. work yet. Received letters from S. P. [Lillie] and mother, quite pleasant indeed. Understand Warren was attacked again at 1 last night, repulsed the attack, and also that the Cavalry has cut the Danville road, &c. (indeed!)[63]

Evening. All so-so this evening. Received my Photograph of Essayons Dramatic Club—much pleased with it.[64]

I notice now, all the soldiers build a bunk when they get in camp as much as they pitch their Shelters, and when a Corps relieves the other, the new-comers tear the late tenants' house to pieces, erecting a new house from the materials thus procured.

Looked over General Barnard's Report, he does not mention the Battalion in either praise or censure—very encouraging indeed![65]

Before Petersburg, Va.

August 26, 1864. Friday, 7 a.m.

A little warmer yesterday. Yesterday afternoon about 3:30 the Battalion went to strengthen the ———— by our former camp near Jones.[66] Went out without anything but guns and belts; had nothing to eat, had (raw) coffee sent to them, with not a cup in the whole command to cook it in! What confounded stupidity.

They returned this morning about 6:30, Grumpy and savage uns. Rumor has it the 2d Corps cut the Lynchburg road but were driven back. The rebs. attacked the 5th five times but were severely repulsed each time.[67] I consider this quite a piece of generalship to force the enemy to come out and fight you on your own ground. I am still at the Topographical Office working; perhaps it may be the intention to keep me there!

If I understand rightly we are a part of the Provisional Brigade, formed of the Head Quarters' Guards, 50th New York and ourselves, and are called out in emergencies, thus it was the Provisional Brigade that carried Guiney's Bridge, May 21st, 1864.

An expression I never heard before this campaign is "coffee-boilers," a class of sometimes shirks and skulkers who cook for the officers of their command, and also those who by any such artifice avoid "going to the front."

Before Petersburg, Va.
August 28, 1864. Sunday, morning.

All so-so, sharp picket-firing about 4 o'clock. A & B are away I think to Warren (A went 25th, B 26th). I continue on at the Topog. Office, may finish my time out there. Quién Sabe!

August 29, 1864. Monday.

Pleasant, though hot. Received a letter from mother to-night. Nothing to write about. I hear there is a railroad to be built along the line.[68] Also, of a huge mortar of the name of "Dictator" coming up on a railroad truck from City Point, which pitches a 232 pound shell into Petersburg.[69] All is so-so, binning away all the while, the weather seems cooler and more like Autumn and Rappahannock Station camp; the pleasant tramp of all my camping days.

On looking over an *Atlantic* to-day I was reminded of a day's march on the Peninsula enlivened by some stray leaves of that excellent magazine found along the road; which I read when bits of opportunities offered, as I was on train guard.

The sound of rifle and cannon seems now to be a part of the natural sounds of the air, as crickets, locusts and other pleasant insects.

>— "The Enlisted men of the Battalion have always done credit to themselves and to their Officers, by the earnestness, rapidity and thoroughness of their labor; and I take pleasure in stating my belief that no better body of Enlisted men can be found in any army."

"Report of Capt. George H. Mendell, Corps of Engineers, U.S. Army, commanding Engineer Battalion," 5 August 1864, in United States War Department, *The War of the Rebellion: A Compilation of the*

Official Records of the Union and Confederate Armies (Washington, DC: Government Printing Office, 1892), ser. 1, vol. 40, part 1, 300.

The Battalion never received its due credit.

I do not know, however, of but one occasion, when the Battalion had a complimentary order read on Parade, and that was not distinctive, as it was when we were brigaded with the Volunteer Engineers, and it was a Brigade Order.[70]

Among the Officers it seemed as though it would be doing like Volunteers; as when the Battalion led the Army of the Potomac at the last Review in Washington, they would not allow the men to take the flowers that the people threw to them! *So* I *heard.*

When the Battalion supported the Batteries at the battle of Antietam, they were told the night before that "the first man who run would be shot in his tracks." It was utterly unnecessary, but it made the men madder than could be imagined, and indignant as well. The officer who had the credit of it was reminded of it when Captain Cross, a brave man, was killed, that "*it was the best men who got shot.*"

The Officers were long in learning that there were a class of men in the ranks such as probably never again will be in the history of the Battalion, for it was a tremendous question at stake, which brought them there. And when their three years had expired, with a few exceptions they laid aside their uniform, and considered they had done their duty, and that was all there was of it. But few re-enlisted, and at the last Review, I venture to say, there were very few of the number who went in out of patriotic motives in 1861.[71]

Yet an old Company A man will say, in 1861 all the individuality and fine character of the Company went out!

I must growl once and awhile.

Before Petersburg, Va.

August 31, 1864. Wednesday, 6 a.m.

Seeming like Fall, cool last night. Very still out at the front indeed, no firing at all. My neighbor says there was a great exchanging of papers among the pickets; perhaps the *Chicago convention* is the why.[72] Fort Morgan taken—by the *Richmond Examiner.*[73] It must be a greater sport for them.

September 2, 1864. Friday, 7:30 a.m.

Cool nights; warm during day however. At Work at Topog. Office. The boys have a gymnastic swing arranged which affords considerable sport and recreation, rarely one gets a bump. My old "bunky" Coolidge is the best performer. D Company generally has one in every camp; I know of no other company doing the same yet. D Company is the only Company I would be in, if choice could get it for me.

Fort Morgan news confirmed; great fuss at the Chicago Convention about "*little* Mac"; if he is any kind of a man, he would deem a mention even from that Convention an insult; perhaps he won't. I think Lincoln will have the majority of votes, even in this army. Some respectable people at Head Quarters had a night of it, over his (Mac's) nomination.

Had a musical evening the 1st, went a little awkward with me; it seemed pleasant however. A gentleman (?) darky favored us with some fine jig dancing. I never saw one who could not dance. If music is not to be had, tapping on the knee with the hands serves the purpose. Negro songs are of a quaint character—natural music I suppose. Wrote to S. P. [Lillie] yesterday, owe a letter to mother. (Ink's out!)

Petersburg, Va.

September 5, 1864. Monday, 6:30 a.m.

Cloudy, just so yesterday morn, which day I slept through, washing a shirt for a variation; grand talk on politics and the situation in the evening. At 12 noon our batteries had a little fun to themselves, slinging shot &c. at obstinate rebs., a band caught the contagion and commenced playing patriotic airs. All this, I suppose to make up for the silence of Sunday. Would have given $50 for a nice letter last night—got none. Atlanta is taken.[74] All looks encouraging.

During the last few days, we (D) have enjoyed ourselves on a gymnastic swing, splendid exercise. John Brown went out a few days ago (3d).[75] It will be nothing but Good Bye—bunky goes in about 20 days.[76]

Before Petersburg, Va.

September 6, 1864. Tuesday, Retreat.

Rainy-like, but only succeeding in an unfortunate drizzle. *Yesterday* at noon D went away in marching order. B Company came in morning, giving one Hurrah as they entered camp. A is back also. It is very lonesome

John H. Brown of
Company B.

in camp—I being yet at work Topoging and occupy my neighbor's house
(Seylandt's) while he is away; there are none to call upon—nothing, only
to ruminate and ask each other how long we have to serve! In fact, the
next two months and a half seem longer than eighteen months did, and I
am not thinking about it as some, who count each day as its hours go by.
My good mother always writes me how many I have to serve, but I soon forget. But I cannot realize that the three years are so near gone, but they are
long, eventful years when I minutely look back upon them. I hope I get
through the rest of my time without injury as my time is so near out. But
I have been extremely lucky so far, both in regards to wounds and health.

I would be promoted to a Sergeant if my time was longer, and I had
reenlisted. I am glad of being so favorably thought of, but still it is not fair
to ignore a man his rightful promotion, even at this time (all *three* of us are
thus included).[77] We ought to have been made last Spring, but I shan't cry
at all, it was not my demerit at all. Harwood inspected Cummins's piece
last muster—who stands next to me—and passed me on by, saluting me;
he has a good opinion of me.

A new event is the railroad from the City Point Railroad round I expect to the Weldon Railroad. It is built as near as possible to the works, and ignores all the rules of engineering in its construction, not being leveled at all, following the curves of the ground, but cars go on it, and the strange sound of a cow whistle is heard now occasionally out in the pasture [in] front of Head Quarters as they peruse "their winding way."[78] That's enterprise. Hear the rebels are also building a railroad to the left of Warren, to avoid wagoning; and *therefore* we shall have to extend our left still more; or *take* the *whole* Weldon Railroad. I anticipate a heavy battle in that quarter yet. They cannot resign it so easily.

Before Petersburg, Va.
September 11, 1864.

Warm, quite a change for warmer weather has taken place since last date. At Topog. Office yet, Companies not back. Finished a bit of a sketch this morning; then with Clarke on a little walk up along the right.[79] Quite a change is noticeable, woods are cut away in a measure, less loafers about, all in the works. Clarke and I were the *only* ones to be seen "gawking about." All so-so.

McClellan *has* accepted a Platform of his own![80] big man!

September 19, 1864. Monday.

Pleasant. Since last date as usual in Topog. Office, all so-so. Cooper, who left last Fall, came to me yesterday, wanted me to take a Captaincy in his Company which he is to leave for a Majority.[81] Thanked him but did not want it; I don't think much of a field officer anyway. There are but few Commissions I would accept at all.

Companies all back; Stevens goes out too-morrow, so the foundations stones are beginning to move at last, I reckon the time of others instead of my own.[82] I am only waiting now—fifty-six days more. All so-so.

Before Petersburg, Va.
September 21, 1864. Evening.

Pleasant. 100 shotted guns fired this morning in honor of Sheridan's victory.[83] Berry of A, shot yesterday afternoon at the front, was buried to-night.[84]

September 25, 1864. Evening.

Pleasant though cool. Blake and others went away this morning.[85] I wanted to go with them. Were paid yesterday, $119. Heavy firing on the James all day; quite severe changes have been made in the position of troops.

Aikens House, near Globe Tavern.
October 6, 1864. Morning.

Warm. Katydids are here; I cannot realize it is October. Fly away quickly I want to see November. The 2d [Corps] moved here, I went with the Topographical party. We have had success at both ends of our line.[86] Bunk with Shibley, built a shanty yesterday.

Aikens House, near Globe Tavern, before Petersburg, Va.
October 8, 1864.

Pleasant, though windy and cool. Yesterday was quite warm. At work at Topog. Office as usual. The Companies alternate in working on Fortification on the Left;[87] a place unknown like "away down East." We are quite near a line of works, and our camp might be uncomfortable if a lively time should occur in front.

Keeping Journal is quite dull business, in fact as the preceding pages testify I have found it particularly so; and should I write, it would be like an Artilleryman's Diary some of our men found; it commenced

"*June* ——— *'64*. Moved up towards Petersburg. *fitin* (!) along the lines."

"*June* ——— '64—fitin along the lines."

"*June* ——— '64. Not all quiet along the lines, some *fitin* along the lines to-day."

And so on for *three months!* No wonder he lost it.

Our picket lines advanced, so I can note "some fitin along the lines today."

Near Globe Tavern, before Petersburg, Va.
October 10, 1864.

Cool, ice in pails, &c., frosty. In one place on the lines last night, there was lively picket-firing and a few artillery shots; it is a peculiar sound those cannon shots at night, something solemn, vindictive, and poetic about their sound; how it would seem in some quiet village to hear such at midnight. It always occasions strange feelings in me that I cannot express; somewhat like hearing music at night, the sound is generally deep and mellow, especially mortars, and reverberating for a long time.

Six weeks from to-night. Gracious! I can't believe it to be so.

Camp Woodbury, before Petersburg.

October 16, 1864. Sunday.

Pleasant; wrote to mother. My old bunky Cummins left this morning, a good fellow, a little dogmatical; he and I always got along finely but were hot-headed on McClellan.[88] Success to him. In about 6 days Rue goes, another bunky, then Coolidge, another; indeed, family bereavements are coming upon me.[89] Laid abed in afternoon. No news. I am still at Head Quarters at work. I may get the position after my time is out.[90] About 5 weeks more—37 days. I realize three years are nearly gone, but I cannot believe I am to go away; that my term of enlistment is so nearly out.

Companies are constantly at work. A Company having gone with bag and baggage up to the right, repairing works.

I find my circle of visiting places are limited. Ames in B, Rue here— that's all.

I haven't been in A Company, since Chipman left at Brandy Station; I know but few of the men now by name; "old hands" are scarce.

Camp Woodbury, Va.

October 17, 1864. Monday.

At Office. General Grant and others, whose names I shall learn in the papers, were at Head Quarters to-day. Admiral Porter also.[91] As usual all round; am well.

A beautiful day it has been; Shib on Guard. Someway I have nothing to write about, and a dozen pages will suffice me for the next two months at the rate I am going on. It is a little odd, that when I have the least time, I write the most in my Journal; on the march, it all comes from something to write about. Perhaps the reason may be plain to-night. Since Sunday morning I have written fourteen pages of letter-writing.

Camp Woodbury, Va.

October 21, 1864. Friday, evening.

Pleasant and Autumn like; rain yesterday. Rue went away this morning—the fine fellow—willing me his frying-pan.

Great cheering last evening over news of another victory by Sheridan, 40 pieces of Artillery captured from Longstreet;[92] also—to-night—a barrel of whiskey came!

I never saw the army in so good humor, full of *vim*, spirits and determination; let their extra feelings "bust" out in a spontaneous bout, then good three cheers for consequential affairs, which goes from here to the north-side of the James. What a line; at the Office I occasionally see a map of our front & rear lines and they resemble an arm reaching out for the Southside Railroad.[93]

Grant was at Head Quarters and with Meade went out to the front; a move may be along soon.

For recreation I endeavor to emulate Ned in his acrobatic feats; hanging by his toes &c., anyway I am growing strong in my arms, and am in excellent health.

Camp Woodbury, Aiken's House, near Weldon Railroad,
    before Petersburg, Va.
Home Month.
November 1, 1864. Tuesday.

A beautiful morning; cool, but clear. I have just finished a breakfast of coffee and fried bread, had a wash; and have so far spent the morning in a sort of glorification that to-day is the commencement of the "Go-home-month." It begins to seem soon like going home. I am feeling a quiet kind of gratification at the event; I should feel different were I with the Company as I have now no Roll-calls to answer, nor even Inspections to attend; I am only boarding here. Probably I have answered my last "Here." I am very glad that my declining days are passing so quietly away; 1st Sergeant Putnam is a man, and may he be blessed too.[94]

I still continue at Topog. work; during my enlistment, I shall have done about eight months' such work altogether.

The army since last date has made a reconnaissance to the Southside Railroad.[95] I was around, but can tell nothing, only it is a worse country than the Wilderness to move in.

First Sergeant Jacob H. Putnam,
Company D.

Built a fire-place yesterday, last evening set by the light ruminating all the time, like a house cat.

I never had so little to write about, all is *so-so* to a most extreme degree. Well, why would it be otherwise after such a summer's campaign? In the morning, all you hear before daybreak are the Reveilles breaking out, one after the other like birds; a little skirmishing up at Fort Hell (Sedgwick), then the sun rises about 9 [and] I go to work, &c.; at dark, bands commence to play, the picket-firing sounds out more distinct; at Tattoo, lie down, hear a brush going on somewhere along the lines, cannon chiming in too, then somebody goes to sleep.

Camp Woodbury, Va.
November 4, 1864. Morning.

Stormy last few days (N.E.), come a S.W. wind up this morning knocking the clouds and rain to smithereens; warm as Spring. Shib on Guard last evening, was consoled during his absence by *three* letters. They will stop bye-by. (J. B. G.,[96] M. A. R., H. G. T.)

I am still at work in Topog. Office. All as usual. Had to put fire out, smoked so; chimney was built for a N.E. wind, so can't manage a S.W. wind.

November 7, 1864. Evening.
Stormy, yet warm. Fine yesterday. Two weeks more to stay to-night. How short the time is becoming, almost coming unexpectedly. Made an addition to our house of another *log* high, Shib put a front façade in to-day. We have a warm house; I shan't enjoy it a great while, an occasion of much regret! Quiet in camp, C being away, and A. Well, I begin to feel alone, and I hope to soon go along, too.

Camp Woodbury, Va.
November 9, 1864. Wednesday.
I am writing this just to kill time. All as usual. Bought an overcoat, washed it before supper—of fried hard tack. Shib and I got to fooling and kept it up like boys until 12 noon—he is on Guard to-night. I am alone. I am waiting for the mail.

November 11, 1864. Friday, evening.
Cooler, but still very pleasant. Am Well. Wrote to mother.
"They Say," the *three-masted schooner* is at the Point!
Saw a Vignette of *Rue*, it was good as looking on the reality a-most, I miss them. Coolidge has had a great reception in Framingham; *silver cup presented!* Whew my old bunky.

Camp Woodbury, Va.
November 20, 1864. Sunday.
Rainy. One day more from Retreat to-day. Wilcutt went this morning.[97] I hope I shall have good weather. All I can write is the above.

Camp Woodbury, Va.
November 21, 1864.

Out of the Service![98]

Well, now I will be sober; although it has been raining for the last three days and no prospect of its clearing.

Although I am glad, of course, to go, yet I do feel a sadness on leaving now those brave fellows I have been associated with for three years; and I may say as while I stood and watched Guard Mount—our Guard Mount—for the last time as a soldier, I had tears in my eyes.

I feel not unlike I did three years ago to-night, when at Thanksgiving I went to two weddings.[99] I feel proud of myself for having done *my* duty and thankful that I have thus safely passed through it all. And as I write this while the cheerful fire is crackling in the fireplace—ours awhile yet—with the rain pattering on the Shelter above; thus closes my Soldier Life.

—✕•✕—

I went up to the Topog. Office to report to Major Duane that "I was unable to finish those Reports, for reason of expiration of service." He laughed at me with "Well, I guess you have got enough of it," he gave me his Autograph, and inquired what I was going to do?

My Character is

Excellent, a good draughtsman

Well Old Journal, you will have to say Mr!

Coming.

Three times have gleamed the fields,
With fruit and golden sheaves,
Three times the winds have swept,
The Autumn's sere and yellow leaves,
Three times from yonder mead I've heard

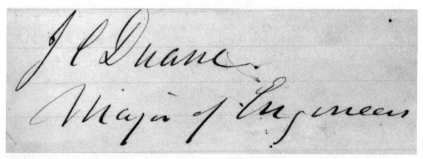

Duane's Autograph. The signature of Major James C. Duane that Thompson collected on November 21, 1864, just before he was mustered out of the service.

The farmer's bravery of harvest mirth.
Three times in gentle noiseless way,
The seasons came and blessed the Earth,
When Spring her garments hung
On vale and hill and mountain height,
I only wished her pretty reign were o'er
And Summer come in lordly right.
Still though balmy airs and gorgeous days,
Charmed my heart the time away,
I longed to hear the November rain
Beating one year out on the window pane.

GT

To my Comrades.

Hours of toil, hours of danger,
Hours of joy, hours of comfort,
'Neath the stars, in the rainstorm,
In the dust, 'neath the tent-roof
And made the days
Into Years,
Since we've been together.

Some hours like days have seemed,
Vexed with groans and dying screams,
Some days like moments went
Lightly on in merriment.
Yorktown's siege, we all remember
The "Seven Days," "Antietam's" splendor.
The long, hard day at Fredericksburg,
And then old thundering at Gettysburg.
Awhile at peace we passed the time,
About the huts at Brandy,
Our "flanks" of late are history's story,
And covered up we are
In dust and glory.
Yet 'tis the hours to come, my boy,
   Our thoughts are ever turning,
When we shall bid "Friend John," good bye,
   And quit our powder burning.

Hopedale. m.   From Memory, Feb. 12½. 1864.   Brandy Sta.

From Memory. Thompson's sketch of what was likely his home in Hopedale, Massachusetts. Made, as the title indicates, from memory in February 1864, while the battalion was encamped at Brandy Station, Virginia.

Gilbert Thompson, December 1864. A photograph of Gilbert Thompson, taken December 24, 1864, in Hopedale, Massachusetts, shortly after his return home.

Siege of Petersburg, Virginia. 1864.

Hopedale, Ma. Home.
December 26, 1864.

Misty and foggy, I ought to have written here before, but who could. I have enjoyed myself in a quiet way, sawing wood, &c. Day after too-morrow I am going back to Head Quarters to work again.

I have found many changes. I begin to realize there is a past; I almost feel I shall have to commence a new series of friends; I have had good times with some old friends at least. Mother is much better than I thought—I rather hate to leave here.

Epilogue

During the last campaign the Battalion moved with Headquarters and was present at Lee's surrender, the officers of the command performing staff duty at Gen. Meade's Headquarters.

After the surrender of Lee the Engineer Battalion took charge of the Engineer trains of the army, and of their shipment to Willets Point.[1] Companies A, B and D arrived at Willets Point in June, 1865, and Company C in December. Company A immediately after its arrival at Willets Point was ordered to West Point, where it remained until September, 1867, when it was again ordered to Willets Point. Company D had been previously sent to San Francisco (August 31).

—LIEUT. TURTLE'S ESSAY

I returned to the Army of the Potomac January 4, 1865, and had a place as Assistant Engineer (civilian) at Head Quarters, Army of the Potomac, and as such I did duty with the Army until the surrender of Lee, after which I was engaged in the Survey of the Battle-Fields of the Army of the Potomac.[2]

I was close up to the Battle of Five Forks, and was in Petersburg the morning of its evacuation.[3]

I was in thirty of the engagements of the Army of the Potomac, and was never wounded, but came very close to it.

I joined the *Society* of the Army of the Potomac in 1883 at Washington, D.C.

Gilbert Thompson,
November 1886.
Photograph of Gilbert
Thompson, dated precisely
twenty-five years after his
enlistment in the US Army.

I joined the Judge McKean Post of the Grand Army of the Republic, at Great Salt Lake City, Utah Territory, 1881. Member of the Lincoln Post, G.A.R., Washington, D.C. 1882–4.

Am a member of the Sons of the American Revolution, 1891.

Am 1st Lieutenant, Commanding Engineer Corps, District of Columbia National Guard, December 15, 1891.

Promoted to Major.

I am Geographer in the U.S. Geological Survey, and I am in charge of the *Appalachian Division*, and its boundaries are as follows: south of Mason's & Dixon's line to the Gulf of Mexico, and from the Mississippi River to the Atlantic Ocean, but it is a peaceful division to command, I have *nine parties*, and in all about *sixty-seven men*! I had a working party one night at Petersburg of over 1,000 men![4]

Gilbert Thompson
Geographer, U.S. Geological Survey
November 22, 1885.

As he noted in his postwar recollections and his final journal entry, Thompson returned to service with the Army of the Potomac in early 1865, but he did not resume his journal and he did not rejoin the Engineer Battalion. The unit's roles from November 1864 through the spring of 1865, however, changed very little in character from those reported in Thompson's wartime record. It continued to build and maintain roads and bridges, improve Union siege works around Petersburg, and serve occasionally as infantry to hold a portion of the lines its men had built or improved. On March 31, 1865, the engineers built a crib bridge over Gravelly Run and corduroyed the approaches to it, continuing the important work of enabling the army's movements, work that the battalion had first commenced during the Peninsula campaign three years earlier. In this case, the battalion's efforts allowed part of Warren's V Corps to move into position for the Battle of Five Forks, which destroyed rebel defenses on their right and allowed Grant to end the siege of Petersburg with a final Federal offensive on April 2. This ultimately drove Lee to abandon both the Cockade City and the Confederate capital.[5]

During the Appomattox campaign that followed, the Engineer Battalion stayed with the head of the Army of the Potomac to keep the roads passable and the Federal army moving. Following Lee's surrender, the unit marched to Washington where it joined the Grand Review before returning to its peacetime stations. Company A returned to West Point, while the three new companies remained at Willets Point, New York, where an Engineer School of Application was established to maintain and develop vital expertise in military engineering.[6]

Thompson, like the battalion, also ended the war performing the same sorts of duties he had carried out earlier in the conflict, albeit in a slightly different manner. Having spent considerable time during his final months in the army working on map surveys, he returned to this type of work when he came back to the Army of the Potomac headquarters as a civilian assistant engineer in early 1865. He continued in this capacity for the rest of the war, traveling with the army's headquarters during its final campaigns. After 1865, he stayed in government service, surveying and mapping the battlefields of Maryland and Virginia for the War Department. He performed this postwar service under Major and Brevet Brigadier General Nathaniel Michler, who had been the Army of the Potomac's chief of mapmaking and under whom Thompson had worked during the war. These maps kept Thompson busy through 1869 or perhaps 1870.[7]

While he helped Michler map the eastern battlefields, Thompson relocated more or less permanently to Washington, DC. He lived there with a new family for the rest of his life, with a few brief exceptions. On September 28, 1869, he married Mary Frances McNeil, daughter of Archibald and Amy McNeil. Originally from Tennessee, Mary was living in the capital with her mother when she and Thompson wed. Three years later, on August 14, 1872, Mary gave birth to the couple's only child, a daughter they named Amy Grier Thompson.[8]

At about the same time as the birth of his daughter, Thompson became involved with some of the expeditions to survey the western United States. In 1871, Lieutenant George Wheeler of the Corps of Engineers began surveying the American Southwest as a prelude to accurately mapping the area. At the end of his initial expedition, he proposed "a systematic topographic survey of the territory of the United States west of the 100th meridian." By the summer of 1872, the chief engineer, the secretary of war, and Congress had all approved the plan, inaugurating a seven-year project known as the Wheeler Survey. The operation formally began in July 1872 with its first surveying expedition. These expeditions continued annually until 1879, lasting generally from mid- or late summer through most of the fall, with the winter, spring, and early summer months reserved for working up the results in Washington and preparing for the next expedition. Thompson joined each of the Wheeler Survey field expeditions from 1872 through 1879 as a topographical assistant.[9]

Building on his wartime and postwar topographical experiences, in 1880 Thompson joined a new branch of the federal government. The United States Geological Survey (USGS) had been organized by Congress the previous year to consolidate all the nation's surveying and mapping projects under the auspices of the Department of the Interior. After the organization of the USGS, the country's western territories were split into four divisions, and Thompson was appointed a topographer in the Division of the Great Basin. As a consequence, he relocated to the division headquarters in Salt Lake City, interrupting for a few years his residence in the national capital. His new duties were similar to those he had executed on the Wheeler Surveys, though he was often the topographer in charge of field expeditions rather than a mere assistant. He remained with the USGS for the rest of his career, though he continued his upward trajectory. In 1882, he was put in charge of the District of the Pacific, which had been established that year to coordinate all field activities in most of California and parts of the Washington and Oregon territories. While the divisions were frequently updated or rearranged, Thompson continued as a senior official in one district or another. In 1884, he became the head of the Appalachian Division, which he mentioned in his memoir and which allowed his return to Washington, DC. By 1890, the name of his department had changed, but Thompson still ran it as the chief geographer of the Southeastern Division. In all of these positions he continued to participate in fieldwork until 1899. In that year, at the age of sixty, he moved into the USGS's Washington office, where he spent the next decade.[10]

As a USGS geographer, Thompson became an active member of the community of scientists in government service, especially after his return to Washington in the mid-1880s. He occasionally published short pieces of scientific interest based on his work with the geological survey, though most of his public writing took a different focus. And while he was not a leading figure in the endeavor, Thompson joined thirty-two other Washington-area scientists at the January 1888 meeting that established the National Geographic Society. Originally intended to share specialized expertise among a small scientific community, a decade later the group's objective shifted to its now-familiar focus of spreading geographic knowledge, broadly defined, to the wider public.[11]

Outside his professional career, Thompson became increasingly interested in the study of the past. The kernel of this pursuit may have always been present; it may have been partially responsible for his decision to keep a journal of his Civil War experiences, and it almost certainly influenced his postwar additions to that early record. One of the ways that Thompson's interest in the past manifested itself later in his life was through genealogical research, as he traced both his maternal and paternal lines. On his mother's side, he was descended from Deborah Sampson Gannett who, prior to her marriage to Benjamin Gannett Jr., served seventeen months in the light infantry company of the Continental Army's 4th Massachusetts under the name of Robert Shurtliff. Thompson also discovered that, through Deborah, he was descended from William Bradford and, possibly, Myles Standish.[12]

Thompson's interest in his family's history may have been simply personal, or it may have been driven by a broader concern for the past that was evidenced by his membership in several historical organizations. In 1891, he joined the Washington, DC, Society of the Sons of the American Revolution. He may have been unique within that organization, obtaining membership in part on the basis of the military service of his great-grand-*mother*, Deborah Sampson. Admittedly, though, his great-grandfather Nathaniel Gilbert also fought in the War for Independence, bolstering his application to the organization. His maternal grandfather, Judson Gilbert, served in a Massachusetts artillery company during the second war with Great Britain, making him eligible for the Washington chapter of the General Society of the War of 1812, and after 1905 Thompson was that group's registrar. He was also an early and active member of the capital city's Society of Colonial Wars, chairing its Committee on Historical Documents and serving as its official historian. Finally, his own role in the Civil War led to his membership in both the Grand Army of the Republic and the Society of the Army of the Potomac.[13]

In addition to his membership and leadership roles in several historical societies, Thompson also produced a few of his own historical works. He wrote two of the first three *Historical Papers of the Society of Colonial Wars*. The first examined the boundaries and geography of Virginia and Maryland throughout their colonial history, and the second, of a more antiquarian bent, was a discussion of powder horns used by military forces in North America. Both were first read before the society, and both also benefited from Thompson's other talents. When he read the paper on Virginia and Maryland in January 1897, it was accompanied by an exhibit of maps that he had drawn, and the examination of powder horns contained several of Thompson's sketches.[14] At the time of his death, he was working on a route map of one of Major General Edward Braddock's columns from the area that later became Washington, DC, through Maryland toward Fort Cumberland.[15]

Thompson's appreciation of history also extended to an awareness of the role that he himself had played in the nation's past. He wrote a history of the Engineer Battalion that drew from his own journals and from the paper on the battalion's history by Lieutenant Thomas Turtle, which provides the chapter epigraphs for this volume. Thompson's history, which was revised and published the year after his death, is a detailed chronicle of the battalion's daily activities during the war, and while much of this information was drawn from his wartime journals, his published account lacks the flavor and personality so evident in that earlier record.[16]

Beyond his written history of the Engineer Battalion, Thompson always maintained a connection with the unit in which he had served. In 1887, he attended the battalion's reunion, which was held as part of that year's national encampment of the Grand Army of the Republic in St. Louis, Missouri. He even brought one of the unit's old flags with him, and afterward, he wrote a brief summary of the event. In cooperation with some of his old friends, Thompson also helped establish an informal group for all former members of the battalion. While his friend Fred Vogel, who had become a Kansas doctor, served as president of the new organization, Thompson was its secretary and historian.[17]

Thompson also retained one final though somewhat tenuous connection with his wartime service in the Corps of Engineers. When the capital city militia was reorganized as the Washington National Guard in 1889, Thompson was tapped to form its engineering contingent. He attracted so many men from the government's scientific bureaus that he managed to raise a four-company engineer battalion. Thompson was himself commissioned a lieutenant in this unit and later promoted to major, despite the many denials of any desire for a commission scattered throughout his Civil War journal.[18]

It seems, then, that he never forgot his military service during the "war for the suppression of the Great Rebellion," as he called it in the introduction to his own record of the conflict. He returned to the war often by revisiting his old journals, in his postwar historical writings, and when he raised a similar unit for Washington's National Guard. In a way, he even returned to it in death; when he died at the age of seventy in 1909, he was laid to rest in Arlington National Cemetery.[19] With his obvious interest in the past and his continuing connections to and memory of his own service with the US Engineer Battalion in the Civil War, it is only a small conceit to suggest that perhaps Gilbert Thompson would have been proud to see the prediction of his friend and eulogist, Marcus Benjamin, come to fruition. Benjamin worked with Thompson for many years in the Society of Colonial Wars, and on Thompson's passing he wrote: "[F]rom [Thompson's] diaries it is probable that a further contribution may be

The 1890 Engineer Battalion Reunion. Standing, L to R: C. M. C. Ferhold, Frederick Vogel, Gilbert Thompson, and John Coughlan. Seated, L to R: William F. Sutherland, William Longstreet, Thomas Molony, James H. Black, and Henry G. Evans. According to the Corps of Engineers Office of History, this is a photograph of the 1890 reunion rather than the one in 1887 that Thompson noted attending. Nevertheless, the small flag in the upper right corner (behind John Coughlan) is either the one that Thompson brought to the 1887 reunion or one very similar to it. This photograph was not included in Thompson's journal or memoir. Courtesy of Office of History, Headquarters, US Army Corps of Engineers.

made to the literature of the Civil War which will give new and interesting details in regard to the special line of work in which he was engaged and at the same time add valuable information concerning the high motives that actuated many young men of that time to offer their services to their country."[20]

It would be a most fitting tribute if this volume could accomplish such lofty goals.

Notes

Editor's Introduction

1. District of Columbia Society of the Sons of the American Revolution, Application for Membership of Prof. Gilbert Thompson, "Sons of the American Revolution Membership Applications, 1889–1970," microfilm, 508 rolls (Louisville, KY: National Society of the Sons of the American Revolution), roll 7, vol. 10, state no. 113; Affidavits of Abbie M. Hadley, 25 October 1904, and Horace C. Adams to Gilbert Thompson, 12 October 1904, both enclosed in Soldier's Certificate No. 1,314,127, Gilbert Thompson, Cos. B & D, US Battalion of Engineers, Civil War and Later Pension Files, Record Group 15, Records of the Department of Veterans Affairs, National Archives and Records Administration, Washington, DC (cited hereafter as RG15).

2. The precise circumstances of William Thompson's life after the mid-1840s are unclear. Born in 1813, he married Hannah Joslin in 1835, and the couple produced one son before Hannah died in 1836. Early the next year, William and Hannah's infant son also died. In November 1837, William married Harriet Gilbert, and Gilbert Thompson was born fifteen months later. William apparently remained with his new family for several years, but by 1850, Harriet and young Gilbert were living alone, and William appeared on the census as the husband of Catharine Thompson and stepfather to her son, Americus Welch. There is, however, no record of a divorce between William and Harriet and no record of a marriage between William and Catharine except for a mid-nineteenth century genealogical study that refers to an 1849 wedding. Given the lack of official records, it is likely that William and Catharine just set up housekeeping together and told census officials in 1850 that they were married. This view is bolstered by Gilbert's estrangement from his father, which is evidenced by the fact that when he went to file his pension application in the early twentieth century, Gilbert did not even know his late father's full name. United States Census 1850, Worcester

County, Massachusetts, population schedule, Blackstone, p. 701, dwelling 372, family 532, William V. and Catharine Thompson, digital image, FamilySearch, accessed June 13, 2016, https://familysearch.org/pal:/MM9.3.1/TH-266|-11285-118746-59?cc=1401638; United States Census 1880, Worcester County, Massachusetts, population schedule, Blackstone, p. 24, dwelling 199, family 264, Americus and Lucy Welch, digital image, FamilySearch, accessed June 14, 2016, https://familysearch.org/pal:/MM9.3.1/TH-1942-25148-19089-50?cc=1417683; Affidavit of Abbie M. Hadley, 25 October 1904, and Horace C. Adams to Gilbert Thompson, 12 October 1904, both enclosed in Soldier's Certificate No. 1,314,127, Gilbert Thompson, RG15; Journal of Gilbert Thompson (a reminiscence not transcribed for this edition), Manuscript Division, Library of Congress, Washington, DC, digital image 319 of 779, accessed February 17, 2016, https://www.loc.gov/resource/mss95752.01/?sp=319; Frederic A. Holden, *Genealogy of the Descendants of Banfield Capron, from A.D. 1660 to A.D. 1859* (Boston, MA: Geo. C. Rand & Avery, 1859), 223.

3. Adin Ballou, *History of the Town of Milford, Worcester County Massachusetts, from Its First Settlement to 1881*, 2 parts (Boston, MA: Franklin Press, 1882), 2:1064; Edward K. Spann, *Hopedale: From Commune to Company Town, 1840–1920* (Columbus: Ohio State Univ. Press, 1992), xi, 120–24; Sarah E. Bradbury, "Community Life as Seen by One of the Young People," in *Hopedale Reminiscences: Childhood Memories of the Hopedale Community and the Hopedale Home School, 1841–1863*, ed. Lynn Gordon Hughes (Providence, RI: Blackstone Editions, 2006), 11.

4. Spann, *Hopedale*, 9.

5. Spann, *Hopedale*, 71; Anna Thwing Field, "Anti-Slavery and Other Visitors to the Community," in *Hopedale Reminiscences*, ed. Hughes, 18; William F. Draper, "Hopedale," in *Hopedale Reminiscences*, ed. Hughes, 67–68.

6. Thwing, "Anti-Slavery and Other Visitors," 18–21; Nellie T. Gifford, "Childhood Days in the Hopedale Community, and Other Recollection," in *Hopedale Reminiscences*, ed. Hughes, 44; Spann, *Hopedale*, 68, 142–43; Patrick Rael, *Black Identity and Black Protest in the Antebellum North* (Chapel Hill: Univ. of North Carolina Press, 2002), 91; Elizabeth Stordeur Pryor, "The Etymology of Nigger: Resistance, Language, and the Politics of Freedom in the Antebellum North," *Journal of the Early Republic* 36, no. 2 (Summer 2016): 210, 214. See also Thompson's February 27, 1862, journal entry. On the racial values of most white Union soldiers, see Joseph T. Glatthaar, *Forged in Battle: The Civil War Alliance of Black Soldiers and White Officers* (New York: Free Press, 1990), 11–12.

7. Spann, *Hopedale*, 10–11, 66, 142, 150–51.

8. Hughes, ed., *Hopedale Reminiscences*, xii; Spann, *Hopedale*, 89–90, 121–23, 152; Bradbury, "Community Life," 11; Gifford, "Childhood Days in the Hopedale Community," 45; William F. Draper, Lizzie B. Humphrey, and William S.

Heywood, "Retrospective Sketch," from "Home School Memorial: A Reunion of Teachers and Pupils of the Hopedale Home School, August 1, 1867," in *Hopedale Reminiscences*, ed. Hughes, 69–70; Ellen M. Patrick, "Our Community School and Its Teacher," in *Hopedale Reminiscences*, ed. Hughes, 34; "Catalogue of the Hopedale Home School," from "Home School Memorial," 82.

9. Ballou, *History of the Town of Milford*, 2:1064; Marcus Benjamin, *Gilbert Thompson*, Memorial Papers of the Society of Colonial Wars in the District of Columbia, no. 5 (n.p.: n.p., 1910), 6; Abbie Ballou Heywood, "Hopedale Community, Founded in 1841: Its Origin and Early History," in *Hopedale Reminiscences*, ed. Hughes, 50.

10. Patrick, "Our Community School and Its Teacher," 34.

11. Richard T. Evans and Helen M. Frye, *History of the Topographic Branch (Division): U.S. Geological Survey Circular 1341* (Reston, VA: US Geological Survey, 2009), 169–70.

12. Gilbert Thompson Journal, Manuscript Division, Library of Congress, Washington, DC, https://www.loc.gov/item/mm81095752/.

13. In 1831, the topographical engineers were moved out of the Corps of Engineers into an autonomous Topographical Bureau, and as part of the 1838 army increase, the "topogs," as they were sometimes known, were reorganized into the Corps of Topographical Engineers. This division was accomplished largely through the efforts of Colonel John J. Abert, an ambitious topographical engineer who served as the head of the new corps from 1838 to 1861. A. A. Humphreys, "Historical Sketch of the Corps of Engineers," *Historical Papers Relating to the Corps of Engineers and Engineer Troops in the United States Army*, Engineer School Occasional Papers, no. 16 (Washington, DC: Press of the Engineer School, 1904), 25, 28; US Army Corps of Engineers, *The History of the US Army Corps of Engineers* (Alexandria, VA: Office of History, US Army Corps of Engineers, 1998), 29; "An Act to increase the present military establishment of the United States, and for other purposes," Chapter 179, 5 July 1838, in A. R. Hetzel, *Military Laws of the United States, Including Those Relating to the Army, Marine Corps, Volunteers, Militia, and to Bounty Lands and Pensions: To Which is Prefixed the Rules and Articles of War, and the Constitution of the United States*, 3rd ed. (Washington, DC: George Templeman, 1846), 262; Thomas F. Army Jr., *Engineering Victory: How Technology Won the Civil War* (Baltimore, MD: Johns Hopkins Univ. Press, 2016), 118.

14. For a thorough examination of the original engineer company's creation, its exploits in the Mexican-American War, and attempts to increase the number of the army's engineer troops between 1846 and 1861, see Mark A. Smith, "The Politics of Military Professionalism: The Engineer Company and the Political Activities of the Antebellum Corps of Engineers," *Journal of Military History*

80, no. 2 (April 2016): 355–87, and Mark A. Smith, "'The Hardest Work and the Hardest Fighting': The Engineer Company in Mexico and the Origins of American Combat Engineering," *Military History of the West* 45 (Fall 2016): 1–46.

15. Gilbert Thompson, *The Engineer Battalion in the Civil War: A Contribution to the History of the United States Engineers*, rev. by John W. N. Schulz, Engineer School Occasional Papers, no. 44 (Washington, DC: Press of the Engineer School, 1910), 1–2; Clayton R. Newell and Charles R. Shrader, *Of Duty Well and Faithfully Done: A History of the Regular Army in the Civil War* (Lincoln: Univ. of Nebraska Press, 2011), 286–87; Timothy D. Johnson, ed., *Memoirs of Lieut.-General Winfield Scott* (Knoxville: Univ. of Tennessee Press, 2015), 309.

16. Thompson, *Engineer Battalion in the Civil War*, 1–2; Newell and Shrader, *Of Duty Well and Faithfully Done*, 287; Winfield Scott to Bvt. Col. Harvey Brown, 1 April 1865, in United States War Department, *The War of the Rebellion: A Compilation of the Official Records of the Union and Confederate Armies*, 4 series, 128 vols. (Washington, DC: Government Printing Office, 1880–1901), ser. 1, vol. 1, part 1, 365–66 (cited hereafter as "*OR*, ser. X, vol. X, part X"); A. J. Slemmer to Col. S. Cooper, 8 January 1861, in *OR*, ser. 1, vol. 1, part 1, 333–34; I. Vogdes to Col. L. Thomas, 7 February 1861, in *OR*, ser. 1, vol. 1, part 1, 357.

17. Thompson, *Engineer Battalion in the Civil War*, 2; Newell and Shrader, *Of Duty Well and Faithfully Done*, 287.

18. Smith, "The Politics of Military Professionalism," 371; "An act for the better Organization of the Military Establishment," 3 August 1861, Chapter 42, in United States, *Statutes at Large of the United States of America, 1789–1873*, 17 vols. (Boston, MA: Little, Brown, and Company, 1845–1873), 12:287–88; Newell and Shrader, *Of Duty Well and Faithfully Done*, 290; Thompson, *Engineer Battalion in the Civil War*, 3–4. See also Army, *Engineering Victory*, for a thorough examination of how both belligerents in the Civil War attempted to meet their respective military engineering needs.

19. "An act to promote the Efficiency of the Engineer and Topographical Engineer Corps, and for other Purposes," 6 August 1861, Ch. 57, *Statutes at Large of the USA*, 12:317–18; Newell and Shrader, *Of Duty Well and Faithfully Done*, 287; Thompson, *Engineer Battalion in the Civil War*, 3–4.

20. Newell and Shrader, *Of Duty Well and Faithfully Done*, 287–88.

21. Corps of Engineers, *History of the Corps of Engineers*, 69–70; Newell and Shrader, *Of Duty Well and Faithfully Done*, 287, 289; "An act to promote the Efficiency of the Corps of Engineers and of the Ordnance Department, and for other Purposes," 3 March 1863, Ch. 78, *Statutes at Large of the USA*, 12:743–44; Army, *Engineering Victory*, 119, 206–8.

22. For this quotation, see Thompson's memoir recollection found on p. 39.

Author's Introduction

1. Thompson himself eventually provided one of these "more correctly and elegant written narratives" when he wrote *The Engineer Battalion in the Civil War*, which was later revised and updated by John W. N. Schulz of the Corps of Engineers and published in 1910 as Number 44 of the Occasional Papers of the Engineer School of the US Army.

1. Off to the Wars with Other Intelligent Men

1. Thompson also noted in his postwar recollections that the original engineer company, Company A, served as part of President-Elect Abraham Lincoln's inaugural escort. He wrote: "At the Inauguration of President Lincoln, Company A was in front of the Presidential carriage. See article by General Stone, *(Scribner's)* Century, July 1883." The article Thompson referenced was General Charles P. Stone, "Washington on the Eve of the War," *Century Illustrated Monthly Magazine*, new ser. 4, 26, no. 3 (July 1883): 458–66. The reference to the engineer company is found on the final page of the article.

2. Thompson commented on Lieutenant Turtle's assertion that the topographical engineer company was not organized during the war, remarking that: "This is probably a mistake. There were two Corps, the Engineers and the Topographical Engineers. We were the Company A of the latter. Shortly after, the two Corps were united, and we were merged in the Engineer Troops. There were 13 of us in all, and there was some feeling about it, but we went in to do our duty no matter where."

It is Thompson, however, who was mistaken. As noted in the introduction, the company of topographical engineers was never fully activated, and in early 1862 its recruits, Thompson included, were transferred into one of the new companies of engineer soldiers that fell under the authority of the Corps of Engineers. This was more than a year before the Corps of Engineers and the Corps of Topographical Engineers were combined into a single organization. Corps of Engineers, *History of the Corps of Engineers*, 70.

Elsewhere in his memoirs, Thompson recorded a song by one of the recruits of the topographical company, Francis E. Beahn. In his lyrics, Beahn identified twelve men who had first joined that company. Either there were only twelve or Beahn simply left one out of his lyrics, which were as follows:

Black, White and Thompson, Currier, Slater, Beahn,
Form the jolliest crowd that you have ever seen,
Miller, Thayer and Fickett, Higgins, Flood and Ames
Also swell the Topog. List with their illustrious names,

Chorus:
Three rousing cheers for the Topographical Engineers, Etc.

Using the battalion returns, the men identified in the first line of Beahn's lyrics were James A. Black, Eben White, Gilbert Thompson, Edward J. Currier, John L. Slater, and Francis E. Beahn. Those in the third line were Daniel H. Miller, Robert C. Thayer, Mariner S. Fickett, Atkins Higgins, James W. Flood, and George Ames. See "Returns from Regular Army Engineer Battalions, Sept. 1846–June 1916" (National Archives Microfilm M690, 10 rolls), Roll 1, "First Battalion, September 1846–June 1849 and December 1861–December 1874," Record Group 94, National Archives and Records Administration, Washington, DC (cited hereafter as "NARA Microfilm M690").

3. Thompson copied large portions of Lieutenant Thomas Turtle's essay on the history of the Engineer Battalion into the memoir portion of his reminisces, and he used it extensively when crafting his own history of the battalion in the American Civil War (Thompson, *Engineer Battalion in the Civil War*). This extensive use makes Turtle's essay an appropriate introduction to the events of each chapter of Thompson's combined journal and memoir, and as such these passages are reproduced as written, without marking errors of spelling or grammar with "[*sic*]." See also Thomas Turtle, "History of the Engineer Battalion, A Paper Read before the 'Essayons Club' of the Corps of Engineers, Dec. 21, 1868," in *Historical Papers Relating to the Corps of Engineers and to Engineer Troops in the United States Army*, Engineer School Occasional Papers, no. 16 (Washington, DC: Press of the Engineer School, 1904).

4. Fort Independence on Castle Island was one of Boston's harbor defenses built as part of the Third System of Coastal Defense.

5. Charlotte Percy was a member of the household of Warren W. Dutcher, a local manufacturer in Milford, Massachusetts, the town where Thompson's home community of Hopedale was located. United States Census 1860, Worcester County, Massachusetts, population schedule, Milford, pp. 121–22, dwelling 644, family 991, Warren and Malinda Dutcher, digital images, FamilySearch, accessed May 5, 2016, https://familysearch.org/pal:/MM9.3.1/TH-1942 -25248-12028-90?cc=1473181 and https://familysearch.org/pal:/MM9.3.1 /TH-1951-25248-10357-57?cc=1473181.

6. In 1860, Adaline Adams was a clerk in the employ of Amos M. Wheelock, an armorer operating out of Worcester, Massachusetts, about 25 or 30 miles from Hopedale, but in 1855 Miss Adams had lived next door to Thompson and his mother. United States Census 1860, Worcester County, Massachusetts, population schedule, Worcester, p. 233, dwelling 1355, family 2009, Amos M. and Bidelia Wheelock, digital image, FamilySearch, accessed May 13, 2016,

https://familysearch.org/pal:/MM9.3.1/TH-1951-25247-28684
-37?cc=1473181; Massachusetts State Census 1855, Worcester County,
population schedule, Milford, p. 129, dwelling 734, family 1094, Abner
and Elizabeth F. Adams, digital image, FamilySearch, accessed June 13,
2016, https://familysearch.org/pal:/MM9.3.1/TH-267-11770-177419-
36?cc=1459987; Massachusetts State Census 1855, Worcester County, population
schedule, Milford, p. 129, dwelling 735, family 1096, Harriet Thompson, digital
image, FamilySearch, accessed June 13, 2016, https://familysearch.org/pal:
/MM9.3.1/TH-267-11770-177419-36?cc=1459987.

7. Hopedale, Massachusetts, was Thompson's home, though it could be
argued that Milford was actually his hometown. The Hopedale community was
founded within the town limits of Milford, Massachusetts, in 1841 as a utopian
experiment. As Thompson noted in his memoir recollections, Hopedale was
established by the Practical Christians under the leadership of the Reverend
Adin Ballou. Their goal was to create a harmonious and Godly mill town that
allowed freedom of conscience, provided equal treatment for all, abhorred
all forms of coercion, and ensured collective control of all property through
a joint stock concern in which members could buy or sell stock. They did not
completely abolish private holdings, as members would, in effect, earn dividends
from their shares, but the joint stock company owned and managed all of the
community's land and resources, a system that has been called Practical Christian
socialism. Five years before the Civil War broke out, however, George Draper
acquired three-quarters of the joint stock and control of the community, ending
the Practical Christian experiment when he turned Hopedale into a company
town to support his textile-based enterprises, the Hopedale Machine Company
and, in partnership with Warren W. Dutcher, the Dutcher Temple Company.
Spann, *Hopedale*, xi, 20–24, 131–34.

8. William F. Draper was a former schoolmate of Thompson's, having come
to the Hopedale community with his family in 1853. As a major in the 36th
Massachusetts, he was shot in the shoulder while attempting to rally his men
from atop Confederate fieldworks during the belated assault of Major General
Ambrose Burnside's IX Corps at the Battle of the Wilderness on the afternoon
of May 6, 1864. His bravery earned Major Draper a promotion to lieutenant
colonel dated May 6, 1864. He was mustered out of service a few months
later in October but was subsequently awarded two brevets, to colonel and
brigadier general. See also Thompson's February 28, 1863, and May 12, 1864,
entries. Draper, "Hopedale," 63; Gordon C. Rhea, *The Battle of the Wilderness,
May 5–6 1864* (Baton Rouge: Louisiana State Univ. Press, 1994), 382, 386;
Francis B. Heitman, *Historical Register and Dictionary of the United States Army,
from Its Organization, September 28, 1789, to March 2, 1903*, 2 vols. (1903; repr.,

Urbana: Univ. of Illinois Press, 1965), 1:383; Adjutant General of Massachusetts, *Massachusetts Soldiers, Sailors, and Marines in the Civil War*, 8 vols. (Norwood, MA: Norwood Press, 1931–35), 3:736.

9. George G. Gay, son of George and Lydia, enlisted and joined Company G of the 2nd Massachusetts Volunteer Heavy Artillery in November 1863. While assigned to garrison duty at Plymouth, North Carolina, in the spring of 1864, nearly all of Company G was captured by a Confederate force under Brigadier General Robert F. Hoke. There were large numbers of southern Unionists and African Americans in Federal service at Plymouth, and many of them were massacred after the engagement, but Gay was sent to the Confederate prisoner-of-war camp at Andersonville, Georgia, along with many of his white compatriots. He died there of diarrhea on September 20, 1864. United States Census 1860, Worcester County, Massachusetts, population schedule, Milford, p. 121, dwelling 643, family 990, Andsel and Mary O. Harlow, digital image, FamilySearch, accessed May 22, 2016, https://familysearch.org/pal:/MM9.3.1/TH-1942 -25248-12028-90?cc=1473181; Weymouth T. Jordan Jr. and Gerald W. Thomas, "Massacre at Plymouth, April 20, 1864," in *Black Flag over Dixie: Racial Atrocities and Reprisals in the Civil War*, ed. Gregory J. W. Urwin (Carbondale: Southern Illinois Univ. Press, 2004), 173–74, 191; Adjutant General of Massachusetts, *Massachusetts Soldiers, Sailors, and Marines in the Civil War*, 5:657, 711, 716; Andersonville Prisoners of War Online Database (Provo, UT: Ancestry.com), accessed May 23, 2016, https://www.ancestry.com/search/collections /andersonville/.

Interestingly, one of the witnesses to the rebel massacre at Plymouth was Gay's comrade in the 2nd Massachusetts Volunteer Heavy Artillery, Warren Lee Goss, who was also a former member of Company B of the US Engineer Battalion. See also Thompson's memoir recollection on p. 65 as well as p. 364n67.

10. While it is not certain, Warren Adams of Milford, Massachusetts, the son of Abner and Elizabeth Adams and older brother of Adaline Adams, may be the Warren L. Adams who enlisted in Company D of the 46th Massachusetts in September 1862 while residing in Chicopee, about seventy miles from Milford, where he was working as a moulder. At Newbern, North Carolina, in April 1863, Adams was discharged for reasons of unspecified disability. United States Census 1850, Worcester County, Massachusetts, population schedule, Milford, pp. 108–9, dwelling 623, family 817, Abner and Elizabeth Adams, digital image, FamilySearch, accessed May 23, 2016, https:// familysearch.org/pal:/MM9.3.1/TH-266-11813-51092-71?cc=1401638 and https://familysearch.org/pal:/MM9.3.1/TH-266-11813-50326-46?cc=1401638; Adjutant General of Massachusetts, *Massachusetts Soldiers, Sailors, and Marines in the Civil War*, 4:361.

11. Eli G. Ball appears in the 1860 census as a needle maker in the household of the Milford manufacturer Warren Dutcher. Ball was mortally wounded on June 3, 1864, as his regiment, the 25th Massachusetts Infantry, assaulted Confederate forces under Major General Joseph B. Kershaw at Cold Harbor during the 1864 Overland Campaign. United States Census 1860, Worcester County, Massachusetts, population schedule, Milford, pp. 121–22, dwelling 644, family 991, Warren and Malinda Dutcher, digital images, FamilySearch, accessed May 5, 2016, https://familysearch.org/pal:/MM9.3.1/TH-1942-25248-12028-90?cc=1473181 and https://familysearch.org/pal:/MM9.3.1/TH-1951-25248-10357-57?cc=1473181; Adjutant General of Massachusetts, *Massachusetts Soldiers, Sailors, and Marines in the Civil War*, 3:11; Gordon C. Rhea, *Cold Harbor: Grant and Lee, May 26–June 3, 1864* (Baton Rouge: Louisiana State Univ. Press, 2002), 349–56.

12. The 1860 census for Milford contains no one by the name of Arthur Johnson, except an eleven-year-old boy. Massachusetts state records list three Arthur Johnsons in service during the Civil War, but none were from Milford, and none of them died in the assault on Cold Harbor. United States Census 1860, Worcester County, Massachusetts, population schedule, Milford, p. 145, dwelling 794, family 1188, Charles C. and Jeminoa Johnson, digital images, FamilySearch, accessed May 25, 2016, https://familysearch.org/pal:/MM9.3.1/TH-1942-25248-12188-81?cc=1473181; Adjutant General of Massachusetts, *Massachusetts Soldiers, Sailors, and Marines in the Civil War*, 1:123, 2:536; 5:797.

13. This is probably a reference to Henry Johnson, a black farm laborer in Milford who was born in slavery in Alabama ca. 1810, and who was one of Milford's handful of black residents. However, the only African American troops participating in the Union assault against Fort Wagner were those of the 54th Massachusetts Infantry (Colored), and the unit's rolls do not include Henry Johnson of Milford. Moreover, only two Johnsons from Massachusetts are listed as having died as a result of the assault against the Confederate Battery Wagner on James Island in July 1863: Peter B. Johnson of Company A from Springfield was reported missing and presumed dead following the action, and Charles H. Johnson of Company F from Warren, Massachusetts, was wounded in the assault, dying of his wounds several months later in September. United States Census 1860, Worcester County, Massachusetts, population schedule, Milford, p. 119, dwelling 628, family 969, Lucy Mason (Boarding House), digital images, FamilySearch, accessed May 25, 2016, https://familysearch.org/pal:/MM9.3.1/TH-1951-25248-10242-1?cc=1473181; Adjutant General of Massachusetts, *Massachusetts Soldiers, Sailors, and Marines in the Civil War*, 4:661, 667.

14. No one by the name Julius Laderer is found on the 1850 or 1860 federal census for Milford, Massachusetts, or in service with the United States Navy during the Civil War.

15. Daniel E. Messenger was a machinist in Milford. He was husband to Eliza M. E. Messenger and father to Hannah, Charles, Adrian, and Lyman. He served in the Army of the Potomac as an enlisted man in Company H of the 1st Massachusetts Volunteer Cavalry from August 1862 until November 1864. United States Census 1860, Worcester County, Massachusetts, population schedule, Milford, p. 123, dwelling 653, family 1004, William and Almira B. Humphry, digital image, FamilySearch, accessed May 22, 2016, https://familysearch.org/pal:/MM9.3.1/TH-1942-25248-12138-57?cc=1473181; Adjutant General of Massachusetts, *Massachusetts Soldiers, Sailors, and Marines in the Civil War*, 6:129, 181, 187.

16. Joseph W. and Henry L. Harlow were sons of Andsel and Mary Harlow of Milford; they, their parents, and their sister Mary were all neighbors of the Gay family whose son George G. died at Andersonville. Joseph does not appear on any of the state's units, but Henry did serve as a corporal in the 19th Unattached Company of Massachusetts Volunteer Infantry from August until November 1864. United States Census 1860, Worcester County, Massachusetts, population schedule, Milford, p. 121, dwelling 642, family 989, Andsel and Mary O. Harlow, digital image, FamilySearch, accessed May 22, 2016, https://familysearch.org/pal:/MM9.3.1/TH-1942-25248-12028-90?cc=1473181; Adjutant General of Massachusetts, *Massachusetts Soldiers, Sailors, and Marines in the Civil War*, 5:246–47.

17. White was probably Eben White, another recruit. Unless otherwise specified, all subsequently provided full names, service activities, illnesses, and deaths of members of the Engineer Battalion are derived from NARA Microfilm M690.

18. Probably Ordnance Sergeant John Parr. See also November 29, 1861, entry. "Post Return of Fort Independence, Mass., commanded by Lieut. Colonel E. Schriver, 11 Inf, for the month of September, 1861," and "Post Return of Fort Independence, Mass., commanded by Capt. C. C. Pomeroy, for the month of April, 1862," both from Returns from US Military Posts, 1800–1916, Records of the Adjutant General's Office 1780s–1917, Record Group 94, National Archives Microfilm Publication M617, roll 508.

19. George L. Ames. Like Thompson, Ames was eventually transferred to Company B of the Engineer Battalion.

20. John L. Slater. Slater, too, was later transferred to Company B.

21. *The Columbia Glee Book* was a compilation of both religious and secular musical pieces by Isaac Baker Woodbury; it was published in 1854 by W. J. Reynolds & Co. See *New York Musical Review and Choral Advocate: A Journal of Sacred and Secular Music* 5, no. 6 (March 16, 1854): 94.

22. Benjamin Franklin Butler was one of the earliest political generals who were granted commissions by Lincoln in his attempt to ensure the support of northern Democrats. Butler, a Massachusetts Democrat, would soon switch his allegiance to the Republican Party.

23. Like Fort Independence, Fort Warren was another of Boston's Third System harbor defenses. During the Civil War, it was used as a prison, housing mainly political prisoners and blockade runners.

24. Sergeant Leas was Thomas H. Leas of Company C.

25. James Mason and John Slidell were southern diplomats; Mason was appointed to represent the Confederacy in Britain, and Slidell was to serve as the southern minister to France. In early November 1861, both men were seized en route to Europe, nearly provoking a diplomatic crisis between the United States and Great Britain. They were incarcerated at Fort Warren in Boston harbor until Lincoln released them in January 1862 to defuse tensions with the British. Allan Nevins, *War for the Union*, vol. 1, *1861–1862: The Improvised War* (New York: Scribner, 1971), 384, 387–94.

26. Lieutenant Charles N. Turnbull was the officer who recruited Thompson. He later served with the Engineer Battalion, including a brief stint as its commander.

27. Thompson recorded his journal entries from November 22 through December 1, 1861, on small, loose sheets of paper that he later inserted into his bound, wartime journal.

28. Chirography means handwriting, particularly to distinguish it from typography, and Thompson's use of the term here may be reflective of his former experience as a printer.

29. These comments from Thompson about his reception in Hopedale on this brief furlough were likely reflective of the pacifist aspects of Practical Christianity as practiced by the community members. See Spann, *Hopedale*, xi, 120–24.

30. The "Topog Chorus" may refer to the song written by Francis Beahn about the dozen men who enlisted in the company of topographical engineers. See also pp. 337–38n2.

31. Thompson and the others who enlisted in the company of topographical engineers were transferred to Company B, Corps of Engineers, in mid-January 1862 as indicated by Thompson's wartime insertion here. Apparently, however, the men were informed of the upcoming transfer a couple of weeks in advance, as Thompson remarked on the change here in his entry for January 1, 1862. See also January 18, 1862, entry.

32. This is probably a reference to the basic infantry drill that the new engineer soldiers had to learn. Facings were turns to the left, right, or rear by

344 Notes to Pages 8–10

individual soldiers. Lieut.-Col. W. J. Hardee, *Rifle and Light Infantry Tactics; for the Exercise and Manoeuvres of Troops of When Acting as Light Infantry or Riflemen*, 2 vols. (Philadelphia, PA: J. B. Lippincott & Co., 1860–61), 1:18, 23.

33. H.R.R. refers to the Hudson Railroad, which runs north from New York City up the east bank of the Hudson River.

34. Sunnyside was Washington Irving's home in Tarrytown, New York.

35. Thompson's mother was Harriet Gilbert Thompson, who he sometimes also identified by her initials, H. G. T.

36. Jacob D. Geyser. Like many others, including Thompson, Geyser was transferred into Company D of the battalion when that company was created in July 1862. The Bowery Boys were one of the most well known of New York City's antebellum gangs, one that was also a political force in the city. Peter Adams, *The Bowery Boys: Street Corner Radicals and the Politics of Rebellion* (Westport, CT: Praeger, 2005).

37. Paying devoirs means formally paying one's respects.

38. Buttermilk Falls was the village immediately south of the US Military Academy at West Point; today it is called Highland Falls. Francis F. Dunwell, *The Hudson River Highlands* (New York: Columbia Univ. Press, 1991), 92.

39. Thompson was using the word elevated as a euphemism for inebriation.

40. Thompson often marked the time of his journal entries using military terms such as those included in this entry. Reveille was the signal marking the start of the day, calling the men to wake, usually at sunrise, though often earlier when on campaign; it was followed immediately by a morning roll call. Retreat marked the end of the work day and was usually sounded at sunset; if flags had been raised, they were lowered at this signal. Tattoo indicated that the soldiers should prepare for the day's end and secure the post or camp; it was followed by the day's final roll call, and the ordering of all men not on duty to their quarters. Taps was the signal for lights out; all men were to be in their bunks (or other sleeping arrangements) and quiet. Each roll call was a full calling of a company's roll to identify all who were absent. *Revised United States Army Regulations of 1861* (Washington, DC: Government Printing Office, 1863), 40; Bell Wiley, *The Life of Billy Yank: The Common Soldier of the Union* (Indianapolis, IN: Bobbs-Merrill, 1952; Garden City, NY: Doubleday, 1971), 45–47.

41. A chevaux de frise was an obstruction that usually consisted of sharpened stakes joined together and secured in place to obstruct and delay the approach of enemy troops. Here, Thompson seems to have been using the term as a generic one for any sort of obstruction with a military purpose, in this case the chain that was strung across the Hudson River during the War for Independence to prevent the British from moving past West Point. D. H. Mahan, *A Treatise of Field Fortification, Containing Instructions on the Method of Laying Out, Constructing,*

Defending, and Attacking Intrenchments, With the General Outlines Also of the Arrangement, the Attack and Defence of Permanent Fortifications, 3rd ed. (New York: John Wiley, 1861), 47.

42. In 1861, the Ordnance Museum, also known as the Ordnance and Artillery Museum, was located on the third floor of West Point's Academic Building, two floors above the chemistry lab that was housed with that department on the first floor of the building. The museum had been established in 1854 to display the trophies captured in the war with Mexico, but it also contained many objects acquired in earlier conflicts, dating back to the War for Independence, thus Thompson's reference to "guns captured at Saratoga, Stony Point, Monterrey, Vera Cruz, &c." Captain Edward C. Boynton, *History of West Point: and the Origin and Progress of the United States Military Academy* (London: Sampson Low, Son, & Marston, 1864), 226, 258, 296–97; Theodore J. Crackel, *West Point: A Bicentennial History* (Lawrence: Univ. Press of Kansas, 2002), 108.

43. Page was Allen Page, Company B. He later went missing during the Battles of the Seven Days.

44. Without further information it is impossible to identify Miss Albee conclusively, but she may have been Harriet Amanda Albee who, born in 1842, was of an age with Thompson and had attended the Hopedale Home School with him. "Catalogue of the Hopedale Home School," in *Hopedale Reminiscences,* ed. Hughes, 75; United States Census 1860, Worcester County, Massachusetts, population schedule, Milford, p. 118, dwelling 624, family 963, Stephen and Harriett M. Albee, digital image, FamilySearch, accessed June 20, 2016, https://familysearch.org/pal:/MM9.3.1/TH-1951-25248-10103-11?cc=1473181.

45. The three performers in this group besides Thompson were Robert C. Thayer, Mariner S. Fickett, and Edward J. Currier, all from the battalion's Company B.

46. This chapel, built in 1836, was just east of the Academic Building that housed, among other things, the museum that Thompson visited and wrote about on January 3, 1861. The guns Thompson mentioned here were trophies from the Mexican-American and Revolutionary wars. Today, this stone structure has been relocated to the West Point cemetery. Stephen E. Ambrose, *Duty, Honor, Country: A History of West Point* (Baltimore, MD: Johns Hopkins Univ. Press, 1966), 339; Boynton, *History of West Point,* 258; Crackel, *West Point,* 108, 178.

47. Fort Putnam was one of the Revolutionary War–era defenses of West Point. It was located on the high ground west of the site where the US Military Academy was later established. Crackel, *West Point,* 16, 20.

48. Just five days after the firing on Fort Sumter inaugurated the Civil War, most of the original engineer company, Company A, was dispatched as part of the reinforcement sent to Fort Pickens on Santa Rosa Island at the entrance to

Pensacola harbor. From mid-April through mid-September 1861, the sappers of Company A oversaw the efforts to make the fort more defensible. The constant work and limited rations imposed by the siege-like conditions resulted in much suffering for the men during this six-month posting. Thompson, *Engineer Battalion in the Civil War*, 1–2; Newell and Schrader, *Of Duty Well and Faithfully Done*, 287.

49. Half seas over was slang for intoxication.

50. Cold Spring, New York, is just across the Hudson River from West Point.

51. Sergeant William Anderson, Company A, Engineer Battalion.

52. This is probably a Mr. F. P. James, a banker in Cold Spring. United States Census 1860, Putnam County, New York, population schedule, Cold Spring and Phillipstown, p. 84, dwelling 241, family 325, F. P. and Julia James, digital image, FamilySearch, accessed April 21, 2016, https://familysearch.org/pal:/MM9.3.1/TH-1942-25265-8267-69?cc=1473181.

53. This may be William H. Morris, son of George Pope Morris of Undercliff, Cold Spring, New York (see also next annotation). However, in early 1862, William Morris was only a captain serving as the assistant adjutant general of the First Brigade, 1st Division, IV Corps, Army of the Potomac. He later rose to the rank of brigadier general and brevet major general. Bvt. Maj.-Gen. George W. Cullum, *Biographical Register of the Officers and Graduates of the U.S. Military Academy at West Point, N.Y., From Its Establishment in 1802, to 1890, with the Early History of the United States Military Academy*, 3rd ed., rev. and exp., 3 vols. (Boston: Houghton, Mifflin and Company, 1891), 2:295–96.

54. Undercliff was the summer home of the George Pope Morris, father of General William H. Morris. The elder Morris was a major cultural figure in New York; he was the co-publisher of the literary and artistic magazine the *New York Mirror* and was himself a relatively popular amateur poet. Dunwell, *Hudson River Highlands*, 77–79.

55. Artificer William Farr, Company A. Like Thompson, Farr transferred to Company D when it was created in July 1862.

56. Robert Ayres, a sergeant in Company A, was also transferred to Company D on its creation. He was promoted to second lieutenant in the 19th US Infantry on December 19, 1862.

57. For a thorough examination of the Mexican-American War activities of the engineer company, also known as Company A, Corps of Engineers, see Smith, "'The Hardest Work and Hardest Fighting,'" 1–46.

58. William Farr of Company A first enlisted in that unit in May 1855 for a five-year term, and he subsequently reenlisted in the spring of 1860 for five more years. At the date of Thompson's entry, he had been with the company for nearly seven years, not eight. Thompson's description of Farr as "an eight year

soldier," however, might have been based on Thompson's misunderstanding of Farr's second enlistment term. It is possible that Thompson thought Farr's reenlistment period was only for three years, like Thompson's, thus meaning that Farr would serve a total of eight years between his two terms. "Register of Enlistments in the US Army 1798–1914," Records of the Adjutant General's Office 1780s–1917, Record Group 94, National Archives Microfilm Publication M233 (cited hereafter as "NARA Microfilm Publication M233"), roll 25, 51:71; NARA Microfilm Publication M233, roll 75, 141:244.

59. Mary Grover belonged to the Committee of Ladies who helped to establish and run the Union Volunteer Refreshment Saloon in Philadelphia, which provided medical care and lodgings to Union soldiers in the city beginning in May 1861. See J. Thomas Scharf and Thompson Westcott, *History of Philadelphia, 1609–1884* (Philadelphia: L. H. Everts & Co., 1884), 1:832.

60. "Annie Lisle" is a ballad written in 1857 by H. S. Thompson. Gilbert Thompson's reference suggests that he and his friends were singing "Auld Lang Syne" to the tune of this other work. John W. Finson, *Voices that Are Gone: Themes in Nineteenth-Century American Popular Song* (Oxford: Oxford Univ. Press, 1994), 89.

61. In January 1862, Chauncey B. Reese was the first lieutenant in command of Company B of the Engineer Battalion.

62. The construction of field fortifications, also known as temporary fortifications or fieldworks, was one of the many technical specialties of engineer troops. Closely related to this responsibility was the construction of siege works, which also fell under the purview of the sappers.

63. Artificer James Latson of Company C was reported in the company rolls as having died of "Congestion of the Brain."

64. This ailing soldier was Private Daniel Miller, Company B.

65. At Dress Parade an entire unit, whether battalion, regiment, or brigade, turned out, and the men went through some of the manual of arms; in addition, reports were made, and orders and announcements were read aloud to the men. Wiley, *Billy Yank*, 46–47.

66. Guard duty was assigned to details in twenty-four hour blocs, with each member of the guard detail standing guard for two of every six hours. In addition to the usual camp guards, members of the Engineer Battalion were also frequently detailed to guard the bridges that they constructed and dismantled as well as the equipment for erecting those bridges. Wiley, *Billy Yank*, 46.

67. "A City of Magnificent Distances" was a nineteenth-century nickname for Washington, DC, and Thompson's subsequent description of the semi-finished nature of the capital city also evokes Charles Dickens's famous deprecating revision of that sobriquet into "A City of Magnificent Intentions." Charles

Dickens, *American Notes, For General Circulation,* 2 vols. (Paris: A. and W. Galignani and Co., 1842), 1:146.

68. Sara ——— may have been Sarah P. Lillie. See February 9, 1862, entry and p. 350n80.

69. Dr. Isaac I. Hayes, an American arctic explorer, led an 1860–61 expedition in search of the Open Polar Sea, a supposedly ice-free zone around the North Pole. After running a hospital during the Civil War, Hayes published a book about his arctic expedition in 1866. See Dennis Drabelle, "Pointing the Way to the Pole," *Pennsylvania Gazette* (Nov/Dec 2011), 41, 43–44.

70. This may be a reference to Joshua Hutchinson from the family that produced the popular antebellum Hutchinson Family Singers, a reform-minded musical group that might have had a special appeal to those like Thompson from the reform-minded Hopedale community. Joshua, however, was not a member of the primary group but another sibling of the main singers, though he did perform in the mid- and late 1840s as part of the Home Branch of the Hutchinson Family while the major group toured Great Britain. Joshua had also visited Thompson's hometown of Hopedale, Massachusetts, before the war, and he even ran a singing school there one winter. At the time of this journal entry, moreover, the Hutchinson Family Singers had just recently been driven out of the Army of the Potomac's encampment by McClellan for singing abolitionist songs and so may have been on Thompson's mind. Without some further information from Thompson, however, this is merely speculation. John Wallace Hutchinson, *Story of the Hutchinsons (Tribe of Jesse),* ed. Charles E. Mann, 2 vols. (Boston: Lee, Shepard, Publishers, 1896), 1:iii, 170–71; Vera Brodsky Lawrence, *Strong on Music: The New York Music Scene in the Days of George Templeton Strong,* vol. 1, *Resonances, 1836–1849* (Chicago, IL: Univ. of Chicago Press, 1988), 347, 412, 490; Nellie T. Gifford, "Childhood Days in the Hopedale Community," 43; Christian McWhirter, *Battle Hymns: The Power and Popularity of Music in the Civil War* (Chapel Hill: Univ. of North Carolina Press, 2012), 8–12.

71. George H. Young, twenty-one, of Milford, Massachusetts, was another a member of the Hopedale community from which Thompson came. United States Census 1860, Worcester County, Massachusetts, population schedule, Milford, p. 125, dwelling 672, family 1030, Charles and Roxanna Young, digital image, FamilySearch, accessed May 13, 2016, https://familysearch.org/pal: /MM9.3.1/TH-1942-25248-12183-68?cc=1473181; Gifford, "Childhood Days in the Hopedale Community," 43.

72. "From Greenland's Icy Mountains" was an early nineteenth-century missionary hymn written by Reginald Heber in 1819 as part of a campaign by the Society for the Propagation of the Gospel. J. R. Watson, ed., *An Annotated Anthology of Hymns* (Oxford: Oxford Univ. Press, 2002), 242–43.

73. It is possible that Thompson's bunkmate at this time was George Ames; see January 28, 1862, entry. It could also have been Thomas Rand, who at the time was a private in Company B like Thompson; later Thompson and Rand definitely shared quarters in camp.

74. One of the many duties of engineer soldiers was the care, protection, deployment, withdrawal, and sometimes destruction of military bridges such as pontoon bridges. The boats that Thompson refers to here were thirty-one feet long and weighed approximately thirteen hundred pounds; it took twenty men to lift each boat from its wagon during the construction of a bridge. A single bridge train consisted of thirty-four such wagons loaded with the pontoon boats and other materials, plus thirty-four additional wagons containing other accoutrements, and two traveling forges. James Chatham Duane, *Manual for Engineer Troops*, 3rd ed. (New York: D. Van Nostrand, 1864), 7–18; Jonathon K. Rice, *Moving Mountains: A Study in Civil War Logistics* (Bloomington, IN: Xlibris, 2011), 44; Ed Malles, ed., *Bridge Building in Wartime: Colonel Wesley Brainerd's Memoir of the 50th New York Volunteer Engineers* (Knoxville: Univ. of Tennessee Press, 1997), 386n; John D. Billings, *Hardtack and Coffee: A Soldier's Life in the Civil War* (1887; repr., Saybrook, CT: Konecky & Konecky, n.d.), 384.

75. Higgins was Atkins Higgins of Company B. The spider Thompson described was some type of cooking implement. Originally, a spider was a frying pan mounted on a tripod, though the term was also used more loosely to refer to a simple cast iron skillet or frying pan, and it is unclear which of these Thompson meant.

76. There were too many Smiths in the battalion to identify this individual conclusively, but it was probably George Smith, who was the only Smith in Company B at the date of this entry. While Thompson could have been writing of someone in another of the battalion's companies, his reference to "our men" suggests, though not conclusively, that he was referring to someone from his own Company B. The Crimean War was a conflict between Russia and the alliance of Britain, France, and the Ottoman Empire from 1853–1856.

77. Thompson was claiming that before joining the Engineer Battalion, Thaddeus K. Pendleton of Company B participated in the Second Opium War of 1856–1860 and served on the HMS *Hero* which returned Albert Edward, Prince of Wales (and the future King Edward VII) to England. In the late summer of 1860, Prince Albert made a state visit to North America. On September 20, having completed his official visit, he entered the United States for a six-week unofficial tour, traveling under one of his lesser titles, the Baron of Renfrew. He entered the United States at Detroit, then swung west and south, turning northwards at Richmond, Virginia, and proceeding from there up the coast to Portland, Maine. On October 20, 1860, he started home aboard the *Hero* under

Captain George H. Seymour, presumably with Thaddeus Pendleton aboard as a member of the ship's crew. Thompson's reference to "H'old H'ngland" here appears to be an attempt to render "old England" in a phonetic British accent of some variety. Ian Radforth, *Royal Spectacle: The 1860 Visit of the Prince of Wales to Canada and the United States* (Toronto: Univ. of Toronto Press, 2004), 3, 6–7, 313–64.

78. Thompson was perhaps referring here to his first stint on guard duty. See also January 23, 1862, journal entry.

79. Thompson confused two of Sir Walter Scott's poems here; he named "The Lady of the Lake" but quoted from "The Lay of the Last Minstrel."

80. This is likely Sarah P. Lillie, a young unmarried schoolteacher from Hopedale whose father had been one of the original members of the joint stock company that founded and administered the community until 1856. Ms. Lillie was a year younger than Thompson and lived only a few doors down from him and his mother. United States Census 1860, Worcester County, Massachusetts, population schedule, Milford, p. 122, dwelling 650, family 998, Henry and Caroline Lilley, digital image, FamilySearch, accessed May 6, 2016, https://familysearch.org/pal:/MM9.3.1/TH-1951-25248-10357-57?cc=1473181; Spann, *Hopedale*, 30, 154; Massachusetts State Census 1855, Worcester County, population schedule, Milford, p. 129, dwelling 732, family 1091, Henry and Caroline Lilly [*sic*], digital image, FamilySearch, accessed June 13, 2016, https://familysearch.org/pal:/MM9.3.1/TH-267-11770-177419-36?cc=1459987; Massachusetts State Census 1855, Worcester County, population schedule, Milford, p. 129, dwelling 735, family 1096, Harriet Thompson, digital image, FamilySearch, accessed June 13, 2016, https://familysearch.org/pal:/MM9.3.1/TH-267-11770-177419-36?cc=1459987.

81. Much of this entry discusses operations in late February 1862 that stemmed from Major General George B. McClellan's attempt to cross the Potomac at Harpers Ferry with portions of his army. His objectives were to clear the rebels out of Winchester, Virginia, and open the Baltimore and Ohio Railroad to restore Washington's connection with the Ohio Valley. In addition to the lighter pontoon bridge that the Engineer Battalion laid over the Potomac (and which Thompson described later in this entry), McClellan intended to construct another, more robust crossing for his heavy supplies. He intended to build this sturdier bridge using canal boats, but they turned out to be too wide to fit through the lift lock connecting the Chesapeake and Ohio Canal with the Potomac River, and McClellan gave up the effort and returned to Washington, leaving Nathaniel Banks behind to cover the construction of a railroad bridge and, eventually, to occupy Winchester. Stephen W. Sears, *To the Gates of Richmond: The Peninsula Campaign* (New York: Ticknor & Fields, 1992), 11; Allan Nevins,

The War for the Union, vol. 2, *1862–1863: War Becomes Revolution* (New York: Scribner, 1971), 42; Stephen W. Sears, *George B. McClellan: The Young Napoleon* (New York: Ticknor & Fields, 1998), 156–58.

82. The Relay House is the site of a junction on the Baltimore and Ohio Railroad where a spur breaks off the main line to run to Washington, DC. In early May 1861, Brigadier General Benjamin Butler seized the junction as part of his attempts to secure Washington. John F. Stover, *History of the Baltimore and Ohio Railroad* (West Lafayette, IN: Purdue Univ. Press, 1987), 39–41, 114; Chester G. Hearn, *When the Devil Came Down to Dixie: Ben Butler in New Orleans* (Baton Rouge: Louisiana State Univ. Press, 1997), 28.

83. Frederick W. Gerber, 1st sergeant of the Engineer Battalion. See also Thompson's memoir recollection following this entry on pp. 25–26 and another memoir passage on p. 77.

84. A balk was a length of wood used to connect pontoon-bridging boats across a body of water. They came in two varieties, the balk and the shorter claw balk. Duane, *Manual for Engineer Troops*, 14, 17–18, 21, 23.

85. Chess is the technical term for the planking used to form a roadway over a pontoon bridge; after it was laid atop the balks that connected the pontoon boats, the chess served as the bridge's flooring. See Duane, *Manual for Engineer Troops*, 14, 23.

86. There were many different methods to throw a bridge over a watercourse, and the selection of any given one depended a great deal on the particular circumstances. There was, however, a general pattern. In all cases, the men were divided into six to eight sections in order to accomplish the many required tasks. One group was detailed to prepare the abutments where the bridge would join the riverbanks. This section established the abutment on the near bank first, then loaded its tools and materials into a pontoon boat, crossed the river, and prepared the abutment on the far bank. Another section, sometimes two, was tasked with constructing the bridge trestles, if any were used. These men moved the supports into position and set the trestles for the bridge. Up to two sections of pontoneers were tasked with placing the bridge's floating supports, whether of pontoons, rafts, or civil craft dragooned into service. The men of these groups would first set two anchor cables, one upstream and another down, or if it was a narrow crossing, they would set a single sheer-line running across the river instead. Once these lines were set, the pontoneers moved the boats into position and secured them to the lines. Another group, sometimes two, handled the balks that connected the pontoons. They unloaded the balks, accompanied them in the pontoons to their position on the bridge, and then lashed them to the boats to form the superstructure of the bridge. A chess section secured the planking that formed the bridge's roadway, and another group installed side

rails to complete it. In certain circumstances, a bridge might be built in parts by connecting three pontoons along the shore. Those larger parts, once complete, would be floated downstream or towed upstream to the crossing spot, where they were would be secured together and to the appropriate abutments and trestles, if used. Duane, *Manual for Engineer Troops,* 19–48; Billings, *Hardtack and Coffee,* 386–87.

87. In February 1862, Major General Nathaniel P. Banks commanded a division in the Army of the Potomac under McClellan's overall command.

88. Thompson was referring to the 1859 raid on the federal arsenal in Harpers Ferry, Virginia, by the abolitionist John Brown and his followers. The fire-engine house at the federal complex in Harpers Ferry was a brick building with thick oak doors, and Brown and his men retreated into it when they were surrounded by local militia forces. It was also this building that was stormed by US Marines under the command of cavalry lieutenant J. E. B. Stuart to end the raid and capture Brown. Thompson's comment that "we were all John Brown men" may reflect the anti-slavery tendencies of his Hopedale, Massachusetts, upbringing. Stephen B. Oates, *To Purge This Land with Blood: A Biography of John Brown* (New York: Harper & Row, 1970), 295, 300.

89. In the American Civil War, northern and southern Zouave units wore distinctive and colorful uniforms that were patterned after the Algerian Zouaves that had fought for France in the Crimean War. In the Union army several of these units were raised from urban fire companies and known as Fire Zouaves. The only such regiment that was part of McClellan's army and present at Harpers Ferry at the date of this entry by Thompson was the 72nd Pennsylvania Infantry Regiment, also known as the Philadelphia Fire Zouaves or Baxter's Philadelphia Fire Zouaves. Their fire company experience may explain why they sought to secure the fire engines that Thompson mentioned. See John T. Fallon, *List of Synonyms of Organizations in the Volunteer Service of the United States during the Years 1861, '62, '63, '64, and '65* (Washington, DC: Government Printing Office, 1885), 44, 104, 149, 170, 223; Frederick H. Dyer, comp., *A Compendium of the War of the Rebellion, Compiled and Arranged from Official Records of the Federal and Confederate Armies, Reports of the Adjutant Generals of the Several States, the Army Registers and Other Reliable Documents and Sources* (Des Moines, IA: Dyer Publishing Company, 1908), 1254, 1259, 1409, 1433, 1597; "Extract Embracing the 'First Period,' from Maj. Gen. George B. McClellan's Report of the Operations of the Army of the Potomac from July 27,1861, to November 9, 1862," *OR,* ser. 1, vol. 5, 48.

90. Sibley tents were conical tents capable of housing twelve men. They were designed in 1856 by Henry Hopkins Sibley a US Army officer who later served as a Confederate brigadier general. Both Union and Confederate forces used Sibley

tents during the Civil War. Capt. Randolph B. Marcy, *The Prairie Traveler: A Hand-Book for Overland Expeditions* (New York: Harper & Brothers, 1861), 142–44.

91. After Virginia militia seized the federal armory at Harpers Ferry in 1861, Confederate forces relocated its valuable machinery to Richmond, then destroyed its main buildings as well as the Baltimore and Ohio Railroad bridge over the Potomac before abandoning the town. This destruction also prompted the first of several evacuations of the area. By the time Thompson and the Engineer Battalion arrived in February 1862, the town was a far cry from its antebellum heyday. The "destroyed bridge at Harpers Ferry" that Thompson mentioned camping near earlier in this entry was the B&O Railroad bridge. See Merritt Roe Smith, *Harpers Ferry Armory and the New Technology: The Challenge of Change* (Ithaca, NY: Cornell Univ. Press, 1977), 319–20.

92. This may refer to the bridge that McClellan planned to construct using canal barges before he realized that they were too wide to pass the locks into the river. See pp. 350–51n81.

93. Colonel John W. Geary led the 28th Pennsylvania Volunteer Infantry.

94. John Edwin Cook first met John Brown in Kansas after the Pottawatomie Massacre in the spring of 1856. Cook eagerly joined Brown's planned raid on Harpers Ferry, even traveling to the area far in advance of the other participants to collect information. During the actual raid, Cook and C. P. Tidd cut the telegraph lines to isolate the town as the others stormed the federal facility. Like several of the raiders, Cook was apprehended, tried, and executed after the failure of the raid. Oates, *To Purge This Land with Blood*, 41, 218–19, 251–52, 302, 350.

95. While the particular passage Thompson references here is unclear, the author he identified is Thomas Babington Macaulay, a British writer and politician.

96. Major General Winfield Scott commanded American forces during the 1847 campaign against Mexico City in the Mexican-American War.

97. Capt. James C. Duane commanded the Engineer Battalion through November 1862.

98. These volunteer engineers were probably the 15th and 50th New York Volunteer Engineers, both of which also served with the Army of the Potomac.

99. Gerber was awarded the Medal of Honor in 1871 to recognize his twenty-five years of service as a non-commissioned officer, a period that included the Mexican-American War, the Civil War, and several Native American conflicts. Frank N. Schubert, *Black Valor: Buffalo Soldiers and the Medal of Honor, 1870–1898* (Lanham, MD: Rowman & Littlefield, 2009), 6.

100. Founded in 1866, the Grand Army of the Republic (GAR) was the largest Union's veterans' organization. Stuart McConnell, *Glorious Contentment:*

The Grand Army of the Republic, 1865–1900 (Chapel Hill: Univ. of North Carolina Press, 1992), 15.

101. "Ned" Coolidge appears on the Engineer Battalion's official monthly rosters as both Edwin H. Coolidge and Edward H. Coolidge, but his pension application identifies him as Edwin. In early 1862, he was an artificer in Company C; he was transferred to Company D when it was established later that summer. "General Index to Pension Files 1861–1934," Records of the Department of Veteran Affairs, Record Group 15, National Archives Microfilm Publication T288 (cited hereafter as "NARA Microfilm Publication T288"), roll 96.

102. Artificer James Latson of Company C who died on January 22, 1862. See that entry and p. 347n63.

103. According to Duane's manual, a flying bridge was "any floating support anchored to a fixed a point (usually in the stream), and driven from shore to shore by the oblique action of the current on its sides." These types of bridges did not open permanent communications across a river, but they could be constructed quickly with relatively few men and they allowed troops of all arms to cross so long as the current was not more than two miles per hour. The flying bridge Thompson described here was thrown over the Shenandoah by the Engineer Battalion on February 28 to allow Union forces to cross the river and deal with a rebel contingent that had been harassing the trains on the Baltimore and Ohio. Duane, *Manual for Engineer Troops*, 34; Sears, *George B. McClellan*, 157–58.

104. In this encounter, Col. John W. Geary commanded his own regiment, the 28th Pennsylvania Infantry, plus a four-gun battery and a battalion of the 1st Michigan Cavalry. These forces crossed the Shenandoah to halt Confederate assaults on the trains using the Baltimore and Ohio Railroad. The very presence of Geary's force threatened the rebels' line of communication and temporarily halted their attacks. Geary also managed to capture a few prisoners during these operations. "Report of Col. John W. Geary, Twenty-Eighth Pennsylvania Infantry, including Operations of his Command to May 6, 1862," in *OR*, ser. 1, vol. 5, 512.

105. Belial is another name for Satan.

106. A pontoon boat train consisted of seventy wagons. There were thirty-four pontoon wagons, so named because the primary load of each of them was a single thirteen-hundred-pound wooden pontoon, though a considerable amount of additional equipment was stored in and around the boat, including balks, lashings, oars, and other materials. There were also twenty-two chess wagons loaded with bridge planking and cables in the train. Twelve wagons were set aside to carry a variety of other materials. The last two components of the train were not wagons, per se, but traveling forges, which were mounted on their own mobile carriages. Duane, *Manual for Engineer Troops*, 17–18.

107. Budd's Ferry was on the Potomac River, about thirty-five miles south of Washington.

108. This march was part of McClellan's movement toward the Confederate position at Manassas, Virginia, west of the Union capital. The movement began on March 10, 1862, and quickly came to a disappointing conclusion when it became clear that rebel forces had withdrawn from Manassas to a new position behind the Rappahannock River. Sears, *George B. McClellan*, 163.

109. An epaulement was a minor field fortification intended mainly to screen troops from the enemy rather than offer substantial protection. D. H. Mahan, *An Elementary Course of Military Engineering*, 2 vols. (New York: John Wiley & Son, 1867), 2:2–3.

110. The Long Bridge over the Potomac River had initially been open only to wagon and pedestrian traffic, but in early 1862 rail tracks were laid across it. The bridge was located in Washington, at the site of the modern Fourteenth Street Bridge. Albert J. Churella, *The Pennsylvania Railroad*, vol. 1, *Building An Empire, 1846–1917* (Philadelphia: Univ. of Pennsylvania Press, 2013), 431.

111. Without further information or some indication of whether Withrop was a first or last name, it is impossible to identify this person.

112. The banquette was the raised walkway (and the slope leading to it) found inside a defensive work on which men and guns could be positioned. A redoubt was any enclosed work capable of defense in all directions. Redoubts also had no re-entering angles, or angles whose apices were directed inwards towards the defensive work itself. Mahan, *A Treatise of Field Fortification*, 12, Plate 1, Fig. 1.

113. See p. 355n108.

114. Greenway Court in the Shenandoah Valley was the home of Thomas, Lord Fairfax, who was a patron of the young George Washington. Ron Chernow, *Washington: A Life* (New York: Penguin Press, 2010), 16, 19–20, 22.

115. Private Edwin A. Kimball was discharged on April 30, 1862.

116. Thompson noted elsewhere in the memoir portions of his reminisces that President Lincoln's visit to the lower Potomac where the Engineer Battalion was at work occurred about March 10, 1862.

2. Uncle Sam's Pontoon Shoes

1. In a postwar comment, Thompson asserted that Turtle's description of the battalion's role at New Bridge during the Battle of Mechanicsville on June 26, 1862, was:

An error, as our army never crossed New Bridge; a detachment did go there, and during the night tried to float the boats and material down the stream, but day coming on before they could get inside the lines, they scuttled them and burned the rest. This was the morning of the day of the battle of Gaines's Mill, Friday the 27th, and when our detachment went into the redoubt by order of Colonel [Barton] Alexander we saw the smoke near New Bridge. They had a close race in as the Rebels began crossing at New Bridge very soon—General [Winfield Scott] Hancock [of the First Brigade, 2nd Division, VI Corps] was asking us in the rifle-pit if we could give an idea how they were moving. We could see them moving that way, their attack in our front was only to keep us in doubt where they were to strike. When they came out to attack us, it was a grand sight. Hancock told us to "fire steady, pick out your man, and if they crowd up on you give them the bayonet." I admired his manner very much.

Of Turtle's claim that Confederate forces appeared on the opposite bank of the Chickahominy River just as the detachment from the battalion finished destroying the bridges on the morning of June 28, 1862, Thompson wrote later: "This I cannot confirm, but it is worthy of note; Lieutenant Turtle received this from Captain Reese."

2. Thompson's remark about the "Bull Run rout-e" was a play on the meanings of the words rout and route.

3. Major General Nathaniel Banks commanded over twenty thousand Union troops of the Army of the Potomac's V Corps that were in the Shenandoah Valley at the date of this entry, and Banks's men would soon be engaged against Confederate forces under Stonewall Jackson's command.

4. As noted earlier, when rebel forces withdrew from Manassas they retreated to a line behind the Rappahannock River, not to Gordonsville some forty miles southwest of the river as this rumor claimed. See also March 11, 1862, entry and p. 355n108.

5. In the late winter of 1862, Brigadier (soon to be Major) General Ambrose E. Burnside was in command of the Burnside expedition, which was establishing Union control of most of the major ports on the North Carolina coast. Despite Thompson's report of Burnside in trouble, the brigadier was consolidating his control over Newbern, North Carolina, at the date of this entry. Sears, *To the Gates of Richmond*, 157; William Marvel, *Burnside* (Chapel Hill: Univ. of North Carolina Press, 1991), 77.

6. After the Confederate withdrawal from Manassas, McClellan's plan to land his army at Urbanna, Virginia, near the mouth of the Rappahannock and flank the rebel position at Manassas while advancing on Richmond was foiled. The general's new plan was to land at Fort Monroe on the Virginia Peninsula between the James and York rivers, avoiding the new Confederate line along the Rappahannock. This allowed him to move against the Confederate capital from the southeast. The first components of his army steamed out of the area around

Washington on this maneuver on March 17, the day after Thompson recorded this entry. Sears, *George B. McClellan*, 131, 163–67.

7. Robert Ayres was a sergeant in Company D.

8. Euchre is a trick-taking card game that was popular in the nineteenth-century United States. Charles Henry Wharton Meehan, *The Law and Practice of the Games of Euchre* (Philadelphia, PA: T. B. Peterson, 1862), 35–43; Wiley, *Billy Yank*, 250.

9. The author of this entry, Frederick Vogel, accompanied the bulk of the battalion to Fort Monroe at the opening of McClellan's 1862 Peninsula campaign, while Thompson was with the detachment that initially stayed behind to continue loading some of the unit's materials. See also next annotation and Thompson's March 30, 1862, entry.

10. In early 1862, Vogel was a member of Company C who, like Thompson, would later be transferred to Company D. His last name was often spelled "Vogl," "Vogel" or occasionally "Vogle" in Thompson's wartime journals and on the battalion's official monthly rolls, but Thompson consistently spelled it "Vogel" in his postwar writings, so that spelling has been adopted. In 1886, Vogel sent copies of his wartime journal to Thompson. Because Vogel's journal entries exist only in Thompson's postwar recollections and show signs of having been edited by Thompson, those entries have also been differentiated in the main text in the same way as Thompson's own postwar writings.

11. Thompson's mention of "the re-enlistment list" was a reference to the relatively small proportion of battalion men who reenlisted for three (or five) more years of service in the regular army, regardless of when the war ended. See also the memoir passage on p. 311 and p. 436n71.

12. Thompson clearly wrote the name Vickus in this March 1862 journal entry, but he was most likely referring to Ordnance Sergeant Thomas Vickers. Born in Derbyshire, England, about 1800, Vickers enlisted in the US Army in 1831. For five years he served in Company E of the 1st Artillery, but when he reenlisted in 1836 he joined the Ordnance Department, where he continued to serve and where he was eventually promoted to the rank of sergeant. At the date of Thompson's entry, Vickers had been in the American army for thirty-one years, and he was stationed in the national capital where Thompson recorded this entry. It is possible that Vickers served in the British army before coming to the United States, and he may have been at Waterloo as Thompson reported, though Vickers would have only been about fifteen years old at the time. It is unlikely that he had served a full fifty years as a soldier by 1862, however, as that would have required him to enlist in the British army at the age of twelve. He ultimately gave thirty-five years of service to the United States, dying of bronchitis

in Washington while still an ordnance sergeant in 1866. NARA Microfilm Publication M233, roll 20, 41:205, 216; NARA Microfilm Publication M233, roll 21, 43:255; NARA Microfilm Publication M233, roll 22, 48:259; NARA Microfilm Publication M233, roll 24, 49:223; NARA Microfilm Publication M233, roll 28, 57:227; NARA Microfilm Publication M233, roll 30, 61:234.

13. Corporal Thompson was James Thompson of Company B.

14. In his postwar recollections, Thompson added the following comment to Vogel's April 5, 1862, journal entry that described the battalion's stay in the same field where Lord Cornwallis surrendered to George Washington following the siege of Yorktown in 1781: "Vogel is wrong here, this camp was made the 8th of May." See also Thompson's journal entry for May 10, 1862.

15. Gabions were cylindrical frameworks made of wicker that were open at both ends. They could be filled with earth for use in constructing field fortifications, and they were particularly useful in siege operations as they could be built in advance and moved into place quickly. Duane, *Manual for Engineer Troops*, 67.

16. Thompson wrote of this entry by Vogel, dated April 12, 1862: "There is a little confusion here, and from the fact that I have Saturday the 12th of April and Vogel Friday. We—the squad—came into the camp on Wormley's Creek the 11th of April per my Journal, and maybe the Battalion did also, only earlier in the day. I may be behind one day's date, but Vogel's journal helps about the camps between Hampton and Yorktown. No. Friday was April 11th." Thompson was correct about the dates. April 11, 1862, was Friday, and the twelfth was Saturday.

17. Thaddeus S. C. Lowe was the primary figure behind the Union's Balloon Corps in the war's early years, and he provided valuable intelligence for the Army of the Potomac during McClellan's Peninsula campaign.

18. Thompson corrected this entry by Vogel, noting that the battalion camped on Wormley's Creek and not, as Vogel reported, Black Creek.

19. These bridges were likely over the many small waterways in the area, and they were placed so that Union forces could bring up and position their heavy artillery. Thompson, *Engineer Battalion in the Civil War*, 10. See also Thompson's entry for April 22, 1862, and p. 358n20.

20. These bridges over Wormley's Creek were built to allow the movement of Union siege guns to their batteries. Sears, *To the Gates of Richmond*, 58.

21. A posé is a place to stop and rest along a portage route.

22. Having enlisted in the regular US Army rather than a volunteer unit, Thompson and his fellow volunteers in the Engineer Battalion had signed up for three years of service rather than three years or the duration of the war, as was the case in many volunteer regiments.

23. Embrasures were openings in the walls, or parapets, of defensive works through which artillery could fire, and the parenthetical number Thompson provided suggests that Battery No. 3 had six of them. Mahan, *Treatise of Field Fortification*, 54.

24. A parallel was a trench used when besieging an enemy position. As is apparent from the name, it paralleled an enemy's defensive works and was connected to the position of one's own forces with communication trenches, or boyaux, that ran generally perpendicular to the position of both forces. To approach an enemy position, multiple parallels would be constructed, each somewhat closer to the enemy's position. The parallel closest to one's own line would be the First Parallel, and the next one would be the Second Parallel, and so forth. Generally, after the First Parallel, the boyaux would be built in a zig-zag pattern to help cover the men. These crooked communications trenches were also known as saps, and they are the origin of the term sapper, which was often used as a synonym for an engineer soldier. Mahan, *Treatise of Field Fortification*, 145–49.

25. At the date of this entry in late April 1862, Edward M. Marshall was a corporal in Company G of the 40th New York, but before the outbreak of the war, he lived in Milford, Massachusetts, where he and Thompson likely knew one another. *Annual Report of the Adjutant-General of the State of New York for the Year 1900. Registers of the Thirty-ninth, Fortieth, Forty-first, Forty-second and Forty-third Regiments of Infantry*, vol. 3, serial no. 23 (Albany: James B. Lyon, State Printer, 1901), 512; Ballou, *History of the Town of Milford*, 1:166.

26. The 40th New York was nicknamed the Mozart Regiment for the Mozart Hall political faction in New York City, then led by Fernando Wood. This faction provided the funds necessary to complete the organization of the unit. Though it carried a New York designation, it included four companies raised in Massachusetts and two raised in Pennsylvania during the early enthusiasm after the attack on Fort Sumter. Thomas E. V. Smith, *Political Parties and Their Places of Meeting in New York City, Read Before the New York Historical Society February 7th, 1893* (New York: n.p., 1893), 18; Frederick Phisterer, comp., *New York in the War of the Rebellion, 1861 to 1865*, 3rd ed., 5 vols. (Albany, NY: J. B. Lyon Company, State Printers, 1912), 3:2213–14.

27. A corduroy road was constructed by covering a road with logs laid perpendicular to the direction of travel and securing them to stringers laid parallel to the direction of travel on either side of the road. The process was employed to allow passage over muddy or marshy roads, and the construction of such a passage was called corduroying. Edward S. Farrow, *A Dictionary of Military Terms*, rev. ed. (New York: Thomas Y. Cromwell Co., 1918), 144.

28. After McClellan spent a month approaching the fortified defenses of Yorktown, Confederate general Joseph E. Johnston abandoned the city on the

night of May 3–4, 1862, before McClellan could open his siege guns against what Johnston believed to be a weak defensive position.

29. The engagement that Thompson described second-hand in this entry was probably the Battle of Williamsburg on May 5, 1862. In this encounter, a rebel division under Major General James Longstreet fought a delaying action against pursuing Union troops while the main Confederate force withdrew up the peninsula. It is also possible, however, that Thompson's confidant had attempted to describe the cavalry skirmishing that occurred during the Confederate withdrawal late on May 4. Sears, *To the Gates of Richmond*, 69–82.

30. There was undoubtedly some skirmishing between Johnston's retreating Confederates and McClellan's pursuing Federals on the evening of May 6, but the main rebel delaying action was fought the day before at the Battle of Williamsburg. Confederate major general John B. "Prince John" Magruder, who had been in charge of Confederate forces at Yorktown when McClellan first arrived on the Peninsula, was not wounded or killed in any of this fighting in early May, nor was his entire force captured, despite Thompson's report. Magruder went on to a long if unremarkable career in the Confederate army, and Thompson realized his error very quickly. He added a wartime notation in the margin of his journal next to his remarks about Magruder's death and his army's capture, describing his own original comment as "A splendid Rumor after all (I guess)." Sears, *To the Gates of Richmond*, 68–85.

31. A parapet was the embankment of a fieldwork that provided the primary protection from enemy fire. Mahan, *Treatise on Field Fortification*, 2.

32. The Battle of Williamsburg on May 5, 1862. See journal entries for May 6 and 7, 1862, and p. 360n29–30.

33. Thompson was mistaken as White House and Cumberland Landings were distinct points on the Pamunkey River, with White House Landing about five river miles west of Cumberland Landing.

34. As noted above, White House Landing is on the Pamunkey River. It is likely that Thompson also mentioned the York because the Pamunkey combines with the Mattapony River to form the York downstream from White House Landing.

35. The White House that Thompson mentioned here was the site of the plantation owned by the widowed Martha Dandridge Custis in 1759 and the location of her wedding to George Washington, but the original house had been destroyed and the building present in 1862 was only about thirty years old. John E. Ferling, *The First of Men: A Life of George Washington* (Knoxville: Univ. of Tennessee Press, 1988), 51, 61–62; Malles, *Bridge Building in Wartime*, 355n10.

36. Probably Theodore Kendall of Company B.

37. Brigadier General Silas Casey (who was promoted to major general a week after Thompson wrote this entry) commanded the 3rd Division, IV Corps, Army of the Potomac in May 1862.

38. At the date of this entry, Brigadier General Henry W. Slocum had only recently been elevated to the command of the 1st Division, VI Corps of McClellan's army on the Peninsula.

39. As McClellan's forces bridged the Chickahominy and prepared to besiege Richmond, the Union commander heard reports that the Confederates were planning to advance a force of seventeen thousand men to Hanover Court House north of Richmond and just south of the Pamunkey River in the right rear of Federal forces on the Peninsula. McClellan sent Fitz John Porter and about twelve thousand men of his V Corps to clear this area, and the resulting Battle of Hanover Court House on May 27 against four thousand Confederates under Lawrence O'Bryan Branch eliminated the threat. Sears, *To the Gates of Richmond*, 114–17.

40. The wounded sapper that Thompson mentioned here was Private Edwin F. Austin of Company A. His wound was not mortal, but Austin was discharged from the company several months later for disability. By early 1864, however, he was well enough to reenlist, and he rejoined his comrades in Company A that May. See also the quoted passage on pp. 56–57 and p. 361n42–44.

41. Fair Oaks, known to southerners as Seven Pines, was Confederate general Joseph Johnston's poorly managed and unsuccessful attempt to drive the Army of the Potomac away from Richmond on May 31, 1862. Late in the engagement, Johnston himself was wounded, leading to his replacement by Robert E. Lee as commander of the Army of Northern Virginia.

42. First Lieutenant Orville E. Babcock, then with Company A of the Engineer Battalion.

43. Thompson added his postwar thoughts to John G. Barnard's report of the battalion soldier "shot through the lungs," noting that: "At first it was thought so, but it was a glancing shot, coming out at the back. E. F. Austin, in charge [of] Lafayette Square, Washington, D.C., 1886–7. He told me he was shot through the Lungs." The battalion's monthly rolls record that Private Edwin F. Austin was "Shot through the right lung" on June 1, 1862.

44. Where the author of this passage, John G. Barnard, noted his relief at learning that it was an enlisted man who had been shot through the lung and not, as he had first thought, Lieutenant Babcock, Thompson added an exclamation mark in the margin, as if to show his surprise that Barnard evinced more concern for an officer than for a simple soldier.

45. Brigadier General John G. Barnard was chief engineer of the Army of the Potomac during the Peninsula campaign, and Brigadier General William F. Barry

was its chief of artillery, as indicated by the source citation for the quotation that Thompson copied into his memoirs.

46. The muddy, boggy banks of the Chickahominy required extensive corduroying of the approaches to the military bridges that the engineers built across the river. J. G. Barnard and W. F. Barry, *Report of the Engineer and Artillery Operations of the Army of the Potomac, From Its Organization to the Close of the Peninsular Campaign by Brig.-Gen. J. G. Barnard, Chief Engineer, and Brig.-Gen. W. F. Barry, Chief of Artillery* (New York: D. Van Nostrand, 1863), 18–21.

47. This was the Lower Trestle Bridge over the Chickahominy River. Thompson, *Engineer Battalion in the Civil War*, 14.

48. The only member of the battalion who died in June 1862 was Nicholas Drum, Company A, who died of typhoid fever; moreover, no one else from the unit took injuries that month matching Thompson's description, so he must have been referring to a member of a working party assisting the battalion and not one of the sappers. See also entry and annotations for June 19, 1862.

49. This was probably Private Peter Kelsey of Company A, who, according to the battalion's monthly rolls, was "shot in the leg" on June 7. However, it could refer to another member of the company who took a wound so slight it was not reported.

50. Private Nicholas Drum died of typhoid on June 17, 1862.

51. Details of the battalion had been put to work building batteries and fieldworks in the days before this entry on June 22, 1862. Thompson, *Engineer Battalion in the Civil War*, 16.

52. In late June 1862, Major General Ambrose Burnside's command was still in North Carolina, but he was about to assume command of the reinforcements for the Army of the Potomac that were gathering in Newport News, Virginia. Brigadier General Henry Prince at this time was about to be ordered to join McClellan's army and may have been with Burnside as a result. By late July, however, Prince had been assigned to command the Second Brigade, 2nd Division, II Corps, of the Army of Virginia under Major General John Pope. Sears, *To the Gates of Richmond*, 157, 162; L. Thomas, Special Orders No. 154, 6 July 1862, in *OR*, ser. 1, vol. 11, part 3, 305; Cullum, *Biographical Register*, 1:613, 2:319.

53. Thompson was quoting from the hymn "Mercy in the Midst of Judgment." Darius E. Jones, *Temple Melodies: A Collection of About Two Hundred Popular Tunes, Adapted by Nearly Five Hundred Favorite Hymns, with Special Reference to Public, Social, and Private Worship* (New York: Mason & Law, 1852), 85.

54. This was the Battle of Mechanicsville, also known as the Battle of Beaver Dam Creek, on June 26, 1862. It marked the beginning of Robert E. Lee's offensive that drove the Army of the Potomac away from Richmond in the Battles of the Seven Days.

55. Sumner's Upper Bridge on the Chickahominy River, built by troops from Major General Edwin Sumner's II Corps, was also known by the local appellation of Grapevine Bridge.

56. Trent's house, which Thompson mentioned here, refers to the home of Dr. Peterfield Trent. This house served for a time as McClellan's headquarters. The bridge near it that Thompson also referenced was built by the volunteer engineers serving with the Army of the Potomac and was also known as Woodbury and Alexander's Bridge or just Alexander's Bridge. Army, *Engineering Victory*, 125–26; Thompson, *Engineer Battalion in the Civil War*, 104.

57. A sink was a latrine.

58. François d'Orleans, Prince de Joinville, was a son of Louis Phillipe, the king of France from 1830 to 1848. De Joinville came to the United States after the Civil War broke out and served as an unofficial member of McClellan's staff.

59. At the time this bridge over the Chickahominy was destroyed, Charles E. Cross of the Engineer Battalion was a first lieutenant, though he was subsequently promoted to the rank of captain.

60. During Robert E. Lee's pursuit of McClellan's retreating army in the wake of the Battle of Gaines's Mill, Lee ordered Stonewall Jackson to cross the Chickahominy on June 29, after rebuilding the Grapevine Bridge (also known as Sumner's Upper Bridge). Reconstructing this bridge took the entire morning, and when complete, it became clear that this bridge was insufficient for Jackson if he wanted to make a rapid crossing of the river. He immediately ordered the reconstruction of Alexander's Bridge (which Thompson identified as Woodbury and Alexander's). This project, however, was not finished until after dark, seriously delaying Jackson's movement across the Chickahominy. As a result, Jackson could not participate in the Battle of Savage's Station on June 29, and Federal forces were able to continue their withdrawal to the James River. Sears, *To the Gates of Richmond*, 250, 261–62, 269, 273–74.

61. The Battle of Gaines's Mill during the Seven Days was fought on June 27, 1862.

62. Thompson's description of the Battle of Gaines's Mill on June 27, 1862, implies that Fitz John Porter held off the rebel attack with a single division all day before withdrawing according to prior plans. In fact, Porter opposed the Confederate assault with the entire V Corps, and he retreated after southerners broke through his lines late in the day.

63. Major General Silas Casey and Brigadier General Darius Couch commanded the 3rd and 1st divisions, respectively, of Major General Erasmus Keyes's IV Corps. The two divisions of Casey and Couch bore the brunt of the Confederate attack at the Battle of Fair Oaks or Seven Pines on May 31, 1862. Sears, *To the Gates of Richmond*, 122–33.

64. The Battle of Malvern Hill was the last of the Battles of the Seven Days on July 1, 1862. After inflicting severe casualties on the attacking Confederates at this engagement, however, McClellan continued his retreat to a secure base on the James River, abandoning his attempt to take Richmond. "Pickett's Division at Gettysburg," of course, is a reference to the poorly conceived rebel attack against the Union center on the third day of the Battle of Gettysburg, an assault made by the Confederate division of George Pickett as well as two others from A. P. Hill's corps.

65. Major General Samuel P. Heintzelman commanded the III Corps of McClellan's army during the Battles of the Seven Days.

66. Any group of cut trees designed to prevent enemy movement was called a slashing. Such an obstacle was easily confused with an abatis. See also entry for July 6, 1862, and p. 367n81. Farrow, *Dictionary of Military Terms*, 562.

67. Warren Lee Goss belonged to Company B of the Engineer Battalion when he was captured during the Seven Days. In mid-November 1862, he was discharged due to health problems, but he subsequently enlisted in the 2nd Massachusetts Volunteer Heavy Artillery. As part of that unit, he was captured at Plymouth, North Carolina, in April 1864 and, after witnessing one of many rebel-perpetrated racial atrocities, Goss was sent to Andersonville (along with George Gay of Hopedale, Massachusetts, who also served in Company G of Goss's regiment). NARA Microfilm Publication M233, roll 27, 55:113; Adjutant General of Massachusetts, *Massachusetts Soldiers, Sailors, and Marines in the Civil War*, 6:716, 730; Warren Lee Goss, *The Soldier's Story of His Captivity at Andersonville, Belle Isle, and Other Rebel Prisons* (Boston, MA: Lee and Shepard, 1867), 60–61; Jordan and Thomas, "Massacre at Plymouth," 173–74. See also Thompson's memoir reminiscence on p. 3 and annotation 9 on p. 340.

68. The articles to which Thompson referred here are Warren Lee Goss, "Battles and Leaders of the Civil War: Recollections of a Private," *Century Illustrated Monthly Magazine* 29, no. 1 (November 1884): 107–13; Warren Lee Goss, "Battles and Leaders of the Civil War: Recollections of a Private," *Century Illustrated Monthly Magazine* 29, no. 2 (December 1884): 179–84; Warren Lee Goss, "Battles and Leaders of the Civil War: Recollections of a Private," *Century Illustrated Monthly Magazine* 29, no. 5 (March 1885): 767–77; Warren Lee Goss, "Recollections of a Private. IV. To the Chickahominy—The Battle of Seven Pines," *Century Illustrated Monthly Magazine* 30, no. 1 (May 1885): 130–36; Warren Lee Goss, "Recollections of a Private. V. Retiring from the Chickahominy," *Century Illustrated Monthly Magazine* 30, no. 4 (August 1885): 633–40; Warren Lee Goss, "Recollections of a Private. Two Days of the Second Bull Run Battle," *Century Illustrated Monthly Magazine* 31, no. 3 (January 1886): 467–74; Warren

Lee Goss, "Recollections of a Private. VII. McClellan at the Head of the Grand Army," *Century Illustrated Monthly Magazine* 32, no. 1 (May 1886): 131–37.

69. Goss, *The Soldier's Story of His Captivity at Andersonville, Belle Isle, and Other Rebel Prisons.*

70. Camp Woodbury was the battalion's camp before Petersburg in the fall of 1864, so Thompson may have meant Camp Lincoln, where the battalion spent a week before the Battle of Savage's Station on June 29, 1862.

71. The battalion rolls for July 1862 list nine men as missing since the fighting around Richmond began. These men included Warren Lee Goss and Allen Page of Company B, Company C's Charles Stoddard, William H. Foss, Albert Hutchinson, Thomas W. Melumby, Benjamin Sparrow, and Edwin H. Damon, as well as William W. Downs of Company A. Two of the nine, Stoddard and Downs, eventually returned to the battalion, though Thompson's entry only mentions Private Downs, who rejoined Company A in early August 1862, while the unit was still at Harrison's Landing. The story about Downs that Thompson relates is possible, as the Union prisoners were first sent to Richmond where, in early August, Confederate major general Gustavus W. Smith oversaw the capital city's defenses. Smith had led the original engineer company, Company A, throughout most of the Mexican-American War, and he may have encountered Private Downs and arranged his release because Downs belonged to the unit that Smith once led. While there is just enough circumstantial evidence to support the plausibility of such an occurrence, there is not enough to confirm it, particularly since Downs enlisted in Company A in November 1861, long after Smith had resigned from the US Army. It is more likely that Downs was merely exchanged or paroled early due to bad health or wounds suffered in action, a supposition supported by the fact that Confederate authorities paroled a number of Union soldiers who were in need of medical care and by Downs's subsequent early discharge from the service in September 1862 due to a fractured pelvis that he suffered prior to his capture, when he fell off a bridge across the Chickahominy while under Confederate fire. In addition to the battalion's monthly rolls, see NARA Microfilm Publication M233, roll 75, 141:200, 205; Leonne M. Hudson, *The Odyssey of a Southerner: The Life and Times of Gustavus Woodson Smith* (Macon, GA: Mercer Univ. Press, 1998), 131–32; Smith, "'The Hardest Work and Hardest Fighting,'" 11; Thompson's entry of July 6, 1862; Sears, *To the Gates of Richmond,* 353; "Certificate of Disability for Discharge, Private William W. Downs," September 2, 1862, enclosed in Widow's Pension Application Certificate No. 354341, William W. Downs (Co. A, US Engineer Battalion), RG15.

72. See also Warren Lee Goss, *Recollections of a Private: A Story of the Army of the Potomac* (New York: Thomas Y. Crowell & Co., 1890).

73. Thompson's "Reminiscences of the Retreat" describe the Army of the Potomac's withdrawal following the Battle of Gaines's Mill on June 27, 1862, from outside Richmond to a new base along the James River.

74. Brigadier General William F. "Baldy" Smith commanded the 2nd Division of the VI Corps of the Army of the Potomac, and his division confronted the only substantial Confederate attack south of the Chickahominy River during the Battle of Gaines's Mill on June 27. Sears, *To the Gates of Richmond*, 247, 384–84.

75. Thompson's mention of "their white battle flag" sounds like the second national Confederate flag known as the Stainless Banner. That flag consisted of a white field with the familiar southern battle flag (based on the St. Andrew's Cross) relegated to the upper corner. This design, however, was not a battle flag, and it was not adopted until May 1, 1863, some ten months after the date of this entry. John Coski, *The Confederate Battle Flag: America's Most Embattled Emblem* (Cambridge, MA: Harvard Univ. Press, 2005), 17.

76. Several Civil War general rode white horses. Joseph Hooker rode one during the Seven Days, and Robert E. Lee's horse, Traveler, was sometimes described as white, though his coat was actually grey. Without additional information, it is impossible to determine precisely whose horse Thompson was referencing. On Hooker's white horse, see Goss, *Recollections of a Private*, 68.

77. Brigadier General Winfield Scott Hancock commanded the First Brigade of Baldy Smith's division and bore the brunt of the division's fighting at Gaines's Mill on June 27. Sears, *To the Gates of Richmond*, 384.

78. Major General Fitz John Porter commanded the still provisional V Corps of McClellan's Army. Thus, Thompson is likely referring to one or all of the three divisions of the V Corps that were under Porter's ultimate command; he may, however, have meant the division that Porter had previously commanded, which, by the date of this entry was led by Brigadier General George W. Morell. Sears, *To the Gates of Richmond*, 382; John J. Hennessy, "Conservatism's Dying Ember: Fitz John Porter and the Union War, 1862," in *Corps Commanders in Blue: Union Major Generals in the Civil War*, ed. Ethan S. Rafuse (Baton Rouge: Louisiana State Univ. Press, 2014), 30.

79. In his memoir recollections above and in his published history of the Engineer Battalion after the war, Thompson identified this bridge as Woodbury and Alexander's Bridge, known more commonly as Alexander's Bridge. The crossing that was usually referred to as Woodbury's Bridge, named for Major Daniel P. Woodbury commanding the Army of the Potomac's Engineer Brigade, was farther upstream. Thompson, *Engineer Battalion in the Civil War*, 17; Sears, *To the Gates of Richmond*, 269; Phillip M. Thienel, *Mr. Lincoln's Bridge Builders: The Right Hand of American Genius* (Shippensburg, PA: White Mane Books, 2000), 59.

80. The second bridge that Thompson mentioned here was the Grapevine Bridge, also known as Sumner's Upper Bridge.

81. An abatis was a careful arrangement of felled trees or large limbs secured to the ground as an obstacle to the advance of an enemy. Mahan, *Treatise of Field Fortification*, 45.

82. Major General John Pope was brought from the western theater and appointed to command the newly created Union Army of Virginia in late June 1862 to deal with the many small Confederate forces operating in northern Virginia and the Shenandoah Valley. While Pope's assignment was reported in northern newspapers in early July, he did not actually take command of his forces until later in the month. Sears, *To the Gates of Richmond*, 349.

83. The date at which Thompson made this insertion was unclear, but judging by placement and handwriting, he did make it sometime during the war, presumably before he filled his first wartime journal and mailed it home on or shortly after October 12, 1862.

84. When the Army of the Potomac reached White House Landing in May 1862, the Richmond and York River Railroad became its main supply line, carrying materials from West Point, Virginia, on the York River to the army. The line functioned in this capacity until the Union retreat from Richmond following the Battle of Gaines's Mill. Sears, *To the Gates of Richmond*, 103–5, 115, 257–58.

85. Job's comforter was slang for a boil.

86. Thompson's mention of seven bells refers to the keeping of time aboard ship by the use of bells rung every half hour in a four-hour cycle. Seven bells was half an hour before the end of the four-hour watch.

87. Each company's first sergeant prepared a daily Morning Report following the day's first roll call, which was held immediately after reveille. Its purpose was to identify all the men present and fit for duty. If only 105 men were fit for duty, as Thompson wrote, then over 160 men were on the sick list, judging by the battalion's July 1862 monthly return. See also Wiley, *Billy Yank*, 45.

88. Thompson was referring to "Rhine Song of the German Soldiers after Victory" by the English poet Felicia Hemans.

89. Contrabands was the term applied by Union soldiers to the enslaved people who ran away from their owners in search of freedom with Union armies. While they were not, at this early stage of the war, set free, many were retained by Union armies and put to work on behalf of the Federal military.

90. Just after midnight on August 1, 1862, Confederate forces on the south side of the James River bombarded Union shipping and supply depots around Harrison's Landing north of the river. Little damage was done to the shipping but ten men were killed and another fifteen wounded. George L. Kilmer, "The

Army of the Potomac at Harrison's Landing," *Battles and Leaders of the Civil War,* vol. 2, part 2 (New York: The Century Co., 1884), 428; "Report of Maj. Gen. George B. McClellan, U.S. Army, commanding Army of the Potomac," August 4, 1863, in *OR,* ser. 1, vol. 11, part 1, 76.

91. After the August 1, 1862, bombardment that Thompson described in his entry of that date, McClellan dispatched a small force to Coggins Point on the south bank of the James. There these men, including Thompson, destroyed the grounds of the Cole House, where some of the Confederate guns had been emplaced, after which they occupied and fortified the position to prevent any further rebel cannonading from that location. Kilmer, "The Army of the Potomac at Harrison's Landing," 428; "Report of Maj. Gen. George B. McClellan, U.S. Army, commanding Army of the Potomac," August 4, 1863, in *OR,* ser. 1, vol. 11, part 1, 76; Ethan S. Rafuse, *McClellan's War: The Failure of Moderation in the Struggle for the Union* (Bloomington: Indiana Univ. Press, 2005), 248.

92. In an attempt to stop general in chief Henry W. Halleck from ordering him to evacuate Harrison's Landing, McClellan sent Major General Joseph Hooker with seventeen thousand men to retake Malvern Hill early on August 5, 1862. Hooker drove off the Confederate outpost there and occupied the hill, but McClellan ordered his withdrawal when Lee began to prepare a large counteroffensive. Sears, *George B. McClellan,* 243–44; Sears, *To the Gates of Richmond,* 354–55.

3. Getting Accustomed to Campaigning

1. In his reminisces following the war, Thompson remarked of the order Turtle described for the battalion to report as infantry after the Battle of Antietam that "My Impression is that this was a general order for all detached commands."

2. After Turtle's mention of Randall's battery in the Antietam campaign, Thompson noted in his postwar memoirs: "Randoll, See Vol. V. p. 106 *Century.*" Thompson's citation, however, is incomplete and inaccurate, as neither *Scribner's Monthly Magazine* nor its successor, *The Century Illustrated Monthly Magazine,* contains any reference to Antietam on page 106 of its volume 5 (either in the original series or new series numbering). In fact, Thompson's spelling itself may be mistaken and the individual in question may have been 1st Lieut. Alanson Merwin Randol of the 1st United States Artillery. See also Heitman, *Register,* 1:815.

3. Berlin, Maryland, is now the town of Brunswick, Maryland.

4. In the late summer of 1862, Orlando Jackson was an artificer in Company D.

5. While Thompson added this comment in his postwar memoir, he wrote his *wartime* journal entries in his own voice but based on Jackson's journal sometime near October 11, 1862, judging by the placement of Thompson's entries in his manuscript journal (see also his journal entry of that date). These entries, however, have been located in chronological order for the reader's convenience; they are indicated here by the inversion of the regular heading order of date followed by day of the week (so that the day of the week is listed first) and by the absence of an entry location on the line above the date.

6. See journal entry for August 5, 1862, and p. 368n91.

7. This movement on August 10, 1862, and the activities Thompson subsequently described were part of McClellan's preparations for the army's withdrawal from the Peninsula, a movement that began in earnest on August 14. Jeffrey D. Wert, *The Sword of Lincoln: The Army of the Potomac* (New York: Simon and Schuster, 2005), 132–33; Sears, *George B. McClellan*, 242–45; Thienel, *Mr. Lincoln's Bridge Builders*, 60–61.

8. Quién Sabe is Spanish for "who knows." Thompson consistently misspelled this phrase as "Quen Sabe" in his journal, but to avoid confusion it has been rendered correctly throughout the text.

9. The USS *Congress* was destroyed by the ironclad CSS *Virginia* in the naval Battle of Hampton Roads on March 8, 1862.

10. Shelter tents, also known as dog tents, were designed to house two men, each of whom carried a half shelter that, when buttoned together and stretched over a horizontally-suspended pole, created an inverted V-shaped tent open at both ends that was approximately five feet long by five feet wide. Wiley, *Billy Yank*, 56; George C. Rable, *Fredericksburg! Fredericksburg!* (Chapel Hill: Univ. of North Carolina Press, 2002), 11.

11. A simoom is a heavy windstorm carrying dust or sand; it is a phenomenon usually associated with North Africa and the Middle East.

12. This bridge at Barrett's Ferry near the mouth of the Chickahominy River was built to allow the Army of the Potomac to move overland from Harrison's Landing to Fort Monroe at the tip of the Virginia Peninsula, where McClellan's forces boarded steamers to return to operations just south of Washington. Thienel, *Mr. Lincoln's Bridge Builders*, 60–61.

13. Privates John H. Sinsabogh and William C. Smith of Company A were reported on the battalion rolls as having deserted on August 24, 1862. Thompson may have erred in recording these desertions on August 21 since he was writing these entries in mid-October based on the journals of other soldiers, or Privates Sinsabogh and Smith may have deserted a few days before they were reported as such officially.

14. Soldiers mustered every other month to provide the information on which their pay was based. Wiley, *Billy Yank*, 48–49.

15. Aquia Landing, where Aquia Creek empties into the Potomac about thirty-five miles below Washington, had been the site of several Confederate batteries that had interrupted travel along the lower Potomac in early 1862 prior to the Peninsula campaign. Rafuse, *McClellan's War*, 189–90; Sears, *George B. McClellan*, 158.

16. Merrill was either Charles Merrill of Company D, who deserted three weeks after the date of this entry, or Paul Merrill, who remained with Company D until November 1863.

17. Thompson, while he may not have known it at the time, was referring to the Second Battle of Bull Run, August 28–30, 1862.

18. Fort Ellsworth was one of the Union defenses of Alexandria, Virginia. This city just south of Washington, DC, was a valuable point of supply for the capital, and Fort Ellsworth guarded the western approaches to it. Benjamin Franklin Cooling III and Walton H. Owen II, *Mr. Lincoln's Forts: A Guide to the Civil War Defenses of Washington* (1988; repr. Lanham, UK: Scarecrow Press, 2010), 9, 47; Ron Field, *American Civil War Fortifications*, vol. 2, *Land and Field Fortifications* (Oxford: Osprey Publishing, 2005), 29–30; Benjamin Franklin Cooling III, *Symbol, Sword and Shield: Defending Washington During the Civil War* (Hamden, CT: Archon Books, 1975), 47.

19. The corporal of the guard did not walk post himself but instead assisted the sergeant of the guard in overseeing the guard detail, chiefly by responding to the calls and queries of the individuals who were actively walking post. It was also the duty of the corporal of the guard to post the reliefs by escorting each man to and from his post during the guard rotation. Each guard contained three times as many privates as there were posts to guard, and each man served two hours on post and then four hours off post. Joseph A. Crowell, *The Young Volunteer: The Everyday Experiences of a Soldier Boy in the Civil War*, 2d ed. (New York: Dillingham Company, 1906), 185; E. Cook to His Parents, October 25, 1862, in Neal E. Wilson, ed., *Echoes from the Boys of Company 'H': The Siege of Charleston, the Assault on Fort Wagner, the Virginia Campaigns for Petersburg and Richmond, and Prison Life in Andersonville, as Chronicled by Civil War Soldiers from the 100th New York State Regiment, Company H* (New York: iUniverse, 2008), 39–40.

20. Major General John Pope was in command of the Union Army of Virginia at Second Bull Run.

21. At Second Bull Run, Major General Fitz John Porter and his V Corps had been detached from the Army of the Potomac to support Pope. Porter, however, did little to aid the Army of Virginia during the fighting on the morning of August 29, 1862, and when Pope ordered him to attack the right flank of

Stonewall Jackson's Confederate corps late that afternoon, Porter continued to sit out the battle. For this latter reason, Porter was later court martialed and cashiered, even though by the time he received Pope's order on the afternoon of the twenty-ninth, Jackson's right was connected to and protected by James Longstreet's corps and not vulnerable to a flank attack.

22. Decatur O. Blake joined Company D of the Engineer Battalion in late October 1862, having previously served with the 8th Michigan Infantry in Major General Ambrose Burnside's IX Corps. Before this regiment joined Burnside's corps, it fought under Brigadier General Henry W. Benham at the Battle of Secessionville, perhaps influencing Blake's and, later, Thompson's views of Benham (see also April 21, 1863, entry and p. 387n4). Blake's original unit, the 8th Michigan, fought on the Union right at Second Bull Run as part of Brigadier General Isaac I. Stevens's 1st Division of the IX Corps. NARA Microfilm Publication T288, roll 116; Charles F. Howlett, "79th New York Infantry Regiment," in Alexander M. Bielakowski, ed., *Ethnic and Racial Minorities in the U.S. Military: An Encyclopedia*, 2 vols. (Santa Barbara, CA: ABC-CLIO, 2013), 2:639; Hazard Stevens, *The Life of Isaac Ingalls Stevens*, 2 vols. (Boston: Houghton Mifflin, 1900), 2:439.

23. Tenallytown was a district of the capital city that is today known as Tenleytown.

24. Probably Battery K, 1st US Artillery, commanded by Captain William Montrose Graham. Heitman, *Register*, 1:469.

25. A Tartar was a stubborn, violent, ill-tempered individual. *Oxford English Dictionary Online*, s.v. "Tartar, n," accessed April 19, 2016, http://www.oed.com/view/Entry/197938?rskey=SnhdPW&result=2&isAdvanced=false.

26. At the Battle of South Mountain, portions of Robert E. Lee's Army of Northern Virginia defended Turner's Gap west of Middletown, Maryland, for nearly a full day on September 14, giving Lee additional time to concentrate his divided forces in the face of McClellan's pursuit.

27. Thompson's report of a minié ball penetrating two quarter-inch-thick pieces of iron and then killing a man behind them seems incredible, particularly as he reported the event years after the fact. Given the accounts of the failure of some Civil War–era body armor made of iron or steel, however, it is possible that Thompson's recollection is accurate, though one still wonders why he waited so long to record such an extraordinary event. See also Sarah Jones Weicksel, "Armor, Manhood, and the Politics of Mortality," in *Astride Two Worlds: Technology and the American Civil War*, ed. Barton C. Hacker (Washington, DC: Smithsonian Institute Scholarly Press, 2016), 180, 183.

28. This bridge was Burnside's Bridge on the southern part of the Antietam battlefield.

29. The fight Thompson mentioned here was the Battle of Antietam on September 17, 1862.

30. A flag of truce did not prevent McClellan from delivering the *coup de grâce* to Lee's Confederate army on September 18, 1862, as Thompson claimed. Historian Ethan Rafuse suggests this failure was the result of the exhaustion of Union reserves caused by the reshuffling of their units that necessitated several long marches, as well as the bout of dysentery that struck McClellan at an inopportune moment. Others, like McClellan biographer Stephen Sears, maintain that the Union commander simply deferred to the preference of his corps commander, Edwin Sumner, rather than make his own decision about whether or not to continue the engagement on the eighteenth. Rafuse, *McClellan's War*, 327–28; Sears, *George B. McClellan*, 319–20.

31. See p. 368n2.

32. Probably Crampton's Gap through South Mountain.

33. The apparent contradiction between Thompson's description of the faces of the dead and his refusal to look at them may stem from the fact that this part of his journal was written several weeks later based on his own memory and the journals of his colleagues. Or, he may simply have meant that he did not leave the wagon he was riding in to inspect the dead Confederates more closely. See also the memoir recollection on p. 72, the journal entry for October 11, 1862, and pp. 369n5 and 374n49.

34. President Lincoln twice offered Major General Ambrose Burnside the command of the Army of the Potomac as the president lost faith in McClellan's abilities during the summer of 1862, but on both occasions, first in late July and again in early September, Burnside declined the offer, arguing instead that McClellan was the more capable man for the job. In his postwar recollection here, Thompson referred to these refusals as recounted on pages 102 and 118 of Augustus Woodbury, *Major General Ambrose E. Burnside and the Ninth Corps: A Narrative of Campaigns in North Carolina, Maryland, Virginia, Ohio, Kentucky, Mississippi, and Tennessee, During the War for the Preservation of the Republic* (Providence, RI: Sidney S. Rider & Brother, 1867). See also Sears, *George B. McClellan*, 235, 264–65, 437n16; Rable, *Fredericksburg! Fredericksburg!*, 51; Marvel, *Burnside*, 99–100, 110–11.

35. Lee's Special Orders No. 191 detailed the division of his army to accomplish necessary objectives as it moved north during the Maryland campaign in the late summer of 1862. A copy of the order was lost and fell into Union hands, giving McClellan the opportunity to defeat Lee's army in detail. The Federal commander, however, could not bestir himself to move quickly enough to take advantage of the opportunity.

36. Thompson was paraphrasing from page 74 of William Swinton, *The Twelve Decisive Battles of the War: A History of the Eastern and Western Campaigns, In Relation to the Actions That Decided Their Issue* (New York: Dick & Fitzgerald Publishers, 1867). The actual quote, which Swinton wrote about the Federal attack on Gideon Pillow's Confederate forces at Fort Donelson, is: "for every step gained by the enemy, a heavy price in blood was exacted."

37. Probably Battery K, 1st US Artillery. See memoir recollection found on p. 78.

38. While McClellan's poorly coordinated attacks at Antietam undoubtedly allowed Lee to maximize his defense by maneuvering men about the battlefield to meet the current point of attack at any given moment, Thompson's claim that the Confederate general managed a numerical superiority at every point of engagement is simply inaccurate. A. Wilson Greene, "'I Fought the Battle Splendidly': George B. McClellan and the Maryland Campaign," in *Antietam: Essays on the 1862 Maryland Campaign*, ed. Gary W. Gallagher (Kent, OH: Kent State Univ. Press, 1989), 69–75.

39. After Antietam, McClellan spent several weeks in camps near the battlefield, including one at Sandy Hook, Maryland, where the Engineer Battalion encamped and which was across the Potomac from Harpers Ferry.

40. Thompson's own original journal entries resume here. See also p. 369n5.

41. In his reconstructed entry for August 14, 1862, Thompson originally described this pontoon bridge over the Chickahominy River at Barrett's Ferry as being 2,100 feet long, but in that entry he subsequently corrected the length to 1,980 feet; however, he never corrected the length he recorded in this entry for September 22, 1862.

42. In this September 22, 1862, journal entry, Thompson was summarizing very briefly the events since his last full contemporary entry on August 5. His entries for August 10 through September 21 were written in mid-October 1862 and were based on his own notes and on the journal of Orlando Jackson. See also opening memoir section of chapter 3 on p. 72 and 369n5.

43. Henry P. Pitcher was a Company D artificer.

44. In the fall of 1862, after the Battle of Antietam but before his removal by Lincoln, McClellan considered a limited campaign against Winchester, Virginia, or in the Shenandoah Valley in general, either of which would require better lines of communication and supply across the Potomac and Shenandoah rivers at Harpers Ferry. Constructing permanent bridges across these two rivers was part of the general's ultimate plan, but in the meantime it seems as if the Engineer Battalion was opening temporary communications across these two rivers. Sears, *George B. McClellan*, 331.

45. In an attempt to prod the cautious McClellan into action, President Lincoln visited the Army of the Potomac during the first four days of October 1862. Sears, *George B. McClellan*, 330; Wert, *Sword of Lincoln*, 175.

46. Colonel Dixon Miles was the commander of the Union garrison at Harpers Ferry in the late summer of 1862, and he surrendered the post to Stonewall Jackson on September 15, 1862, just before the Battle of Antietam.

47. L. B. Humphrey was probably Elizabeth "Lizzie" Bullock Humphrey of the Hopedale community in Milford, Massachusetts. Lizzie was a schoolmate of Thompson's and shared an interest in art with him. She later attended New York's Cooper Union, where she studied art before going on to a successful career illustrating books and magazines. United States Census 1860, Worcester County, Massachusetts, population schedule, Milford, p. 123, dwelling 658, family 1010, William and Almira B. Humphry, digital image, FamilySearch, accessed May 13, 2016, https://familysearch.org/pal:/MM9.3.1/TH-1942 -25248-12138-57?cc=1473181; Patrick, "Our Community School and Its Teacher," 34; April F. Masten, *Art Work: Women in Mid-Nineteenth-Century New York* (Philadelphia: Univ. of Pennsylvania Press, 2008), 157.

48. Jackson was Orlando Jackson, Company D.

49. The entries Thompson mentions here are found in chronological sequence at the beginning of chapter 3. See also the memoir section on p. 72 and annotation number 5 on p. 369.

50. The first of Thompson's three wartime journals ends with this entry; the second journal commences with the next entry.

51. A second entry for this date; it is the first one in Thompson's second wartime journal.

52. Thompson was quoting from Edward Young's "Time, Death, and Friendship," the second of nine nights in the most well-known poem from this eighteenth-century English poet, *The Complaint: Or, Night-Thoughts on Life, Death, and Immortality.*

53. Rue was Charles H. Rue, Company D, and Thompson's use of "ours" in this sentence was a reference to the tent shared by him and his bunkmate, who at the time was Thomas Rand. Thompson also occasionally used "we" in the same way to refer to himself and his bunkmate.

54. Fernald was either William L. or Cassius M. Fernald, both of Company D, and Rand was Thomas Rand, also from Company D.

55. Beahn of "Currier & Beahn" was Francis E. Beahn, Company B.

56. There are too many Roberts in the battalion to identify the person Thompson called Bobby without further information.

57. William D. Walsh, Company A, was the violin player mentioned here.

58. The enterprising restauranteur and clerk Thompson described was Thomas P. Wight, Company D.

59. This pontoon bridge across the Potomac River was laid to enable McClellan to finally lead the Army of the Potomac southward into Virginia more than a month after the Battle of Antietam. Rable, *Fredericksburg! Fredericksburg!*, 8.

60. General Orders No. 154 was designed to fill units of the regular army to their authorized size by recruiting volunteers into them for three years or the remainder of their three-year volunteer term. L. Thomas, General Orders No. 154, 9 October 1862, in *OR*, ser. 3, vol. 2, 654.

61. As a result of the order Thompson mentioned above, over 250 men joined the Engineer Battalion's four companies in late October 1862, according to the unit's monthly rosters.

62. Thompson may be referring to War Department General Orders No. 162, which were probably issued at McClellan's request. These orders modified War Department General Orders No. 154 by prohibiting the enlistment in the regular army of more than ten men from any single volunteer company. See also entry for October 26, 1862, and p. 375n60. L. Thomas, General Orders No. 162, 21 October 1862, in *OR*, ser. 3, vol. 2, 676.

63. Orville E. Babcock commanded Company D in early November 1862, but he was only a first lieutenant at that time. He was, however, promoted to captain the following spring. Heitman, *Register*, 1:178.

64. Throughout his wartime journals, Thompson often fretted about his mother's health, occasionally even worrying that she might not survive until the end of his three-year enlistment. His concerns, however, were misplaced. Harriet Gilbert Thompson lived to be seventy-eight; she died of bronchitis in Hopedale in 1893. "Massachusetts, Death Records, 1841–1915" Online Database, Ancestry .com (Provo, UT: Ancestry.com), accessed February 6, 2017, https://www .ancestry.com/search/collections/madeathrecords/.

65. This may be a reference to Thompson's father's abandonment of him and his mother in the late 1840s. See pp. xiii and 333–34n2.

66. This quote is from the poem "Rock Me to Sleep" by Elizabeth Anne Chase (later Akers, and eventually Elizabeth Akers Allen). She wrote this poem in 1859 under the pen name Florence Percy, hence Thompson's attribution of "F. Percy." Albert Nelson Marquis, ed., *Who's Who in America; A Biographical Dictionary of Notable Living Men and Women of the United States, 1908–1909* (Chicago: A. N. Marquis, 1908), 17.

67. Thompson was writing about Elisha Kent Kane, an American naval officer who participated in two Arctic explorations intended to rescue the lost British explorer (and naval officer) Sir John Franklin. Robert E. Johnson, "Kane, Elisha

Kent," in *Dictionary of Canadian Biography*, vol. 8, University of Toronto /Université Laval, 2003–, accessed April 17, 2016, http://www.biographi.ca /en/bio/kane_elisha_kent_8E.html.

4. We Are for Fredericksburg

1. It is unclear which of Company D's two Geyser brothers, Jacob D. or John B., Thompson meant here. While he later identified these men as either John or Jake, here and in one other instance, he simply used numbers to differentiate them. It seems from later entries that "Geyser 1st" in this journal entry refers to Jacob, while "Geyser 2" in the December 20, 1862, entry refers to John, but this is not entirely certain. NARA Microfilm Publication M233, roll 27, 55:108, 110.

2. The "four pieces" Thompson mentioned was a reference to the half shelter that each man carried, which could be combined with others to make a larger protection. Wiley, *Billy Yank*, 56.

3. In the American Civil War, both sides used yellow flags to mark facilities for treating the wounded.

4. Pruntelles in this entry may be a misspelling of the French word prunelles, which means sloes, the fruit of the blackthorn tree. If so, Thompson is describing a blackthorn wreath.

5. On November 7, 1862, President Lincoln removed McClellan from command of the Army of the Potomac and replaced him with Major General Ambrose E. Burnside. Rable, *Fredericksburg! Fredericksburg!*, 43–44.

6. Private Julian Day died of an unspecified fever on November 14, 1862.

7. Thompson made a second entry for this date.

8. S. P. was Sarah P. Lillie. See February 9, 1862, entry and p. 350n80.

9. In the engineer companies, an artificer was a first-class private, one grade above second-class privates and just below corporals.

10. Thompson seems to have been reporting an unfounded rumor of Captain Duane's arrest. He may have been conflating Duane, one of the Engineer Battalion's former commanders, with a major on General in Chief Henry W. Halleck's staff, Major John J. Key whose brother Thomas was a colonel on McClellan's staff. In late September 1862, President Lincoln learned that Major Key had suggested that the goal of the Union war effort was not to defeat Confederate armies but to drag the war out until a compromise solution could be established to save the Union and maintain slavery, an idea that Lincoln seems to have imputed to McClellan as well. As a result, Lincoln had Major Key cashiered. Thompson may have heard a muddled version of this, leading to the report in his journal about Duane's arrest. Captain Duane was on McClellan's staff, and from September 8 through November 5, 1862, he served as chief

engineer of the Army of the Potomac. On November 19, 1862, however, less than two weeks after McClellan's removal, Duane commenced a tour as chief engineer of the Department of the South, during which he participated in the attacks on Fort McAlister, Georgia, and Union operations in Charleston, South Carolina, before returning to the Army of the Potomac to serve as its chief engineer again in the summer of 1863. Bruce Tap, *Over Lincoln's Shoulder: The Committee on the Congressional Conduct of the War* (Lawrence: Univ. Press of Kansas, 1998), 152–53; Sears, *George B. McClellan*, 326–28; Cullum, *Biographical Register*, 2:344–45; Army, *Engineering Victory*, 209.

11. First Lieutenant Orville E. Babcock and Second Lieutenant Charles R. Suter were both relieved of duty with the battalion's Company D on November 16, 1862. Suter went to serve as the assistant engineer of the newly created Center Grand Division of the Army of the Potomac under Major General Joseph Hooker. Babcock became chief engineer of Major General William B. Franklin's Left Grand Division. Both of these grand divisions were established as part of Major General Ambrose Burnside's reorganization after he took command of the Army of the Potomac in November 1862. Cullum, *Biographical Register*, 2:770, 847; Rable, *Fredericksburg! Fredericksburg!*, 43–44, 59–60.

12. The "Bloomer costume," or sometimes simply bloomers, refers to the billowy trousers worn underneath a knee-length skirt that were designed in 1850 by Elizabeth Smith Miller and popularized by (and named for) Amelia Bloomer. They were worn primarily by women's rights advocates such as Elizabeth Cady Stanton or the Grimké sisters, and they became popular for a time among the women of Thompson's reform-minded home community of Hopedale, Massachusetts. Carol Hymowitz and Michaele Weissman, *A History of Women in America* (New York: Bantam Books, 1978), 102–3; Anna Thwing Field, "Anti-Slavery and Other Visitors to the Community," 18; Draper, "Hopedale," 67.

13. This was the actress Charlotte Crampton, who Thompson mentioned again in his February 12, 1864, journal entry. Crampton was a popular Shakespearean actor before the war, and her bloomer attire was in keeping with her flouting of traditional gender norms by portraying male roles on stage, such as Richard III and Hamlet. Based on a postwar newspaper article that Thompson mentioned in his memoir additions, Crampton was probably following the 14th US Infantry at the time of this journal entry. See also February 12, 1864, journal entry. Tony Howard, *Women as Hamlet: Performance and Interpretation in Theatre, Film and Fiction* (Cambridge: Cambridge Univ. Press, 2007), 77–78; John A. Spring, "With the Regulars in Arizona," *National Tribune*, November 20, 1902, p. 8.

14. Lieutenant Charles E. Cross of Company B took command of the Engineer Battalion after Captain James C. Duane was assigned as chief engineer of the Army of the Potomac in September 1862.

15. The delay in building the pontoon bridge over the Rappahannock that Thompson described here was the result of poor coordination among the army's leadership, which delayed the arrival of the boats. The first pontoons did not make it to Falmouth where the battalion was camped until November 24, and all of them were not on site until November 27, a week and a half later than Burnside had wanted them. See Rable, *Fredericksburg! Fredericksburg!*, 87–88.

16. "Dead March in Saul" is the funeral march in George Frideric Handel's 1738 oratio *Saul*, about the first king of Israel.

17. Daniel H. Miller joined the Engineer Battalion with the baker's dozen, including Thompson, that first enlisted in the company of topographical engineers. Miller remained in Company B of the battalion when Thompson was transferred to the newly created Company D. He died of chronic dysentery on December 5, 1862.

18. Thompson was reporting an inaccurate camp rumor that Major General Joseph Hooker had replaced Burnside in command of the Army of the Potomac. Hooker did eventually replace Burnside but not until late January 1863, nearly two months after this entry.

19. In addition to discussing standard matters of governance in his December 1, 1862, annual message to Congress, President Lincoln also dealt with several matters relating to the war. He tried to motivate the North to continue the struggle. He also proposed a constitutional amendment that would have reimbursed slaveholders in any state that abolished slavery on its own authority and would have funded the resettlement of the newly emancipated slaves and other free blacks. Thompson may have been referring to any of these provisions; he did not elaborate. *Senate Journal*, 37th Cong., 2d Sess., December 3, 1862.

20. The "Democratic triumphs" that Thompson mentioned were that party's victories in the 1862 northern congressional elections. These elections had been fought largely around the issue of slavery and its connection to the war effort, with Democrats adopting tactics that would later be known as race-baiting to score victories (these efforts were one reason Lincoln was willing to continue supporting the notion of colonization for emancipated slaves, as described in the previous annotation—to diffuse white hostility to freed slaves). When the president announced the Emancipation Proclamation in late September, it also became a central issue in these elections. Another related issue was the general progress of the Union war effort, which was hardly inspiring in the fall of 1862. As a result of all these factors, Democrats scored gains in the House of Representatives, though Republicans still retained a majority there. In the Senate, on the other hand, the Republicans actually increased their margin of control.

21. This pontoon bridge over the Rappahannock was thrown at what became known as Franklin's Crossing, after General William B. Franklin whose Left

Grand Division of the Army of the Potomac crossed there before the Battle of Fredericksburg. Rable, *Fredericksburg! Fredericksburg!*, 157–58.

22. George F. Noyes joined the Union army at the outbreak of the Civil War and eventually served as a captain on the staff of Major General Abner Doubleday. At Fredericksburg, Doubleday's 1st Division of the I Corps, Left Grand Division, anchored the left flank of the Union assault on the Confederate position just across from the Engineer Battalion's pontoon bridges at Franklin's Crossing. "Obituary of Col. George F. Noyes," *New York Times*, January 11, 1868; Rable, *Fredericksburg! Fredericksburg!*, 194–95, 250, 441.

23. By "United States Engineers," Noyes meant the US Engineer Battalion.

24. See May 6, 1863, journal entry.

25. The Battle of Fredericksburg, December 13, 1862.

26. Thompson was describing the withdrawal of Franklin's Left Grand Division back to the north side of the Rappahannock as part of Burnside's general retreat following the Battle of Fredericksburg. Rable, *Fredericksburg! Fredericksburg!*, 281–82.

27. Thompson was referring to prisoners taken by Union forces on December 13, 1862, the day of the main Federal attack at the Battle of Fredericksburg.

28. It seems that Thompson was referring to Lee's Army of Northern Virginia on the heights above Fredericksburg in December 1862; if so, that force contained only about seventy-five thousand men at the time of the battle, not the two hundred thousand that Thompson reported.

29. "Geyser 2" probably indicates John B. Geyser, Company D. See also November 5, 1862, entry and p. 376n1.

30. Church was Artificer Charles A. Church of Company D, and Jackson was probably Orlando Jackson of Company D, but it is impossible to be certain of this latter identification, as there were several other Jacksons in Company D and the battalion.

31. Thompson may have been playing on the terms *femme sole* and *femme covert* with his phrase "Free-Coverte." A *femme sole* was an unmarried or widowed woman capable of representing herself publicly, while a *femme covert* was a married woman who, under the law of coverture, was represented publicly by her husband. The implication of Thompson's remark seems to be that once a pair of bunkmates broke up, each man was free to represent himself to others in search of a replacement.

32. Sevastopol (spelled with a "b" rather than a "v" in nineteenth-century English) was Russia's major port on the Black Sea in the mid-nineteenth century, and during the Crimean War it was protected by a series of extremely strong defensive fieldworks. An Allied assault by the combined forces of France and Great Britain defeated the Russian defenders in the open ground in front of

the city in the Battle of Alma. Afterwards, the Allies settled down to an extended siege from October 1854 until September of the following year. After repeated bombardments, the city fell to a major Allied assault in September 1855. Winfried Baumgart, *The Crimean War, 1853–1856* (London: Arnold, 1999), 115–26, 159–62.

33. Benjamin Paul Akers was a sculptor from Maine famous for his statue of a deceased youth, The Dead Pearl Diver (1858). John Carlos Rowe, *The New American Studies* (Minneapolis: Univ. of Minnesota Press, 2002), 99.

34. This quote is from the poem "A Petition to Time" by the British poet Byron Waller Procter, who wrote under the pen name Barry Cornwall. The poem was also set to music by George Loder. John Aikin, *Select Works of the British Poets, with Biographical and Critical Prefaces*, vol. 2, *Southey to Croley* (Philadelphia: Thomas Wardle, 1842), 328; *New York Mirror: A Weekly Gazette of Literature and the Fine Arts* 20, no. 3 (January 15, 1842), 19.

35. "Topoging" (sometimes "Out Topoging" and sometimes hyphenated as "Topog-ing") was Thompson's phrase for performing the surveying duties necessary to the production of maps and topographical charts, a duty to which he was frequently assigned during lulls in active campaigning.

36. Thompson was quoting Shakespeare's *Henry IV, Part II* (act II, scene 1), though he misremembered the final article. The quote should be "uneasy lies the head that wears a crown."

37. Sutlers were campsite vendors; they were civilians who provided goods for sale to the soldiers, and they had a reputation of charging excessive prices for their goods. Bell Irvin Wiley, *The Life of Johnny Reb: The Common Soldier of the Confederacy* (Indianapolis, IN: Bobbs-Merrill, 1943), 100.

38. "Ad libitum" is Latin for "optional" or "at one's pleasure."

39. Edward Currier, an artificer of Company B, was one of the few men who, like Thompson, originally enlisted in the company of topographical engineers before being transferred into Company B of the Engineer Battalion. Henry H. Perkins was another B Company artificer, though not originally a topog. "French leave" was slang for going absent without permission. Artificers Currier and Perkins were reported as having deserted on January 6, 1863. Both men were apprehended and returned to the battalion by the provost marshal on the sixteenth.

40. Sheepskin, as Thompson used it here, is probably a reference to his corporal's warrant, the parchment document naming him to his non-commissioned rank of corporal. See also his May 1, 1864, journal entry.

41. The subsequent description that Thompson provided in this entry recounts his participation in Burnside's "Mud March." This episode was the failed attempt to cross the Army of the Potomac over the Rappahannock above

Fredericksburg and strike Lee's army on its left flank. The march was undone by a torrential downpour that turned the roads into impassable mud.

42. "George B." was a reference to George B. McClellan. Thompson was reporting a false camp rumor that was likely prompted by the fact that Ambrose Burnside had been replaced as commander of the Army of the Potomac by Major General Joseph Hooker. See also journal entry for February 18, 1863, and p. 381n4.

43. According to Thompson's marginal notation in his February 28, 1863, entry, this was an actual ring that had been his mother's but which she had given to him. It apparently broke and Thompson later sent it home to his mother.

5. Camp Life Here Is Quite Pleasant

1. Thompson's "voluminous entry" refers to his very abbreviated entry of February 2, 1863, which is found at the conclusion of chapter 4.

2. Aquia Landing, where Aquia Creek empties into the Potomac River, is about a dozen miles northeast of Fredericksburg, Virginia.

3. Wheeler was Artificer John A. P. Wheeler, Company C.

4. Lincoln replaced Ambrose Burnside as commander of the Army of the Potomac with Major General Joseph Hooker on January 26, 1863. See also the camp rumor that Thompson reported in his January 27, 1863, journal entry.

5. John G. was John B. Geyser of Company D.

6. The non-commissioned officer that Thompson mentioned was Sergeant James C. Wilson, Company C. See also journal entry for February 18, 1863.

7. Thompson was attempting to quote the popular Henry Wadsworth Longfellow poem "A Psalm of Life" (1838). The actual quote is "In the world's broad field of battle / In the bivouac of Life / Be not like dumb, driven cattle! / Be a hero in the strife!" See also Robert L. Gale, *A Henry Wadsworth Longfellow Companion* (Westport, CT: Greenwood Press, 2003), 202.

8. George Draper was a textile manufacturer who relocated to the Hopedale community in Milford, Massachusetts, in 1853. His father had invented some enhancements to the temple, a device used to improve the edges of fabric woven on a loom. He relocated to Hopedale to partner with his brother, Ebenezer Draper, one of the original Practical Christians who established the community. George Draper, however, focused on the industrial potential of the area; he ultimately secured control of 75 percent of the Practical Christian joint stock concern that operated Hopedale, reorienting it from its original utopian objectives to serve his more prosaic capitalist goals. In partnership with Warren W. Dutcher, Draper also managed the Hopedale Machine Company and the Dutcher Temple Company. Spann, *Hopedale*, xi, 132–34.

9. See journal entry and annotation for February 2, 1863.

10. Charlie may be Charles H. Rue of Company D, who was Thompson's bunkmate at the date of this entry.

11. These fieldworks were erected to guard the Richmond, Fredericksburg and Potomac Railroad, including Aquia Creek Station on the Potomac River, and Brooks Station, about halfway between Aquia Creek Station and the city of Fredericksburg on the Rappahannock. Thompson, *Engineer Battalion in the Civil War*, 30; "Map of Northeastern Virginia and Vicinity of Washington," August 1, 1862, Map 1, Plate VIII, and "Central Virginia, showing Lieut. Gen. U. S. Grant's Campaign and Marches of the Armies under His Command in 1864–65," n.d., Map 1, Plate C, both in Major George B. Davis, Leslie J. Perry, and Joseph W. Kirkley, *The Official Military Atlas of the Civil War* (1891–1895; repr., New York: Grammercy Books, 1983).

12. Thompson was referring here to a lull in campaigning that occurred in both major theaters of the Civil War during early 1863. Murfreesboro, also known as Stones' River, was fought between December 31, 1862, and January 2, 1863, in Tennessee, and there was very little news of fighting or progress after this western theater engagement until the start of the Chancellorsville campaign in the East that spring.

13. It is impossible to determine if Thompson meant John B. Geyser or Jacob D. "Jake" Geyser here because at this date, both Geyser brothers shared a tent with Thompson and his bunkmate, Charles H. Rue.

14. This clipping from the *Milford Journal* was pasted into Thompson's wartime journal after the last March 1863 entry; the attribution was added in Thompson's hand.

15. The Long Roll was a drum signal for an attack.

16. See also Thompson's journal entry for February 27, 1862.

17. John B. Geyser remained in service until the expiration of his term of enlistment, which came in September 1864.

18. Louisa H. was Louisa Humphrey, the aunt of Elizabeth "Lizzie" B. Humphrey. See also October 10, 1862, entry and p. 374n47. Ballou, *History of the Town of Milford*, 2:832.

19. The rat that Thompson smelled appears to be the start of an active campaign. In his January 16, 1863, entry, he noted that one of the battalion's men had been tracking the rise and fall of the Rappahannock just a few days before the start of what became known as Burnside's "Mud March." Apparently, with the engineers' bridging responsibilities, some of the battalion's members were tasked with keeping track of the water's depth just prior to the start of a movement. Thompson also used the phrase "smell a rat" on other occasions to indicate the common soldiers' ability to figure out when campaigns were about

to commence. See also Thompson's entries for January 16 and 23, 1863, and his July 30, 1864, entry.

20. *Chronicles of the Canongate* is a collection of short stories by Sir Walter Scott.

21. This was the pontoon bridge at Barrett's Ferry. See also Thompson's entries for August 13–16, 1862.

22. R—— may have been Charles Rue, who had been away on detached duty since late February 1863.

23. It is impossible to identify conclusively these individuals or any others based solely on a set of initials, and unfortunately Thompson's correspondence, which would be invaluable in identifying the people he references in his journal, does not survive. No further mention will be made of individuals referenced only by initials whose identity cannot be determined. Only where additional information allows identification will such initials be annotated.

24. Corporal Sweetland was probably Charles W. Sweetland of Company C, but with two other Sweetlands in the battalion, it is impossible to be certain.

25. Confederate major general J. E. B. Stuart commanded the Army of Northern Virginia's Cavalry Division at the date of this entry.

26. In the main text and his subsequent addition, Thompson was somewhat inaccurately describing the cavalry battle at Kelly's Ford on March 17, 1863. Hooker sent Brigadier General William W. Averell with two thousand cavalrymen to drive a much smaller force of Confederate cavalry under Brigadier General Fitzhugh Lee away from the area around Culpeper Court House. The rebels, even though they were severely outnumbered, reacted aggressively and charged Averell's Federal troopers, launching a four-hour engagement. After Averell's force stopped the last southern attack, he retreated north of the Rappahannock River. Wert, *Sword of Lincoln*, 228–29; Walter H. Hebert, *Fighting Joe Hooker* (1944; repr., Lincoln: Univ. of Nebraska Press, 1999), 186–87.

27. Uncle Charley was Lieutenant Charles E. Cross of Company B.

28. The young woman with whom Thompson had danced and who he reported to be ailing in this entry may be Henrietta Munro, whose death Thompson recorded later. See journal entry for January 17, 1864.

29. Chauncey B. Reese was promoted to captain and took command of the Engineer Battalion in early March 1863. Heitman, *Register*, 1:826.

30. In early March 1863, Congress passed the Enrollment Act to implement conscription for Federal armies. While some men were drafted into Union military service, the primary goal of the law was to encourage more men to volunteer for service with the threat of conscription, and in that, the law was a success.

31. The five-year enlistment term Thompson mentioned here refers to the regular army. In 1861, the term of enlistment in the US Army had been reduced

from five years to three in order to spur recruitment, but on January 1, 1863, that term was returned to five years. In mid-June 1864, however, Congress again approved three-year enlistments for the regular army. "An Act to Increase the Present Military Establishment of the United States," 29 July 1861, ch. 24, *Statutes at Large of the USA*, 12:280–81; "An Act Making Appropriations for the Support of the Army for the Year ending the thirtieth June, and for other Purposes," 15 June 1864, ch. 125, *Statutes at Large of the USA*, 13:130.

32. Private George W. Pedrick of Company D, who was later discharged for disability in August 1863.

33. Artificer John B. Geyser was ill and had been sent to the General Hospital in the capital city on March 14, 1863.

34. At the Battle of Gaines's Mill on June 27, 1862, the detachment of the Engineer Battalion that Thompson described here, of which he was a member, was overseeing the construction of a line of rifle pits in front of Brigadier General William F. "Baldy" Smith's 2nd Division of the VI Corps. As a result, these men were in between the main lines when a Confederate brigade launched a feint at Smith's position, and the engineers loaded their rifle muskets and helped repel the assault. Thompson, *Engineer Battalion in the Civil War*, 17; Sears, *To the Gates of Richmond*, 227, 247. See also Thompson's entry of July 6, 1862, and the memoir recollections on p. 62.

35. The Battle of Austerlitz, on December 2, 1805, is often regarded as the French Emperor Napoleon's most decisive victory. Reportedly, on the morning of the battle the sun broke through the clouds over Austria for the first time in two weeks, revealing the weakness of the combined Austro-Russian forces facing the French. This stroke of fortune is sometimes referred to as "the sun of Austerlitz," and it is in this vein that Thompson's friend Robert Thayer used the phrase here, taking the sun rising above the enemy works as a sign of good things to come. Alan Schom, *Napoleon Bonaparte* (New York: HarperCollins, 1997), 410; Gregory Fremont-Barnes and Todd Fisher, *The Napoleonic Wars: The Rise and Fall of an Empire* (Oxford: Osprey Publishing, 2004), 49.

36. Thompson was referring here to the Grapevine Bridge (also known as Sumner's Upper Bridge). See also memoir recollection on p. 62, the journal entry for July 6, 1862, and p. 367n80.

37. See Thompson's entry of June 25, 1862.

38. Thompson's wartime reminiscence here dealt with events that took place in the early morning of June 28, 1862, following the Battle of Gaines's Mill the previous day. See also his journal entry for July 6, 1862, and the memoir passages just before it on pp. 62–64.

39. The bridge Thompson mentioned here was sometimes known as Alexander's and Woodbury's Bridge, but it was more commonly called

Alexander's. Thompson himself, however, was with the detachment that took down Sumner's Upper Bridge on the morning he was describing here, so he may have misremembered the particular bridge involved in this episode. See also his memoir recollection on p. 62, the entry and annotations for July 6, 1862, and p. 363n55.

40. Thompson's description of "going up to Maryland" was a reference to the campaign that culminated at the Battle of Antietam in September 1862.

41. Thompson was quoting a popular hymn known as either "Kingdom of Christ among Men" or, by its first line, "Lo! What a Glorious Sight Appears." For lyrics, see Jones, *Temple Melodies*, 70.

42. Lieutenant George L. Gillespie commanded the battalion's D Company from mid-November 1862 through late May 1863.

43. Grant was Artificer Alorn Grant, Company C.

44. Grass widows are women whose husbands are away for a prolonged absence, as opposed to actual widows.

45. Elizabeth "Lizzie" B. Humphrey and her aunt, Louisa Humphrey. See also entries for October 10, 1862, and March 12, 1863, as well as pp. 374n47 and 382n18. Ballou, *History of the Town of Milford*, 2:832.

46. Major General Daniel Sickles commanded the III Corps of the Army of the Potomac at the date of this entry.

47. This is probably Elizabeth J. "Lizzie" Adams, who was another former student of the Hopedale Home School that also lived just a couple of doors down from Thompson and his mother in the 1850s. She was also the older sister of Adaline Adams whose wedding Thompson attended just before enlisting. See also entry for November 21, 1861, and p. 338-39n6. "Catalogue of the Hopedale Home School," 74; Massachusetts State Census 1855, Worcester County, population schedule, Milford, p. 129, dwelling 734, family 1094, Abner and Elizabeth F. Adams, digital image, FamilySearch, accessed June 13, 2016, https://familysearch.org/pal:/MM9.3.1 / TH-267-11770-177419-36?cc=1459987.

48. Lincoln's only two surviving children at the date of this entry were Robert Todd Lincoln, then nineteen but *not* part of the president's party on this trip, and Thomas Lincoln, commonly called Tad, who turned ten while visiting the Army of the Potomac with his father and mother. Major General Henry Wager Halleck, at the date of this entry, was the general in chief of all Union armies. Doris Kearns Goodwin, *Team of Rivals: The Political Genius of Abraham Lincoln* (New York: Simon & Schuster, 2005), 7, 120, 131, 419; Hebert, *Fighting Joe Hooker*, 182; Wert, *Sword of Lincoln*, 228.

49. See entry for September 1, 1862, and p. 370n19 on the duties of the corporal of the guard.

50. Sergeant Carney was Barnard Carney of Company A.

51. G. H. Y. may have been George H. Young. See January 30, 1862, entry and p.348n71.

52. Major Duane did *not* return to command the battalion.

53. Captain Turnbull was assigned to Company D, and he also commanded the battalion briefly for part of May and June 1863. He was replaced as battalion commander by Captain George H. Mendell in late June. Mendell continued in command of the Engineer Battalion until August 9, 1864. Lieutenant Gillespie was listed as being in command of Company D on November 16, 1862, and for the next several months he remained with that company (though he was absent for several weeks in January and February). However, he was also listed as having been transferred from C Company to D on May 21, 1863, by order of Captain Turnbull during the latter's command of the battalion. It seems as if Gillespie was briefly transferred to Company C during this command shakeup in April and May 1863, before Turnbull returned him to Company D. All of these command changes to the Engineer Battalion were probably the result of the March 1863 merger of the Corps of Topographical Engineers and the Corps of Engineers into a single organization under the latter name. "An Act to Promote the Efficiency of the Corps of Engineers and of the Ordnance Department and for other Purposes," 3 March 1863, Ch. 78, *Statutes at Large of the USA*, 12:43–44.

54. This cavalry movement was the first attempt by Major General George Stoneman to launch a cavalry raid into Lee's rear that Hooker had ordered. The troopers left camp on April 13, but heavy rains beginning the night of the fourteenth caused Stoneman to delay the operation until late April. Wert, *Sword of Lincoln*, 230, 232; "Report of Lieut. Col. Charles G. Sawtelle, U.S. Army, Chief Quartermaster," May 26, 1863, in *OR*, ser. 1, vol. 25, part 1, 1067–68.

6. Hooker Goes on His Own Hook

1. The method of dismantling a pontoon bridge by conversion was designed for use by a retreating army with an enemy in pursuit. The bridge was disconnected from the abutments on both banks and then, by means of cables, wheeled ninety degrees into the current and floated downstream to some protected position where it could be disassembled under cover. Duane, *Manual for Engineer Troops*, 31.

2. Probably a reference to Major General George Stoneman's cavalry raid that left camp on April 13 but was delayed due to the heavy rain that Thompson described in this entry. See also entry for April 12, 1863, and p. 386n54.

3. The Engineer Brigade consisted of the two volunteer engineer regiments, the 15th and 50th New York Volunteer Engineers, and, on occasion, the US Engineer Battalion. Malles, *Bridge Building in Wartime*, 45.

4. Henry W. Benham was a brigadier general of volunteers and a major in the US Army Corps of Engineers. He commanded the Engineer Brigade from the spring of 1863 through the end of the war. Thompson's remark about "James Island notoriety" refers to the June 16, 1862, Battle of Secessionville (also known as the First Battle of James Island). At this engagement, Benham ignored the near-unanimous counsel of his subordinates and sent sixty-five hundred Union troops in an unwise assault against a well-fortified Confederate position on James Island, South Carolina. Benham's men were repulsed with heavy casualties by a Confederate force with less than half Benham's numbers. As a result of this poor performance, his commission as a brigadier general of volunteers was revoked in August 1862 and not restored until February of the following year. Shelby Foote, *The Civil War, a Narrative*, vol. 1, *Fort Sumter to Perryville* (New York: Random House, 1958), 473; Malles, *Bridge Building in Wartime*, 372–73n; Howlett, "79th New York," in Bielakowski, ed., *Ethnic and Racial Minorities in the U.S. Military*, 2:639.

5. William Howard Russell was a reporter for the *Times* of London. He had covered the Crimean War and Indian Mutiny of 1857 before crossing the Atlantic to report on the American Civil War from early 1861 until early 1862. In 1863, he published a diary of his experiences called *My Diary North and South* (Boston: T.O.H.P. Burnam, 1863). Angela Michelli Fleming and John Maxwell Hamilton, eds., *The Crimean War as Seen by Those Who Reported It* (Baton Rouge: Louisiana State University Press, 2009), ix, xv.

6. Thompson was referring to Franklin's Crossing, where the battalion threw a bridge at the start of the Battle of Fredericksburg and where they would construct another for the Chancellorsville campaign.

7. Stafford Heights is the line of hills across the Rappahannock River from Fredericksburg, Virginia.

8. The method of throwing a pontoon bridge by conversion is similar to that of dismantling one by conversion (see chapter 6 epigraph and p. 386n1). The bridge is assembled parallel to the riverbank upstream from the crossing point. It is then floated down the river into position and wheeled across the river after being anchored to the nearer abutment. Duane, *Manual for Engineer Troops*, 30.

9. A reference to the battalion's role at Fredericksburg in constructing the bridges at Franklin's Crossing, which it completed before the volunteer engineers finished their crossings.

10. At Fredericksburg, the 15th New York Volunteer Engineers constructed a pontoon bridge just west of the one built by the Engineer Battalion. They were delayed by enemy musketry but eventually completed this bridge and another later in the day. Thienel, *Mr. Lincoln's Bridge Builders*, 81–82.

11. Captain Sands was the owner of one of the local homes southeast of Falmouth and about a mile and a half east of Fredericksburg on the north side of

the Rappahannock. The pontoon train was parked near Captain Sands's house in late April 1863.

12. According to this April 3, 1863, report by the Joint Committee on the Conduct of the War, if McClellan had been as successful with the Army of the Potomac as other Union generals had been with their forces, the war would likely already have been decided in favor of the Union. The report blamed McClellan for delaying the start of the Peninsula campaign, adopting the allegedly flawed Peninsular approach, leaving Washington underdefended, causing the defeat of John Pope at Second Bull Run by his lethargic movements in support of Pope, and for letting Lee escape with his army intact after Antietam. See Tap, *Over Lincoln's Shoulder*, 162–63.

13. Thompson's memory of soldier attitudes towards McClellan at the time of the Peninsula campaign (particularly his own attitude about the general) is faulty. In the spring of 1862, Thompson praised McClellan for taking Yorktown with siege operations and, consequently, very few casualties. He also noted his approval of the retreat to Harrison's Landing on the James during that campaign and even reported on the good spirits of men in the army immediately after this movement. Thompson's criticisms of these same developments were all written long after the events themselves. See journal entries for May 4 and July 6, 11, and 25, 1862, as well as pp. 359-60n28.

14. This bridge over the Rappahannock at Franklin's Crossing was part of Hooker's feint against Fredericksburg, which was intended to keep Lee's attention focused there while Hooker took the bulk of his army on a march into the Confederate rear. Lee divined the Union general's purpose, however, and left Fredericksburg in the hands of Major General Jubal A. Early and ten thousand Confederates, while Lee moved west with most of the Army of Northern Virginia to confront Hooker in what became the Battle of Chancellorsville.

15. Balk lashers were tasked with attaching the superstructure of a pontoon bridge to the pontoons themselves before chess, or decking, was laid to form the roadway. Duane, *Manual for Engineer Troops*, 26.

16. Shibley was William Shibley of Company D.

17. Thompson may be remembering events through rose-colored lenses here, as others reported Benham to be inebriated while the Engineer Brigade worked to bridge the Rappahannock in late April 1863. Like Thompson, however, Colonel Wesley Brainerd of the 50th New York Volunteer Engineers, reported in his postwar recollections that Benham's fall and bloody face on April 29 was the result of "a fall from his horse the night previous when he was too much intoxicated to retain his seat in the saddle," implying that he was sober (if perhaps hungover) the day the bridge was thrown. Nevertheless, it is worth noting that Benham's defenders all wrote after the war, while the accusations of

insobriety date from the conflict itself. Stephen W. Sears, *Chancellorsville* (Boston: Houghton Mifflin Company, 1996), 154–55; Stephen M. Weld (Headquarters Engineer Brigade, Camp near Falmouth) to His Father, April 29, 1863, in Stephen M. Weld, *War Diary and Letters of Stephen Minot Weld, 1861–1865* (Riverside Press, 1912), 187–90; Malles, *Bridge Building in Wartime*, 141.

18. This location near Deep Run was Franklin's Crossing.

19. The engineer soldier lampooning General Benham was either Edgar M. Johnson or James Johnson, both of Company D.

20. While the Engineer Battalion and the 15th New York Volunteer Engineers worked to bridge the Rappahannock at Franklin's Crossing on April 29, 1863, a detachment of the 50th New York Volunteer Engineers threw two bridges over the river about three or four miles downstream at the mouth of Pollock's Mill Creek. The 50th New York's work, however, was delayed by enemy fire because no covering party was provided to cross the river and protect the site. As a consequence, Confederate fire kept the 50th New York from finishing its work before noon. Malles, *Bridge Building in Wartime*, 138; H. W. Benham to General S. Williams, May 10, 1863, in *OR*, ser. 1, vol. 25, part 1, 213.

21. Thompson was referring to the first bridge thrown at Franklin's Crossing, which was completed by the Engineer Battalion.

22. Dunham was Private Marcus A. Dunham of Company D.

23. Ebenezer B. Hosmer was a member of Company D, not Company C as Thompson reported here in his postwar recollection.

24. Major General George Stoneman, at the date of this journal entry, commanded the Army of the Potomac's Cavalry Corps and was leading a large Federal cavalry raid toward Richmond. Major General Henry W. Slocum commanded the XII Corps of the Army of the Potomac in the spring of 1863. Thompson's reports of both generals' deaths at Chancellorsville were just rumors.

25. Thompson was still reporting camp rumors. In May 1863, Major General Samuel Heintzelman commanded the XXII Corps of the Department of Washington, where he oversaw the city's defenses. The VIII Corps was commanded by Major General Robert Schenck, and in the spring of 1863 it was operating in Maryland. Major General Erasmus Keyes commanded the IV Corps of the Department of Virginia. None of these forces, however, was moving towards the Army of the Potomac.

26. A reference to Napoleon III, Emperor of France (1852–1870), and his distinctive facial hair, which included a mustache the width of his face and a chin puff of several inches.

27. Sergeants George Yagier and William McGee were both discharged from Company C of the Engineer Battalion to allow them to accept commissions as

second lieutenants in the 5th New Hampshire, Yagier in Company C and McGee in Company E of the New England regiment. Yagier never mustered in to his new unit, and his appointment was revoked on June 2, 1863. McGee, however, joined Company E of the 5th New Hampshire in mid-May 1863 and was promoted to first lieutenant of Company H on November 16 of that year. William Child, *A History of the Fifth Regiment New Hampshire Volunteers, in the American Civil War, 1861–1865*, 2 parts (Bristol, NH: R. W. Musgrove, 1893), 2:123–24, 201.

28. Thomas J. McGrath, "An Eye-Witness and Part Instigator," *Washington National Tribune*, July 4, 1907, p. 6.

29. By the spring of 1863, all Louisiana infantry had become known as Tigers, and at that time there were two brigades of Louisianans in the Army of Northern Virginia, containing ten regiments between them. Only one soldier named Lynch deserted from these units that spring, identifying the man that McGrath wrote about in this newspaper excerpt as Patrick Lynch of Company E, 9th Louisiana Infantry. Terry L. Jones, *Lee's Tigers: The Louisiana Infantry in the Army of Northern Virginia* (Baton Rouge: Louisiana State Univ. Press, 1987), xii, 1, 35, 112, 143–44; "Organization of the Army of Northern Virginia," April 27–May 6, 1863, in *OR*, ser. 1, vol. 25, part 1, 792–93; Andrew B. Booth, comp., *Records of Louisiana Confederate Soldiers and Louisiana Confederate Commands*, 3 vols. (New Orleans, LA: n.p., 1920), vol. 3, part 1, 820.

30. There was no General Nelson in the Union army, so this name is either an error of memory on the part of Thomas J. McGrath, the author of the article, or it is an editorial mistake. Given that McGrath was a corporal in Company K, 102nd Pennsylvania, Third Brigade, 3rd Division, VI Corps, Army of the Potomac, it is likely that this is supposed to be a reference to Major General John Newton, commander of the 3rd Division, VI Corps. Samuel P. Bates, *History of Pennsylvania Volunteers, 1861–65*, 5 vols. (Harrisburg, PA: B. Singerly, State Printer, 1869–71), 3:685; "Organization of the Army of the Potomac, Commanded by Maj. Gen. Joseph Hooker, May 1–6, 1863," in *OR*, ser. 1, vol. 25, part 1, 164–66.

31. L. H. Wilkes, "On the Rappahannock," *Washington National Tribune*, May 6, 1909, p. 8.

32. Thompson was hearing the sounds from the Battle of Chancellorsville several miles west of Fredericksburg.

33. See entry for May 1, 1863, and pp. 389–90n27, on the departure of Sergeants McGee and Yagier.

34. On the morning of May 3, 1863, Major General John Sedgwick, commanding his own VI Corps as well as the I Corps of the Army of the Potomac, crossed the Rappahannock and drove Jubal Early's Confederates from the

heights behind Fredericksburg in an attempt to strike against Lee's rear at Chancellorsville, while Hooker tried to turn the rebel left with three Union corps. Though Sedgwick's Federals took Marye's Heights behind Fredericksburg, Lee sent one of his divisions to stop the Union movement and secure his rear. On the night of May 4–5, Sedgwick abandoned Fredericksburg and recrossed the Rappahannock after fending off a Confederate attack on the afternoon of the fourth. Wert, *Sword of Lincoln*, 232, 246–49.

35. Thompson's description here detailed the relocation of the pontoon bridge from Franklin's Crossing to a point directly opposite the city of Fredericksburg on May 3, 1863.

36. Thompson did not mean to suggest that the Engineer Battalion captured the 18th Mississippi, though his entry appears to imply just that at first glance. Instead, he was referring to Sedgwick's assault on Marye's Heights above Fredericksburg on May 3, 1863. This position was held by the 18th Mississippi of Brigadier General William Barksdale's Confederate brigade and half a dozen artillery pieces, most of which were captured when the regiment was overwhelmed by the Federal assault. "Reports of Brig. Gen. William Barksdale, C.S. Army, commanding brigade," May 15, 1863, in *OR*, ser. 1, vol. 25, part 1, 839–40.

37. Thompson's "bridge builders" were likely the US Military Railroad (USMRR). Organized in early 1862 and administered by Daniel McCallum and Herman Haupt, the USMRR ran and maintained the railroads required for the Union war effort, and its duties included building or rebuilding railroad bridges to keep the lines open. John E. Clark Jr., *Railroads in the Civil War: The Impact of Management on Victory and Defeat* (Baton Rouge: Louisiana State Univ. Press, 2001), 62–63.

38. Deep Run flowed into the Rappahannock River near Franklin's Crossing, while Hazel Dell was farther upriver, closer to Fredericksburg.

39. The events of Monday, May 4, that Thompson recounts here were part of Sedgwick's defense of Marye's Heights that day and his subsequent abandonment of them that night. See also fpp. 390–91n34.

40. See the description of the corporal of the guard's duties on p. 370n19 for information about posting reliefs.

41. The "Seven Sisters" refers to Batteries B and M of the 1st Connecticut Heavy Artillery, which were posted behind Franklin's Crossing during the Battle of Chancellorsville and contained between them seven 4½-inch Parrott rifles (also called 30-pound Parrotts). At the date of this entry by Thompson, Captain Alfred F. Brooker commanded Battery B, and Captain Franklin A. Pratt led Battery M. "A Brave Battery," *Pennsylvania School Journal, Devoted to School and Home Education* 40, no. 5 (November 1891): 227–28; "Report of Bvt. Brig.

Gen. John C. Tidball, Fourth New York Heavy Artillery, Commanding Artillery
Brigade," May 28, 1865, in *OR*, ser. 1, vol. 47, part 1, 1070; J. C. Taylor and S. P.
Hatfield, comp., *History of the First Connecticut Artillery and of the Siege Trains of the
Armies Operating against Richmond, 1862–65* (Hartford, CT: Case, Luckwood, &
Brainard Company, 1893), 156, 210; "Report of Brig. Gen. Henry J. Hunt, U.S.
Army, Chief of Artillery," August 1, 1864, in *OR*, ser. 1, vol. 35, part 1, 246; John
W. Stepp and J. William Hill, eds., *Mirror of War: The Washington Star Reports the
Civil War* (Castle Books, 1961), 184; Bvt. Brig.-Gen. Henry L. Abbot, "History of
the First Regiment C.V. Heavy Artillery," in *The First Regiment Connecticut Heavy
Artillery, in the War of the Rebellion, 1861–1865* (Hartford, CT: Case, Lockwood, &
Brainard Company, 1889), 2.

42. Major General John Dix commanded the Department of Virginia at the
date of this entry; he did *not* reinforce Hooker in the spring of 1863.

43. It is impossible to identify conclusively which of the three men from
Company D named either Clark or Clarke that shared a blanket with Thompson
here. However, based on the association Thompson made between a Clarke and
Charles Rue in the September 11, 1864, journal entry as well as the spelling of
"Clarke" in that later entry, this is probably Melville Clarke of Company D, even
though Thompson spelled the name in this entry without the "e" at its end.
Because of this likelihood, the editor has supplied the final "e" in Clarke's name
in the main text.

44. What Thompson called his commission was probably his corporal's
warrant since he was a non-commissioned officer and, therefore, had no
commission.

45. By the morning of May 6, 1863, Major General Joseph Hooker had started
the withdrawal of his forces north across the Rappahannock after his defeat in
the Battle of Chancellorsville. By day's end, the river was between him and Lee's
rebels, and Hooker was on the same side of the river as the Engineer Battalion,
which was camped at Falmouth. Sears, *Chancellorsville*, 428–29.

46. Thompson was mistaken here, as the Engineer Battalion *was* used to throw
a bridge over the Rappahannock as part of Hooker's feint against Fredericksburg
during the Chancellorsville campaign in late April and early May 1863. See
April 29 and May 1, 1863, journal entries and annotations, as well as the postwar
recollection between those entries.

47. Those portions of the Army of the Potomac that fought the Battle of
Chancellorsville under Hooker's direct command had returned to the camp at
Falmouth, Virginia, on the north bank of the Rappahannock by the date of this
entry.

48. Abbie is likely a reference to Abigail Sayles Ballou Heywood, Thompson's
former teacher at the Hopedale Community School and daughter of the

Hopedale founder, Adin Ballou. She married the Reverend William Heywood in 1851, but she was known to her students, including Thompson, as "Mrs. Abbie." Bradbury, "Community Life," 11; Patrick, "Our Community School and Its Teacher," 34; Gifford, "Childhood Days in the Hopedale Community," 42; Draper, "Hopedale," 63; Ballou, *History of the Town of Milford,* 2:556.

49. What spawned this false rumor of Vicksburg's fall in early May 1863 is unclear, but by the time of this entry, Major General Ulysses S. Grant had marched his Army of the Tennessee down the west bank of the Mississippi River, and Rear Admiral David Dixon Porter had run his gunboats past the Vicksburg batteries and ferried Grant's men to the eastern side of the river, where they embarked on a campaign that would eventually lead to a successful siege of the city.

50. Major General George Stoneman, commanding the Army of the Potomac's Cavalry Corps, led a raid against Richmond during the Chancellorsville campaign. Stoneman achieved little other than frightening Richmonders and depriving Hooker of nearly his entire cavalry force. See also the entry for April 12, 1863, and p. 386n54.

51. In early May 1863, Major General Nathaniel P. Banks was slowly moving towards Port Hudson on the Mississippi in cooperation with Grant's operations against Vicksburg.

52. Grand Gulf, below Vicksburg on the Mississippi, is where Grant had intended to cross his Union army from the western to the eastern bank preparatory to his spring and summer 1863 campaign against Vicksburg. A naval bombardment by Rear Admiral David Dixon Porter's squadron, however, failed to drive away the Confederate defenders on April 29, and Grant was forced to cross the river farther south at Bruinsburg; once his men were east of the river, the rebel position at Grand Gulf was untenable and the Confederates there abandoned it. Allan Nevins, *War for the Union,* vol. 3, *1863–1864: The Organized War* (New York: Scribner, 1971), 51, 63–64.

53. Major General John Peck commanded a Federal division at Suffolk, Virginia, that was besieged by rebel forces under James Longstreet, recently detached from Robert E. Lee's Army of Northern Virginia. While Peck successfully defended Suffolk, Longstreet abandoned the siege, primarily to return to Lee's army at Chancellorsville; Peck certainly did not drive Longstreet fifteen miles up the Blackwater River. Sears, *Chancellorsville,* 391–92.

54. See journal entry for April 12, 1863, and p. 386n54.

55. Without further information, this individual cannot be identified. The name itself may be an alias, as there was no one named Richardson working as a spy, detective, scout, or guide with the Army of the Potomac found in either Entry 36 (Correspondence, Reports, Appointments, and Other Records Relating

to Individual Scouts, Guides, Spies, and Detectives, 1861–1867) or Entry 92 (List of Scouts, Guides, Spies, and Detectives, Showing Stations to Which Assigned) of Record Group 110, Records of the Provost Marshal General's Bureau (Civil War), National Archives and Records Administration, Washington, DC.

56. Thompson and the newspapers were incorrect. Lee had not been reinforced at Chancellorsville but had actually been deprived of two divisions that James Longstreet had taken to thwart Union operations along the Virginia coast. See p. 393n54.

57. See May 9, 1863, entry and p. 393n54.

58. This former British soldier was probably Samuel Graham, who transferred into Company D from a volunteer unit in May 1863.

59. Joseph Cummins, Company D.

60. The specific nature of the good news Thompson had heard is unclear, but on May 14, 1863, Grant's forces had taken Jackson, Mississippi, securing his rear for the campaign against Vicksburg, and on May 16 and 17, Grant's forces had won victories at Champion's Hill and the Big Black River, driving the enemy back into the defenses of Vicksburg.

61. Union enlisted men wore brass service insignia and brass letters identifying their company on either the front or top of their standard headgear, usually a French-style kepi or a similarly-styled forage hat. For the engineers, the service insignia was a small triple-turreted castle of stamped brass. According to Thompson's published history of the battalion, only Company A had worn these insignia in 1861, and they were a marker of that company's status as the original engineer company of the regular army. However, in January 1862, when the new regular companies and the 15th and 50th New York Volunteer Engineers joined the Federal forces around Washington, the battalion's commander, Captain James C. Duane, had the men of Company A remove their brass castles because he felt that if the volunteers could wear them, then they were no longer a symbol of distinction. They were restored to the uniforms of all the battalion's men on Brigadier General Benham's orders while the unit was attached to the Volunteer Engineer Brigade. Ron Field and Robin Smith, *Uniforms of the Civil War* (Guilford, CT: Lynn Press, 2001), 55, 129; Thompson, *Engineer Battalion in the Civil War*, 34; Army, *Engineering Victory*, 77; General Orders No. 8, Engineer Brigade, 18 April 1863, Regimental Order Book, 15th New York Engineers, Book Records of Volunteer Union Organizations, Entry 112–115, Record Group 94, Records of the Adjutant General's Office 1780–1917, National Archives and Records Administration, Washington, DC.

7. All We Knew . . . [Was] That a Battle Was Going On

1. A crib bridge was one whose structure was built by stacking logs atop one another in rows, with the logs of each successive row placed perpendicular to those below it.

2. All the activity Thompson described in this paragraph and the preceding one stemmed from the opening moves of the Gettysburg campaign. When Hooker learned that Lee was moving west up the Rappahannock towards Culpeper, he ordered a bridge thrown at Franklin's Crossing so Major General Sedgwick could reconnoiter towards Fredericksburg with his VI Corps. While Thompson remained on guard duty, the Engineer Battalion and some of the volunteer engineers threw this bridge over the Rappahannock late on June 5, 1863. This was the action that cost Captain Charles Cross, commander of the battalion's B Company, his life. According to Wesley Brainerd of the volunteer engineers, Cross was shot while trying to rally his men, some of whom had attempted to slink to the rear. See also journal entry for June 6, 1863, and p. 172. Hebert, *Fighting Joe Hooker*, 233; Wert, *Sword of Lincoln*, 259–60; Thompson, *Engineer Battalion in the Civil War*, 34–35; Malles, *Bridge Building in Wartime*, 153.

3. At the date of this entry, Brigadier General Alfred Pleasonton had recently taken command of the Cavalry Corps of the Army of the Potomac, and he would soon be promoted to the rank of major general.

4. Charles Dickens's *Bleak House* was first published as a serial novel in the early 1850s.

5. Stevens was Daniel Stevens of Company D.

6. The battalion's wounded on this date, besides Captain Cross, consisted of six men. Private Martin C. Kehoe of Company A, who Thompson mentioned later in this entry, died of his wounds on June 6. Private Charles S. Handy, also of Company A, survived but was discharged in late August due to the severity of his injuries. The other four men all returned to duty and completed their terms of enlistment. They included Private Henry Sliter and Artificer Peter D. Lark of Company A, Sergeant George H. Lovejoy of Company C, and D Company's Artificer John H. Carr, who Thompson also mentioned in this journal entry.

7. Thompson appears to be rendering Captain Cross's distinctive way of calling "Shoulder, Arms" phonetically.

8. Brigadier General George Bayard led the cavalry brigade of the Left Grand Division of the Army of the Potomac at Fredericksburg. He was mortally wounded by shrapnel while near the grand division's headquarters on December 13, 1862.

9. *The Oxonians: A Glance at Society* is a two-volume novel by Samuel Beazley published in New York by J. & J. Harper in 1830. *Barnaby Rudge: A Tale of the Riots of Eighty* is a novel by Charles Dickens.

10. Edwin F. Austin of Company A was shot through the right lung on June 1, 1862, during the Peninsula campaign; he was not killed, but he was discharged due to disability in October 1862. See also Thompson's journal entry of June 2, 1862, and pp. 56-57 and 361n40.

11. This is Thompson's account of the bridge thrown over the Rappahannock at Franklin's Crossing on June 5, 1863, where Captain Cross was killed. While Thompson was on guard duty and not with the battalion during this operation, he probably drew on eyewitness accounts of other members of the battalion to produce this entry. See also entries for June 5 and 6, 1863, and pp. 395n2 and 395n6.

12. This was probably the 2nd Florida, whose men held the rebel rifle-pits at Franklin's Crossing on June 5, 1863. "Army of the Potomac," *Harper's Weekly* 7, no. 339 (June 27, 1863): 405.

13. There are too many Bowens in the battalion to identify this individual without further information.

14. Colchester Ferry is on the Occoquan River, about two and a half miles downstream from the town of Occoquan.

15. The pontoon bridge over the Occoquan River at Colchester Ferry was converted into large rafts made of four pontoon boats each. Thompson, *Engineer Battalion in the Civil War*, 37.

16. The *Sylvan Shore* was a steamboat that towed the pontoon rafts, with the battalion members aboard them, to Alexandria, Virginia. Thompson, *Engineer Battalion in the Civil War*, 37.

17. While it is impossible to be certain, "*a la* Harney" could refer to an officer (Captain Charles Turnbull in this case) having a physical altercation with the men under his command, as was the habit of William S. Harney, an officer in the antebellum regular army. It is unclear, however, precisely how Thompson would have known about Harney, who never served with the Army of the Potomac and who retired from the army a few weeks after the date of this journal entry. Nevertheless, in the decades before the Civil War, Harney earned a reputation for brutal treatment of those under his authority, even by the standards of an army in which officers frequently treated enlisted men with an almost casual cruelty. In 1834, Harney beat to death an enslaved woman named Hannah who had upset him. Throughout his career he repeatedly engaged in fisticuffs with teamsters under his command, and he inflicted such vicious physical maltreatment on soldiers that he was convicted of it by a court-martial in 1845. In the latter case, commanding general Winfield Scott only objected to the court's punishment of Harney because Scott did not think it harsh enough;

he had hoped for Harney's dismissal. It is possible that Thompson was aware of Harney's reputation from the *Atlantic Monthly*, which had described him in March 1859 as "an officer of rude force of character amounting often to brutality," or Thompson may have simply heard about Harney from his fellow enlisted men in the regular army, whose service in some cases predated the onset of the Civil War. George Rollie Adams, *General William S. Harney: Prince of Dragoons* (Lincoln: Univ. of Nebraska Press, 2001), 3, 24–25, 36–37, 47–48, 57, 80–81, 139–40, 152–53, 179, 181, 240; William B. Skelton, *An American Profession of Arms: The Army Officer Corps, 1784–1861* (Lawrence: Univ. Press of Kansas, 1992), 270–73, 335; Samuel J. Watson, *Peacekeepers and Conquerors: The Army Officer Corps on the American Frontier, 1821–1846* (Lawrence: Univ. Press of Kansas, 2013), 223–24, 522n23.

18. This phrase is reminiscent of the Latin, *qui custodiet ipsos custodies*, which translates as the query "who guards the guards themselves."

19. This bridge spanned the Potomac River, and it required the use of three trestles because of a lack of boats, which is not entirely clear from this journal entry due to Thompson's phrasing. Thompson, *Engineer Battalion in the Civil War*, 38.

20. According to both the battalion's monthly rosters and Cullum's *Biographical Register*, Captain Mendell took command of the battalion on June 28, 1863, not June 21 as Thompson reported. Mendell continued to lead the regular engineers through August 9, 1864, when he was replaced by Captain Franklin Harwood. Cullum, *Biographical Register*, 2:473.

21. According to Thompson's postwar published account, the bridge that the battalion built on June 21, 1863, was near the mouth of Goose (not Duck) Creek. See also next journal entry from June 23, 1863. Thompson, *Engineer Battalion in the Civil War*, 38.

22. Thompson may have been referring here to the promotion of Brigadier General Alfred Pleasonton. Hooker had put him in command of the Army of the Potomac's Cavalry Corps about a month prior to this entry, and his constant lobbying eventually led to his promotion to the rank of major general, dating from June 22, 1863.

23. In March 1863, the Army of the Potomac officially adopted a system of cloth badges to identify a soldier's corps. These were sewn to the top of the kepi, the side of a hat, or the left breast of the uniform blouse. The diamond that Thompson drew into his journal here was the badge for the III Corps, though Thompson may not have known which corps the badge represented. The III Corps, first under Major General George Stoneman and later under Major General Daniel E. Sickles, did spend the winter of 1862–1863 stationed in Falmouth, Virginia, where the Engineer Battalion also wintered. The badge for

the XI Corps, which he mentioned by its number, was a crescent; the XII Corps used a star with five points. Philip Katcher, *American Civil War Armies*, vol. 2, *Union Troops* (Oxford: Osprey Publishing, 1986), 11–12.

24. Nathaniel Michler of the engineers spent much of the war's first two years in the western theater, but he was transferred to the Army of the Potomac on June 1, 1863, and spent most of that month en route to his new assignment. On the twenty-eighth, two days after this entry, he was captured at Rockville, Maryland, and released on parole shortly thereafter. Heitman, *Register*, 1:708; Cullum, *Biographical Register*, 2:347–48.

25. Major General George Meade replaced Hooker in command of the Army of the Potomac on June 28, 1863.

26. A reference to Libertytown, Maryland, just ten miles northeast of Frederick.

27. Roger B. Taney, chief justice of the United States Supreme Court from 1836 to 1864, was born in Calvert County, Maryland, lived for a while in Frederick, Maryland, and later in Baltimore, but never in Taneytown in Frederick County. Timothy L. Hall, *Supreme Court Justices: A Biographical Dictionary* (New York: Facts on File, 2001), 91–93.

28. Captain George H. Mendell, who took command of the Engineer Battalion on June 28, 1863, had spent the previous four years teaching physics at the United States Military Academy. During that time, he completed and published a translation of Antoine-Henri Jomini's *The Art of War* in cooperation with Lieutenant William P. Craighill. These experiences were likely the origin of Thompson's opinion of Mendell as "a too good scholar for practical soldiering." See memoir recollection on p. 180 as well as annotation 20 on page 397; Cullum, *Biographical Register*, 2:473–74; R. Steven Jones, *The Right Hand of Command: Use and Disuse of Personal Staffs in the American Civil War* (Mechanicsburg, PA: Stackpole Books, 2000), 11.

29. Clearly, Thompson did not have all the details correct, as Lee was not in Maryland but Pennsylvania, and Longstreet was neither mortally wounded nor captured, but rumors of the Union victory at Gettysburg seem to have already reached the engineer corporal.

30. Lieutenant General Richard Ewell was put in charge of Stonewall Jackson's old corps in May 1863, after Jackson's death.

31. There was no Confederate general officer at Gettysburg named Stewart. This could be a reference to either Brigadier General George H. Steuart, who commanded a brigade in Richard Ewell's Confederate corps, or Confederate major general J. E. B. Stuart and his Cavalry Division of the Army of Northern Virginia, though elsewhere Thompson spelled Stuart's name correctly. The aberrant spelling may reflect the same error in Lieutenant Turtle's essay, used as

the epigraph for this chapter; if so, then Thompson's reference was most likely to the Confederate cavalry commander. At Gettysburg, Brigadier General Steuart was leading a brigade in Richard Ewell's Second Corps, fighting at Gettysburg through July 3 and retreating southwest towards the Potomac thereafter. On July 3, however, Major General Stuart led five thousand Confederate horseman east from Gettysburg down the Hanover Road; they were eventually stopped by Union cavalrymen, but only the Federal victory prevented Stuart's troops from heading south against Westminster, Maryland, where the Engineer Battalion was posted at the Union army's supply base for the campaign. "Report of Lieut. Gen. Richard S. Ewell, C. S. Army, commanding Second Army Corps," in *OR*, ser. 1, vol. 27, part 2, 444–48; Wert, *Sword of Lincoln*, 301–3.

32. On the morning of July 2, General Meade had ordered Brigadier General John Buford to take his cavalry division to Westminster, Maryland, where the Engineer Battalion was then stationed. Edward J. Stackpole, *They Met at Gettysburg*, 3d ed. (Harrisburg, PA: Stackpole Books, 1986), 217, 273.

33. In this brief sentence, "Pickett's attack" refers to the infamous Confederate assault on July 3, 1863, against Meade's center, named for Major General George Pickett whose division played a leading role. Bachelder (which Thompson actually misspelled as "Batchelor" in his manuscript memoir entry) was John B. Bachelder, the most prominent nineteenth-century authority on the battle of Gettysburg, and the one individual who exerted the most control over the physical monuments to the battle that began to emerge there in the 1880s. Thompson's mention of the president is unclear, though it could have referred to Lincoln, who gave his Gettysburg Address at the Soldiers' National Cemetery less than half a mile from the most advanced locations reached by Pickett's charge. Hunt was Brigadier General Henry J. Hunt, Chief of Artillery for the Army of the Potomac, and Stannard was Brigadier General George Stannard, who commanded the Third Brigade, 3rd Division, I Corps, Army of the Potomac at Gettysburg; his brigade helped fend off Pickett's charge. On Bachelder, see Thomas A. Desjardin, *These Honored Dead: How the Story of Gettysburg Shaped American Memory* (Cambridge, MA: Da Capo Press, 2003), 86–87, 103, 154–55.

34. This was the 7th New York State Militia, which was one of the first units to answer the federal government's call for troops when the war broke out in April 1861. On April 19 of that year, its one thousand men turned out, and the unit became one of the first to arrive in the nation's capital amid the growing crisis. It spent most of the war in New York City providing security to one of the most important northern cities, but it did see brief service in Maryland in both 1862 and 1863. Phisterer, comp., *New York in the War of the Rebellion*, 1:547.

35. See entry for May 6, 1863, and pp. 391–92n41 on the Seven Sisters.

36. On July 4, 1863, Confederate lieutenant general John C. Pemberton surrendered Vicksburg, the last significant Confederate stronghold on the Mississippi River, to Major General Ulysses S. Grant.

37. The fighting Thompson mentioned in the evening of July 11, 1863, was probably the result of Union skirmishers coming in contact with rebel forces as the Army of the Potomac crossed South Mountain in pursuit of Lee's Confederates after Gettysburg. Freeman Cleaves, *Meade of Gettysburg* (Norman: Univ. of Oklahoma Press, 1980; repr., 1991), 179; Wert, *Sword of Lincoln*, 306–7.

38. This was Washington Augustus Roebling who, after the war, completed the Brooklyn Bridge in New York City that his father, John A. Roebling, had designed. In the early fall of 1862, the younger Roebling, in Federal military service, had built a suspension bridge over the Shenandoah River at Harpers Ferry. When the Army of Northern Virginia moved north at the start of the Gettysburg campaign, the Confederates damaged this structure, and in mid-July, Roebling was tasked with repairing it. David McCullough, *The Great Bridge: The Epic Story of the Building of the Brooklyn Bridge* (New York: Simon & Schuster, 1972), 159.

39. Warren Whitney Dutcher was a successful manufacturer of weaving equipment who relocated from Vermont to Hopedale, Massachusetts, in 1856 to go into partnership with George Draper. See also Thompson's entry for February 28, 1863, and p. 381n8. United States Census 1860, Worcester County, Massachusetts, population schedule, Milford, p. 121, dwelling 644, family 991, Warren W and Malinda Dutcher, digital image, FamilySearch, accessed April 29, 2016, https://familysearch.org/pal:/MM9.3.1/TH-1942-25248-12028 -90?cc=1473181; E. Everton Foster, ed., *Lamb's Textile Industries of the United States, Embracing Biographical Sketches of Prominent Men and a Historical Resume of the Progress of Textile Manufacture from the Earliest Records to the Present Time*, 2 vols. (Boston, MA: James H. Lamb, 1916), 1:291; Spann, *Hopedale*, 132.

40. For the identification of this quote, see annotation number 41 on p. 385.

8. The Line of the Rappahannock

1. This was the second Battle of Rappahannock Station. See p. 404-5n34 for a brief description.

2. James C. Duane, former commander of the battalion, had been promoted to major since his service with the engineer troops. Heitman, *Register*, 1:384.

3. Chauntecler is a term for a rooster.

4. Thompson chose *not* to reenlist, perhaps because to do so in 1863 would have required him to serve the full reenlistment term of five years in the regular army, regardless of when the war ended. Even though the enlistment period

was subsequently reduced back to three years, Thompson still did not reenlist. He left the service on November 22, 1864, at the expiration of his original term, perhaps because service in the regulars was for a fixed period without the limiting clause of "or the duration of the war" that was included on volunteer enlistments. See also memoir passage on p. 45 as well as annotation number 22 on p. 358.

5. Following a carefully planned campaign of maneuver, Major General William S. Rosecrans and his Army of the Cumberland advanced from Murfreesboro, prompting Confederate general Braxton Bragg to withdraw his Army of Tennessee, first to Tullahoma, and then all the way to Chattanooga in early July 1863.

6. Thompson was writing about the Rappahannock River.

7. A vidette was a mounted sentry.

8. A reference to the fact that Union major general Benjamin F. Butler was cross-eyed.

9. After Lee's Army of Northern Virginia recrossed the Potomac following its defeat at Gettysburg, it settled into position along a line south of the Rappahannock. At the same time, the forces of the Federal Army of the Potomac were reduced by the need to dispatch troops to New York City to quell the draft riots there and to send men to support siege operations along the South Carolina coast. As a result, Meade was limited to patrolling the area between the Rapidan and the Rappahannock rivers and mounting the occasional probe of southern defenses along the latter river. The engagement Thompson describes here was part of an attempt by Meade to threaten the rebel flank. Wert, *Sword of Lincoln*, 312; Cleaves, *Meade of Gettysburg*, 190–91.

10. The United States Military Railroad's Construction Corps was a permanent organization established by Herman Haupt in 1862 to maintain and build railroad lines and bridges for Union armies. Army, *Engineering Victory*, 140–42.

11. "Lethean streams" was a reference to the mythical river Lethe in Hades; drinking from its waters caused total forgetfulness.

12. Thompson may have been referring to the anti-war activities of North Carolina politician William W. Holden. Holden, believing the South could no longer win the war, organized a series of anti-war meetings in the summer of 1863. One effect of these activities was the election of several North Carolina congressmen who reportedly favored seeking an immediate peace with the Union.

13. See journal entry for August 13, 1862, and p. 369n12.

14. According to his published history of the battalion, Thompson repaired this bridge using boards taken from soldiers' huts as well as small trees cut nearby. Thompson, *Engineer Battalion in the Civil War*, 45.

15. The Geyser mentioned here was probably John B. Geyser of Company D, who took an interest in chess. See March 4, 1863, entry.

16. On October 9, 1863, Lee began a brief Confederate offensive when he moved north across the Rapidan River and attempted to turn the Union right. As a result, Meade abandoned Culpeper and retreated north along the Orange and Alexandria Railroad to protect his lines of communication and supply. Both armies continued moving north until the Battle of Bristoe Station on October 14. Wert, *Sword of Lincoln*, 316; Cleaves, *Meade of Gettysburg*, 196–97.

17. Thompson was writing of his second wartime journal, his first having been filled up and sent home in mid-October 1862. See both October 12, 1862, journal entries.

18. Thompson was referring to the Rappahannock and Rapidan rivers.

19. In October 1863, Brigadier General George Armstrong Custer commanded the Second Brigade, 3rd Division of the Army of the Potomac's Cavalry Corps. During the army's retreat from Culpeper, Virginia, in the face of Lee's brief fall offensive, Major General Alfred Pleasanton's Cavalry Corps was surrounded. To fight through the encirclement, the brigades of Custer, Colonel Thomas Devin, and Brigadier General Wesley Merritt assaulted the southern troopers for several hours and eventually fought their way free. According to modern biographers, Custer did not lead his men in a round of "Rally Round the Flag" as he led the charge against the rebel cavalrymen, but instead merely attacked the rebel troopers to the tune of "Yankee Doodle." See October 12, 1863, journal entry. D. A. Kinsley, *Favor the Bold, Custer: The Civil War Years* (New York: Holt, Rhinehart, and Winston, 1967), 171–74; Jay Monaghan, *Custer: The Life of General George Armstrong Custer* (Lincoln: Univ. of Nebraska Press, 1959), 166; Gregory J. W. Urwin, *Custer Victorious: The Civil War Battles of General George Armstrong Custer* (Lincoln: Univ. of Nebraska Press, 1983), 102–3.

20. Based on the handwriting and placement, Thompson's recollection of Custer was almost certainly written during the American Civil War, but it is *not* found in chronological sequence in his journal. Instead, it was recorded on a journal page from mid-June 1863 that had initially been left half blank, indicating that Thomson recorded this impression of General Custer sometime after the events of October 12, 1863, but before he mailed the second of his wartime journals home to his mother on April 16, 1864.

21. The run that Thompson mentioned here was Cedar Run, a tributary of the Occoquan River.

22. The Battle of Bristoe Station took place on October 14, 1863. Elements of the Union II Corps under Major General Gouverneur K. Warren repulsed an assault by Lieutenant General A. P. Hill's Confederate III Corps, bloodying the

southern advance. The next day, Meade adopted a strong position to the north at Centreville, and a few days later Lee ended his fall 1863 offensive and withdrew back behind the Rappahannock without testing Meade's defenses. See also entry for October 12, 1863. Wert, *Sword of Lincoln*, 316–17; Cleaves, *Meade of Gettysburg*, 196–200.

23. George McMillan of Company D was discharged for disability on October 25, 1863.

24. Artificer Thomas H. Leas of Company C was discharged from the Engineer Battalion for disability on June 17, 1862. In September 1863, however, he entered into service in Company D of the 95th New York Infantry, presumably as a substitute. *Annual Report of the Adjutant-General of the State of New York for Year 1902. Registers of the Ninety-fourth, Ninety-fifty, Ninety-sixth, Ninety-seventy, Ninety-eighth, and Ninety-ninth Regiments of Infantry*, vol. 3, serial no. 32 (Albany, NY: Argus Company, 1903), 384.

25. Prior to his service with the Engineer Battalion, Decatur O. Blake served with the 8th Michigan Infantry and fought on the Union right with that unit at Second Bull Run. See also the memoir section on p. 77 and its annotation number 22 on p. 371.

26. The uncompleted railroad that Thompson mentioned is a reference to the defensive position held by Jackson's Confederate corps at Second Bull Run in a railroad cut that formed a pre-made trench. On August 29, 1862, Union major general John Pope assailed this formidable position without success.

27. The 14th Brooklyn probably refers to the 14th New York State Militia, also known as the 84th New York Volunteer Infantry. At Second Bull Run, this regiment served in the 1st Division of Major General Irvin McDowell's III Corps.

28. While Fitz John Porter's V Corps played no role in the fighting at Second Bull Run on August 29, leaving Pope to manage alone, Porter's Corps was responsible for the August 30 Union assault that was repulsed by the enfilading fire of Longstreet's artillery. John J. Hennessy, *Return to Bull Run: The Campaign and Battle of Second Manassas* (Norman: Univ. of Oklahoma Press, 1993), 339–61.

29. The Warrenton Turnpike. John S. Salmon, *The Official Virginia Civil War Battlefield Guide* (Mechanicsburg, PA: Stackpole Books, 2001), 145.

30. With his quote of "when my yoke &c.," Thompson was probably referencing Matthew 11:28–30, which reads "Come unto me, all ye that labour and are heavy laden, and I will give you rest. Take my yoke upon you, and learn of me; for I am meek and lowly in heart: and ye shall find rest unto your souls. For my yoke is easy, and my burden is light." These passages promise spiritual relief, but Thompson appears to have been drawing a parallel to heavy but necessary physical labor or, perhaps, referencing the burden of living under an oppressive social structure, which may have been how military discipline seemed

to the young man, particularly after his comments in his journal entry prior to this one. See also O. Wesley Allen Jr., *Matthew* (Minneapolis, MN; Fortress Press, 2013), 127.

31. According to Thompson's recollections and the monthly returns of the Engineer Battalion, the seven men who started in the Company of Topographical Engineers, were later transferred into one of the Engineer Battalion's companies, and still remained in the battalion at the date of this entry were Thompson himself, Edward J. Currier (who subsequently deserted in December 1863), John L. Slater, Francis E. Beahn, Mariner S. Fickett, Atkins Higgins, and George Ames. Of the five no longer with the battalion, James A. Black had died of disease on September 3, 1862; Robert C. Thayer had been discharged for disability on October 16, 1862; Daniel H. Miller had died of dysentery on December 5, 1862; Eben White had been discharged on September 15, 1863 (and promoted to lieutenant in another unit, see next annotation); and James W. Flood deserted some time prior to July 1864 (in which month he was reported as having returned from desertion).

32. Sergeant Eben White was discharged from the Engineer Battalion on September 15, 1863, to accept a commission as a second lieutenant in the 7th US Colored Infantry. On October 19, 1863, he was murdered by Joseph H. Southoron (sometimes spelled "Sothoron" or "Southern") and his son Webster while White was recruiting men for his new unit outside Benedict, Maryland. "Compiled Military Service Records of Volunteer Union Soldiers Who Served with the United States Colored Troops, 2nd through 7th Colored Infantry, 6th Louisiana (African Descent), 7th Louisiana Infantry (African Descent)," Records of the Adjutant General's Office 1780s–1917, Record Group 94, National Archives Microfilm Publication M1820 (cited hereafter as "National Archives Microfilm Publication M1820"), roll 108.

For a thorough contextualization of the violence faced by white officers of African American units, see James G. Hollandsworth Jr., "The Execution of White Officers from Black Units by Confederate Forces During the Civil War," in *Black Flag over Dixie*, ed. Urwin, 52–64.

33. As Lee withdrew south after the Battle of Bristoe Station, his men tore up the Orange and Alexandria Railroad.

34. Thompson's recapitulation describes the Second Battle of Rappahannock Station on November 7, 1863. In this engagement, Major General John Sedgwick led the V and VI Corps against Confederate defenses just north of the Rappahannock River at Rappahannock Station, while Major General William French led the I, II, and III Corps against rebel works north of the river at Kelly's Ford, which was the part of the action that Thompson described. The result of the entire engagement was an unqualified tactical success for the Federals, who

captured both positions and roughly two thousand prisoners combined at both locations. After the fight, the Engineer Battalion threw two bridges over the Rappahannock at Kelly's Ford. Ethan S. Rafuse, *George Gordon Meade and the War in the East* (Abilene, TX: McWhiney Foundation Press, 2003), 104–5; Wert, *Sword of Lincoln*, 318–19; Thompson, *Engineer Battalion in the Civil War*, 47–48.

35. The 1st Connecticut Heavy Artillery. See also journal entries for May 6 and November 13, 1863, and pp. 391–92n41 and 405n39.

36. The sharpshooters Thompson mentioned were likely the 2nd US Sharpshooters, which served in the 1st Division of Major General William French's III Corps, and the artillery was probably a battery of the 1st Rhode Island Light Artillery. "Report of Lieut. John K. Bucklyn, Battery E, First Rhode Island Light Artillery, of action at Kelly's Ford," November 10, 1863, in *OR*, ser. 1, vol. 29, part 1, 568–69.

37. Confederate major general Robert E. Rodes commanded the division that included the 2nd North Carolina and that held Kelly's Ford during the Second Battle of Rappahannock Station on November 7, 1863 (see p. 404n34). According to his report, his entire division suffered a total of just under three hundred men missing after this engagement. He did note, however, that most of those came from the two regiments that were on picket duty at the time, one of which was the 2nd North Carolina. R. E. Rodes to Lieut. Col. A. S. Pendleton, November 13, 1863, in *OR*, ser. 1, vol. 29, part 1, 232.

38. Thompson was paraphrasing James Fennimore Cooper's *The Pioneers*, which he was reading at the time; the actual line is "hounds should be gaunty to run well."

39. Thompson seems to have been mistaken in his identification of the 2nd Rhode Island. His mention of brass 12-pound howitzers indicates an artillery unit, but the only Rhode Island artillerymen at Kelly's Ford belonged to the 1st Rhode Island Light Artillery, which was probably the unit he encountered. Thompson's remark about the "grim old 32s" was probably a reference to the Seven Sisters, Batteries B and M of the 1st Connecticut Heavy Artillery. See journal entry for May 6, 1863, and pp. 391–92n41. On the identification of the 1st Rhode Island Light Artillery, see "Organization of the Army of the Potomac, Maj. Gen. George G. Meade, U.S. Army, commanding, October 10, 1863," in *OR*, ser. 1, vol. 29, part 1, 216–25; "Report of Capt. George E. Randolph, commanding Artillery Brigade, of action at Kelly's Ford and skirmish at Brandy Station," November 11, 1863, in *OR*, ser. 1, vol. 29, part 1, 566–68.

40. Mountain Run joins Mine Run just before the latter feeds into the Rapidan River about ten miles southeast of Culpeper, Virginia.

41. The meaning of Thompson's abbreviation "Cor." in this entry is uncertain, however given his many musical references and his use of Roman numerals in

this and subsequent entries, he may have been referring to a piece of music that he was writing. Thompson might have been abbreviating the word corps, using it to mean an ensemble piece designed to be played by several instruments. Alternatively, he could have been writing a piece for the cornet, an instrument included in many Civil War military bands. Without further information, it is impossible to be certain. See also Thompson's journal entries for January 11 and February 10 and 11, 1864. Jeremy Montagu, "Military Band and Corps of Drums," *The Oxford Companion to Music*, Oxford Music Online, accessed February 27, 2017, http://www.oxfordmusiconline.com/subscriber/article/opr/t114 /e4418; Niles Eldredge, "Cornet," Grove Music Online, Oxford Music Online, accessed February 27, 2017, http://www.oxfordmusiconline.com/subscriber /article/grove/music/A2256224.

42. On November 26, 1863, Lieutenant George L. Gillespie left the battalion to perform recruiting service.

43. Thompson was writing about Meade's Mine Run campaign, during which the Union general attempted to get the Army of the Potomac around the left flank of the Army of Northern Virginia by making a quick crossing of the Rapidan at Jacob's and Kelly's Fords. Thompson's prediction of success, however, was mistaken. Problems with the weather and the river crossings delayed Meade long enough for Lee to concentrate his army in opposition, and in early December Meade gave up the operation. The Engineer Battalion spent the remainder of the campaign after Thompson's November 30 entry guarding the bridges that its men had thrown.

44. One of the reasons for the delay at the river crossings during the Mine Run campaign was an insufficient number of pontoon boats, which Thompson also reported here in this postwar recollection. His mention of the "horse-shoe nail" alludes to the old nursery rhyme with logistical implications that begins "for want of a nail, the shoe was lost; for want of a shoe, the horse was lost," and continues upward until the loss of a battle and, ultimately, a kingdom. See also Salmon, *Virginia Civil War Battlefield Guide*, 242.

45. Thompson was referring to the provost marshal or provost guard, which was tasked with apprehending deserters. Wiley, *Billy Yank*, 282.

9. Waiting to Do Something

1. Thompson was writing about the end of Meade's Mine Run campaign in late 1863. See journal entry for November 28, 1863, and p. 406n43.

2. From 1859 to 1863, Captain Mendell had been an assistant professor of natural and experimental philosophy (known today as physics) at the US Military

Academy at West Point. Cullum, *Biographical Register*, 2:473–74. See also journal entry for July 5, 1863, and p. 398n28.

3. John Smith was either John T. Smith of Company D or John Smith of Company A. McCormack was Thomas McCormack, Company C.

4. A Martello Tower was a round circular fort, usually intended for coastal defense, with its guns mounted behind or atop stone walls. The name derives from the fortification of this type on Corsica, in the Bay of Martello, which successfully drove off a British naval assault in 1794. The United States built several of them on its coast, most notably in Key West, Florida. Arthur P. Wade, *Artillerists and Engineers: The Beginnings of American Seacoast Fortifications* (McLean, VA: CDSG Press, 2011), 111–12.

5. An anchorite is someone who withdraws from society, usually for religious reasons.

6. A common punishment for minor offenses was to require men to march around the camp while carrying a log. Wiley, *Billy Yank*, 197.

7. "Pitcher of England" was Henry P. Pitcher of Company D.

8. Thompson's bunkmate at this time was Edwin H. "Ned" Coolidge, and this arrest may be the reason that Coolidge was later reduced in rank (see entry for December 20, 1863). Sergeant Taylor was David B. Taylor of Company D.

9. Lieutenant George Gillespie was on recruiting service in December 1863, and Artificer John H. Carr was on detached duty at West Point, New York. Why Thompson believed these men to be in Tennessee is unclear.

10. Edwin J. Sweet of Milford had enlisted as a private in the 40th New York, also known as the Mozart Regiment. By the spring of 1863, Sweet had been promoted to first sergeant, and on June 5, he was commissioned as a second lieutenant. From July 2, 1863, he served as the unit's acting adjutant. Just a few days before his meeting with Thompson, Sweet was again promoted, this time to first lieutenant. See also Thompson's entry of April 28, 1862, and p. 359n26. United States Census 1860, Worcester County, Massachusetts, population schedule, Milford, p. 145, dwelling 795, family 1189, George W. and Roxanna Sweet, digital image, FamilySearch, accessed May 8, 2016, https://familysearch .org/pal:/MM9.3.1/TH-1942-25248-12188-81?cc=1473181; *Annual Report of the Adjutant-General of the State of New York for the Year 1900. Registers of the Thirty-ninth, Fortieth, Forty-first, Forty-second and Forty-third Regiments of Infantry*, vol. 3, serial no. 23 (Albany: James B. Lyon, State Printer, 1901), 633.

11. This is likely a reference to a loss of rank. In his May 20, 1863, entry, Thompson noted that Coolidge was a corporal, but when Ned was discharged in October 1864, he was only an artificer. See also next journal entry and its annotation 12 on p. 408.

12. It is likely that Ned Coolidge had to find a new mess when he was demoted, as the unit's corporals were required to bunk together. See Thompson's entries of May 20, December 20, and December 29, 1863, and annotation 11 on p. 407.

13. L. H. was Louisa Humphrey, and her niece was Elizabeth "Lizzie" Bullock Humphrey, artist and former schoolmate of Thompson's. The school mentioned was the Cooper Union for the Advancement of Science and Art in New York City, established in 1859. See also entries from October 10, 1862, and March 31, 1863, and pp. 374n47 and 385n45.

14. The army successes that Thompson mentioned were probably Union achievements in east Tennessee where Major General Ulysses S. Grant had broken the siege of Chattanooga with the Battle of Lookout Mountain in late November 1863 and Major General Ambrose Burnside had successfully defended his control of Knoxville from a besieging rebel force. The naval accomplishment he wrote about may have been the successful siege of Brownsville, Texas, on the north bank of the Rio Grande by a combined Federal force in late 1863.

15. The message here was Abraham Lincoln's third annual message to Congress of December 8, 1863. Just what Thompson found so significant about this message is difficult to ascertain. In addition to discussing all the mundane matters of government and issues relating to the progress of the war, he also discussed his Ten Percent plan for Reconstruction, which Thompson may have taken as a sign of sorts for the eventual end of the war. *Senate Journal*, 38th Cong., 1st Sess., December 9, 1863.

16. Confederate lieutenant general Richard S. Ewell commanded the II Corps of the Army of Northern Virginia in the winter of 1863–64. Ewell was not, however, in the Shenandoah Valley that winter, though one of his division commanders, Major General Jubal A. Early, had been dispatched to the valley in mid-December 1863 in response to a Federal raid led by Brigadier General William W. Averell. Early was unsuccessful in dealing with Averell, and he afterwards remained in the valley collecting supplies for several weeks. Douglas Southall Freeman, *Lee's Lieutenants: A Study in Command*, vol. 3, *Gettysburg to Appomattox* (New York: Charles Scribner's Sons, 1944), 325–36; Donald C. Pfanz, *Richard S. Ewell: A Soldier's Life* (Chapel Hill: Univ. of North Carolina Press, 1998), 348; Joseph T. Glatthaar, *General Lee's Army: From Victory to Collapse* (New York: Free Press, 2008), 344.

17. G. M. was likely George Munro. See January 17, 1864, journal entry.

18. Corporal John Fitzpatrick of Company D.

19. William Longstreet of Company D had been on furlough since December 29, 1863.

20. M. A. Blunt was likely the printer Michael A. Blunt of Milford, Massachusetts. In his February 25, 1864, entry, Thompson identified Blunt as "my old boss." United States Census 1860, Worcester County, Massachusetts, population schedule, Milford, p. 38, dwelling 212, family 312, Michael A. and Permelia Blunt, digital image, FamilySearch, accessed April 21, 2016, https://familysearch.org/ark:/61903/1:1:MZC9-K45.

21. This club was the Essayons Dramatic Club, which took its name from the motto of the US Army Corps of Engineers: Essayons (French for "we try," though interpreted as "let us try" by the engineers). The club members and battalion officers volunteered funds and labor to construct a theater at Brandy Station, Virginia. Thompson, *Engineer Battalion in the Civil War*, 52.

22. The initials H. G. T. probably refer to Thompson's mother, Harriet Gilbert Thompson.

23. While it is impossible to be certain, Thompson may be exaggerating the results of a reconnaissance by a detachment of 150 men from the 1st Maine Volunteer Cavalry under Major Sidney W. Thaxter. This Union cavalry force captured eight prisoners on its reconnaissance. "Itinerary of the Army of the Potomac," February 1864, in *OR*, ser. 1, vol. 33, 620.

24. Brigadier General Alexander Hayes commanded the 3rd Division, II Corps, Army of the Potomac, at the date of this entry.

25. According to the battalion's monthly returns, in February 1864 alone, nearly ninety-five men from all four of its companies reenlisted, twenty of them from Thompson's Company D.

26. Gleason was Jonas D. Gleason of Company C.

27. See "From Memory," page 320, for this sketch.

28. *Lucrezia Borgia* is an 1833 play by Victor Hugo.

29. See journal entry for November 16, 1862, and p. 377n13 for more on Charlotte Crampton.

30. The lecture by Mr. Rockwell that Thompson described here probably felt familiar to him because his home community of Hopedale, Massachusetts, had sponsored regular lyceums for its members as part of the Practical Christian commitment to education and betterment. Spann, *Hopedale*, 87–88.

31. *The Toodles* is an 1848 comedic play by William E. Burton that was based on the older work *The Broken Heart; or, the Farmer's Daughter*. The 1848 play was one of Burton's biggest successes. Gerald Bordman and Thomas S. Hischak, *The Oxford Companion to American Theater*, 3rd ed. (Oxford: Oxford Univ. Press, 2004), 622.

32. A gander dance was one with no women, in which the men partnered each other. John D. Wright, *The Language of the Civil War* (Westport, CT: Oryx Press, 2001), 123, 284.

33. A violincello, also spelled violoncello, is a four-stringed instrument also known as a bass violin or cello. *Oxford English Dictionary Online*, s.v. "Violoncello, n," accessed May 1, 2016, http://www.oed.com.proxygsu-for1.galileo.usg.edu /view/Entry/223670?redirectedFrom=violincello&.

34. Boreas was the Greek god of the North Wind.

35. As noted in annotation number 10 on p. 357, Frederick Vogel of Company D sent copies of his wartime journal to Thompson in 1886, some of which were reproduced in Thompson's postwar recollections.

36. *Box & Cox* was a one-act comedy from 1848 by John Madison Morton.

37. *Irish Assurance and Yankee Modesty* (1854) was a comedy that was James Pilgrim's most successful play. William H. A. Williams, *'Twas Only an Irishman's Dream: The Image of Ireland and the Irish in American Popular Song Lyrics, 1800–1920* (Champaign: Univ. of Illinois Press, 1996), 98; Shaun Richard, ed., *The Cambridge Companion to Twentieth-Century Irish Drama* (Cambridge: Cambridge Univ. Press, 2004), 22.

38. Fritz was Thompson's nickname for Frederick Vogel of Company D.

39. In 1853, William Collins first enlisted in Company A, Corps of Engineers, for a five-year term, and in 1858 he reenlisted. He deserted in mid-March 1861 but was apprehended nearly three years later in early March 1864, and on the twenty-third of that month, he was reported on the Engineer Battalion's official rolls as having rejoined the unit from desertion. During his three-year absence, Collins served with two volunteer units. About a month after he deserted from Company A in 1861, Collins enlisted in Company K of the 69th New York Volunteer Infantry, one of the Irish Brigade's original regiments. He later served as ordnance sergeant for his brigade and division until the 69th New York was mustered out. He subsequently enlisted as a private in Company D of the 22nd New York Volunteer Cavalry, from which he deserted in February 1864, just before it was attached to the Army of the Potomac's IX Corps and about a month before his apprehension and return to the Engineer Battalion. NARA Microfilm Publication M233, roll 26, 53:286; NARA Microfilm Publication M233, roll 29, 56:29; William Collins, Co. K, 69th New York Infantry, Compiled Military Service Record, Record Group 94, Records of the Adjutant General's Office 1780–1917, National Archives and Records Administration, Washington, DC; D. P. Conyngham, *The Irish Brigade and Its Campaigns: With Some Account of the Corcoran Legion and Sketches of the Principal Officers* (New York: William McSorley & Co., 1867), 467; *Annual Report of the Adjutant General of the State of New York for the Year 1901. Registers of the Sixty-ninth, Seventieth, Seventy-first, Seventy-second, Seventy-third and Seventy-fourth Regiments of Infantry*, serial 28 (Albany, NY: J. B. Lyon Company, 1902), 59; *Annual Report of the Adjutant-General of the State of New York for the Year 1894. Registers of the 20th,*

21st, 22d, 23d, 24th, 25th and 26th Regiments of Cavalry, New York Volunteers in War of the Rebellion (Albany, NY: J. B. Lyon, 1895), 519; Dyer, *Compendium*, 1381, 1430–31.

40. Here Thompson was probably referring to the punishment known as "riding a rail" or "riding the wooden horse," in which a soldier was required to straddle a horizontal beam that was positioned high enough to keep his feet off the ground. Wiley, *Billy Yank*, 197; Billings, *Hardtack and Coffee*, 150.

41. "Old 'Turny'" was Captain Charles N. Turnbull, commanding Company D.

42. *Paddy Miles, the Limerick Boy, A Farce* (1836; rev. ed. 1855) by James Pilgrim.

43. At 25 cents per ticket and a profit of $46.00, the benefit was presented to approximately 184 people.

44. Lieutenant General Ulysses S. Grant was appointed commanding general of Union armies in March 1864, and he traveled with the Army of the Potomac for the rest of the war.

45. When Thompson first joined the Engineer Battalion in early 1862, Godfrey Weitzel commanded its Company A. In April 1864, Weitzel was a captain and brevet major in the US Army Corps of Engineers as well as a brigadier general of volunteers. At the time of this entry, he was on his way to join the 2nd Division, XVIII Corps, Army of the James. Similarly, when Thompson originally enlisted Chauncey B. Reese commanded the battalion's Company B, but by April 1864, Reese was a captain in the US Army Corps of Engineers, and on the twenty-ninth of the month he was appointed as chief engineer of the Army of the Tennessee. Cullum, *Biographical Register*, 2:605–6, 716–17.

46. The Second Battle of Rappahannock Station. See November 12, 1863, entry and pp. 404-5n34.

47. Flick was Captain George H. Mendell, the Engineer Battalion commander.

48. *Corrine, or Italy*, by Madam de Stael (1807).

49. Alphonse de Lamartine, *Memoirs of My Youth* (1849).

50. This is a reference to the titular character of another Alphonse de Lamartine novel, *Graziella* (1852).

51. Joe was likely Corporal Joseph Cummins, one of the four Company D corporals who all shared quarters and also Thompson's bunkmate at the date of this entry.

52. Harmer was Joseph Harmer of Company A.

53. The church that Thompson mentioned may have been the St. James Church, a local landmark in the area around Brandy Station, but it is impossible to be certain. The 45th Massachusetts was a nine-month militia regiment raised in response to the call for additional troops in the summer of 1862; it served briefly in Union military operations along the North Carolina Coast in late 1862 and early 1863. However, there was no officer of any rank named Kirk on the

unit's rolls. Adjutant General of Massachusetts, *Massachusetts Soldiers, Sailors, and Marines in the Civil War*, 4:309–47.

54. In British musical terminology, a crotchet is a quarter note. Corporal Joseph "Joe" Cummins, Thompson's bunkmate, may have been continuing to play music after the evening's entertainment, though with what instrument is unclear. Christine Ammer, *The Facts on File Dictionary of Music*, 4th ed. (New York: Facts on File, 2004), 330.

55. The second of Thompson's three wartime journals ends here, and his final journal commences with the next entry.

56. This was a second entry for this date to begin Thompson's third manuscript journal.

57. Mather was Joseph Mather, who was the battalion's quartermaster sergeant when discharged in November 1864.

58. Michael Daly of Company B. NARA Microfilm Publication M233, roll 29, 58:274.

59. This may be a reference to the Germania Musical Society of the 1840s and 1850s that consisted of young musicians originally from Berlin. The group helped to popularize the symphony orchestra in mid-nineteenth century America. Nancy Newman, *Good Music for a Free People: The Germania Musical Society in Nineteenth-Century America* (Rochester, NY: Univ. of Rochester Press, 2010), xi, 1; Lawrence Levine, *Highbrow/Lowbrow: The Emergency of a Cultural Hierarchy in America* (Cambridge, MA: Harvard Univ. Press, 1988), 110–12.

60. Stephen C. Foster's *The Social Orchestra for Flute or Violin: A Collection of Popular Melodies Arranged as Solos, Duos, Trios, and Quartets* (1854). Harold Vincent Milligan, *Stephen Foster Collins: A Biography of America's Folk-Song Composer* (New York: G. Schirmer, 1920), 81.

61. "Soldier's March" is from Charles Gounod's opera *Faust*. Baumbach may be a reference to the well-known mid-nineteenth century composer of sheet music, Adolph Baumbach. Terese Volk Tuohey, *A Musician and Teacher in Nineteenth-Century New England: Irving Emerson, 1843–1905* (Lanham, MD: Lexington Books, 2015), 7.

62. The following twelve men were discharged from the Engineer Battalion on April 25, 1864, at the end of their three-year enlistments: Buel Chipman of Company A, Edgar M. Johnson of Company D, and ten men from Company B, viz., Charles Burns, Atwood P. Jones, James Lewis, Terence McCabe, William McCarty, Allan McDonald, Charles F. Robes, Isaac Sanborn, James Savage, and Isaac Sozier.

63. Robbins was George H. Robbins of Company D.

64. Thompson's use of meerschaum here referred to a tobacco pipe made of that material.

65. Thompson's amusement likely stemmed from Vogel's exaggerated manner and the unexpected juxtaposition of the slow, stately music of the adagios with the rapid alternating tones of a trill played by Vogel on his flute and represented by the musical notation that Thompson recorded in his journal.

66. Sarah P. Lillie, whose name Thompson usually abbreviated as "S. P." See February 9 and November 15, 1862, entries and pp. 350n80 and 376n8.

67. In the spring of 1864, Major General Ambrose Burnside commanded the IX Corps, recently returned to Virginia from the western theater; because Burnside was Meade's senior officer, he fought in Virginia under Lieutenant General Grant's direct control until May 24, 1864.

68. *Italy, A Poem*, published as book, was by the English Romantic poet Samuel Rogers.

69. Lord Byron's *Childe Harold's Pilgrimage*.

70. Possibly the Romantic poet Robert Burns.

71. It is unclear which brigade Thompson meant by "the Colored Brigade." Brigadier General Edward Ferrero's 4th Division of Major General Ambrose Burnside's IX Corps actually contained two brigades of African American soldiers. Colonel Joshua K. Siegfried's First Brigade included the 27th USCT (United States Colored Troops), the 30th USCT, the 39th USCT, and the 43rd USCT. The Second Brigade, commanded by Colonel Henry G. Thomas, was composed of the 19th USCT, the 23rd USCT, a battalion of the 28th USCT, the 29th USCT, and the 31st USCT. Dudley Taylor Cornish, *The Sable Arm: Black Troops in the Union Army, 1861–1865* (1956; repr., Lawrence: Univ. Press of Kansas, 1971), 273.

72. Thompson was partially mistaken here. Since 1838, Joseph Gilbert Totten had served as chief engineer of the US Army, and he died on 22 April 1864 (at the rank of brigadier general and brevet major general), necessitating the appointment of a replacement. As a result, Brigadier General Richard Delafield was elevated to the post. Brigadier General Montgomery C. Meigs, however, while he did belong to the regular army engineers, continued to serve as quartermaster general of Union armies rather than becoming chief engineer as Thompson suggested. Thompson's pride at having Totten's signature on his corporal's warrant was probably a reflection of Totten's well-known contemporary reputation as a talented engineer. Cullum, *Biographical Register*, 1:66, 181, 496.

73. Lieutenant Benyaurd was First Lieutenant William H. H. Benyaurd of Company C.

10. Something Earnest Is Intended

1. Brigadier General Godfrey Weitzel was the chief engineer of Major General Benjamin F. Butler's Army of the James. The source Turtle quoted here appears to have been in error about the identity of the particular volunteer engineers involved in building this bridge. At the time this bridge was thrown, the 1st US Veteran Volunteer Engineers was participating in Sherman's Atlanta campaign as part of the Army of the Cumberland. It is possible that the men Turtle described were from the 1st *New York* Volunteer Engineers that belonged to Butler's Army of the James and that built the approaches to the James River crossing in mid-June 1864. Thompson, however, repeated Turtle's error in his postwar history of the Engineer Battalion, perhaps because of his reliance on Turtle's earlier work. Army, *Engineering Victory*, 257, 269; Thienel, *Mr. Lincoln's Bridge Builders*, 172.

2. The Penates were the household gods of ancient Rome.

3. The cavalry mentioned here was likely Brigadier General Daniel Gregg's cavalry division, which moved south from near the Rappahannock River on May 3 as the Army of the Potomac got underway for the 1864 Overland Campaign. Gregg's troopers passed through Richardsville where Thompson recorded this entry on the very day that he wrote it; later that night the cavalrymen crossed the Rapidan at Ely's Ford just a couple of miles south of the Engineer Battalion's camp. Rhea, *Battle of the Wilderness*, 60–61.

4. Thompson was referring to the Federal assault on the Mule Shoe Salient in the Confederate lines around Spotsylvania. For more information see quoted entry for May 12, 1864, on p. 263 as well as p. 417n27.

5. Thompson's wording in the opening phrases of this sentence is unclear, but he and those with him spent the morning of May 6 in the rifle pits to the rear of the VI Corps, and in the late afternoon they moved forward to construct defensive works in front of the V Corps, near its junction with the VI Corps. See Thompson, *Engineer Battalion in the Civil War*, 57.

6. The Battle of the Wilderness was fought on May 5 and 6, 1864. On the first day, Lee had planned to strike the Army of the Potomac as it moved through the heavily wooded area, but Confederate and Federal forces collided earlier than the southern general had planned, and Grant's northerners managed to hold the crossroads that they needed to continue moving southward. On the sixth, the day that Thompson wrote about here, a Federal assault on the rebel right almost overran Lee's headquarters before Lieutenant General James Longstreet's corps halted the advance. That afternoon, a Confederate attack by Brigadier General John B. Gordon drove the Union right back about a mile; this part of the Union line had been held by elements of Major General John Sedgwick's VI Corps, including the 4th New York Heavy Artillery, which Thompson mentioned. Just

before Gordon's Confederate assault, the Engineer Battalion had been sent to build fieldworks in front of the right of Major General Gouverneur K. Warren's V Corps near its right-angle junction with the VI Corps of Sedgwick. When the rebels attacked Sedgwick and his corps fell back, the engineers were caught between the enemy onslaught and the V Corps soldiers who faced to their right to meet the potential threat as the VI Corps gave way. The battalion's sappers managed to extricate themselves and rally a number of Federal troops to help stem Gordon's attacking rebels. See also Thompson's "Postwar Sketch Map of the Wilderness"; Rhea, *Battle of the Wilderness*, 416; Thompson, *Engineer Battalion in the Civil War*, 57–58.

7. Brigadier Charles Griffin commanded the 1st Division of Warren's V Corps; at the Wilderness on May 6, Griffin's division was instrumental in restoring order to the Union right after Gordon's rebel assault. See also previous annotation.

8. This was part of the general skirmishing along the lines on May 7, 1864, as Grant prepared to move towards Spotsylvania to the southeast.

9. The Lacy House served as the headquarters for Gouverneur Warren's V Corps at the start of the Battle of the Wilderness. Rhea, *Battle of the Wilderness*, 131.

10. Major William F. Draper of the 36th Massachusetts was shot in the shoulder on May 6, 1864. See memoir recollection See memoir recollection on p. 3 as well as annotation 8 on pp. 339-40.

11. While Jackson's arm was interred somewhere near the Lacy House (also known as Ellwood), he did not die there, but in an outbuilding on the nearby Chandler House. Charles Royster, *The Destructive War: William Tecumseh Sherman, Stonewall Jackson, and the Americans* (New York: Random House, 1991), 223; Robert M. Dunkerly, Donald C. Pfanz, and David R. Ruth, *No Turning Back: A Guide to the 1864 Overland Campaign, from the Wilderness to Cold Harbor, May 4–June 13, 1864* (El Dorado Hills, CA: Savas Beatie, 2014), 7.

12. A rod is a measure of distance equal to sixteen and a half feet or five and a half yards.

13. See May 7, 1864, quoted entry on pp. 255–56 and pp. 414n5 and pp. 414–15n6 for a description of the Battle of the Wilderness and the Engineer Battalion's role in it.

14. Brigadier General David G. Birney commanded the 3rd Division of Major General Winfield Scott Hancock's II Corps at the Battle of Spotsylvania Court House.

15. Here Thompson described Lee's refusal to assault the strong defensive position adopted by Meade at Centreville, Virginia, in mid-October 1863 at the end of Lee's Bristoe Station offensive. See also journal entry for October 14, 1863, and pp. 402–3n22.

16. The Battle of Chancellorsville, April 30–May 6, 1863.

17. Immediately following the Battle of the Wilderness, as Grant initiated a move to Spotsylvania to attempt to get around the Confederate right, most soldiers in the Army of the Potomac expected a withdrawal or at least a significant pause in operations. When they turned south towards Spotsylvania instead of north towards the Rappahannock, Union morale brightened considerably at the prospect of continuing the campaign despite the lack of immediate success in the Wilderness.

18. Major General Winfield Scott Hancock commanded the II Corps, Army of the Potomac at the Battle of Spotsylvania Court House in early May 1864, and his corps was positioned near Todd's Tavern on the ninth of that month.

19. Major General Philip Sheridan commanded the Army of the Potomac's Cavalry Corps; the engagement Thompson referenced here was Sheridan's attempt to clear the Union army's route to Spotsylvania Court House on May 7, 1864. Gordon C. Rhea, *The Battles of Spotsylvania Court House and the Road to Yellow Tavern, May 7–12, 1864* (Baton Rouge: Louisiana State Univ. Press, 1997), 29–30.

20. Major General John Sedgwick led the Army of the Potomac's VI Corps from the start of the Overland Campaign until his death on May 9, 1864. Despite the claim of William "Shib" Shibley that Thompson recorded here, General Sedgwick was, in fact, killed by a sharpshooter at the Battle of the Wilderness.

21. As a first lieutenant in the Corps of Engineers, Orville Babcock had commanded Company D of the Engineer Battalion from July 1862 through mid-November of that year. During the Overland Campaign of 1864, he was a lieutenant colonel of volunteers serving as an aide to Grant. Cullum, *Biographical Register*, 2:770.

22. This was Colonel Emory Upton's May 10, 1864, attack on the Mule Shoe Salient in the Confederate line near Spotsylvania. For more information, see quoted journal entry for May 12, 1864, on p. 263 and p. 417n27.

23. As a captain, James Chatham Duane had commanded the Engineer Battalion until November 1862. During the 1864 Overland Campaign in Virginia, Duane was a major (and brevet colonel) of engineers serving as chief engineer of the Army of the Potomac. Cullum, *Biographical Register*, 2:344–45.

24. "The loving are the daring" is the last line of Bayard Taylor's poem, "The Song of the Camps" about the siege of Sevastopol in the Crimean War.

25. This was probably Captain Samuel F. Stone of the 86th New York Volunteer Infantry, a regiment that was part of Hancock's II Corps. Captain Stone was likely killed in the fighting on May 10 as Grant tried to pry Lee out of his defensive works near Spotsylvania Court House. Brigadier General J. H. Hobart Ward's brigade of Hancock's corps managed to establish a lodgment in

Confederate works on the rebel left, but at a heavy cost to the 3rd Maine and 86th New York regiments. "Return of Casualties in the Union forces commanded by Lieut. Gen. Ulysses S. Grant, from the Rapidan to the James River, May–June 1864," in *OR*, ser. 1, vol. 36, part 1, 152; "Report of Brig. Gen. P. Regis de Troiband, U.S. Army, commanding First Brigade," 20 October 1864, in *OR*, ser. 1, vol. 36, part 1, 470; Earl J. Hess, *Trench Warfare under Grant and Lee: Field Fortifications in the Overland Campaign* (Chapel Hill: Univ. of North Carolina Press, 2007), 50–53.

26. Probably Captain Cornelius C. Billings of Company I, 151st New York, First Brigade, 3rd Division, VI Corps. Captain Billings was mortally wounded at the Wilderness. Helena Adelaide Howell, comp., *Chronicles of the One Hundred Fifty-First Regiment New York State Volunteer Infantry, 1862–1865, Contributed by Its Surviving Members* (Albion, NY: A. M. Eddy, 1911), 272, "Organization of the Forces Operating against Richmond, under Lieut. Gen. Ulysses S. Grant, U.S. Army, on the Morning of May 5, 1864," in *OR*, ser. 1, vol. 36, part 1, 112.

27. At the Battle of Spotsylvania Court House on the morning of May 12, 1864, Major General Winfield Scott Hancock launched a Federal assault with his II Corps against a bulge in the Confederate lines known as the Mule Shoe Salient. Hancock's attack was based on the partial success of Colonel Emory Upton's smaller assault two days earlier; Upton had led twelve regiments arrayed in four successive lines against the same bulge in the rebel lines and successfully penetrated the southern defenses, but he could not hold his gains. On May 12, Hancock tried to repeat and exploit the feat with his entire corps. The larger assault secured a lodgment in the Confederate lines, but like Upton, Hancock was unable to exploit it. The rebels resisted tenaciously for nearly a full day, separated from their assailants by just a single earthen parapet, while Confederate engineers prepared a new, shorter defensive line across the base of the salient. Hess, *Trench Warfare under Grant and Lee*, 55–61, 64–82.

28. As indicated in his entry on November 17, 1862, Thompson often took brief hurried notes when he did not have time to write in his journal. He later copied these notes into his journal, putting them in quotation marks, as he did for his May 7–12, 1864 entries; these are the "pencil notes" he mentioned here. The *Remarks* sections following each of his May 7–12 entries were added later, on May 19. See also entry for May 19, 1864, and p. 416n46.

29. Edward C. Barnard was an assistant topographer with the US Geological Survey in 1887. The first two letters following his name are likely a reference to his degree; he graduated from Columbia College (now University) in 1884 with an Engineer of Mines degree. The second set of letters likely references his services with the Geological Survey. Evans and Frye, *History of the Topographic Branch*, 151; Columbia College in the City of New York, *Officers and Graduates*

of Columbia College, Originally the College of the Province of New York known as King's College: General Catalogue, 1745–1894 (New York, 1894), 384.

30. The Brown House, where one of the divisions of Major General Hancock's II Corps was stationed, also served as the starting position of Hancock's assault on the Mule Shoe Salient. See also the quoted entry for May 12, 1864, and the following memoir section, all on p. 263, and p. 417n27. Hess, *Trench Warfare under Grant and Lee*, 60.

31. Thompson was describing the fighting at the Mule Shoe Salient at Spotsylvania Court House on May 12, 1864. See also his journal entry for May 12, 1864, on p. 263, and p. 417n27.

32. Patrick H. Flood was first sergeant of Company D.

33. While it does not identify the IX Corps Hospital, per se, "Map of the Battle-Field of Spotsylvania C.H., Va.," Map 2, Plate LV of Davis, Perry, and Kirkley, *The Official Military Atlas of the Civil War*, does identify the Gayle House which, according to Thompson's May 14, 1864, entry, was near the site of the hospital established by Burnside's corps.

34. In the May 12, 1864, assault on the Mule Shoe Salient (see quoted entry for May 12, 1864, and p. 417n27), Major General Ambrose Burnside's IX Corps advanced to the left of Hancock's II Corps. The leading brigade of Burnside's assault took some rebel rifle pits and part of the main Confederate line on the eastern side of the salient, capturing two rebel guns in the process. This attack struck elements of the Army of Northern Virginia's III Corps, and the only artillery of that corps opposing Burnside's Federals were the battalions of Lieutenant Colonel William T. Poague and Lieutenant Colonel William J. Pegram, but which of these two batteries lost guns to Burnside's advance is unclear from the official reports. It is also possible that the captured pieces came from the Rockbridge Artillery, a company of the 1st Virginia Artillery that had originally been commanded by William N. Pendleton (the name on the relic that Thompson removed from one of the caissons). On May 12, the Rockbridge Artillery was stationed to the left rear of Pegram's battalion. Rhea, *Battles for Spotsylvania Court House and the Road to Yellow Tavern*, 245–46, 404n101; Marvel, *Burnside*, 363; "Report of Brig. Gen. William N. Pendelton, C.S. Army, Chief of Artillery," February 28, 1865, in *OR*, ser. 1, vol. 36, part 1, 1045; "Report of Brig. Gen. Robert B. Potter, U.S. Army, commanding Second Division," August 1, 1864, in *OR*, ser. 1, vol. 36, part 1, 928; Monroe F. Cockrell, ed., *Gunner with Stonewall: Reminiscences of William Thomas Poague, Lieutenant, Captain, Major and Lieutenant Colonel of Artillery, Army of Northern Virginia, CSA, 1861–65, A Memoir Written for His Children in 1903* (Jackson, TN: McCowat-Mercer Press, 1957), 92.

35. Major General Joseph Hooker commanded the XX Corps of the Army of the Cumberland in the western theater during the spring of 1864. Thompson was merely reporting inaccurate rumors here.

36. In the spring of 1864, the VIII Corps, under Major General Lew Wallace, was operating in Maryland, and *not* moving towards Grant's forces in Virginia.

37. The Battle of the Wilderness, May 5–6, 1864.

38. The 7th Maine Battery was a green unit; it was organized on January 1, 1864, and after completing its training, the battery joined the 3rd Division, IX Corps, on April 25. Its captain was Adelbert B. Twitchell. A. S. Twitchell, *History of the Seventh Maine Light Battery, Volunteers in the Great Rebellion. Containing a Brief Daily Account of Its Services, Without Comments or Attempt to Criticise or Praise the Brave Boys in This Command; Also, Personal Sketches of a Large Number of Members, Portraits, Illustrations and Poems* (Boston, MA: E. B. Stillings & Co., 1892), 9, 20.

39. Thompson was correct that the reports he had just recorded about the capture of Atlanta and some of the defenses of Richmond were all just rumors.

40. Assuming that Abbie D—— lived relatively close to Thompson's home in Worcester County, Massachusetts, and that she was probably close to his own age, it is possible this was Abigail M. Davis, daughter of Solomon and Lucy Davis, of Worcester, Massachusetts, but this is far from certain. United States Census 1860, Worcester County, Massachusetts, population schedule, Ward 7 Worcester, p. 176, dwelling 989, family 1298, Solomon W. and Lucy M. Davis, digital image, FamilySearch, accessed May 16, 2016, https://familysearch.org/pal:/MM9.3.1/TH-1951-25262-10647-82?cc=1473181.

41. *Good Society, or Contrasts of Character* is an 1863 novel by Elizabeth Caroline Grey.

42. The Anderson family house was a major landmark on the Spotsylvania Court House battlefield, but there were no Andersons serving in either house of the Confederate Congress from Virginia. The only congressmen of that name were Clifford Anderson, who was born in Virginia but had relocated to Macon, Georgia, in the late 1840s, and James Patton Anderson, born in Tennessee but representing Florida in the Confederate House. Ezra J. Warner and W. Buck Yearns, *Biographical Register of the Confederate Congress* (Baton Rouge: Louisiana State Univ. Press, 1975), 4–6.

43. Fuller was Private James Fuller, Company D.

44. Jeff was the battalion's former dog. See March 28, 1863, entry.

45. The Spotsylvania Turnpike was probably the Fredericksburg Road, along which the Union II and VI Corps launched an assault towards the new Confederate line behind what had been the Mule Shoe Salient on May 18, 1864. Hess, *Trench Warfare under Grant and Lee*, 48, 87–89; Thompson, *Engineer Battalion in the Civil War*, 59.

46. Thompson was referring to the *Remarks* sections that follow his copied notes of May 7–12 found on pp. 255–63 under his general May 12, 1864, entry.

47. The pike mentioned here was likely the same Fredericksburg Road that Thompson referenced in his May 18, 1864, entry, and which he identified in his published history of the battalion's activities as the Fredericksburg Turnpike. Thompson, *Engineer Battalion in the Civil War*, 59.

48. Captain George Gordon Meade Jr. served as an *aide de camp* to his father from June 1863 until the end of the war. George Gordon Meade Jr., ed., *The Life and Letters of George Gordon Meade, Major-General United States Army*, 2 vols. (New York: Charles Scribner's Sons, 1913), 1:vi.

49. While Thompson used both Guiney's and Guinea's at various times to describe this bridge and the nearby Guiney's Station, the correct wartime spelling of Guiney's has been adopted here. Today, however, the name has been altered to Guinea.

50. Captain Williams was probably Henry C. Williams, captain of Company I, 8th Pennsylvania Volunteer Cavalry. Bates, *History of Pennsylvania Volunteers*, 3:141.

51. The movement Thompson described here was part of Grant's attempt to move south from Spotsylvania around Lee's right in order to reach the North Anna River and draw the rebels out of their fieldworks. Thompson's subsequent mention of Guiney's Station in his note indicates that these headquarters units were following Major General Winfield Scott Hancock and the II Corps, which passed through Guiney's Station about dawn on May 21, 1864. The exchange that Thompson recorded between Turnbull and Crawford was probably a reference to the fact that the headquarters' forces, including the Engineer Battalion, had performed the function of skirmishers for Crawford's division by driving off the rebel cavalry before they could destroy Guiney's Bridge over the Poni River. Hess, *Trench Warfare under Grant and Lee*, 88, 121–22; Thompson, *Engineer Battalion in the Civil War*, 62.

52. Apparently Proutz and Lieutenant Howell of the Engineer Battalion accompanied Major General Philip Sheridan's Union cavalry raid toward Richmond in early May 1864. This raid by Sheridan's Cavalry Corps led to the Union victory at Yellow Tavern north of the city on May 11, followed by additional confrontations east and south of the Confederate capital before Sheridan rejoined the Army of the Potomac on the twenty-fourth. Allan Nevins, *The War for the Union*, vol. 4, *1864–1865: The Organized War to Victory* (New York: Scribner, 1971), 37.

53. At the Battle of Yellow Tavern, about four hundred captured Union prisoners of war were reclaimed by Sheridan's cavalry force. *The Union Army: A History of Military Affairs in the Loyal States, 1861–65—Records of the Regiments in the Union Army—Cyclopedia of Battles—Memoirs of Commanders and Soldiers*, vol. 3, *New Jersey, Indiana, Illinois, and Michigan* (Madison, WI: Federal Publishing Company, 1908), 417.

54. Sir Percy Wyndham was an English soldier of fortune who had
served in several European military forces, most recently those of Giuseppe
Garibaldi in Italy. He eventually came to the United States and joined the
Union army. He was the colonel of the 1st New Jersey Cavalry until wounded
at Brandy Station in June 1863. His career with the Union military, however,
was dogged with controversy. He spent some time commanding Union cavalry
forces in Washington before finally being mustered out of the army on July
5, 1864, just a month and a half after Thompson's entry. Robert F. O'Neill,
*Chasing Jeb Stuart and John Mosby: The Union Cavalry in Northern Virginia
from Second Manassas to Gettysburg* (Jefferson, NC: McFarland & Company
Publishers, 2012), 256–58.

55. The Battle of Williamsburg on May 5, 1862, was one of the battles of
the Peninsula campaign. It resulted from the Army of the Potomac's pursuit of
Confederate forces that were withdrawing from Yorktown.

56. As the Appomattox River is south of Richmond, Thompson can only
have heard about this episode from someone who accompanied Major General
Sheridan's raid in that direction in early May, though at least one member of the
Engineer Battalion, William Proutz, did participate in the raid. See entry for May
25, 1864, and p. 420n52.

57. First Sergeant Henry K. Turner, Company B.

58. Thompson's mention of "The Golden Farm" refers to the June 27–28,
1862, engagement known as the Battle of Garnett's and Golding's Farm. It was a
Union defensive victory during the Battles of the Seven Days. Brigadier General
William F. "Baldy" Smith repulsed an ill-conceived attack by two Confederate
brigades. Sears, *To the Gates of Richmond,* 258–59, 427n9.

59. Thompson was right to add a question mark after his assertion of
Confederate major general James Ewell Brown Stuart's final resting place. Stuart
was buried in Richmond's Hollywood Cemetery after he died from wounds
received at the Battle of Yellow Tavern. Burke Davis, *Jeb Stuart: The Last Cavalier*
(New York: Rhinehart, 1957), 421.

60. The Battle of Haw's Shop on May 28, 1864, was primarily a cavalry
engagement, though both sides fought dismounted. After a prolonged fight
with little tactical finesse, the Federal troopers eventually overwhelmed the rebel
horsemen and sent them into a disorganized route. Hess, *Trench Warfare under
Grant and Lee,* 139; Wert, *Sword of Lincoln,* 361; Rhea, *Cold Harbor,* 61–88.

61. In his postwar memoirs, Thompson added a reference here to page 178
of Andrew A. Humphreys's *The Virginia Campaign of '64 and '65; The Army of
the Potomac and the Army of the James* (New York: Charles Scribner's Sons, 1883),
which describes the beginnings of Grant's movement to Cold Harbor late on
June 1, 1864.

62. Major General Phillip Sheridan's Federal cavalrymen seized the road junction called Cold Harbor on May 31, 1864, after driving off rebel troopers under Fitzhugh Lee. Sheridan held the position until he was reinforced the next day. Around 6 p.m. on June 1, the Union VI and XVIII Corps advanced against Confederate positions around Cold Harbor to little effect because Federal delays had given the southerners the time they needed to entrench their lines strongly. Rhea, *Cold Harbor*, 233–34, 266–70.

63. Major General Lew Wallace's VIII Corps was still in Maryland at the date of this entry.

64. Thompson was describing the assault by three Union Corps (the II, VI, and XVIII) against the well-fortified Confederate line at Cold Harbor early on the morning of June 3, 1864. The attack stalled after the Federal forces suffered heavy casualties, and following this failure, Grant had his men fortify their positions close to the rebels and initiated the use of siege warfare against Lee's Confederate forces. Hess, *Trench Warfare under Grant and Lee*, 153, 155, 158–60, 162.

65. In the spring of 1864, Major General William F. "Baldy" Smith commanded the XVIII Corps of Major General Benjamin F. Butler's Army of the James, which had been sent to reinforce the Army of the Potomac at Cold Harbor.

66. The work Thompson wrote about here was the opening of trench warfare in this 1864 Virginia campaign as the Federals began to fortify a new position considerably closer to the rebel lines and to employ siege approaches. The Federal assault Thompson recounted was doubtless part of the heavy skirmishing that continued after the initial engagement was over and as the Federals continued to advance their lines closer to the Confederate position. Wert, *Sword of Lincoln*, 365–66; Hess, *Trench Warfare under Grant and Lee*, 162–65, 168–69; Bruce Catton, *Grant Takes Command* (Boston: Little, Brown, and Company, 1968), 267; Rhea, *Cold Harbor*, 359, 362.

67. Quincy A. Gillmore was a major of engineers and a major general of volunteers; in the spring of 1864, he led the X Corps of Major General Benjamin F. Butler's Army of the James. Thompson's mention of Morris Island referred to Union operations against Charleston, South Carolina, in the summer of 1863. At that time, Gillmore commanded the Department of the South, and he oversaw the Union occupation of Morris Island, the Federal assault on Battery Wagner on the island, and the bombardment and reduction of Fort Sumter from Morris Island. Cullum, *Biographical Register*, 2:368.

68. Confederate general Pierre Gustave Toutant Beauregard commanded the Department of North Carolina and Southern Virginia in the spring of 1864, and as such, he was responsible for defending the Confederate capital

from Butler's Union Army of the James. Beauregard achieved his objective by bottling Butler's forces up near Bermuda Hundred, about thirty miles south of Richmond.

69. This location heading by Thompson is an unclear reference to the headquarters of the XVIII Corps commander, Major General William F. "Baldy" Smith, and of Brigadier General Thomas Neill of the 2nd Division, VI Corps.

70. Private Nathaniel "Joe" Storms of Company K, 10th New York Volunteer Artillery, was killed at Cold Harbor on June 5, 1864. *Annual Report of the Adjutant-General of the State of New York for the Year 1897. Registers of the Ninth and Tenth Artillery in the War of the Rebellion* (Albany, NY: Wynkoop Hallenbeck Crawford Co., State Printers, 1898), 758.

71. Herbert Bennett, of Milford, Massachusetts, was a private in Company B of the 25th Massachusetts Volunteer Infantry, the same unit in which Eli Ball, also of Milford, served. See also the memoir recollection on p. 3, as well as the June 20, 1864, journal entry, and pp. 341n11 and 426n9. United States Census 1860, Worcester County, Massachusetts, population schedule, Worcester, p. 229, dwelling 1171, family 1874, Minerva Bennett, digital image, FamilySearch, accessed May 16, 2016, https://familysearch.org/pal:/MM9.3.1/TH-1951 -25248-9546-54?cc=1473181; Adjutant General of Massachusetts, *Massachusetts Soldiers, Sailors, and Marines in the Civil War,* 3:11.

72. Hayes was Jeremiah Hayes of Company D.

73. Captain Francis Ulric Farquhar, US Army Corps of Engineers, was chief engineer of the XVIII Corps. Cullum, *Biographical Register,* 2:812.

74. The John that Thompson mentioned here was reference to the generic southern soldier, usually known as Johnny Reb. Thompson used several variations for this purpose, such as John, Johny, and Johnny, and his choice of appellation and spelling is followed throughout.

75. This railroad was the Virginia Central. In early June, Grant sent Sheridan's cavalry west to link up with Major General David Hunter at Charlottesville; together they were to menace Richmond from the west. While on his way to join Hunter, Sheridan had instructions to destroy as much of the Virginia Central Railroad as he could.

76. Thompson was probably trying to identify the community of Providence Forge, Virginia, on the Chickahominy River.

77. The movement on June 12 that Thompson described here was the opening of Grant's shift toward the James River southeast of Richmond. Once across that river, Grant hoped to take Petersburg, where several rail lines converged south of the Confederate capital. If successful, such a move would have cut Lee's supply lines and forced him to either abandon Richmond or

attempt to defend the city without a dependable source of supplies. Wert, *Sword of Lincoln*, 369–71.

78. This was the James River, which was being bridged near the tip of the Weyanoke Peninsula, just south of Charles City, Virginia, so Grant's Union forces could move against Petersburg to the south of Richmond.

79. This was the longest pontoon bridge of the Civil War, and it was thrown by roughly equal sized detachments of the Engineer Battalion and the 50th New York Volunteer Engineers. Earl J. Hess, *In the Trenches at Petersburg: Field Fortifications and Confederate Defeat* (Chapel Hill: Univ. of North Carolina Press, 2009), 9, 16–17.

80. For Mendell's report on the pontoon bridge across the James at Weyanoke Landing in the spring of 1864, see "Report of Capt. George H. Mendell, Corps of Engineers, U.S. Army, commanding Engineer Battalion," August 5, 1864, in *OR*, ser. 1, vol. 40, part 1, 300–302.

81. Thompson was partly mistaken. None of Grant's children were old enough to serve in the military during the war. Thompson may have encountered Colonel Lewis Addison Grant, who at the time of this entry was a brigade commander in the Army of the Potomac's VI Corps but was no relation to the commanding general.

82. John G. Barnard was a lieutenant colonel of engineers and a brigadier general of volunteers by this date, and at the time he served as chief engineer of Grant's personal staff.

83. The CSS *Atlanta* was a converted blockade runner that was captured by the Union navy off coastal Georgia in June 1863; she had been incorporated into the Union navy as the USS *Atlanta*, and in the late spring of 1864, she was serving on the James River.

84. Probably Edward M. Marshall of the 40th New York Volunteer Infantry, which was with the II Corps of the Army of the Potomac before Petersburg in mid-June 1864. See also Thompson's journal entry of April 28, 1862. *Annual Report of the Adjutant-General of the State of New York for the Year 1900. Registers of the Thirty-ninth, Fortieth, Forty-first, Forty-second and Forty-third Regiments of Infantry*, vol. 3, serial no. 23 (Albany: James B. Lyon, State Printer, 1901), 512; Dyer, *Compendium*, 1418–9.

85. The "Georgetown spree" that Thompson mentioned here refers to the brawl involving several Company D men and Captain Turnbull, the company commander, while in Georgetown during the 1863 Gettysburg campaign. See also the journal entry for June 18, 1863, and pp. 396–97n17.

11. Engaged on Fortification

1. Fort Stedman, which Turtle misspelled, was on the right of the Army of
the Potomac's position before Petersburg, west of the city and south of the
Appomattox River. Fort Sedgwick was almost due south of Petersburg on the east
side of the Jerusalem Plank Road. See also entry for July 24, 1864, and
p. 430n31. Hess, *In the Trenches at Petersburg*, 143.

2. On October 27 and 28, 1864, at the First Battle of Hatcher's Run, also
known as the Battle of Burgess Mill or the Battle of Boydton Plank Road, thirty
thousand Union troops tried unsuccessfully to move around the Confederate
right. While the major movement was by Major General Winfield Scott Hancock's
II Corps, the IX Corps of Major General John G. Parke was also engaged along
the Boydton Plank Road in support of Hancock's movement. As a result, Parke's
Corps was pulled from the Union lines just west of Peebles's Farm. Covering that
position during the battle was Brigadier General Nelson Miles's 1st Division,
II Corps, with the assistance of the Engineer Battalion, which held Fort Fisher.
Catton, *Grant Takes Command*, 381; Hess, *In the Trenches at Petersburg*, 190–92;
Thompson, *Engineer Battalion in the Civil War*, 90–91.

3. The Second Battle of Hatcher's Run, sometimes called just Hatcher's Run,
was an attempt by Major General Gouverneur K. Warren to extend the Union
left to the Boydton Plank Road with his V Corps on February 6 and 7, 1865.
After two days of heavy fighting, the Federal line was extended westward some
four miles. During the battle, the Engineer Battalion again went to the aid of
Miles's division of the II Corps (under a new corps commander, Major General
Andrew A. Humphreys). This time the battalion held a section of the Federal
lines near Fort Howard. Hess, *In the Trenches at Petersburg*, 229–32.

4. Thompson's location for this journal entry referred to the house of James
A. Dunn, which was behind the Confederate Dimmock Line east of Petersburg
and just south of Jordan's Point Road. This line was also east of the Union works
depicted on the map of "Federal Siege Works at Petersburg, 1864," having been
located between them and the future site of the US Military Railroad, though the
Dimmock Line is not depicted on the map. Hess, *In the Trenches at Petersburg*, 19,
22, 256.

5. Grant succeeded in getting his army to Petersburg ahead of Lee, and
from June 15 to 18, 1864, Union forces attempted to break through the city's
defenses with little success. By the eighteenth, Lee's army had begun to arrive in
the southern works around Petersburg, and on the nineteenth Grant began to
formally besiege the city. Wert, *Sword of Lincoln*, 371–75.

6. In general, walking post refers to the two hours of active guard service when
a soldier was on guard duty, in contrast to his four-hour shift off post, during

which he could be found in the guard tent. Here, someone has been assigned extra guard duty as a punishment, which was sometimes done by reversing their hours on and off post, so that a soldier being punished would spend four hours walking post and two in the guard tent. Wiley, *Billy Yank*, 46; Billings, *Hardtack and Coffee*, 149, 190–91.

7. The works Thompson and his colleagues surveyed on June 19 were the original, weaker field fortifications built by the rebels to defend Petersburg; they included the Dimmock Line, which was taken by Major General William F. "Baldy" Smith's XVIII Corps on June 15, and the Hagood Line, which was behind the Dimmock Line and was abandoned by the Confederates for the stronger Harris Line to its rear on the night of June 17–18. Hess, *In the Trenches at Petersburg*, 18–19, 23–28.

8. Bran is the husk of a grain after being ground, and it is generally quite coarse. Thompson seems to have been making a humorous reference to all the low-quality food he had just consumed.

9. There is no indication that Eli G. Ball, a private in the 25th Massachusetts, had been offered an officer's commission before he was mortally wounded in a Federal assault on June 3, 1864, at the Battle of Cold Harbor. See also the memoir section on p. 3 and annotation 11 on p. 341. Adjutant General of Massachusetts, *Massachusetts Soldiers, Sailors, and Marines in the Civil War*, 3:11.

10. The Jones House on the west side of the Jerusalem Plank Road served as the headquarters of the Union II Corps. "Reports of Maj. Gen. Winfield S. Hancock, U.S. Army, commanding Second Army Corps," September 21, 1865, in *OR*, ser. 1, vol. 40, part 1, 318.

11. In the originals of Thompson's journal, the days of the week in the headings of his entries for June 15 through June 23, 1864, were incorrect; he had inadvertently advanced them by one day. These days, however, have been silently corrected in the main text of this edition to avoid confusion.

12. Nathaniel Michler was actually a major in the Corps of Engineers by the early summer of 1864; at the time, he oversaw the Army of the Potomac's Topographical Department. In the last year of the war, Michler earned three brevets, to lieutenant colonel, colonel, and brigadier general, and as a result, Thompson frequently refers to him as General Michler in his memoirs. Regardless of his rank, Michler spent the two years after the war conducting surveys and producing maps of the various military movements and battlefields of the Army of the Potomac, assisted by Gilbert Thompson and others. Cullum, *Biographical Register*, 2:347–48; Davis, Perry, and Kirkley, *Official Military Atlas of the Civil War*, "Antietam," Map 2, Plate XXIX; "Fredericksburg," Map 1, Plate XXXIII; "Richmond, Va.," Map 1, Plate LXXVII; "Petersburg and Five Forks,

Va.," Map 2, Plate LXXVII; "Bermuda Hundred, Va.," Map 3, Plate LXXVII; "Jetersville and Sailor's Creek, Va.," Map 4, Plate LXXVII; "Appomattox Court-House, Va.," Map 2, Plate LXXVIII; "High Bridge and Farmville, Va.," Map 4, Plate LXXVIII; "The Battle-Field of Chancellorsville," Map 2, Plate XCIII; "Map of the Battle-Field of the Wilderness, Va.," Map 1, Plate XCVI; "Map of the Battle-Field of North Anna, Va.," Map 2, Plate XCVI; "The Battle-Field of Totopotomoy, Va.," Map 6, Plate XCVI; "Map of the Battle-Field of Cold Harbor, Va.," Map 2, Plate XCVII.

13. The action Thompson described here was the result of Grant's attempt to interrupt the Weldon and Petersburg Railroad, which brought supplies into Petersburg from the south. He sent three Federal corps toward this line on June 22, but a Confederate counterattack drove the northerners back in confusion when it took them by surprise at a gap between two Union corps. While some of these Federal troops managed to reach the railroad the next day, June 23, they could not hold it. Hess, *In the Trenches at Petersburg*, 38–39; Wert, *Sword of Lincoln*, 376.

14. Major General David Hunter commanded the Department of West Virginia at the date of this entry; he was operating in the Shenandoah Valley in the late spring and summer of 1864.

15. The Cockade City was a nickname for Petersburg, Virginia.

16. Rocinante was the name of Don Quixote's horse in Cervantes' seventeenth-century novel, *The Ingenious Gentleman Don Quixote of La Mancha*.

17. Ferdinand Theilkuhl, sometimes spelled Thielkuhl, was formerly a first lieutenant of topographical engineers who, by the date of this journal entry, was serving as a civilian assistant in the Army of the Potomac's Topographical Department under Major Nathaniel Michler. He also worked with Michler and Thompson after the war to survey and map the operations of the Army of the Potomac. See pp. 426–27n12. C. C. Suydam, General Orders No. 29, October 3, 1863, in *OR*, ser. 1, vol. 29, part 2, 247; "Report of Maj. Nathaniel Michler, Corps of Engineers, U.S. Army, Acting Chief Engineer," October 20, 1864, in *OR*, ser. 1, vol. 36, part 1, 294; Davis, Perry, and Kirkley, *Official Military Atlas of the Civil War*, "Antietam," Map 2, Plate XXIX; "Fredericksburg," Map 1, Plate XXXIII; "Richmond, Va.," Map 1, Plate LXXVII; "Petersburg and Five Forks, Va.," Map 2, Plate LXXVII; "Bermuda Hundred, Va.," Map 3, Plate LXXVII; "Jetersville and Sailor's Creek, Va.," Map 4, Plate LXXVII; "Appomattox Court-House, Va.," Map 2, Plate LXXVIII; "High Bridge and Farmville, Va.," Map 4, Plate LXXVIII; "The Battle-Field of Chancellorsville," Map 2, Plate XCIII; "Map of the Battle-Field of the Wilderness, Va.," Map 1, Plate XCVI; "Map of the Battle-Field of North Anna, Va.," Map 2, Plate XCVI; "Map of the Battle-Field of Spotsylvania Court-House, Va.," Map 3, Plate XCVI; "The Battle-Field of

Totopotomoy, Va.," Map 6, Plate XCVI; "Map of the Battle-Field of Cold Harbor, Va.," Map 2, Plate XCVII.

18. Also known as mercurial ointment, anguintum was a rub applied externally to soothe irritation and sometimes to kill lice. Enos Ballard Vail, *Reminiscences of a Boy in the Civil War* (n.p.: n.p., 1915), 96.

19. Thompson was on the right track with this camp rumor, but he named the wrong commander when he asserted that Ewell was operating in the Shenandoah. Lieutenant General Richard S. Ewell, commanding the II Corps of the Army of Northern Virginia, had something of a breakdown in late May after the Battle of North Anna, and Lee replaced him with Lieutenant General Jubal A. Early. It was Early that Lee sent into the Shenandoah Valley in June 1864, and in early July (shortly after the date of this entry) Early's forces crossed the Potomac into Maryland and menaced Washington.

20. In his postwar recollections, Thompson identified this field fortification as Fort Davis. Originally named Fort Warren, it was located on the west side of the Jerusalem Plank Road where the V Corps held the left of the Army of the Potomac in July 1864. Hess, *In the Trenches at Petersburg*, 55–57.

21. The United States Sanitary Commission, which Thompson referenced here, was a northern voluntary association formed early in the war to improve soldiers' health by promoting camp sanitation and providing medical assistance. It also frequently sent food and clothing to the men along with medical supplies, and on July 3, 1864, four days before this entry by Thompson, the *New York Times* reported that the commission had distributed over forty thousand pounds of fruits and vegetables to Federal soldiers around Petersburg, including the lemons that Thompson enjoyed. See also *New York Times*, July 4, 1864.

22. In mid-June 1864, Lee sent his II Corps under Lieutenant Jubal A. Early into the Shenandoah Valley to clear it of Federal forces (see also entry for July 5, 1864, and p. 428n19). During this campaign, Union troops abandoned Harpers Ferry and withdrew north into Maryland, burning the bridges over the Potomac to prevent Early from using them. The rebels, however, crossed elsewhere and launched a raid that threatened Washington on July 11. West, *Sword of Lincoln*, 386; Benjamin Franklin Cooling III, *Jubal Early: Robert E. Lee's "Bad Old Man"* (Lanham, MD: Rowman & Littlefield, 2014), 64–65.

23. At the date of Thompson's journal entry, this fort was an unnamed redoubt. As Thompson noted in his postwar addition, it was later dubbed Fort Bross. The work was part of the secondary refused line of works built in July 1864 to the southeast of the main positions on the right of the Union line. Hess, *In the Trenches at Petersburg*, 58.

24. On July 10, 1864, Captain Charles Turnbull was relieved of the command of Engineer Battalion's Company D and replaced by Captain Franklin Harwood.

25. This work was probably Fort Prescott, where the new secondary line described in the previous annotation began. This work, however, could also refer to the construction of rifle-pits connecting Forts Bross and Prescott. See memoir section on p. 294. Thompson, *Engineer Battalion in the Civil War*, 76; Hess, *In the Trenches at Petersburg*, 57–58, 143–44.

26. Fort Howard was not a part of the same secondary Union line that included Fort Bross and was described in annotation 23 on page 428. It is likely that Thompson named the wrong fieldwork; the work referenced here was probably Fort Prescott, which was part of the newly built secondary Federal line, and which Thompson identified in his published history of the battalion as the work connected to Fort Bross by the rifle-pits built during the night of July 13–14, 1864. Hess, *In the Trenches at Petersburg*, 143; Thompson, *Engineer Battalion in the Civil War*, 76.

27. The fiasco to which Thompson referred was the Battle of the Crater on July 30, 1864. In an attempt to overcome the Confederate defenses of Petersburg, Union troops from Major General Ambrose Burnside's IX Corps tunneled underneath the rebel position and detonated four tons of gunpowder. Originally, Burnside's African American division was slated to lead the Union assault that was organized to follow the explosion, and its men received special training for the operation. However, just before the battle, Meade instructed Burnside to send in his white divisions first, even though they lacked the proper training. As a result, many of Burnside's unprepared men charged into the crater left by the explosion where they became easy targets for rebels around its edges. After all three of Burnside's white divisions entered the fray, he sent in his black division just in time to oppose a Confederate counterattack. Many of these African American troops were subsequently massacred by Confederate soldiers after suffering wounds or attempting to surrender. Hess, *In the Trenches at Petersburg*, 83–106; Edwin C. Bearss with Bryce A. Suderow, *The Petersburg Campaign*, vol. 1, *The Eastern Front Battles, June–August 1864* (El Dorado Hills, CA: Savas Beatie, 2012), 215–37; Bryce A. Suderow, "The Battle of the Crater: The Civil War's Worst Massacre," in *Black Flag over Dixie*, ed. Urwin, 204.

28. Adam Reed served in Company F of the 4th US Colored Infantry from August 1863 until February 1866. In the war's final year, the 4th USCT served in the lines around Petersburg with the 3rd Division, XVIII Corps, Army of the James. The 3rd Division was an all African American one led by Brigadier General Edward Hinks, and as part of it, the 4th USCT took heavy casualties assaulting the works before Petersburg on June 15, 1864, while most of the Army of the Potomac was still moving into position. The regiment spent much of July in the trenches east of the city, during which time Reed served on a working party under Thompson. At the Battle of the Crater, Reed's regiment, along with

the rest of Hinks's division and the 1st Division of the XVIII Corps, held the trenches on Burnside's front but did not participate in the Federal assault. After the war, Reed served as company cook for several months before mustering out, perhaps giving him the experience that helped secure him a similar position later with Thompson's postwar survey party. NARA Microfilm Publication M1820, roll 43; John David Smith, ed., *Black Soldiers in Blue: African American Troops in the Civil War Era* (Chapel Hill: Univ. of North Carolina Press, 2002), 56; John R. Mass, *The Petersburg and Appomattox Campaigns, 1864–1865* (Washington, DC: Government Printing Office, 2015), 19; "Report of Maj. Gen. Edward O. C. Ord, U.S. Army, commanding XVIII Corps, of operations July 30," August 3, 1864, in *OR*, ser. 1, vol. 40, part 1, 706–8.

29. A covered way was usually a path around the outer edge of the ditch found in front of a fortification. It was covered from direct enemy fire by the fort's outworks and could serve as either an external defensive position or a place to assemble an offensive force hidden from the enemy's sight and fire. The particular covered ways Thompson referenced here were not mere make-work projects as he surmised. Instead, they were being built by the Engineer Battalion for use by Federal forces in the assault at in the Battle of the Crater. See also memoir section on p. 294 and p. 429n27. Mahan, *Treatise on Field Fortification*, 3, 136; Hess, *In the Trenches at Petersburg*, 53.

30. Metamora could be a reference to the popular 1829 play by John Augustus Stone, *Metamora, Or the Last of the Wampanoags*. Or Thompson could be referring to some unrecorded incident of the battalion's history from the time it traveled on the steamer *Metamora*. See also Thompson's entries for August 10, 13, 20, and 21, 1862. Priscilla F. Sears, *A Pillar of Fire to Follow: American Indian Dramas, 1808–1859* (Bowling Green, OH: Bowling Green Univ. Popular Press, 1982), 8–9, 35.

31. Thompson was writing of a Federal fort east of Petersburg. Originally called Roeblings Redoubt, it was later renamed Fort Sedgwick, though it was also referred to colloquially by Union troops as Fort Hell. It was located across the Jerusalem Plank Road from Fort Warren, which was later known as Fort Davis. See also Thompson's entry of July 7, 1864, and p428n20. Hess, *In the Trenches at Petersburg*, 57, 266.

32. Thompson was suggesting here that the Confederates would not arrange soldiers' truces with black Federals like those he had just described between the rebels and white Union soldiers, a pattern replicated throughout the conflict. See also Peter S. Carmichael, *The War for the Common Soldier: How Men Thought, Fought, and Survived in Civil War Armies* (Chapel Hill: Univ. of North Carolina Press, 2018), 71.

33. Thompson made a second entry for this date.

34. By the summer of 1864, James Birdseye McPherson was simultaneously a captain of engineers, a brigadier general of the line in the regular US Army, and a major general of volunteers. That summer, he was in command of the Union Army of the Tennessee, one of three armies moving against Atlanta under the overall command of Major General William T. Sherman. At the Battle of Atlanta, on July 22, 1864, McPherson ran into group of enemy soldiers and was killed. While the battle could certainly be considered a Union victory, it did not lead immediately to the fall of the city, which held out until September.

35. This battery was Fort Sedgwick southeast of Petersburg and just east of the Jerusalem Plank Road. Thompson sometimes identified it by the number of its gun emplacements as the Eighteen-Gun Battery. Because it was so close to Confederate lines and therefore exposed to rebel fire, it was also known to Union soldiers colloquially as Fort Hell. Hess, *In the Trenches at Petersburg*, 57, 59, 298–99; Thompson, *Engineer Battalion in the Civil War*, 78.

36. See the final sentence of the first journal entry for July 24, 1864, and p. 430n32, for an explanation of this activity on Burnside's front.

37. On July 11 and 12, 1864, as part of Jubal Early's Confederate raid on the Union capital, his rebels skirmished with the defenders of Washington. On the twelfth, some of this fighting took place in front of Fort Stevens, one of the capital city's many defensive works, and one that President Abraham Lincoln visited during the engagement. See also July 5 and 9, 1864, journal entries and annotations 19 and 22 on p. 428.

38. Cuyler was First Lieutenant James W. Cuyler of Company C.

39. See entry for July 28, 1864, and pp. 431–32n42.

40. Seylandt was John B. Seylandt of Company D.

41. First Lieutenant William H. H. Benyaurd, formerly of Company C, was in command of Company A on June 10, 1864.

42. In late July 1864, Brigadier General Robert S. Foster's Third Brigade, 1st Division, X Corps of the Army of the James held a fortified bridgehead called Deep Bottom immediately north of the James River. Just prior to midnight on the twenty-fifth of that month, Major General Joseph B. Kershaw's division of the Army of Northern Virginia's I Corps drove in Foster's pickets, launching the First Battle of Deep Bottom. Grant, however, took this opportunity to launch his own offensive. He reinforced Foster with the II Corps under Major General Winfield Scott Hancock and two cavalry divisions under Major General Philip Sheridan to retake the lost ground and launch a cavalry raid towards Richmond. Confederate defenses were too strong for Hancock to outflank them or for Sheridan to mount a successful raid on the capital city, and the movement was abandoned on the twenty-ninth. These actions, however, convinced Lee to move more of his forces north of the James River, reducing his numbers in front of

Petersburg just before the Battle of the Crater. See also entry for July 30, 1864, and pp. 432n43–45. Catton, *Grant Takes Command*, 318–20; Hess, *In the Trenches at Petersburg*, 79–83.

43. Here Thompson described the unsuccessful Union offensive at the Battle of the Crater. See also memoir section on p. 294 and annotation number 27 on p. 429.

44. Thompson's postwar correction was considerably more accurate. The detonation of the mine at the start of the Battle of the Crater blasted a thirty-foot-deep hole in the ground that was about 125 feet long and 50 feet wide. The resulting crater would have covered an area of a little more than 6,000 square feet, considerably less than three acres, which is approximately 130,000 square feet. Hess, *In the Trenches at Petersburg*, 91.

45. Burnside's IX Corps made the Union assault at the Battle of the Crater. See also annotation 27 on p. 429.

46. Brigadier General William F. Bartlett commanded the First Brigade, 1st Division of Burnside's IX Corps, which made the Union assault at the Crater. Bartlett had lost a leg at Yorktown in 1862, and at the Crater he was wounded again and had his wooden leg shot away in the fighting, forcing him to surrender himself as he could not withdraw with his men; he did not, however, surrender his entire brigade as Thompson reported here.

47. Thompson's contention that Major General Benjamin F. Butler's Army of the James achieved some advantage during the Battle of the Crater was either a false camp rumor or wishful thinking on Thompson's part. During Burnside's ill-fated Federal assault, various components of the Army of the James either supported the attack or held the Union lines behind it; none of Butler's forces achieved any advantage that day. "Itinerary of the Army of the Potomac and Army of the James, &c," in *OR*, ser. 1, vol. 40, part 1, 211–18.

48. Major General Burnside wanted to continue the attack at the Battle of the Crater that Thompson was discussing here, and Burnside even asked Meade to order Major General Gouverneur K. Warren to advance with his V Corps on Burnside's left. Had Meade agreed, Warren would have met little opposition as the rebels had stripped their lines to the right of the Crater for reinforcements to blunt Burnside's assault. Grant, however, ordered Meade to end the attack without sending Warren's corps forward. Marvel, *Burnside*, 405–6.

49. Dick Turpin was a famous eighteenth-century English highwayman, and Newgate was a London prison.

50. See entry for July 26, 1864, and annotation 35 on p. 431, for the identification of this work.

51. Thompson was referring to the battalion's role in countermining activities near Forts Sedgwick and Morton at Petersburg in early August 1864.

Countermining is an activity both combatants pursued; shafts and listening galleries were dug in an attempt to locate and intercept enemy mines like the Union one whose detonation touched off the Battle of the Crater on July 30, 1864. For the rest of the campaign at Petersburg, the battalion pursued countermining at a variety of points along the Union lines. Hess, *In the Trenches at Petersburg*, 115–17, 122, 185–86.

52. The work being built here was either the Taylor Battery or Fort Morton. The Taylor Battery was built by men from the Engineer Battalion and the 50th New York Volunteer Engineers about a hundred yards beyond Fort Morton. These same detachments also improved Fort Morton at about the same time, adding some new embrasures to this work which had also been known as the Fourteen-Gun Battery. Hess, *In the Trenches at Petersburg*, 53, 110, 358n28; Thompson, *Engineer Battalion in the Civil War*, 81.

53. Thompson was referring here to the five-hour march on the evening of October 10, 1863. See also October 11, 1863, journal entry. Thompson, *Engineer Battalion in the Civil War*, 46.

54. A second entry for this date.

55. Thompson was describing the opening stages of the Second Battle of Deep Bottom. Major General Hancock's II Corps boarded steamers and pretended to embark for Washington on August 13; then it moved up the James in the dark and landed near Deep Bottom while two X Corps divisions and a cavalry division also crossed to the north bank of the James near Deep Bottom. These forces were stymied by rebel defenses on the fourteenth, but over the next few days, they distracted Confederate forces while Major General Warren moved against the Weldon and Petersburg Railroad with his V Corps. See also entry for August 20, 1864, and p. 434n61. Hess, *In the Trenches at Petersburg*, 124–29.

56. Buel Chipman, Company A. Chipman's service expired and he was discharged in early April 1864.

57. See July 14, 1864, journal entry and p. 428n23.

58. Major General Gouverneur K. Warren's V Corps pulled out of its trenches around Petersburg on the night of August 14, 1864, in preparation for a movement toward the Weldon and Petersburg Railroad that culminated in the Battle of Globe Tavern (see also August 20, 1864, journal entry and p. 434n61). The IX Corps under Major General John G. Parke took over those Union trenches vacated by Warren's V Corps. Major General David G. Birney's X Corps of the Army of the James was still north of its namesake river on August 16 engaged in the Second Battle of Deep Bottom. See entry for August 14, 1864, and p. 433n55. Hess, *In the Trenches at Petersburg*, 128–29.

59. In the photo titled "A Group of Us," which Thompson preserved and labeled in his memoirs, he identified the third man from the left in the very

front row as "Kelley, A [Company] (lost a leg at Ft. Hell)," and he identified the same person in a slightly different photo found in his published history of the battalion as G. Kelley. However, according to the battalion's monthly roll for August 1864, the man shot in the knee on August 18, 1864 was Artificer Robert Kelly of Company A, and it happened in front of Fort Morton, not Fort Sedgwick. Either way, Kelly's left leg was amputated as a consequence of the wound, and he remained on the sick list until his enlistment expired in late January 1865, at which time he was discharged. In 1881, when he was only forty years old, Kelly died of paralysis that his widow Margaret attributed to the wound he received before Petersburg and which pained him for the rest of his life. Thompson, *Engineer Battalion in the Civil War*, 81; Enoch P. Lawrence, "Physicians Affidavit," October 17, 1885, and Enoch P. Lawrence, M.D., to Allen Rutherford, October 22, 1881, both enclosed in Widow's Pension Application Certificate No. 287,315, Robert Kelly (Co. A, US Engineer Battalion), RG15.

60. *Rara avis* is a Latin phrase meaning a rarity; it translates literally as "rare bird."

61. Thompson was describing the Battle of Globe Tavern, from August 18 to 21, 1864. On the eighteenth, Major General Gouverneur K. Warren advanced his V Corps to a position astride the Weldon and Petersburg Railroad, one of Lee's supply lines into the city. Through the use of well-placed artillery and extensive fieldworks that included abatis and wire entanglements, Warren fended off several Confederate attempts to retake the railroad over the next few days. Hess, *In the Trenches at Petersburg*, 128–35.

62. See August 20, 1864, entry and p. 434n61.

63. The Danville Road was also known as the Richmond and Danville Railroad. It ran southwest from Richmond and crossed the Southside Railroad about forty miles west of Petersburg. It was *not* cut by on cavalrymen in late August 1864, but remained open throughout operations around Petersburg. Thompson, however, may have been recording somewhat stale news. In late June, the Federal cavalry divisions of brigadier generals James H. Wilson and Augustine V. Kautz led a raid westward along the Southside Railroad toward its junction with the Danville Road. While the Union troops did manage to tear up portions of the Southside and Danville lines, the Federal raid was ended by Confederate cavalry under Major General Wade Hampton and the destruction was merely a temporary inconvenience for Lee's Confederates. Hess, *In the Trenches at Petersburg*, 38, 135; Bears and Suderow, *The Eastern Front Battles*, 199, 202; Wert, *Sword of Lincoln*, 375–77; Catton, *Grant Takes Command*, 296–97.

64. The picture Thompson mentioned here is one of several similar group photographs taken around the same time as the one titled "A Group of Us." See

also second August 10, 1864, entry and Thompson, *Engineer Battalion in the Civil War*, 51.

65. Thompson's comment about "General Barnard's report" may refer to J. G. Barnard and W. F. Barry, *Report of the Engineer and Artillery Operations of the Army of the Potomac, From Its Organization to the Close of the Peninsular Campaign by Brig.-Gen. J. G. Barnard, Chief Engineer, and Brig.-Gen. W. F. Barry, Chief of Artillery* (New York, D. Van Nostrand, 1863). In collecting his memoirs after the war, Thompson sometimes quoted from this work, which contained, as is evident from the title, the report of Brigadier General John G. Barnard, who served as chief engineer of the Army of the Potomac during McClellan's Peninsula Campaign of 1862. See also the memoir selection following Thompson's June 2, 1862, wartime journal entry and found on pp. 56–57.

66. Thompson was writing of the Jones House just east of the Jerusalem Plank Road; the Engineer Battalion had camped in this vicinity from late June through early July 1864. The work whose name Thompson omitted in his journal was Fort Davis. See also July 7, 1864, entry and p. 428n20. Thompson, *Engineer Battalion in the Civil War*, 82.

67. Thompson's reference to the Lynchburg Road is likely an error on his part. He may have meant the Southside Railroad, but the battle he describes here is the August 25, 1864, Battle of Reams's Station, in which Hancock's II Corps took a portion of the Weldon and Petersburg Railroad as part of an attempt to secure control of that line farther south of Petersburg than the lodgment achieved by Warren's V Corps in the Battle of Globe Tavern a few days earlier (see Thompson's August 20, 1864, journal entry and p. 434n61). At Reams's Station, Hancock was not able to hold his position on the railroad in the face of several determined Confederate assaults, and he withdrew after dark on the twenty-fifth. Hess, *In the Trenches at Petersburg*, 11, 135–40, Wert, *Sword of Lincoln*, 388–89.

68. This rail line was the US Military Railroad. Not to be confused with the organization of the same name, this particular line carried supplies to the Army of the Potomac from the City Point Railroad. It ran from that latter line behind the Union fortifications around Petersburg. In early September 1864, it was extended to the Weldon and Petersburg Railroad at Globe Tavern. For the most part it was simply built along the existing contours of the ground without any grading, a fact that Thompson remarked on later. See also his September 6, 1864, journal entry. Hess, *In the Trenches at Petersburg*, 11, 146; A. Wilson Greene, *The Final Battles of the Petersburg Campaign: Breaking the Backbone of the Rebellion*, 2d ed. (Knoxville: Univ. of Tennessee Press, 2008), 42.

69. The Dictator was a 13-inch mortar that could throw a shell weighing over two hundred pounds for more than two miles. It was the largest mortar in use at

Petersburg, and its monstrous size required that it be mounted on a railroad car so that it could be moved. Hess, *In the Trenches at Petersburg,* 75; Albert Manucy, *Artillery through the Ages: A Short Illustrated History of Cannon, Emphasizing Types Used in America* (Washington, DC: National Park Service, 1949), 61.

70. See Thompson's journal entry for May 15, 1863.

71. While Thompson's assertion may seem to be a defensive attempt to justify his own failure to reenlist, it is actually borne out by the battalion's monthly rolls. Only 96 of its members chose to reenlist in 1864, while during that same year, 185 of them, including Thompson, were discharged at the expiration of their term.

72. Thompson was writing of the 1864 Democratic National Convention, which met from August 29 to 31, 1864, and ultimately nominated George B. McClellan on a peace platform (which McClellan later repudiated). See also September 11, 1864, journal entry and p. 437n80. Nevins, *The Organized War to Victory,* 98–102.

73. On August 5, 1864, Union flag officer David G. Farragut steamed his flotilla past the forts protecting the entrance to Mobile Bay and defeated a Confederate force inside the bay. Once in command of Mobile Bay, however, Farragut had to secure the three forts that guarded its entrance or he would find himself isolated. Fort Powell had an open gorge that was exposed to Union naval bombardment from within the bay, so Confederate forces abandoned it the night after Farragut entered the bay. Fort Gaines on Dauphin Island surrendered on August 8 after a combined naval and land bombardment of several days. The last to fall was Fort Morgan on Mobile Point, which Thompson mentioned here. It surrendered on August 23 after a two-week siege and bombardment that threatened to detonate its powder magazines. With Morgan's fall, Union forces had complete control over Mobile Bay and it was no longer a viable port for Confederate blockade runners. Mark A. Smith, *Engineering Security: The Corps of Engineers and Third System Defense Policy, 1815–1861* (Tuscaloosa: Univ. of Alabama Press, 2009), 184–86.

74. After failing to stop Major General William T. Sherman from severing the last rail line into Atlanta at Jonesboro on August 31, 1864, Lieutenant General John Bell Hood evacuated the city, and Sherman's forces occupied it on September 2.

75. On September 3, 1864, Artificer John H. Brown's three-year term of enlistment expired, and he was discharged from Company B.

76. Thompson's bunkmate in the late summer of 1864 was Corporal Decatur O. Blake, and Blake's enlistment term expired on September 25, 1864.

77. This parenthetical is a reference to the three Company D corporals, none of whom had reenlisted and so none of whom were eligible for promotion

under the policy Thompson had just described. Decatur O. Blake was discharged September 25, 1864; Joseph Cummins went out on October 16; and Thompson himself left on November 22.

78. Thompson was describing the US Military Railroad built to supply Union forces before Petersburg. See also journal entry for August 29, 1864, and annotation 68 on p. 435.

79. If Thompson's spelling of personal names is reliable here, which was admittedly not always the case, then he went for a walk with Melville Clarke of Company D. See also May 6, 1863, entry.

80. In his letter accepting the Democratic nomination, which came after the fall of Atlanta and the capture of Mobile Bay, McClellan rejected the platform plank branding the war a failure but accepted its call for a negotiated peace by stating that he was willing to commence talks with the Confederacy whenever its leaders showed any signs of being prepared to rejoin the Union. Nevins, *The Organized War to Victory*, 101–2.

81. Artificer John S. Cooper of Company A was discharged from the battalion on November 3, 1863, so he could accept a commission as a captain of Company D, 8th US Colored Infantry. Shortly after the date of this entry, Captain Cooper was shot in the arm during the fighting around Petersburg, and two months later he was discharged from the 8th USCT and the regular army, so he could accept a commission as the lieutenant colonel of the 107th Ohio Volunteer Infantry. "Complied Military Service Records of Volunteer Union Soldiers Who Served with the United States Colored Troops: Infantry Organizations, 8th through 13th, including the 11th (New)," Records of the Adjutant General's Office 1780s–1917, Record Group 94, National Archives Microfilm Publication M1821, roll 4; Whitelaw Reid, *Ohio in the War: Her Statesmen, Generals, and Soldiers*, 2 vols. (Cincinnati, OH: Moore, Wilstach, & Baldwin, 1867), 2:576.

82. Stevens was Daniel Stevens of Company D; he was discharged at the end of his term of service on September 20, 1864.

83. On September 19 and 22, 1864, Major General Philip Sheridan and his Army of the Shenandoah defeated Confederate forces in that valley under Lieutenant General Jubal A. Early at the Battles of Winchester and Fisher Hill. Following these Union victories, Sheridan followed Grant's instructions to destroy the Shenandoah as a source of food for Confederate armies, though Early would return to the valley in October for a final confrontation.

84. According to the battalion's monthly rolls, Private Thomas Berry of Company A died of his wounds on September 22, 1864, so either Thompson's journal dates are off slightly or the date of Berry's death was misrecorded in the unit's rosters. In his published history of the battalion, Thompson reported that Berry was shot in the head just as his company finished work on a magazine for

Fort Morton late on September 20, 1864. Thompson, *Engineer Battalion in the Civil War*, 85–86.

85. Decatur O. Blake, Thompson's bunkmate, and six others from Company D were discharged on September 25, 1864. The others included James Fuller, Charles Cross, Esquire Burton, Joshua Noah, Orange P. Noah, and Richard Varness.

86. The success Thompson mentioned here was a reference to Grant's fifth major offensive at Petersburg in late September and early October 1864, which achieved gains on both flanks of the Union lines around Petersburg and Richmond. Major General Benjamin Butler's Army of the James captured some of Richmond's Outer Line defenses north of the James River, while Meade's Army of the Potomac extended its lines westward south of the river and Petersburg, seizing the Confederates' line of works along Squirrel Level Road. Hess, *In the Trenches at Petersburg*, 160–66.

87. These fortifications were new fieldworks being erected in the area seized by the Federal offensive a week earlier (see October 6, 1864, entry and annotation number 86, above). The line of these new works ran west from Fort Wadsworth on the Weldon and Petersburg Railroad to a point just beyond the Pegram House where the line then curved to the south and then turned back to the east, running all the way back to Fort Dushane on the railroad. This formed a large, elongated U-shape, whose northern arm faced the rebel works around Petersburg, while the southern arm secured the Union rear. Hess, *In the Trenches at Petersburg*, 166–69.

88. Joseph Cummins was discharged at the end of his enlistment term on October 16, 1864.

89. Charles H. Rue left the service on October 21, 1864, and Edwin H. "Ned" Coolidge was discharged on October 24, 1864.

90. Thompson did, in fact, get the position he mentioned here. After his discharge in November 1864 and a brief visit home, he returned to the Army of the Potomac's Headquarters as a civilian assistant engineer in early January 1865, remaining in that position until the end of the war. See also his final journal entry, dated December 26, 1864.

91. Rear Admiral David Dixon Porter commanded Union naval forces on the James River.

92. On October 19, 1864, Confederate general Jubal A. Early launched a surprise attack on Major General Philip Sheridan's Federal forces in the Shenandoah Valley at the Battle of Cedar Creek. The rebels initially caught Sheridan's forces by surprise and drove them into a disorganized retreat down the valley. However, Sheridan, who was absent when the battle started, arrived and reorganized his forces, enabling him to launch a counterattack in the

afternoon that defeated Early's rebels and sent them into a chaotic retreat out of the valley.

93. The Southside Railroad ran west from Petersburg towards Lynchburg along the southern bank of the Appomattox River, and it was one of the Confederates' major supply lines at Petersburg. As the Union lines extended westward beyond the city and turned slightly north, they moved towards this rail line.

94. Jacob H. Putnam was the first sergeant of Company D.

95. This was the movement that led to the First Battle of Hatcher's Run on October 27 and 28, 1864. See p. 425n2.

96. This may be John B. Geyser, formerly of the Engineer Battalion's Company D. John Geyser was discharged from the unit at the end of his term of enlistment on September 13, 1864. It is, however, impossible to be certain solely from the three initials Thompson recorded.

97. Elbridge Wilcutt was discharged at the end of his enlistment term on November 20, 1864.

98. According to the battalion's monthly rosters, Thompson was officially discharged the next day, November 22, 1864, not the twenty-first.

99. See Thompson's journal entries for November 21, 1861 and 1862.

Epilogue

1. The Fort at Willets Point, New York, (later named Fort Totten) was one of the last Third System coastal defenses to be constructed, and it became the station of the Engineer Battalion after the war. It also served as an Engineer School after the United States Military Academy was removed from the purview of the Corps of Engineers in 1866. Smith, *Engineering Security*, 131; Corps of Engineers, *History of the Corps of Engineers*, 72.

2. See also pp. 326–27 below as well as Thompson's journal entry for June 23, 1864, and p. 426n12.

3. On April 1, 1865, Grant's Federals and Lee's Confederates fought the Battle of Five Forks, which led to the end of the siege of Petersburg. A Union attack on the Confederate right successfully penetrated into the rebel rear, prompting Grant to launch a massive advance the next day that finally drove Lee to withdraw his army from the works around Petersburg and put it on the road that led to its eventual surrender at Appomattox Court House.

4. See Thompson's July 14, 1864, entry and the memoir recollection found on p. 294.

5. Thompson, *Engineer Battalion in the Civil War*, 92–95; Newell and Shrader, *Of Duty Well and Faithfully Done*, 290; Hess, *In the Trenches at Petersburg*, 258–64.

6. Thompson, *Engineer Battalion in the Civil War*, 95–99; Newell and Shrader, *Of Duty Well and Faithfully Done*, 290; R. R. Raymond, "The Engineer School," *Professional Memoirs: Engineer Bureau, United States Army* 1, no. 2 (April–June 1909), 183–87; Corps of Engineers, *History of the Corps of Engineers*, 72.

7. Benjamin, *Gilbert Thompson*, 7; Davis, Perry, and Kirkley, *Official Military Atlas of the Civil War*, "Antietam," Map 2, Plate XXIX; "Fredericksburg," Map 1, Plate XXXIII; "Richmond, Va.," Map 1, Plate LXXVII; "Petersburg and Five Forks, Va.," Map 2, Plate LXXVII; "Bermuda Hundred, Va.," Map 3, Plate LXXVII; "Jetersville and Sailor's Creek, Va.," Map 4, Plate LXXVII; "Appomattox Court-House, Va.," Map 2, Plate LXXVIII; "High Bridge and Farmville, Va.," Map 4, Plate LXXVIII; "The Battle-Field of Chancellorsville," Map 2, Plate XCIII; "Map of the Battle-Field of the Wilderness, Va.," Map 1, Plate XCVI; "Map of the Battle-Field of North Anna, Va.," Map 2, Plate XCVI; "The Battle-Field of Totopotomoy, Va.," Map 6, Plate XCVI; "Map of the Battle-Field of Cold Harbor, Va.," Map 2, Plate XCVII; Army, *Engineering Victory*, 251; Cullum, *Biographical Register*, 2:347–48; N. Michler to A. A. Humphreys, August 1, 1869, in A. A. Humphreys, "Report of the Chief of Engineers," October 25, 1869, in *H. Ex. Doc. 1, part 2*, 41st Cong., 2d Sess. (1870), 649–50; A. A. Humphreys, *Annual Report of the Chief of Engineers to the Secretary of War for the Year 1870* (Washington, DC: Government Printing Office, 1870), 88.

8. Affidavit of Mary A. Judson, in Mary F. Thompson, Widow's Pension Application Certificate No. 923,292, Gilbert Thompson (Cos. B and D, US Engineer Battalion), RG15; A Transcript from Record of Marriage, Col. B, p. 214, Trinity Church, Washington, DC, in Mary F. Thompson, Widow's Pension Application Certificate No. 923,292, Gilbert Thompson (Cos. B and D, US Engineer Battalion), RG15; Declaration for Widow's Pension, in Mary F. Thompson, Widow's Pension Application No. 1,099,057, Gilbert Thompson (Cos. B and D, US Engineer Battalion), RG15; Certificate of Death of Gilbert Thompson, Record No. 186,506, District of Columbia, in Mary F. Thompson, Widow's Pension Application Certificate No. 923,292, Gilbert Thompson (Cos. B and D, US Engineer Battalion), RG15; Ballou, *History of the Town of Milford*, 2:1065.

9. George M. Wheeler, *Report Upon United States Geographical Surveys West of the One Hundredth Meridian, In Charge of Capt. Geo. M. Wheeler, Corps of Engineers, U.S. Army, Published by Authority of the Honorable Secretary of War, In Accordance with Acts of Congress of June 23, 1874, and February 15, 1875*, 7 vols. (Washington, DC: Government Printing Office, 1875–89), 1:659, 662, 664–66, 668–69, 672–73, 676–77, 680–81, 683, 686–87, 690–91, quote from 682; Evans and Frye, *History of the Topographic Branch*, 2–3.

10. Evans and Frye, *History of the Topographic Branch,* 5–9, 12, 14, 38, 169–70; Benjamin, *Gilbert Thompson,* 8–9.

11. Gilbert Thompson, "An Indian Dance at Jemez, New Mexico," *American Anthropologist* 2, no. 4 (October 1889): 351–55; Gilbert Thompson, "An Hypothesis for the So-called Encroachment of the Sea upon the Land," *Science,* n.s., 15, issue 382 (May 30, 1890), 333; Evans and Frye, *History of the Topographic Branch,* 36; Benjamin, *Gilbert Thompson,* 14.

12. District of Columbia Society of the Sons of the American Revolution, Application for Membership of Prof. Gilbert Thompson, roll 7, vol. 10, state no. 113; Benjamin, *Gilbert Thompson,* 4–5, 10; Alfred F. Young, *Masquerade: The Life and Times of Deborah Sampson, Continental Soldier* (New York: Random House, 2004), 24, 86–88, 93–94, 97, 171, 205, 256; A. C. Peale, *Register of the Society of Colonial Wars in the District of Columbia* (Washington, DC, 1904), 171–72; Ruth Gardiner Hall, comp., *Descendants of Governor William Bradford (Through the First Seven Generations)* (n.p.: n.p., 1951), 157; Myles Standish, M.D., *The Standishes of America,* 2nd ed. (Boston, MA: Press of Samuel Usher, 1895), 10.

13. Benjamin, *Gilbert Thompson,* 4–5, 10, 14; District of Columbia Society of the Sons of the American Revolution, Application for Membership of Prof. Gilbert Thompson, roll 7, vol. 10, state no. 113; *The Constitution and Register of the General Society of the War of 1812* (Philadelphia, PA: n.p., 1908), 169, 182; Peale, *Register of the Society of Colonial Wars in the District of Columbia,* 5–8.

14. Gilbert Thompson, "The Geography and Political Boundaries of Virginia and Maryland, From Their Earliest Date to the Beginnings of the American Revolution, April 19, 1775," *Historical Papers of the Society of Colonial Wars in the District of Columbia,* 1 (n.p.: n.p., 1898); Gilbert Thompson, "Historical Military Powder Horns," *Historical Papers of the Society of Colonial Wars in the District of Columbia,* no. 3 (n.p.: n.p., 1901); Benjamin, *Gilbert Thompson,* 10–11.

15. Benjamin, *Gilbert Thompson,* 12–13. Marcus Benjamin's published eulogy of Thompson contains a reproduction of this map by Thompson that accurately depicts the route followed by Colonel Thomas Dunbar and his 48th Regiment from just north of Alexandria to Fort Cumberland. See also David L. Preston, *Braddock's Defeat: The Battle of the Monongahela and the Road to Revolution* (Oxford: Oxford Univ. Press, 2015), 87–89.

16. Thompson, *Engineer Battalion in the Civil War;* Turtle, "History of the Engineer Battalion." Curiously, Thompson's history of the battalion provides, unattributed, almost the entire chapter on the unit's history during the Civil War that is found in "The History of the First Engineers, 1776–1918," Entry 1001, 1st Battalion, Engineers 1846–1918, RG391.

17. Gilbert Thompson, *Report of the Reunion of the Veterans of the U.S. Engineer Battalion, at St. Louis, Mo. September 26–29, 1887* (n.p., n.d.), 1–2, 9.

18. Benjamin, *Gilbert Thompson*, 9.

19. Certificate of Death of Gilbert Thompson, Record No. 186,506, District of Columbia, in Mary F. Thompson, Widow's Pension Application Certificate No. 923,292, Gilbert Thompson (Cos. B and D, US Engineer Battalion), RG15; Benjamin, *Gilbert Thompson*, 15–16.

20. Benjamin, *Gilbert Thompson*, 7.

Works Consulted

To provide a bibliography, even a judiciously selected one, that covers all the battles, campaigns, and activities in which Gilbert Thompson participated would require more than a single volume in its own right. As a result, what follows here is a list of all specialized works consulted in the transcription and annotation of Thompson's combined journal and memoir.

Manuscript Sources

Book Records of Volunteer Union Organizations. Record Group 94, Records of the Adjutant General's Office 1780s–1917. National Archives and Records Administration, Washington, DC.

Civil War and Later Pensions Files. Record Group 15, Records of the Department of Veterans Affairs. National Archives and Records Administration, Washington, DC.

Correspondence, Reports, Appointments, and Other Records Relating to Individual Scouts, Guides, Spies, and Detectives, 1861–1867. Record Group 110, Records of the Provost Marshal General's Bureau (Civil War). National Archives and Records Administration, Washington, DC.

List of Scouts, Guides, Spies, and Detectives, Showing Stations to Which Assigned. Record Group 110, Records of the Provost Marshal General's Bureau (Civil War). National Archives and Records Administration, Washington, DC.

Online Resources

Andersonville Prisoners of War. Online Database. Provo, UT: Ancestry.com. https://www.ancestry.com/search/collections/andersonville.

Dictionary of Canadian Biography. Toronto: University of Toronto/Université Laval, 2003. http://www.biographi.ca.

Grove Music Online. In Oxford Music Online. Oxford: Oxford University Press.
    http://www.oxfordmusiconline.com.
Massachusetts, Death Records, 1841–1915. Online Database. Provo, UT: Ancestry
    .com. https://www.ancestry.com/search/collections/madeathrecords/.
Massachusetts. Worcester County. United States Census 1850, population Sched-
    ule. Digital Images. FamilySearch. https://www.familysearch.org/search
    /collection/1401638.
———. Massachusetts State Census 1855, population schedule. Digital Images.
    FamilySearch. https://www.familysearch.org/search/collection/1459985.
———. United States Census 1860, population schedule. Digital Images. Family-
    Search. https://www.familysearch.org/search/collection/1473181.
———. United States Census 1880, population schedule. Digital Images. Family-
    Search. https://www.familysearch.org/search/collection/1417683.
New York. Putnam County. United States Census 1860, population schedule.
    Digital Images. FamilySearch. https://www.familysearch.org/search
    /collection/1473181.
Oxford Companion to Music. In Oxford Music Online. Oxford: Oxford University
    Press. http://www.oxfordmusiconline.com.
Oxford English Dictionary Online. Oxford: Oxford University Press. http://www
    .oed.com.
Thompson, Gilbert. Journal. Manuscript Division, Library of Congress, Washing-
    ton, DC. https://www.loc.gov/item/mm81095752/.

Microfilm Collections

Compiled Military Service Records of Volunteer Union Soldiers Who Served
    with the United States Colored Troops, 2nd through 7th Colored Infantry,
    6th Louisiana (African Descent), 7th Louisiana Infantry (African Descent).
    National Archives Microfilm Publication M1820. Record Group 94, Records
    of the Adjutant General's Office 1780s–1917. National Archives and Records
    Administration.
Compiled Military Service Records of Volunteer Union Soldiers Who Served with
    the United States Colored Troops: Infantry Organizations, 8th through 13th,
    including the 11th (New). National Archives Microfilm Publication M1821.
    Record Group 94, Records of the Adjutant General's Office 1780s–1917.
    National Archives and Records Administration.
General Index to Pension Files, 1861–1934. National Archives Microfilm Publi-
    cation T288. Record Group 15, Records of the Department of Veterans Affairs.
    National Archives and Records Administration.

Register of Enlistments in the US Army 1798–1914. National Archives Microfilm
Publication M233. Record Group 94, Records of the Adjutant General's Office
1780s–1917. National Archives and Records Administration.

Returns from Regular Army Engineer Battalions, Sept. 1846–June 1916. National Archives Microfilm Publication M690. Record Group 94, Records of
the Adjutant General's Office 1780s–1917. National Archives and Records
Administration.

Returns from US Military Posts, 1800–1916. National Archives Microfilm Publication M617. Record Group 94, Records of the Adjutant General's Office
1780s–1917. National Archives and Records Administration.

Sons of the American Revolution Membership Applications 1889–1970. Louisville, KY: National Society of the Sons of the American Revolution.

Periodicals

Atlantic Monthly
The Century Illustrated Monthly Magazine
Harper's Weekly
National Tribune
New York Mirror: A Weekly Gazette of Literature and the Fine Arts
New York Musical Review and Choral Advocate: A Journal of Sacred and Secular Music
New York Times
Scribner's Monthly Magazine
Washington National Tribune

Published Materials

Abbot, Henry L. "History of the First Regiment C.V. Heavy Artillery." In *The First
Regiment Connecticut Heavy Artillery, in the War of the Rebellion, 1861–1865*, 1–4.
Hartford, CT: Case, Lockwood, & Brainard, 1889.

Adams, George Rollie. *General William S. Harney: Prince of Dragoons*. Lincoln: University of Nebraska Press, 2001.

Adams, Peter. *The Bowery Boys: Street Corner Radicals and the Politics of Rebellion*.
Westport, CT: Praeger, 2005.

Adjutant General of Massachusetts. *Massachusetts Soldiers, Sailors, and Marines in
the Civil War*. 8 vols. Norwood, MA: Norwood Press, 1931–35.

Aikin, John. *Select Works of the British Poets, with Biographical and Critical Prefaces*.
Vol. 2, *Southey to Croley*. Philadelphia: Thomas Wardle, 1842.

Allen, O. Wesley, Jr. *Matthew*. Minneapolis, MN; Fortress Press, 2013.

Ambrose, Stephen E. *Duty, Honor, Country: A History of West Point.* Baltimore, MD: Johns Hopkins University Press, 1966.

Ammer, Christine. *The Facts on File Dictionary of Music.* 4th ed. New York: Facts on File, 2004.

Annual Report of the Adjutant-General of the State of New York for the Year 1894. Registers of the 20th, 21st, 22d, 23d, 24th, 25th and 26th Regiments of Cavalry, New York Volunteers in War of the Rebellion. Albany, NY: J. B. Lyon, 1895.

Annual Report of the Adjutant-General of the State of New York for the Year 1897. Registers of the Ninth and Tenth Artillery in the War of the Rebellion. Albany, NY: Wynkoop Hallenbeck Crawford, 1898.

Annual Report of the Adjutant-General of the State of New York for the Year 1900. Registers of the Thirty-ninth, Fortieth, Forty-first, Forty-second and Forty-third Regiments of Infantry. Vol. 3, serial no. 23. Albany: James B. Lyon, 1901.

Annual Report of the Adjutant-General of the State of New York for the Year 1901. Registers of the Sixty-ninth, Seventieth, Seventy-first, Seventy-second, Seventy-third and Seventy-fourth Regiments of Infantry. Serial no. 280. Albany, NY: J. B. Lyon Company, 1902.

Annual Report of the Adjutant-General of the State of New York for Year 1902. Registers of the Ninety-fourth, Ninety-fifty, Ninety-sixth, Ninety-seventy, Ninety-eighth, and Ninety-ninth Regiments of Infantry. Vol. 3, serial no. 320 Albany, NY: Argus Company, 1903.

Army, Thomas F., Jr. *Engineering Victory: How Technology Won the Civil War.* Baltimore, MD: Johns Hopkins University Press, 2016.

Ballou Adin. *History of the Town of Milford, Worcester County Massachusetts, from Its First Settlement to 1881.* 2 parts. Boston, MA: Franklin Press, 1882.

Barnard, J. G., and W. F. Barry. *Report of the Engineer and Artillery Operations of the Army of the Potomac, From Its Organization to the Close of the Peninsular Campaign by Brig.-Gen. J. G. Barnard, Chief Engineer, and Brig.-Gen. W. F. Barry, Chief of Artillery.* New York: D. Van Nostrand, 1863.

Bates, Samuel P. *History of Pennsylvania Volunteers, 1861–65.* 5 vols. Harrisburg, PA: B. Singerly, 1869–71.

Baumgart, Winfried. *The Crimean War, 1853–1856.* London: Arnold, 1999.

Bearss, Edwin C., with Bryce A. Suderow. *The Petersburg Campaign.* Vol. 1, *The Eastern Front Battles, June–August 1864.* El Dorado Hills, CA: Savas Beatie, 2012.

Benjamin, Marcus. *Gilbert Thompson.* Memorial Papers of the Society of Colonial Wars in the District of Columbia 5. n.p.: n.p., 1910.

Billings, John D. *Hardtack and Coffee: A Soldier's Life in the Civil War.* George M. Smith & Co, 1887. Reprinted, Saybrook, CT: Konecky & Konecky, n.d.

Booth, Andrew B., comp. *Records of Louisiana Confederate Soldiers and Louisiana Confederate Commands.* 3 vols. New Orleans, LA: n.p., 1920.

Bordman, Gerald, and Thomas S. Hischak. *The Oxford Companion to American Theater.* 3rd ed. Oxford: Oxford University Press, 2004.

Boynton, Edward C. *History of West Point: And the Origin and Progress of the United States Military Academy.* London: Sampson Low, Son, & Marston, 1864.

Bradbury, Sarah E. "Community Life as Seen by One of the Young People." In *Hopedale Reminiscences,* edited by Hughes, 10–12.

"A Brave Battery." *Pennsylvania School Journal, Devoted to School and Home Education* 40, no. 5 (November 1891): 216–30.

Carmichael, Peter S. *The War for the Common Soldier: How Men Thought, Fought, and Survived in Civil War Armies.* Chapel Hill: University of North Carolina Press, 2018.

"Catalogue of the Hopedale Home School." From "Home School Memorial: A Reunion of Teachers and Pupils of the Hopedale Home School, August 1, 1867." In *Hopedale Reminiscences,* edited by Hughes, 74–83.

Catton, Bruce. *Grant Takes Command.* Boston: Little, Brown, and Company, 1968.

Chernow, Ron. *Washington: A Life.* New York: Penguin Press, 2010.

Child, William. *A History of the Fifth Regiment New Hampshire Volunteers, in the American Civil War, 1861–1865.* 2 parts. Bristol, NH: R. W. Musgrove, 1893.

Churella, Albert J. *The Pennsylvania Railroad.* Vol. 1, *Building an Empire, 1846–1917.* Philadelphia: University of Pennsylvania Press, 2013.

Clark, John E., Jr. *Railroads in the Civil War: The Impact of Management on Victory and Defeat.* Baton Rouge: Louisiana University Press, 2001.

Cleaves, Freeman. *Meade of Gettysburg.* Norman: University of Oklahoma Press, 1980. Reprinted, 1991.

Cockrell, Monroe F., ed. *Gunner with Stonewall: Reminiscences of William Thomas Poague, Lieutenant, Captain, Major and Lieutenant Colonel of Artillery, Army of Northern Virginia, CSA, 1861–65, A Memoir Written for His Children in 1903.* Jackson, TN: McCowat-Mercer Press, 1957.

Columbia College in the City of New York. *Officers and Graduates of Columbia College, Originally the College of the Province of New York known as King's College: General Catalogue, 1745–1894.* New York: n.p., 1894.

The Constitution and Register of the General Society of the War of 1812. Philadelphia, PA: n.p., 1908

Conyngham, D. P. *The Irish Brigade and Its Campaigns: With Some Account of the Corcoran Legion and Sketches of the Principal Officers.* New York: William McSorley, 1867.

Cooling, Benjamin Franklin, III. *Jubal Early: Robert E. Lee's "Bad Old Man".* Lanham, MD: Rowman & Littlefield, 2014.

———. *Symbol, Sword and Shield: Defending Washington During the Civil War.* Hamden, CT: Archon Books, 1975.

————, and Walton H. Owen II. *Mr. Lincoln's Forts: A Guide to the Civil War Defenses of Washington.* Shippensburg, PA: White Man Publishing, 1988. Reprinted, Lanham, UK: The Scarecrow Press, 2010.

Cornish, Dudley Taylor. *The Sable Arm: Black Troops in the Union Army, 1861–1865.* New York, Longmans, 1956. Reprinted, Lawrence: University Press of Kansas, 1971.

Coski, John. *The Confederate Battle Flag: America's Most Embattled Emblem.* Cambridge: MA: Harvard University Press, 2005.

Crackel, Theodore J. *West Point: A Bicentennial History.* Lawrence: University Press of Kansas, 2002.

Crowell, Joseph A. *The Young Volunteer: The Everyday Experiences of a Soldier Boy in the Civil War.* 2nd ed. New York: Dillingham Company, 1906.

Cullum, George W. *Biographical Register of the Officers and Graduates of the U.S. Military Academy at West Point, N.Y., From Its Establishment in 1802, to 1890, with the Early History of the United States Military Academy.* 3rd ed. 3 vols. Boston: Houghton, Mifflin and Company, 1891.

Davis, Burke. *Jeb Stuart: The Last Cavalier.* New York: Rhinehart, 1957.

Davis, George B., Leslie J. Perry, and Joseph W. Kirkley. *The Official Military Atlas of the Civil War.* Washington, DC: Government Printing Office, 1891–1895. Reprinted, New York: Grammercy Books, 1983.

Desjardin, Thomas A. *These Honored Dead: How the Story of Gettysburg Shaped American Memory.* Cambridge, MA: Da Capo Press, 2003.

Dickens, Charles. *American Notes, For General Circulation.* 2 vols. Paris: A. and W. Galignani, 1842.

Drabelle, Dennis. "Pointing the Way to the Pole." *Pennsylvania Gazette* (Nov/Dec 2011): 41–45.

Draper, William F. "Hopedale." In *Hopedale Reminiscences,* edited by Hughes, 61–68.

————, Lizzie B. Humphrey, and William S. Heywood. "Retrospective Sketch." From "Home School Memorial: A Reunion of Teachers and Pupils of the Hopedale Home School, August 1, 1867." In *Hopedale Reminiscences,* edited by Hughes, 69–71.

Duane, James Chatham. *Manual for Engineer Troops.* 3rd ed. New York: D. Van Nostrand, 1864.

Dunkerly, Robert M., Donald C. Pfanz, and David R. Ruth. *No Turning Back: A Guide to the 1864 Overland Campaign, from the Wilderness to Cold Harbor, May 4–June 13, 1864.* El Dorado Hills, CA: Savas Beatie, 2014.

Dunwell, Francis F. *The Hudson River Highlands.* New York: Columbia University Press, 1991.

Dyer, Frederick H., comp. *A Compendium of the War of the Rebellion, Compiled and Arranged from Official Records of the Federal and Confederate Armies, Reports of the*

Adjutant Generals of the Several States, the Army Registers and Other Reliable Documents and Sources. Des Moines, IA: Dyer Publishing Company, 1908.

Evans, Richard T., and Helen M. Frye. *History of the Topographic Branch (Division): U.S. Geological Survey Circular 1341.* Reston, VA: US Geological Survey, 2009.

Fallon, John T. *List of Synonyms of Organizations in the Volunteer Service of the United States during the Years 1861, '62, '63, '64, and '65.* Washington, DC: Government Printing Office, 1885.

Farrow, Edward S. *A Dictionary of Military Terms.* Rev. ed. New York: Thomas Y. Cromwell, 1918.

Ferling, John E. *The First of Men: A Life of George Washington.* Knoxville: University of Tennessee Press, 1988.

Field, Anna Thwing. "Anti-Slavery and Other Visitors to the Community." In *Hopedale Reminiscences,* edited by Hughes, 17–21.

Field, Ron. *American Civil War Fortifications.* Vol. 2, *Land and Field Fortifications.* Oxford: Osprey Publishing, 2005.

———, and Robin Smith. *Uniforms of the Civil War.* Guilford, CT: Lynn Press, 2001.

Finson, John W. *Voices that Are Gone: Themes in Nineteenth-Century American Popular Song.* Oxford: Oxford University Press, 1994.

Fleming, Angela Michelli, and John Maxwell Hamilton, eds. *The Crimean War as Seen by Those Who Reported It.* Baton Rouge: Louisiana State University Press, 2009.

Foote, Shelby. *The Civil War, a Narrative.* Vol. 1, *Fort Sumter to Perryville.* New York: Random House, 1958.

Foster, Everton, ed. *Lamb's Textile Industries of the United States, Embracing Biographical Sketches of Prominent Men and a Historical Resume of the Progress of Textile Manufacture from the Earliest Records to the Present Time.* 2 vols. Boston, MA: James H. Lamb, 1916.

Freeman, Douglas Southall. *Lee's Lieutenants: A Study in Command.* Vol. 3, *Gettysburg to Appomattox.* New York: Charles Scribner's Sons, 1944.

Fremont-Barnes, Gregory, and Todd Fisher. *The Napoleonic Wars: The Rise and Fall of an Empire.* Oxford: Osprey Publishing, 2004.

Gale, Robert L. *A Henry Wadsworth Longfellow Companion.* Westport, CT: Greenwood Press, 2003.

Gifford, Nellie T. "Childhood Days in the Hopedale Community, and Other Recollection." In *Hopedale Reminiscences,* edited by Hughes, 42–47.

Glatthaar, Joseph T. *Forged in Battle: The Civil War Alliance of Black Soldiers and White Officers.* New York: Free Press, 1990.

———. *General Lee's Army: From Victory to Collapse.* New York: Free Press, 2008.

Goodwin, Doris Kearns. *Team of Rivals: The Political Genius of Abraham Lincoln.* New York: Simon & Schuster, 2005.

Goss, Warren Lee. *Recollections of a Private: A Story of the Army of the Potomac.* New York: Thomas Y. Crowell, 1890.

————. *The Soldier's Story of His Captivity at Andersonville, Belle Isle, and Other Rebel Prisons.* Boston, MA: Lee and Shepard, 1867.

Greene, A. Wilson. *The Final Battles of the Petersburg Campaign: Breaking the Backbone of the Rebellion.* 2d ed. Knoxville: University of Tennessee Press, 2008.

————. "'I Fought the Battle Splendidly': George B. McClellan and the Maryland Campaign." In *Antietam: Essays on the 1862 Maryland Campaign,* edited by Gary W. Gallagher, 56–83. Kent, OH: Kent State University Press, 1989.

Hall, Ruth Gardiner, comp. *Descendants of Governor William Bradford (Through the First Seven Generations).* n.p.: n.p., 1951.

Hall, Timothy L. *Supreme Court Justices: A Biographical Dictionary.* New York: Facts on File, 2001.

Hardee, W. J. *Rifle and Light Infantry Tactics; for the Exercise and Manoeuvres of Troops of When Acting as Light Infantry or Riflemen.* 2 vols. Philadelphia, PA: J. B. Lippincott, 1860–61.

Hearn, Chester G. *When the Devil Came Down to Dixie: Ben Butler in New Orleans.* Baton Rouge: Louisiana State University Press, 1997.

Hebert, Walter H. *Fighting Joe Hooker.* Indianapolis, IN: Bobbs-Merrill, 1944. Reprint, Lincoln: University of Nebraska Press, 1999.

Heitman, Francis B. *Historical Register and Dictionary of the United States Army, from Its Organization, September 28, 1789, to March 2, 1903.* 2 vols. Washington: Government Printing Office, 1903. Reprinted, Urbana: University of Illinois Press, 1965.

Hennessy, John J. "Conservatism's Dying Ember: Fitz John Porter and the Union War, 1862." In *Corps Commanders in Blue: Union Major Generals in the Civil War,* edited by Ethan S. Rafuse, 14–60. Baton Rouge: Louisiana State University Press, 2014.

————. *Return to Bull Run: The Campaign and Battle of Second Manassas.* Norman: University of Oklahoma Press, 1993.

Hess, Earl J. *In the Trenches at Petersburg: Field Fortifications and Confederate Defeat.* Chapel Hill: University of North Carolina Press, 2009.

————. *Trench Warfare under Grant and Lee: Field Fortifications in the Overland Campaign.* Chapel Hill: University of North Carolina Press, 2007.

Hetzel, A. R. *Military Laws of the United States, Including Those Relating to the Army, Marine Corps, Volunteers, Militia, and to Bounty Lands and Pensions: To Which is Prefixed the Rules and Articles of War, and the Constitution of the United States.* 3rd ed. Washington, DC: George Templeman, 1846.

Heywood, Abbie Ballou. "Hopedale Community, Founded in 1841: Its Origin and Early History." In *Hopedale Reminiscences,* edited by Hughes, 48–60.

Hollandsworth, James G., Jr. "The Execution of White Officers from Black Units by Confederate Forces During the Civil War." In *Black Flag over Dixie: Racial Atrocities and Reprisals in the Civil War*, edited by Gregory J. W. Urwin, 52–64. Carbondale: Southern Illinois University Press, 2004.

Howard, Tony. *Women as Hamlet: Performance and Interpretation in Theatre, Film and Fiction.* Cambridge: Cambridge University Press, 2007.

Howell, Helena Adelaide, comp. *Chronicles of the One Hundred Fifty-First Regiment New York State Volunteer Infantry, 1862–1865, Contributed by Its Surviving Members.* Albion, NY: A. M. Eddy, 1911.

Howlett, Charles F. "79th New York Infantry Regiment." In *Ethnic and Racial Minorities in the U.S. Military: An Encyclopedia*, edited by Alexander M. Bielakowski, 639–40. 2 vols. Santa Barbara, CA: ABC-CLIO, 2013.

Hudson, Leonne M. *The Odyssey of a Southerner: The Life and Times of Gustavus Woodson Smith.* Macon, GA: Mercer University Press, 1998.

Hughes, Lynn Gordon, ed. *Hopedale Reminiscences: Childhood Memories of the Hopedale Community and the Hopedale Home School, 1841–1863.* Providence, RI: Blackstone Editions, 2006.

Humphreys, A. A. *Annual Report of the Chief of Engineers to the Secretary of War for the Year 1870.* Washington, DC: Government Printing Office, 1870.

———. "Historical Sketch of the Corps of Engineers." In *Historical Papers Relating to the Corps of Engineers and Engineer Troops in the United States Army.* Engineer School Occasional Papers 16. Washington, DC: Press of the Engineer School, 1904.

———. *The Virginia Campaign of '64 and '65; The Army of the Potomac and the Army of the James.* New York: Charles Scribner's Sons, 1883.

Hutchinson, John Wallace. *Story of the Hutchinsons (Tribe of Jesse).* Edited by Charles E. Mann. 2 vols. Boston: Lee, Shepard, 1896.

Hymowitz, Carol, and Michaele Weissman. *A History of Women in America.* New York: Bantam Books, 1978.

Johnson, Robert Underwood, and Clarence Clough Buel, eds. *Battles and Leaders of the Civil War.* 4 vols. New York: Century, 1887–88.

Johnson, Timothy D., ed. *Memoirs of Lieut.-General Winfield Scott.* Knoxville: University of Tennessee Press, 2015.

Jones, Darius E. *Temple Melodies: A Collection of About Two Hundred Popular Tunes, Adapted by Nearly Five Hundred Favorite Hymns, with Special Reference to Public, Social, and Private Worship.* New York: Mason & Law, 1852.

Jones, Steven. *The Right Hand of Command: Use and Disuse of Personal Staffs in the American Civil War.* Mechanicsburg, PA: Stackpole Books, 2000.

Jones, Terry L. *Lee's Tigers: The Louisiana Infantry in the Army of Northern Virginia.* Baton Rouge: Louisiana State University Press, 1987.

Jordan, Weymouth T., Jr., and Gerald W. Thomas. "Massacre at Plymouth, April 20, 1864." In *Black Flag over Dixie: Racial Atrocities and Reprisals in the Civil War*, edited by Gregory J. W. Urwin, 153–202. Carbondale: Southern Illinois University Press, 2004.

Katcher, Philip. *American Civil War Armies*. Vol. 2, *Union Troops*. Oxford: Osprey Publishing, 1986.

Kinsley, D. A. *Favor the Bold, Custer: The Civil War Years*. New York: Holt, Rhinehart, and Winston, 1967.

Lawrence, Vera Brodsky. *Strong on Music: The New York Music Scene in the Days of George Templeton Strong*. Vol. 1, *Resonances, 1836–1849*. Chicago, IL: University of Chicago Press, 1988.

Levine, Lawrence. *Highbrow/Lowbrow: The Emergency of a Cultural Hierarchy in America*. Cambridge, MA: Harvard University Press, 1988.

Mahan, D. H. *An Elementary Course of Military Engineering*. 2 vols. New York: John Wiley & Son, 1867.

———. *Treatise of Field Fortification, Containing Instructions on the Method of Laying Out, Constructing, Defending, and Attacking Intrenchments, With the General Outlines Also of the Arrangement, the Attack and Defence of Permanent Fortifications*. 3rd ed. New York: John Wiley, 1861.

Malles, Ed, ed. *Bridge Building in Wartime: Colonel Wesley Brainerd's Memoir of the 50th New York Volunteer Engineers*. Knoxville: University of Tennessee Press, 1997.

Manucy, Albert. *Artillery Through the Ages: A Short Illustrated History of Cannon, Emphasizing Types Used in America*. Washington, DC: National Park Service, 1949.

Marcy, Randolph B. *The Prairie Traveler: A Hand-Book for Overland Expeditions*. New York: Harper & Brothers, 1861.

Marquis, Albert Nelson, ed. *Who's Who in America; A Biographical Dictionary of Notable Living Men and Women of the United States, 1908–1909*. Chicago: A. N. Marquis, 1908.

Marvel, William. *Burnside*. Chapel Hill: University of North Carolina Press, 1991.

Mass, John R. *The Petersburg and Appomattox Campaigns, 1864–1865*. Washington, DC: Government Printing Office, 2015.

Masten, April F. *Art Work: Women in Mid-Nineteenth-Century New York*. Philadelphia: University of Pennsylvania Press, 2008.

McConnell, Stuart. *Glorious Contentment: The Grand Army of the Republic, 1865–1900*. Chapel Hill: University of North Carolina Press, 1992.

McCullough, David. *The Great Bridge: The Epic Story of the Building of the Brooklyn Bridge*. New York: Simon & Schuster, 1972.

McWhirter, Christian. *Battle Hymns: The Power and Popularity of Music in the Civil War*. Chapel Hill: University of North Carolina Press, 2012.

Meade, George Gordon, Jr., ed. *The Life and Letters of George Gordon Meade, Major-General United States Army.* 2 vols. New York: Charles Scribner's Sons, 1913.

Meehan, Charles Henry Wharton. *The Law and Practice of the Games of Euchre.* Philadelphia, PA: T. B. Peterson, 1862.

Milligan, Harold Vincent. *Stephen Foster Collins: A Biography of America's Folk-Song Composer.* New York: G. Schirmer, 1920.

Monaghan, Jay. *Custer: The Life of General George Armstrong Custer.* Lincoln: University of Nebraska Press, 1959.

Nevins, Allan. *War for the Union.* 4 vols. New York: Scribner, 1959–71.

Newell, Clayton R., and Charles R. Shrader. *Of Duty Well and Faithfully Done: A History of the Regular Army in the Civil War.* Lincoln: University of Nebraska Press, 2011.

Newman, Nancy. *Good Music for a Free People: The Germania Musical Society in Nineteenth-Century America.* Rochester, NY: University of Rochester Press, 2010.

Oates, Stephen B. *To Purge This Land with Blood: A Biography of John Brown.* New York: Harper & Row, 1970.

O'Neill, Robert F. *Chasing Jeb Stuart and John Mosby: The Union Cavalry in Northern Virginia from Second Manassas to Gettysburg.* Jefferson, NC: McFarland & Company Publishers, 2012.

Patrick, Ellen M. "Our Community School and Its Teacher." In *Hopedale Reminiscences,* edited by Hughes, 33–35.

Peale, A. C. *Register of the Society of Colonial Wars in the District of Columbia.* Washington, DC, 1904.

Pfanz, Donald C. *Richard S. Ewell: A Soldier's Life.* Chapel Hill: University of North Carolina Press, 1998.

Phisterer, Frederick, comp. *New York in the War of the Rebellion, 1861 to 1865.* 3rd ed. 5 vols. Albany, NY: J. B. Lyon Company, 1912.

Preston, David L. *Braddock's Defeat: The Battle of the Monongahela and the Road to Revolution.* Oxford: Oxford University Press, 2015.

Pryor, Elizabeth Stordeur. "The Etymology of Nigger: Resistance, Language, and the Politics of Freedom in the Antebellum North," *Journal of the Early Republic* 36, no. 2 (Summer 2016): 203–45.

Rable, George C. *Fredericksburg! Fredericksburg!* Chapel Hill: University of North Carolina Press, 2002.

Radforth, Ian. *Royal Spectacle: The 1860 Visit of the Prince of Wales to Canada and the United States.* Toronto: University of Toronto Press, 2004.

Rael, Patrick. *Black Identity and Black Protest in the Antebellum North.* Chapel Hill: University of North Carolina Press, 2002.

Rafuse, Ethan S. *George Gordon Meade and the War in the East.* Abilene, TX: McWhiney Foundation Press, 2003.

———. *McClellan's War: The Failure of Moderation in the Struggle for the Union.* Bloomington: Indiana University Press, 2005.

Raymond, R. R. "The Engineer School." *Professional Memoirs: Engineer Bureau, United States Army* 1, no. 2 (April–June 1909): 183–87.

Reid, Whitelaw. *Ohio in the War: Her Statesmen, Generals, and Soldiers.* 2 vols. Cincinnati, OH: Moore, Wilstach, & Baldwin, 1867.

Rhea, Gordon C. *The Battle of the Wilderness, May 5–6 1864.* Baton Rouge: Louisiana State University Press, 1994.

———. *The Battles of Spotsylvania Court House and the Road to Yellow Tavern, May 7–12, 1864.* Baton Rouge: Louisiana State University Press, 1997.

———. *Cold Harbor: Grant and Lee, May 26–June 3, 1864.* Baton Rouge: Louisiana State University Press, 2002.

Rice, Jonathon K. *Moving Mountains: A Study in Civil War Logistics.* Bloomington, IN: Xlibris, 2011.

Richard, Shaun, ed. *The Cambridge Companion to Twentieth-Century Irish Drama.* Cambridge: Cambridge University Press, 2004.

Rowe, John Carlos. *The New American Studies.* Minneapolis: University of Minnesota Press, 2002.

Royster, Charles. *The Destructive War: William Tecumseh Sherman, Stonewall Jackson, and the Americans.* New York: Random House, 1991.

Salmon, John S. *The Official Virginia Civil War Battlefield Guide.* Mechanicsburg, PA: Stackpole Books, 2001.

Scharf, J. Thomas, and Thompson Westcott, *History of Philadelphia, 1609–1884.* 3 vols. Philadelphia: L. H. Everts & Co., 1884.

Schom, Alan. *Napoleon Bonaparte.* New York: HarperCollins, 1997.

Schubert, Frank N. *Black Valor: Buffalo Soldiers and the Medal of Honor, 1870–1898.* Lanham, MD: Rowman & Littlefield, 2009.

Sears, Priscilla F. *A Pillar of Fire to Follow: American Indian Dramas, 1808–1859.* Bowling Green, OH: Bowling Green University Popular Press, 1982.

Sears, Stephen W. *Chancellorsville.* Boston: Houghton Mifflin Company, 1996.

———. *To the Gates of Richmond: The Peninsula Campaign.* New York: Ticknor & Fields, 1992.

———. *George B. McClellan: The Young Napoleon.* New York: Ticknor & Fields, 1998.

Skelton, William B. *An American Profession of Arms: The Army Officer Corps, 1784–1861.* Lawrence: University Press of Kansas, 1992.

Smith, John David, ed. *Black Soldiers in Blue: African American Troops in the Civil War Era.* Chapel Hill: University of North Carolina Press, 2002.

Smith, Mark A. *Engineering Security: The Corps of Engineers and Third System Defense Policy, 1815–1861.* Tuscaloosa: University of Alabama Press, 2009.

―――. "'The Hardest Work and the Hardest Fighting': The Engineer Company in Mexico and the Origins of American Combat Engineering." *Military History of the West* 45 (Fall 2016): 1–46.

―――. "The Politics of Military Professionalism: The Engineer Company and the Political Activities of the Antebellum Corps of Engineers." *Journal of Military History* 80, no. 2 (April 2016): 355–87.

Smith, Merritt Roe. *Harpers Ferry Armory and the New Technology: The Challenge of Change.* Ithaca, NY: Cornell University Press, 1977.

Smith, Thomas E. V. *Political Parties and Their Places of Meeting in New York City, Read Before the New York Historical Society February 7th, 1893.* New York: n.p., 1893.

Spann, Edward K. *Hopedale: From Commune to Company Town, 1840–1920.* Columbus: Ohio State University Press, 1992.

Stackpole, Edward J. *They Met at Gettysburg.* 3rd ed. Harrisburg, PA: Stackpole Books, 1986.

Standish, Myles, M.D. *The Standishes of America.* 2nd ed. Boston, MA: Press of Samuel Usher, 1895.

Stepp, John W., and J. William Hill, eds. *Mirror of War: The Washington* Star *Reports the Civil War.* n.p.: Castle Books, 1961.

Stevens, Hazard. *The Life of Isaac Ingalls Stevens.* 2 vols. Boston: Houghton Mifflin, 1900.

Stover, John F. *History of the Baltimore and Ohio Railroad.* West Lafayette, IN: Purdue University Press, 1987.

Suderow, Bryce A. "The Battle of the Crater: The Civil War's Worst Massacre." In *Black Flag over Dixie: Racial Atrocities and Reprisals in the Civil War,* edited by Gregory J. W. Urwin, 203–9. Carbondale: Southern Illinois University Press, 2004.

Swinton, William. *The Twelve Decisive Battles of the War: A History of the Eastern and Western Campaigns, In Relation to the Actions That Decided Their Issue.* New York: Dick & Fitzgerald Publishers, 1867.

Tap, Bruce. *Over Lincoln's Shoulder: The Committee on the Congressional Conduct of the War.* Lawrence: University Press of Kansas, 1998.

Taylor, J. C., and S. P. Hatfield, comps. *History of the First Connecticut Artillery and of the Siege Trains of the Armies Operating against Richmond, 1862–65.* Hartford, CT: Case, Luckwood, & Brainard, 1893.

Thienel, Phillip M. *Mr. Lincoln's Bridge Builders: The Right Hand of American Genius.* Shippensburg, PA: White Mane Books, 2000.

Thompson, Gilbert. *The Engineer Battalion in the Civil War: A Contribution to the History of the United States Engineers.* Revised by John W. N. Schulz. Engineer School Occasional Papers 44. Washington, DC: Press of the Engineer School, 1910.

————. "The Geography and Political Boundaries of Virginia and Maryland, From Their Earliest Date to the Beginnings of the American Revolution, April 19, 1775." *Historical Papers of the Society of Colonial Wars in the District of Columbia* 1 (1898): 1–8.

————. "Historical Military Powder Horns." *Historical Papers of the Society of Colonial Wars in the District of Columbia* 3 (1901) : 1–16.

————. "An Hypothesis for the So-called Encroachment of the Sea upon the Land." *Science* n.s., 15, issue 382 (30 May 1890): 333.

————. "An Indian Dance at Jemez, New Mexico." *American Anthropologist* 2, no. 4 (October 1889): 351–55.

————. *Report of the Reunion of the Veterans of the US Engineer Battalion, at St. Louis, Mo. September 26–29, 1887.* n.p., n.d.

Tuohey, Terese Volk. *A Musician and Teacher in Nineteenth-Century New England: Irving Emerson, 1843–1905.* Lanham, MD: Lexington Books, 2015.

Turtle, Thomas. "History of the Engineer Battalion, A Paper Read before the 'Essayons Club' of the Corps of Engineers, Dec. 21, 1868." In *Historical Papers Relating to the Corps of Engineers and to Engineer Troops in the United States Army.* Engineer School Occasional Papers 16 (Washington, DC: Press of the Engineer School, 1904).

Twitchell, A. S. *History of the Seventh Maine Light Battery, Volunteers in the Great Rebellion. Containing a Brief Daily Account of Its Services, Without Comments or Attempt to Criticise or Praise the Brave Boys in This Command; Also, Personal Sketches of a Large Number of Members, Portraits, Illustrations and Poems.* Boston, MA: E. B. Stillings, 1892.

The Union Army: A History of Military Affairs in the Loyal States, 1861–65—Records of the Regiments in the Union Army—Cyclopedia of Battles—Memoirs of Commanders and Soldiers. Vol. 3, *New Jersey, Indiana, Illinois, and Michigan.* Madison, WI: Federal Publishing Company, 1908.

United States Army. Corps of Engineers. *The History of the US Army Corps of Engineers.* Alexandria, VA: Office of History, US Army Corps of Engineers, 1998.

United States Congress. *Statutes at Large of the United States of America.* 17 vols. Boston, MA: Little, Brown, and Company, 1845–1873.

United States Congress. Senate. *Journal of the Senate of the United States of America.* Washington, DC, 1820–.

United States War Department. *Revised United States Army Regulations of 1861.* Washington, DC: Government Printing Office, 1863.

————. *The War of the Rebellion: A Compilation of the Official Records of the Union and Confederate Armies.* 4 series, 128 vols. Washington, DC: Government Printing Office, 1880–1901.

Urwin, Gregory J. W. *Custer Victorious: The Civil War Battles of General George Armstrong Custer.* Lincoln: University of Nebraska Press, 1983.

Vail, Enos Ballard. *Reminiscences of a Boy in the Civil War.* n.p.: n.p., 1915.

Wade, Arthur P. *Artillerists and Engineers: The Beginnings of American Seacoast Fortifications.* McLean, VA: CDSG Press, 2011.

Warner, Ezra J., and W. Buck Yearns. *Biographical Register of the Confederate Congress.* Baton Rouge: Louisiana State University Press, 1975.

Watson, J. R., ed. *An Annotated Anthology of Hymns.* Oxford: Oxford University Press, 2002.

Watson, Samuel J. *Peacekeepers and Conquerors: The Army Officer Corps on the American Frontier, 1821–1846.* Lawrence: University Press of Kansas, 2013.

Weicksel, Sarah Jones. "Armor, Manhood, and the Politics of Mortality." In *Astride Two Worlds: Technology and the American Civil War,* edited by Barton C. Hacker, 157–90. Washington, DC: Smithsonian Institute Scholarly Press, 2016.

Weld, Stephen M. *War Diary and Letters of Stephen Minot Weld, 1861–1865.* Riverside Press, 1912.

Wert, Jeffrey D. *The Sword of Lincoln: The Army of the Potomac.* New York: Simon and Schuster, 2005.

Wheeler, George M. *Report Upon United States Geographical Surveys West of the One Hundredth Meridian, In Charge of Capt. Geo. M. Wheeler, Corps of Engineers, US Army, Published by Authority of the Honorable Secretary of War, In Accordance with Acts of Congress of June 23, 1874, and February 15, 1875.* 7 vols. Washington, DC: Government Printing Office, 1875–89.

Wiley, Bell Irvin. *The Life of Billy Yank: The Common Soldier of the Union.* Indianapolis, IN: Bobbs-Merrill, 1952. Reprinted, Garden City, NY: Doubleday, 1971.

———. *The Life of Johnny Reb: The Common Soldier of the Confederacy.* Indianapolis, IN: Bobbs-Merrill, 1943.

Williams, William H. A. *'Twas Only an Irishman's Dream: The Image of Ireland and the Irish in American Popular Song Lyrics, 1800–1920.* Champaign: University of Illinois Press, 1996.

Wilson, Neal E., ed. *Echoes from the Boys of Company 'H': The Siege of Charleston, the Assault on Fort Wagner, the Virginia Campaigns for Petersburg and Richmond, and Prison Life in Andersonville, as Chronicled by Civil War Soldiers from the 100th New York State Regiment, Company H.* New York: iUniverse, 2008.

Woodbury, Augustus. *Major General Ambrose E. Burnside and the Ninth Corps: A Narrative of Campaigns in North Carolina, Maryland, Virginia, Ohio, Kentucky, Mississippi, and Tennessee, During the War for the Preservation of the Republic.* Providence, RI: Sidney S. Rider & Brother, 1867.

Wright, John D. *The Language of the Civil War.* Westport, CT: Oryx Press, 2001.

Young, Alfred F. *Masquerade: The Life and Times of Deborah Sampson, Continental Soldier.* New York: Random House, 2004.

Index